German foreign policy
since unification

MANCHESTER
UNIVERSITY PRESS

ISSUES IN GERMAN POLITICS
Edited by
Professor Charlie Jeffery, Institute for German Studies
Dr Charles Lees, University of Sussex

Issues in German Politics is a major new series on contemporary
Germany. Focusing on the post-unity era, it presents concise,
scholarly analyses of the forces driving change in domestic politics
and foreign policy. Key themes will be the continuing legacies of
German unification and controversies surrounding Germany's role
and power in Europe. The series includes contributions from political
science, international relations and political economy.

Already published:
Bulmer, Jeffery and Paterson: *Germany's European diplomacy:*
Shaping the regional milieu
Harding and Paterson (eds): *The future of the German economy:*
An end to the miracle?
Harnisch and Maull: *Germany as a Civilian Power?*
The foreign policy of the Berlin Republic
Hyde-Price: *Germany and European order:*
Enlarging NATO and the EU
Lees: *The Red–Green coalition in Germany:*
Politics, personalities and power

German foreign policy since unification

Theories and case studies

edited by Volker Rittberger

MANCHESTER UNIVERSITY PRESS
Manchester and New York
distributed exclusively in the USA by Palgrave

Copyright © Manchester University Press 2001

While copyright in the volume as a whole is vested in Manchester University Press,
copyright in individual chapters belongs to their respective authors, and no chapter
may be reproduced wholly or in part without the express permission in writing of both
author and publisher

Published by Manchester University Press
Oxford Road, Manchester M13 9NR, UK
and Room 400, 175 Fifth Avenue, New York, NY 10010, USA
http://www.manchesteruniversitypress.co.uk

Distributed exclusively in the USA by
Palgrave, 175 Fifth Avenue, New York, NY 10010, USA

Distributed exclusively in Canada by
UBC Press, University of British Columbia, 2029 West Mall,
Vancouver, BC, Canada V6T 1Z2

British Library Cataloguing-in-Publication Data
A catalogue record for this book is available from the British Library

Library of Congress Cataloging-in-Publication Data applied for

ISBN   0 7190 6039 7   *hardback*
0 7190 6040 0   *paperback*

First published 2001

10   09   08   07   06   05   04   03   02   01   10   9   8   7   6   5   4   3   2   1

Typeset by Carnegie Publishing, Lancaster
Printed in Great Britain by Bell & Bain Ltd, Glasgow

Contents

Part IV Comparative analysis

Figures and tables

Contributors

Volker Rittberger, b. 1941, is Professor of Political Science and International Relations, and Director of the Center for International Relations/Peace and Conflict Studies of the University of Tübingen. He has been Special Fellow at the United Nations Institute for Training and Research (1978–98) and Visiting Professor at Stanford University (1986), at the Graduate Faculty of Political and Social Sciences, New School for Social Research, New York City (1992–93), and at the Institut d'Etudes Politiques de Paris (1999/2000). His recent publications include *Theories of International Regimes* (1997), *The United Nations System and its Predecessors* (1997), *Regime Theory and International Relations* (1993) and *International Regimes in East–West Politics* (1990).

Rainer Baumann, b. 1968, was Research Associate at the Center for International Relations/Peace and Conflict Studies of the University of Tübingen (1997–99), and is now Research Associate and Lecturer at the Institute for Comparative Politics and International Relations at the University of Frankfurt a.M.

Henning Boekle, b. 1966, was Research Associate at the Center for International Relations/Peace and Conflict Studies of the University of Tübingen (1996–2000) and is now Research Associate at the Chair for International Relations and Foreign Policy at the University of Trier.

Corinna Freund, b. 1969, was Research Associate at the Center for International Relations/Peace and Conflict Studies of the University of Tübingen (1997–2000). She is currently writing her doctoral dissertation under the supervision of Professor Rittberger, financed by a grant from the Heinrich Boell Foundation.

Dirk Peters, b. 1971, was Research Associate at the Center for International Relations/Peace and Conflict Studies of the University of Tübingen (2000) and is now Research Associate and Lecturer at the Department of Political Science at the University of Mainz.

Wolfgang Wagner, b. 1970, was Research Associate at the Center for International Relations/Peace and Conflict Studies at the University of Tübingen (1997–99), and is now Research Associate and Lecturer at the Institute for Comparative Politics and International Relations at the University of Frankfurt a.M.

Abbreviations

AMF	Allied Command Europe Mobile Force
A/RES	Resolution of the United Nations General Assembly
ARRC	Allied Command Europe Rapid Reaction Force
AS-MR	Arbeitsstab Menschenrechte (human rights staff)
AWACS	Airborne Warning and Control System
BDI	Bundesverband der Deutschen Industrie (umbrella organization of German Industry)
BMBF	Bundesministerium für Bildung und Forschung (Federal Ministry of Education and Research)
BML	Bundesministerium für Ernährung, Landwirtschaft und Forsten (Federal Ministry of Food, Agriculture and Forestry)
BMVg	Bundesminister der Verteidigung (Federal Ministry of Defence)
BMWi	Bundesministerium für Wirtschaft und Technologie (Federal Ministry of Economics and Technology)
BVerfGE	Entscheidungen des Bundesverfassungsgerichts (Decisions of the Federal Constitutional Court)
CAP	Common Agricultural Policy
CDU	Christlich-Demokratische Union (Christian Democratic Union)
CFSP	Common Foreign and Security Policy
CHR	(United Nations) Commission on Human Rights
CICC	Coalition for an International Criminal Court
CSCE	Conference on Security and Cooperation in Europe
CSU	Christlich-Soziale Union (Christian Social Union)
DBV	Deutscher Bauernverband (German Farmers' Association)

DG	Directorate-General (of the EC/EU Commission)
DGAP	Deutsche Gesellschaft für Auswärtige Politik (German Society for Foreign Affairs)
DGB	Deutscher Gewerkschaftsbund (Association of German Trade Unions)
DIHT	Deutscher Industrie- und Handelstag (umbrella organization of the German Chambers of Industry and Commerce)
EC	European Community
ECJ	European Court of Justice
EMU	European Monetary Union
EP	European Parliament
ERDF	European Regional Development Fund
EU	European Union
EUZW	*Europäische Zeitschrift für Wirtschaftsrecht (European Journal for Economic Law)*
FAZ	*Frankfurter Allgemeine Zeitung*
FDP	Freie Demokratische Partei (Free Democratic Party)
FMR	Forum Menschenrechte (Human Rights Forum, umbrella organization of human rights non-governmental organizations in Germany)
FRG	Federal Republic of Germany
FRY	Federal Republic of Yugoslavia
GA	(United Nations) General Assembly
GATS	General Agreement on Trade in Services
GATT	General Agreement on Tariffs and Trade
GG	Grundgesetz (Basic Law)
GNP	gross national product
HCHR	(United Nations) High Commissioner for Human Rights
ICC	International Criminal Court
ICJ	International Court of Justice
IFOR	Implementation Force
IGC	intergovernmental conference
IGM	Industriegewerkschaft Metall (Metalworkers' Union)
IHT	*International Herald Tribune*
ILC	(United Nations) International Law Commission
KFOR	Kosovo Force
KVM	Kosovo Verification Mission
LMG	Like-Minded Group

NATO	North Atlantic Treaty Organization
NGO	Non-Governmental Organization
NZZ	*Neue Zürcher Zeitung*
OECD	Organization for Economic Cooperation and Development
OHCHR	Office of the United Nations High Commissioner for Human Rights
OJ	*Official Journal* (of the EC/EU)
OSCE	Organization for Security and Cooperation in Europe
PAS	political-administrative system
PDS	Partei des Demokratischen Sozialismus (Party of Democratic Socialism)
PR	Permanent Representation of Germany at the EC/EU
QMV	qualified majority voting
R&D	research and development
SACEUR	Supreme Allied Commander Europe
SC	(United Nations) Security Council
SEA	Single European Act
SFOR	Stabilization Force
SPD	Sozialdemokratische Partei Deutschlands (Social Democratic Party)
S/RES	Resolution of the United Nations Security Council
STANAV-FORLANT	Standing Naval Force Atlantic
SZ	*Süddeutsche Zeitung*
TEC	Treaty Establishing the European Community
TEU	Treaty on European Union
UN	United Nations
WEU	Western European Union
WTO	World Trade Organization
ZVEI	Zentralverband der Elektrotechnik- und Elektronikindustrie (Association of the Electrical and Electronics Industry in Germany)

as its independent variables and accounts for a state's foreign policy behaviour as norm-consistent foreign policy. It posits that especially those norms which have a high degree of specificity and which are widely shared among a community of actors will shape a state's foreign policy behaviour. If international and societal norms pertaining to a specific issue converge, they are expected to exert a particularly strong influence. The theory identifies indicators for international and societal norms and thus makes it possible to derive predictions about a state's behaviour in a given situation which can be empirically tested.

To put these three theories to an empirical test, we selected four issue areas of German foreign policy, each representing a case study: German *security policy* within the North Atlantic Treaty Organization (NATO); German *European Union (EU) constitutional foreign policy*; German *foreign trade policy* within the EU and the General Agreement on Tariffs and Trade (GATT); and German *human rights policy* within the United Nations (UN). This selection provides a representative cross-section of German foreign policy. It includes both issues of 'high politics' (e.g. security policy) and of 'low politics' (e.g. foreign trade policy), and thus 'easy' and 'hard' cases for neorealism and its prediction that post-unification Germany will step up its pursuit of power politics. Also, the four case studies include cases from all three main policy areas in international politics: 'security' (security policy), 'welfare' (foreign trade policy) and 'system of rule' (EU constitutional policy and human rights policy).

In order to be able to compare German foreign policy behaviour before and after unification, we selected one to three cases within each case study. Each case consists of a pair or a series of observations of Germany's foreign policy behaviour before and after unification. Thus the case study on German security policy within NATO analyses two cases: the integration of Germany's armed forces in NATO's military structures and Germany's participation in military out-of-area operations. The study of EU constitutional foreign policy focuses on Germany's stance towards an extension of qualified majority voting (QMV) in the Council, towards the strengthening of the European Parliament's (EP's) legislative powers, and towards the size of Germany's net contributions to the EU budget. German foreign trade policy was examined with respect to Germany's position on the liberalization of agricultural trade in the GATT Uruguay round negotiations and to its stance towards the liberalization of public procurement in the European Community's (EC's) telecommunications sector. Finally, the case study on German human rights policy within the UN analysed Germany's position with respect to the strengthening of existing and the establishment of new human rights institutions within the UN. Thus we were able to test hypotheses from our three theories against eight cases of German foreign policy.

Our (re)construction of three foreign policy theories and the case studies applying these theories are presented in this volume. Before the theories are presented, chapter 2 gives a structured account of the public debate on the future direction of German foreign policy. Focusing on the debate inside Germany, the chapter shows that the direction of Germany's foreign policy was disputed and that considerable scope for change was seen. By showing that one of the main dividing lines in this debate lay between authors who recommended that the more powerful Germany pursue a more assertive, less cooperative foreign policy and others who opposed such a change, it highlights the importance that neorealist thinking had in the public discourse on German foreign policy. Neorealism, therefore, is the starting point for our effort to uncover possible causes of continuity and change in German foreign policy. Chapter 3 presents the neorealist theory of foreign policy. Utilitarian liberalism and constructivism follow in chapters 4 and 5. Chapters 6 to 9 are devoted to the case studies in which the three theories are applied to German foreign policy. Finally, chapter 10 compiles the theoretical and empirical findings and puts them into perspective. Based on a summary of chapters 2 to 9 and on methodological reflections, this concluding chapter draws inferences with respect to both the general development of German foreign policy behaviour – does continuity or change prevail? – and to the testing of the three theories – which theory was most successful in explaining Germany's foreign policy?

The book will make it clear that the expectations that unification could result in a major turn in German foreign policy and could lead Germany to step up its pursuit of power politics have been exaggerated. There have been almost no signs that Germany would turn away from its multilateral, cooperative approach to foreign policy, and thus neorealist foreign policy theory fares quite badly in explaining German foreign policy behaviour. To be sure, some of our cases do point towards German efforts to increase Germany's influence within international institutions and may thus be well explained by modified neorealism. However, international and societal norms seem best to explain German foreign policy behaviour after unification. While utilitarian liberalism's explanatory power varies according to the issue under consideration, constructivism's explanatory record across all eight cases is not without flaws but is still fairly impressive. German foreign policy after unification, it seems, is best explained as norm-consistent foreign policy behaviour.

A project like this can, of course, not achieve its goals without help from outside. Many have contributed to its completion, and it is impossible to single out everyone who has helped in one way or another. We gratefully acknowledge the generous funding provided for this project by the German Science Association (Deutsche Forschungs-gemeinschaft/DFG). Our research benefited much from four review workshops which we were able to convene over the course of the project. Therefore, our thanks are due to those who participated in one or more of those workshops: Harald Barrios, Sebastian Bartsch, Thomas Bernauer, Marijke Breuning, Tanja Brühl, Gunther Hellmann, Hartwig Hummel, Markus Jachtenfuchs, Martin List, Peter Moser, Thomas Nielebock, Ingo Peters, Hans Peter Schmitz and Bernhard Zangl. Their 'view from the outside' was an important stimulation for our work. Andrew Moravcsik contributed to our theoretical discussions by engaging in an instructive dialogue on liberalism and constructivism. Derk Bienen, Helmut Breitmeier, Martin Mogler, Frank Schimmelfennig and Christian Westhoff were temporary members of the research team in Tübingen. We are grateful for their invaluable contribution to the project. We would also like to thank Simon Gajer, Daria Nashat and Tatjana Reiber who contributed their parts as research assistants to the success of the project.

A final word of thanks goes to Manchester University Press and the editors of the series 'Issues in German Politics', Charlie Jeffery and Charlie Lees, for publishing this volume. Tony Mason, Politics and Economics Commissioning Editor at Manchester University Press, has been an unfailing source of encouragement and support.

Part I
Discourse analysis

2

The debate about a new German foreign policy after unification

Dirk Peters

Introduction

For observers from outside Germany, the international dimension of German unification has always been its crucial aspect. Would post-unification Germany remain a predictable and reliable partner of Western states? Or would it break with the foreign policy traditions of the West German state and maybe even fall back into the foreign policy behaviour of the German *Reich*, return to seesaw politics (*Schaukel-politik*), drift towards the East or try to set itself up as a world power? Although Germans themselves were primarily occupied with the internal consequences of unification, soon after unification a debate on future foreign policy began inside Germany, too.

The debate centred around the question of how the increase in power experienced by Germany after the Cold War and through unification would affect German foreign policy behaviour (see Staack 2000: 23; Hellmann 1998: 265). Almost all contributors agreed that unification had opened up new opportunities for German foreign policy, including opportunities to break with the foreign policy traditions of the 'old' Federal Republic and to pursue a more assertive foreign policy. Yet they disagreed as to whether it would be a wise choice for Germany to do so.

This chapter will present a reconstruction of this debate, which reached its peak in the early to mid-1990s and eased off somewhat afterwards. It will focus on those contributions to the public debate inside Germany, in which recommendations for German foreign policy makers were formulated. In this debate, two basic positions can be distinguished.[1] Some authors held that Germany, through unification and through the end of the Cold War, had regained the status of a European great power. They argued that this necessitated adjustments in Germany's foreign policy, i.e. that Germany had to bring its foreign policy in line with its improved power position. While all authors of this group agreed that German foreign policy had to become more power conscious and more assertive, there were disagreements about how far these changes were to be taken, especially with regard to Germany's relations with its Western allies. Other authors, however, entirely rejected this analysis and argued that a change towards a more assertive foreign policy would be inadequate, if not outright self-defeating. While some of this latter group reasoned that a basic continuity in German foreign policy would be the best choice for German foreign policy makers, others recommended a change towards a 'civilizing' foreign policy.

In the remainder of this chapter, the arguments of these groups of authors – advocates and critics of a more assertive foreign policy – will be presented in more detail.[2] The distinction is, of course, rough and cannot do justice to all aspects of the debate and to all arguments of the authors cited. It will, nonetheless, prove useful for reconstructing and highlighting the major controversies of a rather complex debate.

Advocates of a more assertive foreign policy

Germany is well-advised to consider itself a great power in Europe – something our neighbors have done for long – and to adjust its foreign policy accordingly within the framework of the Euro-Atlantic institutions.

Gerhard Schröder[3]

The first group of authors regard all international politics as power politics. From their viewpoint, the increase in German power induced by unification profoundly altered Germany's position in the international system, and thus fundamentally changed the general conditions of German foreign policy: Germany has become a European great power again and has to adjust its foreign policy accordingly. While there are some disagreements among the authors grouped together here, as we shall see below, they all conclude that post-unification Germany should turn towards a more assertive foreign policy.

From the viewpoint of these advocates of a more assertive foreign policy, the end of the Cold War represents a sea change in the international distribution of power which will have far-reaching consequences for world politics in general and for German foreign policy in particular.

In three respects, this is a change that leads 'back to the future', as John Mearsheimer (1990) put it. First, bipolarity, which had structured world politics since the end of World War II, disappeared, leaving behind a multipolar Europe. This entailed a return from an exceptional situation that had lasted a mere forty years to 'normality' in the European system (Weißmann 1996: 309f.). This return to multipolarity entailed a loss of significance for the two former 'superpowers', the USA and the Soviet Union/Russia, whereas the European great powers regained their weight – a change which is of importance particularly for Germany. France and Great Britain had not completely lost their great power status during the Cold War but retained it at least partially. Germany's power, however, had been considerably restricted after World War II and West Germans had even grown accustomed to viewing their state as a 'small state'.[4] Thus, for Germany, the shift from bipolarity to multipolarity implied a particularly significant transformation, i.e. the promotion from a state with a seriously restricted autonomy to a great power of European, or even global, significance (Schwarz 1994a: 9f.). Secondly, and parallel to this restoration of multipolarity, a process of renationalization has taken place in Europe since 1989/90, i.e. the world of nation states reconstitutes itself there. Those nations in Eastern and Central Europe which had been held together in multi-ethnic states during the Cold War are anxious to create their own nation states (Hacke 1998: 16, 23), just as the nation that had been divided since 1949 now reclaims its own unified state: 'German unification in itself is an example for ... the trend towards re-nationalisation of the old continent' (Schöllgen 1994: 44). Moreover, existing nation states are determined to preserve their status and are by no means willing to give up their sovereignty – witness the reluctance of EU member states to extend European integration to the realm of foreign and security policy or to shift decision-making competences from the Council to truly supranational organs such as the EP (Hacke 1998: 14f.; Schwarz 1994a: 32–5). On top of these developments, which point towards the re-emergence of a multipolar system of nation states in Europe, the wars in Yugoslavia and in the former republics of the Soviet Union demonstrate that war has again become a means of politics in Europe. All this suggests that the stable Cold War order had been a historical interlude and that after 1989/90 Europe returned to the 'normal anarchy' (Alten 1994) of a world of nation states.

   In this new Europe, Germany's geopolitical situation has changed significantly and its new position in important respects resembles that held by the German *Reich* after 1871 (Baring 1994: 1). Most importantly,

Germany – no longer divided, nor located at the fault line of a global conflict – is now again locked in its *Mittellage*, its position in the middle of the continent. This geographical position, the inescapable basic condition of German foreign policy (Schwarz 1994b: 94–7), impacts on Germany in two respects. First, it makes it particularly vulnerable. The fact that it shares borders with nine countries, more than any other country in Europe, makes its security particularly precarious not only in military terms (Gillessen 1994: 25), but also makes it a prime target of migratory movements (Thies 1993: 528f.). Second, the *Mittellage* makes Germany an especially important player in European politics. It can act both as a bridge and as a barrier between the two parts of the continent which had been strictly separated during the Cold War (Winkler 1995: 105). Its huge capabilities, i.e. its population, territory, economic and military capabilities, over which it has regained full sovereignty, as well as its cultural influence, add to its significance for European and world politics (Schöllgen 1993: 26–31). These capabilities and its geographical position make Germany the 'central power' of Europe (Schwarz 1994a),[5] a fact that was recognized by the other great powers immediately, while Germans themselves – having grown unaccustomed to viewing their own position in terms of power during the Cold War – were slow to become aware of it (Schwarz 1994a: 8; Thies 1993: 524).

Hence post-unification Germany has to cope with two fundamental challenges in its foreign policy: with a peculiar vulnerability and, since every foreign policy action of the central power will impact on Europe at large, with new responsibility. The old West German foreign policy strategies will not suffice to meet these challenges.

West German foreign policy strategies had been marked by a peculiar German *Machtvergessenheit* – Germany had been oblivious of its power (Schwarz 1985). This had created no problems as long as others, i.e. the US and NATO, were ready to protect Germany's security. After the Cold War, however, there is no reason left for the US and other Western powers to protect the country. Therefore, post-unification Germany will have to use its own capabilities and take care of its security by itself (Feldmeyer 1993). Yet it is not only Germany itself that would be affected if the country continued to be oblivious of its power, but also its European neighbours. Ignoring Germany's power and continuing with the low-profile foreign policy of West Germany would have no more benign effects on them than an abuse of German power:

It is certain that every German decision or non-decision will have the strongest effects on the entire European environment. The infirmity of a centrally-located state has consequences as grave as those of such a state's calm efforts to shape its surroundings or its irritating lack of restraint, of which Germans themselves, as well as their neighbors, have tasted enough in the more distant past. (Schwarz 1994a: 11)

Thus Germany's status as the central power of Europe condemns it to make the right use of its power. Hence after unification Germany needs to adjust its foreign policy accordingly. There is, however, some disagreement among advocates of a more assertive foreign policy about how far reaching these adjustments in German foreign policy must be. On the one hand, there is a small group of authors who have adopted the label 'the new democratic right' (Zitelmann 1996). They argue for a fundamental reconsideration of even the most basic foreign policy orientations of the 'old' Federal Republic. On the other hand, most advocates of a more assertive foreign policy are more moderate and do not call into question fundamental foreign policy orientations such as Germany's *Westbindung*. When it comes to concrete policy recommendations, however, these two lines of thought converge, as will become clear below.

The 'new democratic right' is quite a small group of authors, many of whom were born after World War II and are writing as publicists for conservative newspapers, most notably *Die Welt*. In the debate about a new German foreign policy, they received attention only until the mid-1990s. Their writings aim primarily at Germany's internal conditions, but they also have some important implications for Germany's foreign policy. The 'new right' claims that the inadequate low-profile approach to foreign policy, which West Germany had pursued, had been caused by a disturbed relation of Germans to their past. During the Cold War, history had been utilized both by outside powers and by the left inside the Federal Republic to break German national self-confidence. German history was essentially reduced to the time of Nazi rule, thus preventing any German national self-confidence from rising again. For the allied powers, harnessing recent German history this way was a most effective means of breaking national self-confidence in order to prevent Germans from starting yet another destructive war (Röhl 1996: 93f.). Since at least the late 1960s, this strategy has met with sympathy from inside Germany. Leftist groups, most prominently the proponents of Critical Theory, have used recent German history to create 'self-hatred' and 'national masochism' among Germans (Röhl 1996: 95–7) and to justify German division and the existence of a socialist German state in East Germany (Seebacher-Brandt 1996: 47f.). The resulting lack of German self-confidence has translated into an extremely defensive and cautious foreign policy (Inacker 1996: 366).

Based on this analysis, the 'new democratic right' recommends that Germans, first of all, regain a 'normal' national self-confidence. Most of these authors do not deny that the crimes of the Nazi era cannot be justified and make up a particularly dark chapter of German history that must not be forgotten (e.g. Seebacher-Brandt 1996: 49). Yet to reduce German history to this chapter, and thus to justify a peculiar German approach to the concept of the nation or to foreign policy, would be to claim a special role for Germans in Europe again. Instead, Germans should aim at becoming a 'normal' nation, i.e. at regaining a sober national self-confidence and love for their country (Röhl 1996: 99f.; Schwilk and Schacht 1996: 11f.). For foreign policy, this implies that Germans should accept the realities of international politics and no longer retreat to a merely passive role (Inacker 1996: 364f.). In contrast to foreign policy up to unification, there should be no taboos, but only rational decisions that weigh up costs and benefits of different courses of action (Großheim, Weißmann and Zitelmann 1993: 10). This concerns even the most basic foreign policy orientations of West Germany. It implies, for instance, that German *Westbindung*, which had become a matter of course for West Germans, must be reconsidered. It should not be justified simply by reference to a Western 'community of values' of which Germany would be a part. Rather, the pros *and* cons of German ties to the West must be weighed up, and then a rational decision in favour of or against cooperation with, and integration in, the West has to be made (Großheim, Weißmann and Zitelmann 1993).

Other advocates of a more assertive foreign policy, many of them conservative historians or political scientists with a primarily historical research focus, are more moderate in their recommendations. They too dismiss the 'timidity' (Schwarz 1994a: 15) of the 'old' West German foreign policy, yet they do not speculate about German identity, but trace the roots of Germany's now inadequate approach to foreign policy back primarily to the specific German situation after World War II (Schöllgen 1998: 28f.).

Due to its defeat in World War II, Germany had lost its foreign policy autonomy and, as a divided front-line state in the Cold War, the Federal Republic depended on the backing of other states to guarantee its security. Multilateralism was the strategy most adequate under these circumstances. Through its integration in Western multilateral institutions, most notably the EC and NATO, West Germany gradually re-gained autonomy in foreign affairs and was assured of the assistance of the Western powers in safeguarding its survival. The Western allies, in turn, were willing to provide this protection in order to secure their own position in the global conflict. Hence the Federal Republic was able to act as a 'free rider' in the issue area of security and to pursue chiefly welfare goals under Western protection. Thus the cornerstones of West German foreign policy – multilateralism, *Westbindung* and self-restraint in military affairs – resulted from the special position of West Germany in the international system during the East–West conflict (Alten 1994: 288f.).

Since the end of the East–West conflict brought an end to this special position, post-unification Germany has to rethink its foreign policy strategies. In contrast to the 'new democratic right', however, most moderate advocates of a more assertive foreign policy regard some basic orientations, e.g. *Westbindung*, as incontestable prerequisites of West German foreign policy which should not be given up (Hacke 1994: 77; Schwarz 1994a: 16). They do not reflect on a distinct German identity but, more pragmatically, hold that every course of foreign policy that would imply a loosening of German ties with the West would alienate the powerful Western states. It would raise fears of renewed German unilateralism or of attempts to create a mid-European sphere of German influence and would therefore most probably set the Western powers against Germany (Schöllgen 1993: 127–30), a situation unfavourable for a country in Germany's exposed geopolitical position.

Writers of the 'new democratic right' see this danger, too, and thus, when they perform the reconsideration of *Westbindung* they demand, their result usually is that Germany should *not* pursue a unilateral foreign policy or alienate Western countries, especially the US (Hahn 1996: 337–41; Feldmeyer 1993: 473; Großheim, Weißmann and Zitel-mann 1993: 16). Eventually, then, both groups of authors arrive at similar conclusions although they start out from different assumptions. Both call for a more assertive and more power-conscious German foreign policy. Both, however, do not call for more German unilateral-ism. Rather, they argue that Germany should pursue a foreign policy similar to that of the other European great powers, Britain and France, and should, instead of loosening its ties with the West, use them to its own advantage.

It is uncontested among all advocates of a more assertive foreign policy that Germany should utilize these ties, first of all to stabilize

Eastern Europe, since Germany's security at the fault line between Eastern and Western Europe depends above all on the stability of its Eastern neighbours and Russia (Baring 1994: 12). The basic strategy with respect to Eastern Europe, therefore, should be to invite the Eastern European countries into the formerly Western institutions (Hacke 1998: 22f.). With this strategy, Germany could support its Eastern neighbours economically and thus prevent instability at its eastern border and an influx of migrants from there (Brunner 1996: 384f.). At the same time, this multilateral strategy of stabilizing Eastern Europe would prevent suspicion from Germany's Western partners that Germany intended to build up a mid-European sphere of influence (Schöllgen 2000: 12).

Also, in other issue areas of foreign policy, Germany should put more emphasis on its own national interests. There are several important issues in which a German foreign policy simply continuing the old Federal Republic's strategies would jeopardize German interests in the long run. The first and most frequently discussed issue is European integration. Proceeding from the assumption that all European great powers pursue their own national interests in their foreign policies, the authors criticize the German tendency to equate German interests with the deepening of European integration too rashly instead of soberly weighing the costs and benefits of integration for Germany (e.g. Hacke 1994: 81). Especially with respect to the Maastricht Treaty of 1992, many authors sharply criticize Germany for giving up autonomy without gaining much in return (e.g. Watzal 1993). The more reserved, 'British approach' to European integration of the Schröder government is thus applauded by these authors (e.g. Schwarz 1999: 2f.). The tendency to continue multi-lateral foreign policy strategies without paying due attention to Germany's national interests is also criticized with respect to German UN policy. While other great powers, notably the US and France, use the UN to push through their own national interests, German foreign policy tends to overestimate the potential of the UN as an independent actor in world politics (Korte 1998: 10), thus leaving out opportunities to secure influence and to push through its own interests (Inacker 1996: 379). Germany should instead try to influence the UN utilizing its financial contributions and its close relations to the permanent members of the Security Council, Britain and France (Gillessen 1994: 32f.).

To pursue the rational foreign policy of a great power implies an adjustment not only of German foreign policy goals, but also of the means applied in foreign policy. As a normal European great power, Germany – like France or Britain – must be ready to use military force in certain circumstances. Post-unification Germany should no longer stand aside in multilateral military operations in which German interests are at stake (Schwarz 1994a: 15f.). Therefore, the advocates of a more assertive foreign policy approve of the gradual development in post-unification Germany's foreign policy towards full participation in NATO out-of-area operations, and of German participation in the air strikes against Yugoslavia in particular (Schöllgen 2000; Schwarz 1999: 6).

The general line of argument can be extended to every major foreign policy issue: After the Cold War, Germany has re-emerged as the central power of Europe. As such, it has a particular responsibility with which it will cope best if it self-confidently defines its national interests and asserts them in its foreign policy, taking into account the persistence of nation states and the fact that international politics will always be power politics.

Critics of a more assertive foreign policy

Although their contributions have attracted great attention, the advocates of a more assertive foreign policy have remained a minority in the German public debate (see Banchoff 1999a: 181f.). Their underlying assumption, that Europe after the Cold War in important respects resembles Europe after 1871, is sharply criticized by many authors. Even in geopolitical terms, it is argued, the analysis is flawed. In contrast to the end of the nineteenth century, US influence now reaches deep into Europe, and Germany and Russia do not have a common border (Arnim 1995: 470f.). Yet more importantly, critics of a more assertive foreign policy argue that those who speak of the re-emergence of a multipolar system of nation states in Europe ignore central features of the new international system: nowadays the systemic constraints and incentives resulting from multipolarity are countered by the effects of interdependence (e.g. Czempiel 1999: 56). Depending on the extent to which these authors see interdependence shape world politics and to which they anticipate interdependence will intensify in the future, their recommendations for German foreign policy vary. While one subgroup emphasizes continuities between the time before and the time after 1989/90, a second subgroup points to the dynamics of an underlying civilizing process that will lead to further increasing levels of interdependence and that will necessitate adjustments in German foreign policy. But they all agree that for Germany to pursue a more assertive foreign policy would be the wrong way to turn.

Advocates of continuity

> Considering the high degree of dependence of Germany in foreign
> affairs and taking into account our history, continuity and reliability
> are primary, not secondary virtues in German foreign policy. We can
> preserve the trust and predictability which the old Federal Republic
> has built up in 50 years of cautious foreign policy only if we continue
> the policy of prudent self-restriction and multilateral pursuit of our
> interests.
>
>   Joschka Fischer[6]

Apart from 'normality', 'continuity' is probably the notion invoked most
often in the debate about post-unification Germany's foreign policy. As
we have already seen, moderate advocates of a more assertive foreign
policy recommend a certain degree of continuity as they regard some
elements of West German foreign policy, most notably *Westbindung*, as
indisputable prerequisites of Germany's foreign policy after unification.
As we will see in the next section, advocates of a civilizing foreign policy
also emphasize that they do not demand a complete turn-around of
German foreign policy and that they consider continuity in some
respects desirable for Germany's post-unification foreign policy. There
is one group of authors, however, who make continuity the *core concern*
of their foreign policy recommendations. In contrast to the other
groups, these authors do not primarily highlight what needs to be
changed in German foreign policy, but instead they stress what should
remain unaltered and demand only some minor adjustments, if any.
Those authors may therefore be labelled advocates of continuity in
German foreign policy.

In contrast to the advocates of a more assertive foreign policy, most
of whom would not object to being called 'conservatives', the advocates
of continuity cannot be easily grouped together on the political spectrum, with some leaning towards the conservative and others towards
the social democratic side. Most authors in this group have training in
the social sciences and in policy analysis, and many are actively involved
in policy consulting and institutionally tied to foreign policy think tanks,
such as the Deutsche Gesellschaft für Auswärtige Politik (DGAP) or the
Foundation of Science and Policy. These advocates of continuity in
German foreign policy do accept and use much of the vocabulary
employed by advocates of a more assertive foreign policy. They too
regard states as the most important actors in world politics and assume
that material power is of particular importance in international politics.

They count Germany among the major actors of international politics and accord it a peculiar responsibility, especially inside Europe.

Yet, in contrast to advocates of a more assertive foreign policy, the authors of concern here do not accept the claim that post-unification Germany's position in the international system can meaningfully be compared with the position it held after 1871. Rather, they point to certain continuities which reach from the Cold War to the post-Cold War world and which make post-unification Germany's situation resemble more the situation of the old West German state than that of the *Kaiser's Reich*. Most importantly, the increase in power which is emphasized strongly by the advocates of a more assertive foreign policy is held to be not as significant as it is often perceived to be. Some authors flatly reject the assessment that there is any increase in power at all (Bühl 1994: 179). Others point out that, with respect to military capabilities, Germany's power remains limited, because it continues to forgo the possession of weapons of mass destruction and has strictly limited the size of its armed forces (Kreile 1993: 49). Nor did East Germany's economic capabilities add much to West Germany's, so that Germany's power position did not improve much either in the economic realm (Kaiser 1991: 124). All things considered, the German increase in power seems to exist more in the perceptions of the outside world and some people inside Germany than in material reality (Kreile 1993: 50). This is not to deny that post-unification Germany, due to its capabilities, will play a prominent role in Europe and that German room for manoeuvre has widened through unification, but this change is not as far reaching as is suggested by some.

The most important factor, however, making for continuity is interdependence, i.e. the existence of transnational relations and close economic ties that link Germany to its international environment (Kaiser 1993: 543). Interdependence, from the viewpoint of these authors, does *not* entail the dissolution of the state as policy-making authority or a severe restriction on its ability to make binding decisions (Link 1998: 61–9). In this respect, advocates of continuity accept the notion of sovereign states acting in the international realm in the interest of their societies. Yet interdependence does imply that post-unification Germany cannot attain its goals by itself but only in cooperation with its international environment. Due to its economic linkages and the multilateral institutions it is integrated in, post-unification Germany is as firmly embedded in the Western world as West Germany was (Bühl 1994: 176; Haftendorn 1994: 131). Most issues ranking high on

Germany's foreign policy agenda cannot successfully be tackled by one state alone (Bertram 1997: 14f.): as a trade-dependent nation, for instance, Germany needs to ensure a smooth functioning of world markets, which it cannot achieve without the cooperation of other states. The same holds for the stabilization of Eastern Europe, the management of migration and the protection of the environment, to name but a few: all central German interests require common action, at least by the European states (Langguth 1993: 19).

To be sure, national interests will not cease to exist in the post-Cold War world and they will continue to guide the foreign policies of states. But by creating vulnerabilities which can be tackled successfully only by intergovernmental cooperation (Kaiser 1991: 118), interdependence *forces* states to act jointly (Kaiser 1995: 36). Therefore, instead of attempting to assert its interests in the international system, Germany should aim at finding ways in which itself and its partners can attain their goals jointly; how they can connect their interests and develop common strategies for pursuing them (Stürmer 1994: 59). This, in turn, is not so different from the multilateral strategy pursued by West Germany. Thus, from this point of view, it is not a reinvention of German foreign policy that is needed, but continuity with respect to the basic foreign policy orientations of West Germany.

The international institution which lies at the heart of such a foreign policy is the EU. The EU is a prime example of an organization in which states formulate common interests and pursue common policies. As the biggest country in the Union, Germany is accorded particular importance for the future of European integration (Kuper 1999: 419), but at the same time it is emphasized that Germany will not be able to push through progress in European integration all by itself (Kreile 1993: 54–60). In this, as in other respects, it will have to join forces with other states, most notably France (Haftendorn 1993: 40f.; Link 1993: 18–20). Germany should thus acquire the role of a 'co-leading power' (*Mitführungsmacht*) in Europe (Link 2000: 26; Link 1999: 140–2).

The common denominator of what these authors suggest about Germany's European integration policy is that a further advance of European integration will serve German interests best. This advance implies, first, a further deepening of European integration (Haftendorn 1994: 140). To be successful in the interdependent world, EU member states will have to be ready to agree to a further loss of sovereignty in favour of joint decision making in the EU (Kaiser 1991: 104). In remarkable contrast to the advocates of a more assertive foreign policy, therefore, the establishment of European Monetary Union (EMU) is evaluated positively (Bertram 1997: 16, 23). The Maastricht and Amsterdam Treaties are considered steps in the right direction, although further steps towards deeper integration are considered necessary (Link 2000: 25f.), e.g. the further development of the Common Foreign and Security Policy (CFSP) (Langguth 1993: 25) and ultimately, as a positive vision at least, the creation of a federal Europe (Link 1992: 606f.). Second, a further advance of European integration also implies the extension of the EU. Germany should support the admission of Eastern European states into the Union, since this is likely to promote their economic development and will thus have a stabilizing effect on Germany's Eastern neighbours. This is the best way for Germany to promote stability at its eastern border without alienating its Western allies (Kaiser 1991: 106f.). Although there may be tensions between the extension and the deepening of the EU, these two goals are not regarded as mutually exclusive. Rather, German foreign policy needs to accomplish the task of combining these two goals (Link 2000: 25; Haftendorn 1993: 42).

Although much of what these authors write is dedicated to Germany's European policy, they also have some advice for German foreign policy beyond Europe. Under the conditions of worldwide interdependence, Germany would be well advised to continue its cooperation with other states as well, especially to preserve its close links with the US (Haftendorn 1994: 143–5) and to maintain its commitments to institutions which have proven their effectiveness in the past, most notably NATO in the issue area of security (Bertram 1997: 21; Bühl 1994: 183). There may well, however, be a tension between strengthening the EU, on the one hand, and maintaining the close relationship with the US, on the other, which may make it difficult for Germany to define its position between its European partners, especially France, and the US (Haftendorn 1999a; Haftendorn 1999b: 8–11). These possible tensions are often not reflected in the texts, and those authors who discuss them disagree about the best way to resolve them. Their suggestions range from building new transatlantic institutions (Weidenfeld 1996: 115) to balancing the hegemonic ambitions of the US by further advancing European integration (Link 2000: 28f.).

In the economic realm, Germany, as a nation dependent primarily on exports for its material prosperity, should continue to support the liberalization of world trade, which entails the necessity to lobby for this goal inside the EU (Langguth 1993: 26). Moreover, German foreign policy makers should be aware of the fact that Germany is linked not only to industrialized but also to Third World countries through an interdependent relationship: while the latter need the economic support of industrialized countries, the former need Third World countries' cooperation to manage global environmental problems and migratory movements (Bühl 1994: 189; Kaiser 1991: 120f.). Germany should, therefore, step up its foreign aid efforts (Bühl 1994: 200f.). While this, in fact, would imply a change in German foreign policy, it would be one that is in line with the more general tradition of a cooperative and multilateral German foreign policy. It is thus another instance of the basic recommendation of the authors grouped together here; i.e. that post-unification Germany should take care to continue the key foreign policy traditions of West Germany.

Advocates of a civilizing foreign policy

> Taking into consideration the new economic, technological, social and ecological challenges, [the federal government] will formulate its foreign and security policy to help safeguard the global future. It will make every effort to develop and implement effective strategies and instruments in order to prevent crises and to ensure the peaceful resolution of conflicts. It will be guided by the obligation to further civilize international relations and to institutionalize the rule of law, to limit and reduce armament, to establish an economic, ecological and socially just balance of the interests of world regions, and to ensure a worldwide observance of human rights.
>
> Coalition Agreement of SPD and Bündnis 90/Die Grünen [7]

Among those authors who reject the recommendation that Germany pursue a more assertive foreign policy and who stress the importance of interdependence in the international system, there are some who regard mere continuity as insufficient for Germany's post-unification foreign policy. They suggest that Germany take the challenges of interdependence even more seriously and engage in a 'civilizing' foreign policy. Their recommendations are rooted in the assessment that increasing levels of interdependence are currently transforming the international system and that they necessitate corresponding adjustments in the foreign policies of industrialized states.

Like the advocates of continuity, most of the authors concerned here have training in the social sciences. Some, yet not all of them, have a background in peace research and lean towards the left side of the political spectrum or are actively engaged in policy consulting for parties of the left. Similarly to the advocates of continuity, they dismiss the assumption of the advocates of a more assertive foreign policy that 1989/90 signifies the return to a 'normal', anarchic world of nation states. In fact, they regard the 'new normality' invoked by these authors as a misperception or even an attempt to justify the re-militarization of German foreign policy (Bahr and Mutz 1998; Wette 1996: 68–70; Wette 1994). For them, 1989/90 does not signify a return to 'normality', but a further step forward in a process of increasing interdependence. This 'complex interdependence'[8] – and here their assessment differs from that of the advocates of continuity too – impinges more and more on the ability of the state to independently make and implement policy decisions. Hence the significance of societal actors increases, at least in industrialized states, and transnational relations become ever more important: a 'world of societies' gains significance beside the 'world of states' (Czempiel 1993: 105–7), and transnational linkages between economic actors and civil societies increasingly 'qualify' the sovereignty of the state (Senghaas 1994: 171–3).

This is a secular process which had begun before 1989/90 and may even be regarded as one of the causes of the breakdown of the socialist systems in the Soviet Union and Central and Eastern Europe (Senghaas 1994: 31f.; Maull 1992: 269). Yet bipolarity had for some time set incentives strong enough to overrule some of the constraints and incentives created by international interdependence (Lübkemeier 1998: 33; Wolf 1998: 370). The disappearance of bipolarity left interdependence as the single most important structural feature of the international system and thus the single most important challenge for foreign policy makers in Europe and around the world.

This is considered to have at least two important implications. First, world politics after the Cold War will probably be more conflict ridden than before (e.g. Schmillen 1995: 512f.). Internationally, increasing interdependence creates additional opportunities for conflict (Senghaas 1994: 18). Moreover, inside many states the changes of 1989/90 have accelerated social change, which has polarized societies and confronted policy making with insurmountable difficulties, creating additional conflicts and aggravating existing ones. In a word, since 1989/90, the world has become more 'turbulent' (Maull 1997: 1,246f., citing Rosenau 1990). Second, conflicts will increasingly impact on states that are not directly involved in them. The more dependent economies become on exports and imports, and the easier borders can be crossed by persons and goods, the more palpable disturbances of the trade exchange become

and the greater the impact of migratory movements caused by violent
conflicts or human rights violations in other countries will be (Bahr
and Mutz 1998: 241; Wolf 1998: 369).

Therefore, the most important challenge for world politics, and thus
also for German foreign policy in an increasingly interdependent world,
is to find ways to manage conflicts peacefully. From these authors'
viewpoint, traditional power politics are ill suited to achieve this end.
A more promising model of conflict management can be found in the
'OECD world', where not only has no war occurred since 1945 but war
has become virtually unthinkable. Among the democracies of the OECD
world, the security dilemma has actually been resolved (Senghaas 1993:
682), just as it has been overcome *inside* democratic states where
violence (in general) is not regarded a legitimate means of resolving
conflicts.

This analogy between the international and domestic realms informs
much of the writings of the authors grouped together here. It can be
traced back to the writings of Norbert Elias (1985, 1969). Elias argues
that, inside societies, a civilizing process took place which was set in
motion by functional differentiation between members of society (and
hence increasing interdependence between them) and which eventually
led to the creation of institutions of non-violent conflict resolution
inside states. With increasing levels of interdependence between states,
this civilizing process can be expected to occur in the international
realm as well. Finding out how the interdependent members of domestic
societies developed civilized ways of resolving their conflicts will lead
to suggestions as to how the increasingly interdependent members of
international society will be able to resolve their conflicts peacefully as
well. This domestic lesson is threefold: conflicts are settled peacefully
in societies in which the use of force is strictly constrained by law; in
which the freedom of individuals is protected; and in which there are
no gross inequalities (Senghaas 1994: 37–43). These three observations
translate into three general recommendations for a civilizing German
foreign policy.

First, Germany's post-unification foreign policy should promote
efforts to *constrain the use of force* in the international realm. By analogy
with the domestic realm, this can be achieved by creating an international legal order in which the right to authorize the use of force is
reserved for a supra-state authority. Therefore, Germany should aim at
strengthening the UN, the international organization which has been
created to represent just such an authority (Maull 1999: 10; Schmidt

1995: 322). It is recommended that Germany increase its financial contributions to the UN (Statz 1993a: 104) and support a UN reform to prop up the organization and make it a more important player in global politics (Messner and Nuscheler 1996a: 9f.; Roth 1993: 228). It is not a strengthening of German influence inside the UN *per se* that is required from German foreign policy (e.g. by means of a permanent seat in the Security Council), but a strengthening of the organization itself (Maull 1997: 1,253; Rittberger and Mogler 1997; Senghaas 1993: 684f.). The strengthening of international law also implies that Germany should support the building up of an international judicial system based on international conventions (Messner and Nuscheler 1996a: 10; Projektgruppe UNO von WEED 1995: 465).

The establishment of an adequate legal framework, however, must be complemented by other measures which directly help to contain the use of force in international politics, i.e. by the development and promotion of non-military ways of conflict resolution (Wolf 1995; Projektgruppe UNO von WEED 1995: 460) and by a reduction of the number of weapons (Czempiel 1999: 204–14). Therefore, Germany should strengthen its commitment to international organizations such as the Organization for Security and Cooperation in Europe (OSCE), whose primary mission is to promote non-military ways of conflict resolution, and put less emphasis on primarily military organizations such as NATO and the Western European Union (WEU) (Lutz 1999: 56f.; Bahr and Mutz 1998: 245f.; Hamann, Matthies and Vogt 1995: 363; Schmillen 1993: 88). Recommendations for Germany to support efforts at de-militarization include both the downscaling of Germany's own military potential and the support of international disarmament efforts. The latter goal requires Germany not only to support international agreements, but also to cut down its own arms exports (Hofer 1993). As a matter of fact, many authors demand a complete prohibition of the export of weapons (e.g. Schmillen 1995: 524f.; Roth 1993: 216; Statz 1993a: 97).

Yet not all recommendations for Germany's post-unification foreign policy to restrict the use of force in the international realm find unanimous support from all advocates of a civilizing foreign policy. In particular, the question of whether Germany should be ready to use force itself in order to stop violations of international law and to restore international peace is heavily disputed among the authors concerned. This dispute is peculiar to the authors of this group, whereas the question does not pose a problem to other authors who proceed from different assumptions. Advocates of a more assertive foreign policy regard military intervention as a normal means of conflict management in the anarchic international system and recommend German participation in such interventions as long as it serves Germany's national security interest. Advocates of continuity regard participation in multilateral military interventions as one element of Germany's multilateral commitments among others and therefore recommend participation in such operations (e.g. Link 1999: 129; Bertram 1997: 23). Advocates of a civilizing foreign policy, however, face a dilemma because the question of German participation in multilateral military operations, from their viewpoint, boils down to the question of whether Germany should *use* force in order to help *restrain* the use of force in the international realm. Although there is general agreement that military means must always be subordinate to civilian ways of conflict management (Statz 1993a: 98) and that Germany must never act militarily on its own, but only together with other nations and with the authorization of the UN Security Council (Müller and Schoch 1999: 45f.; Senghaas 1993: 685), there are some authors who hold that military interventions should *never* be used to promote peace. They consider such interventions dysfunctional (Projektgruppe UNO von WEED 1995: 459), because especially inner-state conflicts cannot be resolved militarily by outsiders (Hamann, Matthies and Vogt 1995: 359f.). Moreover, they argue that the capabilities necessary for the pursuit of military strategies are likely to be interpreted as threats by others and thus will counter the effects of confidence-building measures and practices; in addition, the building up and maintenance of these military capabilities may result in a neglect of non-military means of conflict resolution (Nassauer 1993: 81). On the other hand, there are authors who suggest that, in rare cases, it may be necessary in an imperfect world to rely on military means to implement a civilizing foreign policy, especially if massive violations of human rights cannot otherwise be stopped (Müller and Schoch 1999: 41f.; Maull 1992: 273). From these authors' viewpoint, the use of force has to adhere strictly to several basic principles. It must be confined to cases clearly defined in advance (Senghaas 1993: 685) and conform with the principles laid down in the *bellum iustum* doctrine, especially the principles of just cause, last resort, reasonable expectation of success and proportionality (see Wolf 1993: 201).

Beside the aim directly to restrict the use of force in the international system, a civilizing foreign policy also needs to *promote the freedom of individuals*. This recommendation is backed up not only by the domestic

analogy (there is less civil strife in free countries). Advocates of a
civilizing foreign policy also cite the result of the 'democratic peace'
literature in conflict research:[9] democracies do not wage war against
one another. Hence one of the ways for a democracy to promote peace
is to support democratization in other countries. Therefore Germany
should make human rights concerns a central focus of its foreign policy
(Schmillen 1995: 525; Weißhuhn 1993: 196). Since the observance of
basic human rights standards inside states is considered a prerequisite
for international peace, the violation of human rights can no longer be
considered a state's internal affair. It is a legitimate focus of foreign
policy and a state's sovereignty may no longer be invoked to reject
condemnations of human rights violations (Czempiel 2000: 18–21; Wolf
1993: 206). This extenuation of the institution of sovereignty is considered justified because sovereignty has *de facto* been weakened by
increasing levels of interdependence anyway (Schmillen 1995: 526f.).
The main forums for the promotion of human rights are, again,
international organizations such as the UN, the OSCE and the Council
of Europe (Senghaas 1993: 675). Yet not only states but also international and supranational organizations should adhere to democratic
principles. Therefore Germany should aim at strengthening democratic
accountability at the international and supranational level and the
involvement of transnational actors in international decision making
through its UN policy (Messner and Nuscheler 1996a: 9f.) as well as its
EU policy (Wolf 1998: 380). Consequently, the more reserved approach
towards a deepening of European integration and a weakening of the
intergovernmental level in the EU displayed by Chancellor Schröder,
welcomed by advocates of a more assertive foreign policy, meets
with criticism from advocates of a civilizing foreign policy (Czempiel
2000: 15).[10]

Third, a civilizing foreign policy should also *address gross inequalities*
in the international system. Large gaps in welfare are considered fault
lines for potential conflicts and should therefore be bridged (Rittberger
1992: 227). Hence Germany's foreign aid policy should be geared
towards a generous support of poor countries (Hamann, Matthies and
Vogt 1995: 363) with the eventual aim of overcoming the North–South
divide (Albrecht 1993: 65f.). In supporting developing countries, however, Germany should not lose sight of the other general aims of a
civilizing foreign policy. Foreign aid flows must be carefully directed to
support not militarization, but democratization (Hamann, Matthies and
Vogt 1995: 365). The same strategy should be applied to Eastern

European countries (Senghaas 1993: 675f.), where German foreign policy makers should take care to avoid the mistakes of the foreign aid policy towards the South made in the decades before 1989/90 (Statz 1993b: 145f.).

A foreign policy pursuing these goals is considered to meet the challenges posed by today's international system and to support the civilizing process. Some authors accord Germany particular importance in this process and they do so for two reasons. On the one hand, Germany has become more significant in world politics through unification, because its material capabilities have risen (Schmidt 1995: 314), or at least because it is perceived by other nations to have become a more important actor in world politics (Maull 1997: 1,249). On the other hand, the foreign policy tradition of West Germany already contained elements of a civilizing foreign policy (Maull 1992: 276f.), especially German multilateralism and its willingness to 'pool' or 'delegate' part of its sovereignty in favour of supranational organizations (Senghaas 1993: 679, 681). Germany is thus ascribed both a particular responsibility and a peculiar qualification to develop foreign policy strategies for the new era. Germany may therefore be able to play the role of a 'civilian power' (Maull 1992, 1990) in international politics, and thus be a role model for a foreign policy which meets the challenges of the post-Cold War era. Nonetheless, as the recommendations outlined above suggest, a considerable change in German foreign policy will be needed (less reliance on military organizations, extension of foreign aid, end to arms exports, etc.), even though some elements of a civilizing foreign policy had already been realized before unification (Maull 1992: 275f.).

Conclusion

After unification, the future of German foreign policy was the object of a heated domestic debate. The main dividing line in this debate was between advocates of a more assertive foreign policy and their critics. Within these two groups, there were additional differences which are summarized in tables 2.1 and 2.2.

Table 2.1 Advocates of a more assertive foreign policy

	'New right'	Moderate advocates of assertiveness
Prominent authors	Michael Großheim, Karlheinz Weißmann, Rainer Zitelmann	Arnulf Baring, Gregor Schöllgen, Hans-Peter Schwarz
Assessment of the situation after 1989/90	Post-Cold War Europe resembles Europe after 1871 • Renationalization • Multipolarity Germany is a 'normal great power' in the centre of Europe	
Policy advice	• Reconsider Westbindung	• Proceed from Westbindung
	• No further deepening of European integration	
	• Extend EU to stabilize Eastern neighbours	

Table 2.2 Critics of a more assertive foreign policy

	Advocates of continuity	Advocates of a civilizing foreign policy
Prominent authors	Helga Haftendorn, Karl Kaiser, Gerd Langguth	Hanns Maull, Dieter Senghaas, Albert Statz
Assessment of the situation after 1989/90	Interdependence counters effects of multipolarity in Europe	
	Important continuity: • no significant increase in power • embeddedness in international institutions and dependence on international environment	Growing importance of complex interdependence: • international relations become more conflict prone • conflicts impact on states not directly involved in them
Policy advice	Basic continuity: • support European integration (deepening and extension of EU) • maintain transatlantic ties (e.g. within NATO)	Support civilizing process, be 'civilian power': • contribute to restricting the use of force • support democratization • improve foreign aid and human rights policies

Nonetheless, there appear to be a few points which were accepted by almost all contributors to this debate. First, most authors agreed that Germany has gained a more prominent status in international politics through unification, due either to an increase in its material capabilities or to the changed perceptions of others. Second, everyone agreed that unification and, even more importantly, the end of the bipolar world order opened up new foreign policy options for Germany because the country was freed from the constraints of a front-line state in the Cold War. Finally, there was wide agreement that the new situation would not require Germany *completely* to change its foreign policy. Only very few authors, for instance, recommended a reconsideration of Germany's *Westbindung*, while most agreed that this basic orientation should be carried over to the foreign policy of post-unification Germany.

Within these limits, however, considerable scope for change was seen, and disagreement prevailed as to which courses of foreign policy would be best for German foreign policy makers to choose. Accordingly, the range of recommendations for German foreign policy makers was wide. It ranged from the advice to become more assertive vis-à-vis its main allies to the recommendation to intensify integration, and from support for a strengthening of international law to advice to utilize international institutions in order to push through Germany's interests. Whether German foreign policy makers eventually chose to continue with the foreign policy strategies of West Germany or whether they seized the opportunities for change is a question which has to be settled empirically in the light of pertinent theories of foreign policy behaviour.

Notes

1 For analyses which structure the debate from a different viewpoint, see Hellmann (1999, 1996) for the debate about Germany's post-unification foreign policy in general, and both Janning (1996a) and Wessels (1999) for the debate about post-unification Germany's EU policy.

2 In what follows, the arguments will be stated as they were put forward by the authors cited. This does not imply that the author endorses the views expressed. All quotes from German texts were translated by the author.

3 Gerhard Schröder 1999, 'Eine Außenpolitik des "Dritten Weges"?', in *Gewerkschaftliche Monatshefte* 50: 7/8, 392–6. Internationally, Chancellor Schröder's characterization of Germany as a great power (*große Macht*) has been noted with interest (see *International Herald Tribune (IHT)*, 13 September 1999, p. 6).

4 Already before unification, most of the authors concerned here were highly critical of the then West German foreign policy. They conceded that West Germany's position in the international system was severely constrained during the Cold War but held that West Germans tended to exaggerate these constraints and to cherish 'small-state virtues' instead of seizing the opportunities of their position and of pursuing the foreign policy of a middle power (e.g. Schwarz 1985).

5 A number of other terms are used to express the significance of Germany for European and world politics. Jochen Thies (1994: 72), for instance, describes Germany as being 'back to the semi-hegemonial position of 1871', Gregor Schöllgen (1998: 32) calls Germany a 'great power with global weight', and Christian Hacke (1988) characterized Germany (even before unification) as a 'world power'. Hacke, however, recently indicated that he now prefers Schwarz's term, 'central power of Europe' (Hacke 1999: 201).

6 Foreign Minister Joschka Fischer in his speech to the general meeting of the German Society for Foreign Affairs, Bonn, 24 November 1999; <http://www.auswaertiges-amt.de/6_archiv/99/r/r991124a.htm> (26 September 2000).

7 'Aufbruch und Erneuerung – Deutschlands Weg ins 21. Jahrhundert', Koalitionsvereinbarung zwischen der Sozialdemokratischen Partei Deutschlands und Bündnis 90/Die Grünen, Bonn, 20 October 1998, <http://www.spd.de/politik/koalition/download/vertrag.doc> (26 September 2000).

8 Some of the authors use this term, coined by Robert Keohane and Joseph Nye (1977), to indicate that, from their point of view, increasing levels of interdependence do not merely imply the intensification of mutual dependencies between states, but transform world politics so that societal or transnational actors increasingly gain significance beside states in world politics.

9 See Chan (1997) for an overview over this literature.

10 Also, German participation in the NATO air strikes against Yugoslavia in 1999 is criticized, not only because the international legal basis of the air strikes was questionable but also because it damaged efforts at democratization both inside Yugoslavia and at the international level (Czempiel 2000: 14; Lutz 1999: 48–51).

Part II
Theories

3

Neorealist foreign policy theory[1]

*Rainer Baumann, Volker Rittberger
and Wolfgang Wagner*

Introduction

Although neorealists frequently analyse state behaviour, neorealism lacks an explicit theory of foreign policy. Waltz's theory (1979) is one of international politics, not of foreign policy, since its dependent variable is not the behaviour of individual states but the properties of various international systems, such as their stability or proneness to war. Waltz himself regards his theory as ill suited as a theory of foreign policy (Waltz 1996), although he stresses that the structure of the international system encourages states to adopt a power-political mode of behaviour (Waltz 1993: 61–70). By contrast, we follow Colin Elman, who has maintained that none of the arguments made by neorealists to substantiate the impossibility of a neorealist theory of foreign policy are convincing, and that there is therefore nothing to prevent the formulation of a neorealist theory of foreign policy (Elman 1996a; cf. Waltz 1996 and Elman 1996b). If we are to come to theoretically substantiated and empirically testable predictions, however, neorealist foreign policy theory not only has to be reconstructed but, in certain aspects, still to be constructed.

Neorealism holds that the interactions of states can be explained by the distribution of power in the international system. In order to formulate a neorealist foreign policy theory, the systemic variable 'international distribution of power' has to be transformed into the positional variable 'relative power position' of a certain state (see Billing et al. 1993: 167). Above all, however, it has to be shown how the relative power position of a state determines its foreign policy behaviour. For this purpose, the fundamental assumption of a specific actor disposition (which underlies any foreign policy theory) will have to be explicated.

A state's foreign policy behaviour as postulated by neorealism depends on its (power) position in the international system, which is thus the independent variable. A state's power position is the function of its share in certain resources available in the international system and the number of poles in that system. In the case of the dependent variable, 'foreign policy behaviour', autonomy-seeking policy and influence-seeking policy can be distinguished as two forms of power politics. In order to formulate neorealist predictions, gains or losses in autonomy and influence must be weighed against each other. To do this, we identify possible forms of autonomy and influence and relate them to different policy options. However, weighing can only be done from a theoretical perspective. Within the neorealist school of thought, there has recently been a debate about the weighing of gains in autonomy and influence, from which two competing views have emerged. We shall attempt to do justice to this development within neorealism by distinguishing between neorealism and modified neorealism. In the final section, we turn to Germany's foreign policy after unification. Based on the empirical measurement of the development of Germany's power position, general predictions about post-unification German foreign policy can be formulated.

States' disposition to action in neorealist foreign policy theory

In the neorealist view, a state's foreign policy behaviour is determined by its power position in the international system (Waltz 1993: 45). However, for a neorealist theory of foreign policy, it first has to be clarified why states gear their foreign policy behaviour to the systemic conditions. This relationship between 'power position' and 'foreign policy' can only be established by specifying the state's disposition to action. Here, neorealism rests on a rationality assumption.[2] According to this assumption, states make their decisions on the basis of cost–benefit calculations. The structure of the international system creates certain restrictions and incentives that states take into account when pursuing their aims. While some neorealists concede that states occasionally violate this 'systemic logic' (e.g., when a state fails to protect itself against more powerful states), they emphasize that this behaviour will soon have negative consequences for that state, and in an extreme case could mean its disappearance (see Layne 1993: 9–10). As states are aware of this danger and are interested in their survival, they will generally act according to the structural constraints of the international system: 'The situation provides enough incentive to cause most of the actors to behave sensibly. Actors become "sensitive to costs", which for convenience can be called an assumption of rationality' (Waltz 1986: 331). For a neorealist theory of foreign policy, in particular, the assumption of rationality is the decisive link between the structure of the international system and actor behaviour (see Keohane 1986: 167). In order to arrive at any expectations about the concrete action of individual states, however, the utility functions of states must be examined more closely.

In the anarchic international system, all states must first safeguard their own survival, i.e. their security. The pursuit of manifold, issue-area-specific aims is only possible on the basis of a sufficient degree of security. In addition, the anarchic structure of the international system implies that the better their power position relative to other states, the more successfully states can pursue their various aims. As a structural characteristic, therefore, 'anarchy' plays a crucial role in neorealist foreign policy theory, since it gives rise to two fundamental interests underlying states' foreign policies: interest in their security and interest in as much power as possible (see Schweller 1996: 106–8; Spirtas 1996: 387–9, 395; Mearsheimer 1995: 11; Gilpin 1986: 304–5). A precondition for the formulation of a neorealist foreign policy theory is that these terms are explicated and their interrelationship clarified.

'Security' means 'the ability of states and societies to maintain their independent identity and their functional integrity' (Buzan 1991: 18–19). From a neorealist point of view, there can never be complete security for states in the anarchic international system. Given the permanent scarcity of this resource, states will always strive to preserve and increase their own security. The security interest is a fundamental interest for every state, and it persistently determines states' behaviour.

Another central concept of neorealism, which is related to that of security, is the concept of autonomy. 'Autonomy' is understood as de facto, rather than simply formal, independence from other actors. The less a state's capacity for action is restricted by other states and international institutions, the more autonomous it is. In the neorealist view, the struggle for autonomy is a consequence of the anarchic structure of the international system. The lack of an effective superordinate dispute arbitrator means that states have to rely on self-help. In order to pursue self-help strategies successfully, states have to safeguard their autonomy (see Grieco 1995: 27; Mearsheimer 1995). A state will above all strive for autonomy in those policy areas in which its security is most likely to be threatened.

While closely related, 'security' and 'autonomy' have to be separated analytically. The distinction is important, because other resources competing with 'autonomy' may also serve to protect a state's security. 'Influence' is such a resource, and it is frequently named as such by neorealists. The reason given for this is that every state must pursue its security interests in a competitive and potentially hostile environment. Thus every state will endeavour to gain as much influence as possible on that environment (Gilpin 1981: 94–5).

Furthermore, the concept of power is of central significance for neorealism. Yet neorealists frequently use the term ambiguously. 'Power' is conceived of as *control over resources* when determining the power position of a state. When attention turns to state behaviour, however, the term is often also used in the sense of *control over actors* and *control over outcomes* (Hart 1976). In this chapter, we will attempt to differentiate the concepts more precisely by distinguishing 'power' from 'influence'. '*Power*' is the ability to assert one's interests in the international system. In the neorealist view, this ability is based on the possession of capabilities conducive to such assertion. The power of a state results from the relationship of its own capabilities to those of other states. 'Influence', in contrast, is the measure of control a state has over its international environment. Without this conceptual distinction, contradictions would be inevitable. It would be unclear whether power refers to a state's capabilities or to the pursuit of control over the international environment as a result of the state's capabilities (Zakaria 1992: 194).

Neorealists assume that power provides a state with the means for securing and enhancing its autonomy. Autonomy therefore presupposes power. At the same time, the neorealist concept of 'power' in the sense of control over resources means that 'power' itself already presupposes a certain degree of autonomy. The territory of a state, for example, can only serve the state as a capability if it effectively controls that territory. In neorealism, therefore, autonomy is both a precondition and the result of power. However, this circularity only exists in exceptional cases, e.g. if a state's foreign policy is aimed at ending a status of occupation. The autonomy it gains thereby improves its power position and gives it increased opportunity to strive for further autonomy (in the sense of freedom of action). As a rule, however, gains in autonomy (such as withdrawal from international organizations) can scarcely increase a state's capabilities and can thus only marginally improve its power position.

While, in the neorealist view, the autonomy of a state is a measure of how little control other states and international organizations (i.e. its environment) can exercise over it, its influence is a measure of how strongly it can itself impact its environment, in particular the behaviour of other states and the collective decision making in, and action of, international organizations. Influence is also linked with a state's security interests, but the relationship between influence and security is a more indirect one than that between autonomy and security. Autonomy losses directly imply a higher exposure to threats from other states. If a state loses influence on its environment, other states may increase their influence instead, which may in turn make them more threatening to the state (Gilpin 1981: 86).

A state is interested in influencing the behaviour of other states or collective actions of international organizations to suit its purposes. Otherwise, other states, which are potentially threatening, could shape these actions and decisions to suit their purposes, which would run contrary to the state's security interests. Hence every state is interested in transforming its capabilities into influence.

In order to maintain its security a state will strive for both autonomy *and* influence. Power is a precondition of both. The more powerful a state, the more autonomy and influence it can achieve. Consequently, when formulating a neorealist theory of foreign policy, the assumption should be made that all states in the international system are interested in as much power as possible. This position is not undisputed within neorealism. While 'offensive neorealists' fully subscribe to it (see Mearsheimer 1995: 11–12; Zakaria 1992: 190–6), proponents of 'defensive neorealism' (also called 'defensive positionalism') stress that the international system only induces states to attempt to avoid power losses. They admit, however, that states may go beyond this point and seek to enhance their power position (Grieco 1988a; Gilpin 1981: 87–8; Waltz 1979: 91–2, 118).[3] These authors allow a certain indeterminacy concerning states' disposition to action. This indeterminacy of defensive neorealism has not been remedied so far.[4] This may be acceptable for a theory of international politics, but not for a foreign policy theory. In such a theory, it must be possible to take the theoretical premises as a basis for predicting whether a given state is striving to preserve or to extend its autonomy and its influence. The assumption that states are interested in as much power as possible is more clear-cut than the defensive neorealist position. Furthermore, this assumption is also the most logical one. If a state prefers its current power position, P^0, to a weaker power position, P^{-1}, because this allows it to assert its security and other interests better, then it will also prefer P^{+1} to P^0 and P^{+2} to P^{+1}.[5] It must be emphasized that this assumption refers to states' fundamental interest in increasing power and not to the style of state behaviour. Analysts frequently fail to make this distinction. The assumption of interest in as much power as possible by no means always involves the expectation of aggressive or expansionist behaviour.

So far, we can state that the following are central tenets of a neorealist theory of foreign policy: it follows from the anarchic structure of the international system that all states (as egoistic and instrumentally rational actors) strive for security. As their security grows with increasing autonomy and influence, states strive for autonomy and influence. However, although this disposition to action is the same for all states, it does not result in all states behaving similarly, as states can only pursue a policy geared to autonomy and influence within the limits of the possibilities for action at their disposal as a result of their relative power position. The stronger a state's power position, the more its foreign policy will be autonomy and influence oriented; in other words, it will pursue more vigorously policies aimed at increasing autonomy and influence (= power politics).

A state's power position as an independent variable

According to neorealism, the international system has three structural characteristics, two of which (anarchy and states as units of the system) are constant. When explaining variance in cases of international inter-action, special significance is attached to the third, variable, characteristic, i.e. the distribution of *capabilities* among states. When explaining the foreign policy behaviour of a state, its relative power position has to be derived from the international distribution of power. A state's relative power position is the product of the polarity of the system and the share of capabilities the state (in relation to other states) has at its disposal. Taken in combination, they decisively influence the state's foreign policy behaviour:

> The behavior of individual states, regardless of their domestic political characteristics, is constrained by their own capabilities and the distribution

of power in the system as a whole. The external environment will inevitably pressure states to move toward congruity between commitments and capabilities. (Krasner 1993a: 21)

Capabilities

In the neorealist view, power is based on the availability of political, economic and military capabilities which allow a state to assert its interests in dealings with other actors. Capabilities are seen as highly fungible (Art 1996; Waltz 1986: 333–4; Waltz 1979: 131), meaning that power is a general potential which can be used in disparate areas of policy.

Although 'power' is a central analytical category in neorealism, no neorealist author has yet indicated satisfactorily what exactly has to be regarded as a significant capability and how this is to be measured. Concerning the concept of capabilities, neorealism does not display any more conceptual rigour than classical realism. Morgenthau (1973, 1948) spoke of eight central elements of national power: geography, natural resources (foodstuffs, minerals), industrial capacity, military prepared-ness (technology, leadership, quantity and quality of armed forces), population, national character, national morale and quality of diplo-macy. Waltz names seven different capabilities: 'size of population and territory, resource endowment, economic capability, military strength, political stability and competence' (Waltz 1979: 131). Neither he nor any other neorealist author explicates or operationalizes these terms, let alone brings them together in a coherent and consistent construct (see Grieco 1995, 1990; Mearsheimer 1995, 1990). For Gilpin, power is based on a state's military, economic and technical capabilities (Gilpin 1981: 13). He stresses that there are other important factors as well (which are, however, very difficult to measure) that help to influence political events, such as public morale or the quality of political leadership. He uses the term 'prestige' to sum up these factors (Gilpin 1981: 13, 30). Although Waltz's concept of power includes material and immaterial, psychological factors, he only pays attention to the former when it comes to their application (cf. Waltz 1993, 1986).

Joseph Nye, whose writings have shown many affinities with neo-realism, investigates immaterial capabilities in more detail. He distinguishes between *command power* (or *hard power*) and *co-optive power* (or *soft power*) (Nye 1990: 31–2). The former rests on the usual capabilities, such as population, territory and economic and military strength, while the latter is based on factors such as the attractiveness of ideas and the state's ability to set agendas. Hard power can be used to influence the actions of others, while soft power is aimed at their preferences (Nye 1990: 267). It can be employed in order to influence what others think and desire. Obviously, Nye's concept of soft power is a long way from neorealism. It includes ideas and ideologies, changeable preferences and inter subjectively marked conceptions of the world, i.e. categories which neorealists usually refuse to consider. It would thus be problematic to include aspects of this soft power when determining the power position of a state from a neorealist perspective.

Hence we cannot fall back on a generally accepted canon of capabilities. It is undisputed, however, that neorealists attach particular importance to a state's economic and military strength as core components of its power. To measure economic strength, neorealists generally consider Gross national product (GNP) and export volume, while military spending, the size of the armed forces and the possession of nuclear weapons are often regarded as indicators of military strength. For neorealists, population and territory are capabilities, too. Population size determines how many people can be mobilized as workers and, if necessary, as soldiers. The size and position of a state's territory not only determine how difficult it will be to conquer that state, but may also limit or extend a state's freedom of manoeuvre (e.g. by making nuclear tests possible on that territory). As 'power' is a relative concept, any measurement of a state's power must always take into account the relative size of its capabilities in comparison with those of other states. In this regard, a state's major competitors constitute the reference group.

Polarity of the international system

Neorealists not only regard the polarity of the international system as the decisive determinant of the durability and proneness to war of the system (Waltz 1979: 134–8), but also vest it with great significance for the power positions of the various states. Polarity is determined by the number of (power) poles, i.e. of great powers in the system. Above all, neorealists distinguish between bipolar and non-bipolar systems.[6] Neorealists, however, have not given any criteria to define when a state has sufficient capabilities at its disposal to qualify as a pole in the system. Waltz contents himself with the assertion that it is usually immediately clear who are the great powers in the system (Waltz 1979: 131). For Mearsheimer, who attributes particularly great importance to military capabilities, the necessary and sufficient criterion is the 'reasonable prospect' of defending oneself independently against the leading state in the system (Mearsheimer 1990: 7).

The polarity of the international system influences a state's power position because the number of great powers determines the freedom for manoeuvre of all states in the international system and thus also how states can employ their capabilities. For most states, for example, increasing their own share in capabilities in the international system under conditions of bipolarity has fewer consequences than if they do so under non-bipolarity. In bipolarity, a state with a share in capabilities at its disposal that is significant but remains far behind those of the two leading powers will have little prospect of itself becoming a pole in the system and thus of being able independently to safeguard its own survival. Its security will remain contingent on protection from one great power by the other. In a non-bipolar system, in contrast, this dependence is far less evident, and the state can act independently to a greater degree. When employing its capabilities it is not (or at least is to a lesser degree) restricted by a protective great power. When a bipolar system falls apart, therefore, the power position of such a state improves even if its share in the capabilities available in the international system has not increased.

The forms of power politics: autonomy-seeking policy and influence-seeking policy

Turning away from the independent variable 'power position', we now come to the dependent variable of neorealist foreign policy theory. As, in the neorealist perspective, states use their given power position to strive for autonomy and for influence, we will distinguish two forms of power politics: autonomy-seeking policy and influence-seeking policy.

Autonomy-seeking policy serves to maintain or reinforce a state's independence from other states or, to put it another way, to prevent new, or reduce existing, dependence on other states. A state can pursue an autonomy-seeking policy when gains in autonomy vis-à-vis other states are possible or when there is a risk of losing autonomy. In this context, international institutions are above all significant as restraints on state independence and freedom of action.[7] A number of modes of behaviour can therefore be identified as manifestations of autonomy-seeking policy:

- non-compliance with, or the withdrawal from, existing obligations resulting from bilateral or multilateral international agreements;
- the refusal to accept new obligations of this nature;
- the refusal to transfer national material resources to international or supranational institutions, or the attempt to win back these resources;
- the refusal to transfer national decision-making powers to international or supranational institutions, or the attempt to win back these powers;
- the refusal to cooperate whenever cooperation threatens to create or reinforce asymmetric interdependence, i.e. dependence to the state's disadvantage;
- the formation of an alliance against a third state.

At first glance, it may appear counter-intuitive that, in the case of alliances, cooperation is regarded as enhancing a state's autonomy. From the neorealist point of view, however, alliances have the sole purpose of warding off dominance by a third state which is threatening one's independence. It is important to note that not every form of cooperation among allies conforms with neorealism. According to the neorealist alliance theory, states only accept the minimum loss of autonomy necessary for the alliance in order to prevent the threat of a far greater loss of autonomy which would result from the dominance of a powerful third country.

Selective cooperation or even non-cooperation due to the anxiety of becoming (more) dependent on another state also has to be regarded as autonomy-seeking policy. This includes non-cooperation as a result of *relative-gains* considerations. A state will above all wish to avoid relative losses vis-à-vis another state in order to escape the danger of a loss of autonomy. The neorealist literature dealing with relative gains always speaks of a close relationship between states' anxiety due to relative losses and states' struggle for autonomy. However, it does not contend that states forgo any cooperation whatsoever because of their anxiety about relative losses. If A emerges from its cooperation with B with an absolute gain, then, even if A itself has suffered a relative loss in comparison with B, it can still have made a relative gain in comparison with third parties C, D and E (see Milner 1992; Snidal 1991). What is decisive for a state is the significance it accords to power-position considerations vis-à-vis a specific other state. In Grieco's well-known utility function, this is given as factor k (sensitivity for relative gains and losses) (Grieco 1988b). The value of k is the greater, the higher a state estimates the danger that the other state will limit its autonomy (in the form of dependence in economic or security policy or other relationships) through its relative gains from cooperation.

While states use autonomy-seeking policy in their attempt to elude the influence of their environment, *influence-seeking policy* helps them to exert influence on that environment. When pursuing influence-seeking policy, states attempt to shape interaction processes with other states and the resulting policy outcomes in their own interest, or they attempt to secure and extend the resources enabling them to do so. International institutions are the most important arena for influence-seeking policies of states (Rittberger, Mogler and Zangl 1997: 25–45). Only exceptionally do states control entire international institutions as this requires a preponderance of capabilities. International institutions are of special importance for less powerful states because they benefit from formalized decision making enhancing their voice opportunities (see Grieco 1995: 34). At the same time, it must be noted that not every strengthening of an international institution enhances a state's influence (see below). Influence-seeking policy may also take place in bilateral relations. In relations with a great power a state will seek voice opportunities. In relations with a less powerful state, however, a state will try to acquire a maximum of control over this state's behaviour. The following can be regarded as manifestations of influence-seeking policy:

- an increase in voice opportunities in international organizations by increasing the state's own share in intra-organizational resources (e.g. voting rights);

- preference for those multilateral institutions which yield the most voice opportunities;

- securing voice opportunities regarding the policies of powerful states and groups of states;

- the establishment, maintenance or reinforcement of the dependence of weaker states (i.e. of influence on these states).

The stronger a state's power position, the more its foreign policy will be characterized by both autonomy-seeking policy and influence-seeking policy. In the neorealist view, a small state is too weak to pursue a strong autonomy- and influence-seeking policy with any prospect of success (cf. Waltz 1979: 194). Its interest in autonomy and influence is by no means smaller than that of a great power, but its opportunities for actually pursuing autonomy- and influence-seeking policy are far fewer.

The relationship between the struggles for autonomy and influence: neorealism and modified neorealism

Formulating neorealist predictions requires an ability to decide when a state will prefer autonomy-seeking policy and when it will prefer influence-seeking policy. It thus has to be clarified how the two fundamental dispositions to action, the struggle for autonomy and the struggle for influence, are related to each other. To prevent various modes of behaviour being attributed *ad hoc* to either autonomy seeking or influence seeking, and to enable us to make unequivocal predictions even when faced with two potentially competing dispositions to action, this section aims to define as precisely as possible the conditions under which autonomy seeking or influence seeking can be expected. Our first task is further to clarify what neorealism regards as a gain or a loss in autonomy or influence. We then go on to examine modes of foreign policy behaviour systematically for gains or losses in autonomy or influence. Thereby, we attempt to identify types of behaviour as systematically as possible, so that in applying the theory empirically we can attribute the behavioural options under discussion to the corresponding types. This enables us to determine gains or losses in autonomy or influence in a uniform fashion. Still, a third step is necessary for making predictions. Only a weighing of the various forms of gains or losses in autonomy or influence will allow us to deduce neorealist expectations of behaviour. It will become clear here that a distinction has to be made between two variants of neorealist foreign policy theory, which we designate as 'neorealism' and 'modified neorealism'.

Forms of autonomy and influence

In this section, we want to arrive at as precise an understanding as possible of what neorealists mean by 'autonomy' and by 'influence'. For this purpose, table 3.1 lists possible forms of autonomy and influence.

Table 3.1 Forms of autonomy and influence

	Forms of autonomy	Forms of influence
Positive obligations (obligations to display a certain mode of behaviour)	a) Procedures: freedom from obligation to: • consult with or inform certain actors • accept and implement the decisions of international organizations • accept and implement the judgements of international or supranational courts b) Specific actions: freedom from obligation to comply with concrete duties	Obliging other states to: • consult with or inform oneself • accept and implement the decisions of international organizations reached with the state's participation
Negative obligations (prohibitions of certain modes of behaviour)	Freedom from obligations such as: • the prohibition to produce or acquire certain goods (e.g. nuclear weapons) • the prohibition to use certain tools or resources (e.g. tariffs or certain types of weapon) • the prohibition of certain modes of behaviour vis-à-vis a country's own population (e.g. in human rights regimes) • the prohibition of certain modes of behaviour vis-à-vis other states (e.g. ban on the proliferation of weapons of mass destruction)	Imposing obligations on other states such as: • prohibiting them to produce or acquire certain goods (e.g. nuclear weapons) • prohibiting them to use certain tools or resources (e.g. tariffs or certain types of weapon) • prohibiting certain modes of behaviour vis-à-vis a country's own population (e.g. in human rights regimes) • prohibiting certain modes of behaviour vis-à-vis other states (e.g. ban on the proliferation of weapons of mass destruction)
Restrictions on a state's freedom of action	Freedom from restrictions such as: • dependence in the sense of asymmetric interdependence to the state's disadvantage (e.g. concerning markets or imports)	Restricting other states' freedom by: • dependence in the sense of asymmetric interdependence to the state's advantage (e.g. concerning markets or imports)

• (possibility of) military threat	• (possibility of) military threat
• military action (e.g. the mining of a state's ports)	• military action (e.g. the mining of a state's ports)
• economic sanctions	• economic sanctions

The table makes it clear that autonomy and influence are, by and large, 'mirror images', i.e. one actor's gain in influence involves another actor's loss of autonomy. However, there is an important exception to this strict mirror-image relationship: while, normally, A's gain in influence is B's autonomy loss and vice versa, both A and B may lose autonomy when they *delegate* authority to an international or supranational actor, i.e. when international or supranational actors are permitted to take autonomous decisions without an intervening inter-state vote or unilateral veto (see Moravcsik 1998: 67). An agreement to strengthen the position of the International Court of Justice (ICJ) or the European Commission, for example, represents an influence gain for these international bodies and an autonomy loss for the states concerned.

Options for behaviour to increase autonomy and influence

After listing the various manifestations of autonomy and influence, we now must categorize types of foreign policy behaviour according to their implications for gains or losses in autonomy or influence. Basically, every foreign policy action can cause autonomy or influence to grow, remain the same or diminish. Any combination of the two variables 'autonomy gain/loss' and 'influence gain/loss' is conceivable. However, different types of foreign policy option will tend to give rise to characteristic combinations of the two variables.

In general, withdrawal (or even exit) from international institutions involves a loss of influence and a concomitant gain in autonomy. On the one hand, it exempts a state from obligations arising from membership but, on the other hand, it deprives it of opportunities to have its own preferences taken into account and to oblige other member states to comply with resulting joint decisions. If international institutions exert influence on third countries, withdrawal from such an international institution may also lower the withdrawing state's influence on these third countries. At the same time, however, the withdrawing state may gain enhanced opportunities of influencing these third countries bilaterally. Thus whether withdrawal yields gains or losses vis-à-vis third countries has to be examined case by case. As a general rule, however, reduced influence within the international institution combined with reduced influence on third states exerted through the institution together outweigh enhanced bilateral influence. Analogously, non-participation in multilateral actions (such as military actions) represents a gain in autonomy, since the deployment of the state's own resources (its troops in this case) is not subject to any multilateral decision making. At the same time, the state loses the opportunity of influencing the execution and results of the collective action. International institutions whose decisions are also binding for non-members are a special case. Thus, withdrawing from the UN will not increase a state's autonomy because decisions of the Security Council acting under chapter VII are binding for non-members as well as members.

The strengthening of international institutions will generally mean that a member state will forfeit autonomy and, at the same time, gain influence, since it will be given enhanced voice opportunities over decisions affecting other member states. It is, however, difficult to assess situations in which a state sacrifices some autonomy in order to preserve its autonomy in the long run, e.g. when it forms an alliance against a powerful third state. While an 'investment' of autonomy of this nature involves a loss of autonomy vis-à-vis the status quo, the alternative (not joining an alliance) would, from the neorealist perspective, result in a considerably greater loss of autonomy. Joining an alliance has therefore to be attributed to the 'autonomy loss/influence gain' category, but it has to be considered whether this action does not represent a gain in autonomy compared with the alternatives. Regardless of this, delegating authority to supranational institutions (e.g. the European Court of Justice (ECJ) or the European Commission) is always a special case. When supranational organs are strengthened, there is a considerable loss of autonomy without any concomitant gain in influence. Only the supranational institutions gain influence, while it is withheld from the member states.

A state will increase its influence without an attendant loss of autonomy if it is granted a greater share of inner-organizational resources. The most important inner-organizational resources include shares of votes and seats in decision-making bodies of an international or supranational institution. The scope of possible gains in influence is determined by the mandate, competence and decision-making procedures of the institution. Additional votes in the Council of the EU, for example, enhance a state's influence more than additional seats in the

EP because, in EU decision making, the Council is the more important organ. An increase in a state's share of an international institution's administrative staff, particularly of top-ranking officials, however, may bring about additional prestige but hardly changes a state's influence within the institution.

Relations with weaker states are characterized by the dependence of the latter. Powerful states can instrumentalize this dependence, e.g. by tying development aid or the provision of diplomatic support to conditions. By having positive and negative sanctions at their disposal, states can increase their influence on weaker states, yet their level of autonomy remains unaffected. If relations with weaker states are coordinated multilaterally among powerful states (e.g. when development aid is granted by multilateral organizations), the more powerful states forfeit part of their freedom and thus lose some autonomy. At the same time, they lose the opportunity of tying resource transfers to weaker states to conditions in their favour, and so there is also a loss of influence (in their dealings with weaker states).

Table 3.2 systematically structures the types of foreign policy behaviour described above according to gains or losses in autonomy or influence. However, it does not claim to give a complete picture of the individual cases.

Weighing of gains in autonomy and influence in neorealist foreign policy theory

Table 3.2 includes cases where a state's options for behaviour only vary in respect of 'autonomy' as well as those where they only vary in respect of 'influence'. In such cases, the power-political scale is one dimensional. In other cases, both the anticipated autonomy gains and the anticipated influence gains vary. In one group of cases, autonomy and influence gains vary in the same direction, i.e. a gain in autonomy is linked with a gain in influence and vice versa (e.g. when development aid is given on a bilateral basis).[8] The striving for both autonomy and influence would then translate into the same foreign policy behaviour. The power-political scale would again be one dimensional, and a neorealist prediction could easily be formulated.

As can be seen from table 3.2, however, the strivings for autonomy and influence can occasionally conflict with each other. Within international institutions especially, a policy of increasing autonomy can cost a state influence, while a policy of increasing influence can lead to a

Table 3.2 Options for foreign policy behaviour

	Gain in influence	Influence stays the same	Loss of influence
Gain in autonomy	Bilateralization of relations with weaker states	Weakening of supranational institutions	Withdrawal/exit from international organizations/ bodies whose decisions apply to member states only
			Non-participation in multilateral actions
Autonomy stays the same	Joining international organizations/bodies whose decisions are also binding for non-member states	Preservation of status quo	Withdrawal from international organizations/bodies whose decisions are also binding for non-member states
	Increase of own share of inner-organizational resources		Decrease of own share of inner-organizational resources
	More frequent use of positive/negative sanctions		Less frequent use of positive/negative sanctions
Loss of autonomy	Strengthening of international organizations/bodies in which the state itself participates	Strengthening of supranational institutions	Multilateralization of relations with weaker states
	Participation in multilateral actions		

loss of autonomy. For such cases, a neorealist theory of foreign policy must specify what importance states (within the bounds of their power-political possibilities) will attach to gains or losses in autonomy and influence. As we shall see, Waltz's neorealist theory clearly gives priority to autonomy gains, whereas recent neorealist writings have in part deviated from this. We therefore have to distinguish between two variants of neorealist foreign policy theory.

A foreign policy theory which closely follows Waltz and Mearsheimer will always give clear preference to an increase in autonomy and thus to autonomy-seeking policy. From this point of view, a state's security is always precarious in the international system. As autonomy is more directly linked with a state's security than any possible influence on other actors, special emphasis is placed on preserving and increasing autonomy. International institutions are above all regarded as constraints on state autonomy, which states should attempt to evade if possible (see Schweller and Priess 1997: 3). According to this theory, a state will pursue influence-seeking policy if, and only if, it either preserves/increases autonomy at the same time or if neither gains in autonomy are to be made nor losses in autonomy feared. States are especially concerned to preserve and increase autonomy when facing issues of high politics.

More recently, a number of neorealists have expressed doubts about granting autonomy such absolute priority. As Brooks (1997) argues, the priority of autonomy over influence which Waltz asserts is only possible because Waltz assumes that states always operate on the basis of *worst-case* scenarios. Here, the potential threat by a state is sufficient ground for having to protect oneself against this threat. Potential threat already exists if another state or alliance of states has more capabilities at its disposal. Given such *worst-case* scenarios, voice opportunities seeking vis-à-vis more powerful states seems extremely risky and unwise. Only a foreign policy that does not jeopardize a state's autonomy is regarded as rational.

Brooks goes on to show that this disposition to action is by no means a necessary consequence of neorealist assumptions about the anarchic structure of the international system. He distinguishes here between 'neorealism' and 'post-classical realism': from the neorealist point of view, the permanent possibility of the use of force in the international system means that states operate with *worst-case* scenarios. From the post-classical realist point of view, by contrast, a state's policy is influenced by the probability of the use of force, i.e. by variable *security pressures*. Security pressures do not simply result from the distribution of capabilities in the international system but also from other material factors such as technology, geography and economy, which may reduce the probability for a state of being attacked and thus might lower the security pressures on the state (Brooks 1997: 458). Thus even in the anarchic international system, a state may face low security pressures at times.

From a heuristic point of view, Brooks's distinction between two variants of modern realist theory is very fruitful when (re)constructing neorealist foreign policy theory. However, the term 'post-classical realism' is unfortunate, since realists such as Waltz and Mearsheimer also go beyond the classical realism of Carr and Morgenthau, and are thus 'post-classical' themselves. Instead, we shall speak of neorealism, on the one hand, and modified neorealism, on the other. Moreover, it remains unclear whether Brooks assumes that, in modified neorealism, states do not pursue power politics under certain conditions, or whether he simply assumes a different form of power politics for this theory.

Our considerations so far have shown that the connection between a state's capabilities and its inclination to pursue power politics also applies to a modified neorealist theory of foreign policy. However, the theory can lead to different expectations as to which form of power politics (autonomy- or influence-seeking policy) a state will primarily pursue within the bounds of its capabilities. The higher the security pressures on a state, the greater its concern will be to preserve or even extend its autonomy. In contrast, the lower the security pressures on a state, the more it will be ready to accept autonomy losses for gains in influence. For a modified neorealist theory, therefore, it is essential that the variable 'security pressures' be defined.

Various neorealist authors have identified variables which have an impact on security pressures. Reference is made to technological, geographical and economic factors which may temper the acuteness of the security dilemma resulting from anarchy (see Snyder 1996: 168–71). For instance, Barry Buzan has introduced 'interaction capacity in the international system' as a variable (Buzan 1993a: 69–80). This refers, first and foremost, to the communications and transport technology available and usable in the international system. His argument is that, as the interaction capacity increases, the anarchic international system will forfeit its self-help character. Robert Jervis and Charles Glaser have emphasized the modifying effect of certain military technologies. Security becomes more precarious as the available military technology gives the offence the advantage (Glaser 1995: 61–2; Jervis 1978) and as offensive weapons and policies become difficult to distinguish from defensive weapons and policies (Glaser 1995: 62). Geography is a factor that plays a significant role in Stephen Walt's balance-of-threat theory. According to Walt, a state does not necessarily have to regard another, very powerful state as a serious threat, if its territory is far away (Walt 1987: 17–33). In such a case, a state may choose influence-seeking instead of autonomy-seeking policy. Finally, Robert Gilpin has referred to economic factors. He emphasizes that the costs of territorial expansion are very high for industrialized countries which are highly integrated in the global economy, and that for this reason these states primarily attempt to achieve political influence on other states and a dominant position in the global economic system (Gilpin 1981: 132–3). It follows from this argument that, other things being equal, a state surrounded by modern industrialized nations will be under less serious threat of military attack than one whose neighbouring states may expect to gain from territorial expansion.

According to these authors, international institutions can, to a greater extent than allowed by neorealism, be used by states as arenas for converting capabilities into influence. This is reminiscent of the variant of the theory of hegemonic stability (Gilpin 1981) which takes the idea of a *coercive hegemon* (see Hasenclever, Mayer and Rittberger 1997: 90–2; Snidal 1985a) as its starting point. In a similar way, Stephen Krasner has pointed out that regimes can themselves be a source of power (Krasner 1983a: 364–5; Krasner 1991; cf. Hasenclever, Mayer and Rittberger 1997: 108). Finally, Joseph Grieco's *voice-opportunity* hypothesis stresses that even weaker states may be successful in using institutions to secure influence by binding a stronger state (Grieco; 1995).[9]

There are similarities between modified neorealism and what has been termed the 'rationalist variant of institutionalism' (see Hasenclever, Mayer and Rittberger 1997: 23–82). The latter claims that international institutions can temper the cooperation-inhibiting effect of anarchy (Keohane 1989b; Axelrod and Keohane 1985). Institutions help to solve collective action problems, to monitor and sanction compliance, and to redress the unequal distribution of gains and losses resulting from international cooperation. Institutions thus allow states to pursue their own interests in coordination with other states. Within a modified neorealist foreign policy theory, too, institutions may have an instrumental character for states. In contrast to rationalist institutionalism, however, modified neorealism always regards the individual state's power position as the decisive independent variable providing the main explanation for its behaviour, since the interaction processes within institutions are determined by power politics (see Krasner 1991). Modified neorealism does not necessarily predict cooperative policies within international institutions. Rather, this variant of neorealist foreign policy theory also predicts that the state will pursue power politics in line with its power position.[10] Facing high security pressures, a state will prefer autonomy over influence (as neorealism would always predict). The lower the security pressures, the more a state will be prepared to forgo gains in autonomy for gains in influence.

As the relative power position of a state remains the independent variable for modified neorealism, technology, geography and economics are intervening variables. They affect a state's disposition to action, i.e. whether it will prefer to strive for autonomy or for influence. The difference between a neorealist and a modified neorealist theory of foreign policy is shown as in figure 3.1.

Figure 3.1 Neorealism and modified neorealism

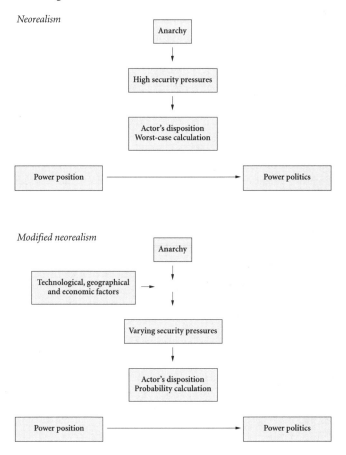

Basically, the following can be stated with regard to the weighing of autonomy and influence in modified neorealism: the lower the security pressures on a state, the greater the relative importance of influence will be as compared with autonomy, and the more that state will be ready to accept autonomy losses in return for substantial gains in influence. If a state faces high security pressures, autonomy will be extremely significant, while influence will be of subordinate importance. Here, the predictions of modified neorealism and those of neorealism will converge. Conversely, if a state is under low security pressures, influence will be very important, whereas less emphasis is put on autonomy. Then, there are again clear priorities concerning autonomy and influence, in this case in favour of influence-seeking policy.

In order to arrive at testable predictions, of course, security pressures as well as gains in influence and autonomy have to be measured with at least a minimum of precision.[11] Unfortunately, the neorealist literature has not given much attention to the operationalization and measurement of these concepts. In our view, however, the following criteria plausibly ensue from a modified neorealist perspective:

- Material obligations outweigh procedural obligations.

- Influence gains vis-à-vis more powerful states are more important than influence gains vis-à-vis less powerful states.

- An obligation to comply with decisions made by international organizations or bodies involves less of an autonomy loss if the state is itself a member.

- An obligation to comply with decisions made by international organizations or bodies involves less of an autonomy loss if the state has the right to veto.

- An obligation to comply with the provisions of a treaty involves less of an autonomy loss if the treaty's binding interpretation is not given by an independent arbitral or juridical authority but by each of the participating states themselves.

- The higher the costs of implementing obligations the more severe the loss of autonomy.

Post-unification Germany and power politics

We can now take the two neorealist variants as a basis for generating predictions about post-unification German foreign policy. Though specific predictions will be derived in the case studies (chapters 6 to 9), general predictions will be presented here (p. 65). Yet we first have to establish the value of the independent variable over time, i.e. to examine how the German power position has changed from the time before unification and the end of the East–West conflict in the 1980s up to the mid- or late 1990s.

The development of Germany's power position

We pointed out above that there are two important factors determining a state's power position: first, its capabilities in comparison with those of other states and, second, the polarity of the international system in which the state operates.

Capabilities

To assess the development of Germany's power position since unification and the end of the East–West conflict, we first have to look at those capabilities which neorealism regards as decisive, comparing them with those of the 'old' Federal Republic of Germany (FRG). Attention should be devoted not to the absolute magnitude but to Germany's share of capabilities in the international system. Following the neorealist theory, other powerful states will be treated as the reference group. When considering capabilities, therefore, we will always examine the German share within the reference group comprising Germany and its major competitors, i.e. the US, the USSR/Russia, France, the UK and Japan. In each case, data from the period 1985–89 will be compared with those from the period 1991–98.[12] Concerning 'population' and 'territory', the situation is clear even without presenting precise data.

We begin with the economic capabilities. Between 1985 and 1989, German GNP made up an average of 10.2 per cent of the total GNP of the reference group in the international system (table 3.3). Between 1991 and 1995, the average German share came to just below 12 per cent. As the data show, this relative increase is above all due to the collapse of the Soviet/Russian economy.

The German economy's export strength is often cited as an important aspect of the country's economy-based power (see Waltz 1993). Between 1985 and 1989, the German share of exports within the reference group fluctuated between 23.5 per cent and 27.8 per cent, with a mean of just below 26 per cent (table 3.4). Since unification (1991–97), the German share has undergone similar fluctuations (23.8 per cent to 26.1 per cent), with a mean of just below 25 per cent. Annual fluctuations notwithstanding, overall Germany's export strength has remained fairly constant.

Table 3.3 GNP (US $ billions, prices of 1995)

	FRG	France	UK	Japan	US	USSR/ Russia	German share (%)	German share (without USSR/ Russia) (%)
1985	1,689	1,226	895	3,849	5,758	2,903	10.35	12.59
1986	1,728	1,260	934	3,952	5,920	3,003	10.29	12.53
1987	1,754	1,290	974	4,123	6,085	3,039	10.16	12.33
1988	1,818	1,349	1,019	4,381	6,321	3,130	10.09	12.21
1989	1,894	1,407	1,040	4,592	6,533	3,170	10.16	12.25
1990	1,998	1,438	1,037	4,811	6,625	3,057	10.53	12.56
1991	2,095	1,449	1,016	5,018	6,555	2,797	11.07	12.99
1992	2,120	1,461	1,022	5,084	6,729	868	12.27	12.91
1993	2,071	1,449	1,044	5,076	6,881	794	11.96	12.54
1994	2,131	1,488	1,084	5,106	7,106	693	12.10	12.60
1995	2,172	1,521	1,110	5,153	7,247	664	12.16	12.63

Source: US Arms Control and Disarmament Agency, *World Military Expenditures and Arms Transfers*, Washington, DC, US Arms Control and Disarmament Agency 1996.

Figures for Russia (from 1992): rough estimates; figures for 1995: estimates for all except FRG, US.

Table 3.4 Exports (US $ billions)

	FRG	France	UK	Japan	US	German share (%)
1985	183.993	101.674	101.252	177.164	218.815	23.50
1986	243.326	124.948	107.093	210.757	227.158	26.64
1987	294.369	148.382	131.257	231.286	254.122	27.79
1988	323.323	167.787	145.165	284.856	322.427	26.00
1989	341.231	179.397	152.345	273.932	363.812	26.03
1990	410.104	216.588	185.172	287.581	393.592	27.47
1991	402.843	217.100	184.964	314.786	421.730	26.13
1992	422.271	235.871	190.003	339.885	448.164	25.81
1993	382.472	209.349	180.180	362.244	464.773	23.92
1994	429.722	235.905	204.923	397.005	512.627	24.14
1995	523.802	286.738	242.042	443.116	584.743	25.18
1996	524.198	288.468	260.746	410.901	625.073	24.85
1997	512.427	289.842	281.513	420.957	688.697	23.36

Source: IMF, *International Financial Statistics Yearbook 1998*, Washington, DC, IMF.

Indicators of military capabilities show a comparable pattern. Between 1985 and 1989, the German share of military spending in the reference group averaged 6.18 per cent, while it came to an average of 8.13 per cent in the years 1991–98 (table 3.5). This relative increase (but slight decline in absolute terms) is again due to the collapse of the Soviet Union/Russia.

Table 3.5 Military spending (US $ millions, prices and exchange rates of 1993)

	FRG	France	UK	Japan	US	USSR/ Russia	German share (%)	German share (without USSR/ Russia) (%)
1985	41,960	42,450	42,563	31,390	337,800	188,604	6.13	8.46
1986	41,460	42,540	42,014	32,880	357,900	190,528	5.86	8.02
1987	43,572	44,218	42,881	34,580	374,644	194,584	5.93	8.07
1988	46,056	44,175	40,952	36,250	366,324	197,236	6.30	8.63
1989	47,579	44,750	41,099	37,770	362,441	179,296	6.67	8.92
1990	49,188	44,537	40,075	39,130	346,315	165,568	7.18	9.47
1991	45,409	44,792	40,278	40,460	300,410	142,012	7.40	9.63
1992	43,013	43,436	35,907	41,330	320,391	25,203	8.45	8.89
1993	38,902	42,819	34,712	41,730	302,993	19,725	8.09	8.44
1994	36,310	43,000	33,362	41,000	286,370	16,440	7.95	8.25
1995	35,581	40,931	30,676	41,886	272,067	14,100	8.17	8.45
1996	35,040	40,188	30,817	42,400	259,133	14,600	8.30	8.60
1997	34,184	40,566	28,879	42,600	257,811	15,000	8.16	8.46
1998	34,088	39,595	28,958	42,571	246,345	7,000	8.55	8.71

Source: Bonn International Centre for Conversion, January 2000.

Troop strength shows a similar picture. Here, the average German share increased from 6.4 per cent (1985–89) to 7.6 per cent (1991–98) (table 3.6). Again, in spite of an absolute decline, this relative gain results exclusively from the dramatic decline in figures for Russia compared with those for the Soviet Union.

Table 3.6 Armed forces (active duty military personnel without reserve forces, thousands)

	FRG	France	UK	Japan	US	USSR/ Russia	German share (%)	German share (without USSR/ Russia) (%)
1985	495	563	334	241	2,244	3,900	6.36	12.77
1986	495	558	331	245	2,269	3,900	6.35	12.70
1987	495	559	328	244	2,279	3,900	6.34	12.68
1988	495	558	324	245	2,246	3,900	6.37	12.80
1989	503	554	318	247	2,241	3,800	6.56	13.02
1990	545	550	308	250	2,181	3,700	7.23	14.21
1991	457	542	301	250	2,115	3,600	6.29	12.47
1992	442	522	293	242	1,919	2,600	7.35	12.94
1993	398	506	271	242	1,815	2,300	7.20	12.33
1994	362	506	257	242	1,715	1,900	7.27	11.75
1995	352	504	233	240	1,620	1,685	7.59	11.92
1996	339	501	221	236	1,575	1,430	7.89	11.81
1997	335	475	218	236	1,539	1,200	8.36	11.93
1998	333	449	216	243	1,518	1,120	8.57	12.05

Source: Bonn International Centre for Conversion, January 2000.

Although it has the capability to develop and produce such weapons, Germany still has no nuclear weapons of any kind. On the whole, the indicators of military capabilities also reveal constancy, or show at best minor German growth.

In contrast, the German position has clearly improved concerning the indicators 'population' and 'territory'. Of course, what is more important than the absolute and relative growth in both areas is the fact that, with unification, Germany was for the first time given full control over its own territory. The special rights and responsibilities of the Allied Powers (*Alliierte Vorbehaltsrechte*) and the special status and exposed position of Berlin put exceptional constraints on the 'old' FRG (see Haftendorn and Riecke 1996). Unification put an end to these two considerable disadvantages for Germany. Given the crucial importance of economic and military capabilities, it is evident that, while on the whole the German share of capabilities has increased, this growth has only been modest.

Polarity of the international system

From a neorealist point of view, however, the structure of the international system has changed radically. The 'old' FRG acted within a bipolar system with two great powers, the US and the Soviet Union. It depended on the one great power for protection from the other and, despite its considerable capabilities, had no prospect of ever becoming a great power, i.e. an independent power pole in the system.

Now that this bipolar structure has vanished, one can best speak of a unipolar transition phase. Layne claims that there is unipolarity, since the US currently occupies a clear position of dominance (Layne 1993: 5). Krasner sees the international system as both more unipolar and less hierarchical than during the East–West conflict, since the US had also suffered a loss of power (Krasner 1993a: 22). Waltz (1993) and Mearsheimer (1990) maintain that the bipolar system is drawing to a close. The current power configuration has also been described as 'unipolarity without hegemony' (Wilkinson 1999). From the neorealist perspective, however, such a unipolar system can scarcely remain stable. Rather, it will now provide other powerful states with a strong incentive to balance against the US. For Germany, the altered polarity of the international system means that it is less dependent on the US and less in need of its protection. These *de facto* constraints on action have disappeared. Of course, several of Germany's competitors, such as France or the UK, have also benefited from this change. Still, Germany's power position has improved due to the changes in the polarity of the international system, regardless of the relative increments in its capabilities.

Summary

On the whole, we can conclude that Germany's power position has improved, albeit less dramatically than some neorealists assume (see Krasner 1993a: 22; Layne 1993: 37; Waltz 1993: 62–4). The data show that Germany has not become a new superpower (Bergner 1991) or a world power (Hacke 1997). Nor has Germany lost power (Maull 1997: 1249). The development of German capabilities, coupled with the collapse of the bipolar structure of the international system, suggests a moderate increase in German power. This gives rise to expectations of a moderate increase in power politics in Germany's foreign policy behaviour. To arrive at more specific predictions, however, we have again to distinguish between neorealism and modified neorealism.

General neorealist predictions for German foreign policy

Since, for *neorealism*, states prefer autonomy over influence, it expects German foreign policy behaviour to be shaped by a balancing strategy vis-à-vis the US. Such a balancing strategy implies a weakening (and in the mid term, a termination) of institutionalized transatlantic cooperation, as this would allow Germany to achieve the greatest gains in autonomy. After all, as the sole remaining great power, the US, with its currently unparalleled capabilities, is the greatest threat to other states (Layne 1993). The fact that a weakening of transatlantic cooperation would involve the loss of opportunities to influence US decision making is far less important than the gains in autonomy it yields. The attempt to preserve, or even extend, possibilities of co-decision making with the US would mean having to rely on US benevolence, although its (so far peaceful) attitude could change at any time. Moreover, Germany will also be very sensitive to losses of autonomy vis-à-vis European states, thus putting the deepening of European integration on hold.

For *modified neorealism*, in contrast, it is crucial that, after unification and the end of the East–West conflict, the security pressures on Germany have declined drastically. While technological factors have largely remained constant, geographical variables affecting the security pressures on Germany have changed significantly. Whereas, during the East–West conflict, the FRG was at the frontline of the Iron Curtain, now the opposing alliance has disappeared altogether. Though Russia has admittedly kept a significant nuclear force, its conventional forces had been completely removed from German territory and from countries adjacent to Germany by the end of 1994. The effect of these geographical factors is intensified by economic changes. In contrast to the period before unification, Germany is now centrally located in a region of established or incipient market economies. Hence it is surrounded by states that will strive for better positions in the global economy rather than for territorial expansion.[13] Even though we cannot measure the security pressures in exact terms, it is clear that, in the case of Germany, the changes are so profound that modified neorealism expects not only a move towards more power politics, but also a shift in its weighing of autonomy and influence in favour of the latter. Admittedly, the dominant power position of the US is also significant for modified neorealism but, as long as the likelihood of a confrontation with the US, or indeed of a military attack on Germany, can be regarded as negligible, there is no need for Germany to pursue a balancing strategy vis-à-vis the US.

Germany will, to a much lesser extent than assumed by neorealism, be sensitive to losses of autonomy in its dealings both with the US and with European states. Greater significance will be accorded to substantial influence gains. For the time being, Germany will not attempt to withdraw from common institutions, but attempt to exert more influence on the joint decisions within them. This does not mean that preserving and extending autonomy have become insignificant for Germany. It will not accept significant losses of autonomy in return for small gains in influence. Nevertheless, Germany will above all strive for gains in influence, and will also be prepared to accept losses in autonomy in return for substantial gains in influence.

Thus the two neorealist theories lead to the following general predictions for German foreign policy:

Neorealism

- As its power position has moderately improved, post-unification Germany will step up its pursuit of power politics.

- By means of intensified autonomy-seeking policy, post-unification Germany will attempt to increase its autonomy, and by means of intensified influence-seeking policy it will attempt to increase its influence. If there is a conflict between autonomy and influence, post-unification Germany will prefer autonomy over influence.

Modified neorealism

- As its power position has moderately improved, post-unification Germany will step up its pursuit of power politics.

- By means of intensified autonomy-seeking policy, post-unification Germany will attempt to increase its autonomy, and by means of intensified influence-seeking policy it will attempt to increase its influence. As the security pressures on Germany have decreased, post-unification Germany will prefer substantial influence over autonomy, if there is a conflict between influence and autonomy.

Notes

1 An extended version of this chapter has been published in German in the *Zeitschrift für Internationale Beziehungen* (Baumann, Rittberger and Wagner 1999).

2 Lebow (1994: 273–4) takes a different view, seeing an evolutionary selection mechanism in neorealism. Elman, by contrast, stresses that, in the
   end, Waltz works with a rationality assumption, although he concedes: 'in
   much of his work it is unclear whether Waltz is relying on rationality,
   evolutionary selection or socialization' (Elman 1996b: 43). Keohane
   (1989a: 160) even attributes the assumption of substantive rationality as
   defined by Herbert Simon to both realists and neorealists. Grieco maintains that the assumption of states' substantive and instrumental rationality
   is an essential feature of the neorealist research programme (Grieco 1995:
   27).

3 Gilpin is often regarded as an offensive realist, however.

4 By explaining the striving for maximum power with subsystemic variables,
   Snyder (1991) has effectively left the tenets of neorealism (see Legro and
   Moravcsik 1999: 23–5; Zakaria 1992). Schweller (1998, 1996, 1994) has
   adopted Carr's (1939) and Morgenthau's (1948) distinction between status
   quo states and revisionist states (see also Buzan 1991: 298–303), but he
   cannot give any clear criteria as to when a state is revisionist and when it
   is status-quo oriented (see Legro and Moravcsik 1999: 27–32).

5 Surprisingly, even Grieco, who coined the term 'defensive positionalist',
   assumes in his model of the state utility function in international cooperation that benefits rise with increasing relative gains (see Grieco 1988b:
   607–9): $U = V–k(W–V)$, where V = the player's payoff, W = the other
   player's payoff, and k = player's sensitivity for gaps in gains. A rational
   actor with this utility function will strive for relative gains and not only to
   avoid relative losses.

6 With regard to non-bipolar systems, neorealists are mostly concerned with
   multipolar systems, but they have also identified unipolar international
   systems (see Layne 1993). In terms of proneness to war, unipolarity is
   regarded as especially stable by neorealist proponents of hegemonic
   stability theory, such as Gilpin. However, most neorealists emphasize the
   extreme instability of unipolar systems in terms of durability: unipolarity
   is only seen as a transition stage on the path to a bipolar or multipolar
   system. For neorealists, therefore, the most important distinction is the
   'bipolarity/non-bipolarity' dichotomy, where non-bipolarity generally
   signifies a multipolar system and, in exceptional cases, a unipolar transitory
   system.

7 At first glance, neorealists' view on international institutions seems somewhat contradictory. On the one hand, they deny a significant influence of
   international institutions on state behaviour, while, on the other hand,
   they assume that states avoid any commitments vis-à-vis international
   institutions. This apparent contradiction may be solved, however: though
   neorealists do not attribute any independent influence to international
   institutions, they regard them as instruments at the disposal of powerful

states (Mearsheimer 1995: 13). By avoiding commitments vis-à-vis inter-national institutions, states in fact avoid commitments vis-à-vis other states which may indeed endanger a state's autonomy.

8 Gains in autonomy and influence do not have to be made vis-à-vis the same state or group of states. In the present example, autonomy would be gained vis-à-vis other donor countries, and influence vis-à-vis recipient states.

9 However, Grieco cannot predict under what conditions a state will prefer balancing and when it will prefer voice-opportunities seeking (cf. Grieco 1995: 40). To do this, the above-mentioned variables would have to be specified.

10 We agree with Jeffrey Legro and Andrew Moravcsik's (1999) critique that contemporary realists such as Charles Glaser, Joseph Grieco, Randall Schweller, Jack Snyder, Stephen Walt and others advance arguments which are at times in opposition to the basic assumptions of their own school of thought. Our (re)construction of modified neorealism, while building up on thoughts of these neorealist scholars, is not subject to this critique, as in modified neorealism a state's foreign policy is determined by its relative power position.

11 Otherwise, observed state behaviour might easily be attributed to modified neorealist hypotheses in a post-hoc fashion, and neorealism might become a degenerative research programme (see the discussion between Vasquez (1997) and Waltz (1997), Christensen and Snyder (1997), Elman and Elman (1997), Schweller (1997), and Walt (1997). As we shall discuss later, it is possible to establish with sufficient precision the changing of security pressures that Germany is facing.

12 Concerning GNP, reliable data were available for the period up to 1995, and concerning exports, up to 1996.

13 The increased possibility of poverty-induced mass migration to Western Europe is sometimes seen as a new security threat. However, such a broad conceptualization of security is inconsistent with the neorealist focus on the military dimension of security.

4

Utilitarian-liberal foreign policy theory

Corinna Freund and Volker Rittberger

Introduction

In contrast to neorealism, liberalism does not regard states as unitary actors with a 'national interest' that can be derived from the international condition of anarchy and the distribution of power among states. Instead, liberalism explains states' foreign policy behaviour on the basis of domestic factors. Utilitarian liberalism combines this basic liberal tenet with the premise of rational actors attempting to maximize their utility, which it treats as exogenously given. The core hypothesis of utilitarian-liberal foreign policy theory is that domestic interests shape the foreign policy behaviour of a country.

In order to allow for the formulation of predictions about foreign policy behaviour across issue areas, both neorealism and constructivism each offer a theoretical conceptualization of their independent variables – power in the case of neorealism, social norms in that of constructivism. Also, both theories posit a direct connection between their independent variables and policy behaviour. It is our aim here to develop a similarly parsimonious utilitarian-liberal approach towards theorizing about foreign policy. We will offer a model for the explanation of German foreign policy behaviour on the basis of domestic interests. And we will suggest ways of identifying domestic interests which are applicable to all issue areas of German foreign policy.

To this end, the basic assumptions of utilitarian liberalism as a school of thought in international relations will be described and different currents of utilitarian-liberal foreign policy theory will be discussed. Here, a distinction will be made between structural and agency-based explanations of foreign policy. After having shown that agency-based explanations are more suitable, especially for the longitudinal study of

German foreign policy, the policy network approach will be introduced as the conceptual basis for a utilitarian-liberal analysis of German foreign policy. The chapter then focuses on showing how network analysis helps to identify the domestic interests which shape German foreign policy. This is done in four steps. First, the foreign policy preferences of domestic actors are derived from their basic interests. Second, the dominant domestic actors – those actors who are capable of asserting their preferences most successfully in the foreign policy-making process – will be identified. Third, on the basis of the composition of the set of dominant actors, the policy network structure will be established. On the basis of the network structure and the preferences of the dominant actors, it is then possible to ascertain those domestic interests which are most likely to shape foreign policy behaviour in a given issue area of foreign policy. Following on from this, we describe some general features of foreign policy networks in Germany. Finally, we formulate a general prediction for German foreign policy behaviour after unification.

Basic assumptions of utilitarian liberalism

A central concern with individual actors is the common denominator uniting all utilitarian-liberal analytical approaches (e.g. Buchanan 1989; Buchanan and Tullock 1962: 1ff.). Utilitarian liberalism is therefore indebted to the tradition of methodological individualism. It is always individuals, not collectives, that act. While individuals may form collective units, every observed action is attributable to the preferences of individuals.

In addition to this fundamental methodological decision, utilitarian liberalism makes an assumption about the behavioural disposition of actors which harks back to the classical utilitarians of the early nineteenth century, such as Jeremy Bentham and John Stuart Mill. According to the concept of *homo oeconomicus* (Kirchgässner 1991: 13ff.; Downs 1967: 2; Buchanan and Tullock 1962: 17ff.), all actors seek to maximize their utility. In order to do so, they gear their actions towards achieving their aims with the minimum of effort or cost, i.e. they act rationally. However, both 'rationality' and 'utility' are highly abstract concepts which can be operationalized in different terms. A utilitarian-liberal theory of foreign policy cannot therefore avoid explicating the concepts of rationality and utility on which it is based.

There are two possible understandings of 'rationality': *substantive rationality* and *procedural rationality*. Our construction of a utilitarian-liberal foreign policy theory makes use of the concept of substantive rationality, which posits that an actor will choose from among the objectively available alternatives for action the one which maximizes his utility (Simon 1985: 294). This concept does not take account of the uncertainty, or restrictions on available information, which an actor has to face. We have chosen this understanding of rationality because the concept of procedural rationality presents problems for both theory construction and empirical research that are extremely difficult to resolve. If an actor is assumed to behave according to procedural rationality or 'bounded rationality', he chooses the utility-maximizing alternative from among the behavioural alternatives known to him subjectively, and does so in the face of other constraints, such as uncertainty. In this case, the alternatives for action which are available from the actor's point of view have to be known, as do the restrictions on an actor's information and his information processing.

The assumption of utility maximization also needs to be specified in more detail. When the concept of substantive rationality is taken as the point of departure, the utility of actors is defined *a priori*, i.e. in objective terms, by the analyst. In order to do this, however, additional theoretical assumptions are needed (Simon 1985: 294–6). As is commonly done in political science, we will distinguish between two variants of utility: 'power' and 'plenty'.[1] Accordingly, actors are assumed to strive for both financial means (i.e. income and assets) and policy-making power. In earlier public choice approaches, utility was usually modelled as solely dependent on financial means: the more financial means an actor had at his disposal, the higher his level of utility was assumed to be. However, the restriction of utility to financial means has proved too narrow in political science. It has thus been extended to include increases in actors' policy-making power, such as the appointment to political office (Buchanan 1989: 41f.; Blair and Maser 1978: 12).

The assumption of utility maximization also leads directly to the previously mentioned concepts of *interests* and *preferences*. An actor's presumed orientation to maximizing his utility is his interest. Ensuring survival – in the narrow physical as well as in the larger social sense – must be regarded as the fundamental interest of any actor, as only then can other utility-increasing goals be pursued. In the following, all those interests whose pursuit directly serves to secure an actor's survival will be regarded as basic interests. According to the individual utility function, in certain structural circumstances and contexts of action (in a given issue area of foreign policy, for example) more specific policy preferences can be derived from these basic interests. While actors' basic interests tend to show little variation over time, policy preferences can change if the context of action changes. This is especially the case when incentives for, or restrictions on, action arise or disappear.

Variants of utilitarian-liberal explanations of foreign policy

There are two main types of utilitarian-liberal approach to foreign policy: structural and agency-based approaches. While structural explanations of foreign policy behaviour refer to domestic structures, agency-based explanations attribute pre-eminence to domestic interests. Below, we give a brief description of the main features of both approaches. We argue that agency-based approaches are more suitable, especially for a longitudinal analysis of foreign policy behaviour, and will therefore form the point of departure for our utilitarian-liberal foreign policy theory.

Structural explanations of foreign policy

Structural utilitarian-liberal approaches to foreign policy deduce predictions about a state's foreign policy directly from its domestic structures.

One domestic structure which is referred to is a state's *level of modernity*. Here, the internal differentiation of a state's socio-economic structure forms the point of departure. Due to a higher level of internal differentiation, 'modern' states are assumed to pursue a more peaceful and cooperative foreign policy than 'traditional' states (Wachtler 1983). Another structural explanation of a state's foreign policy hinges on the classification of states as *democratic* or *authoritarian*. It is argued that democratic states will pursue a more cooperative foreign policy than authoritarian ones. This consideration is based on the idea that a liberal-democratic domestic order will encourage the peaceful settlement of conflicts, whereas in an authoritarian state conflicts tend to be settled by the threat or use of violence (Russett 1993). Finally, some authors view the relative *strength or weakness of the state vis-à-vis its domestic society* as the decisive determinant of a state's foreign policy (Katzenstein 1978; Krasner 1978). However, there is no consensus in the literature as to how a state's strength affects its foreign policy behaviour. Some authors believe that, due to a highly centralized policy-making process, strong states are more likely to support international cooperation.

Others contend that weak states will pursue a more cooperative foreign policy, as the dispersion of policy-making competence renders trans-governmental coalitions more likely (Zürn 1993: 304).

Due to their high level of aggregation, structural explanations of foreign policy are useful primarily for cross-country comparisons: when differences between the foreign policies of different states are to be explained, a high level of aggregation is justified, for the intention is to explain the foreign policy style or typical foreign policy patterns of a state. In contrast, structural approaches are not suited for a longitudinal analysis of a state's foreign policy behaviour. They are not sufficiently differentiated to allow for predictions of the foreign policy behaviour of *one* state in various issue areas of foreign policy over time.

Agency-based explanations of foreign policy

Agency-based analytical approaches attribute pre-eminence to domestic interests for explaining states' foreign policy behaviour, imparted via foreign policy preferences. The explicit consideration of domestic interests is rooted in liberal *state theory*, which accords primacy to domestic interests: 'Liberal theory rests on a ... view of politics in which the demands of individuals and societal groups are treated as analytically prior to politics' (Moravcsik 1997a: 517).

Agency-based analytical approaches do not neglect domestic structures. While they take domestic interests as the independent variable shaping foreign policy behaviour, they concede that domestic structures act as intervening variables since they constitute opportunities for, and barriers to, individual or group action. In particular, a state's structures of interest intermediation influence foreign policy behaviour by allowing certain domestic actors to assert their political preferences more successfully than others (Moravcsik 1997a: 518).

In contrast to structural approaches, agency-based approaches are well suited for the longitudinal study of the foreign policy of a country because they allow for a highly disaggregated analysis of foreign policy. It is possible to investigate the interests of domestic actors and the structures of interest intermediation on a policy-specific basis. In order to be able to do so, however, we need a heuristic model of interest intermediation which is initially non-committal concerning which domestic actors are able to assert themselves most successfully[2]. In the following sections, we will develop such a model by taking recourse to the policy network concept.

The policy network concept

In the literature, the emergence of the policy network concept at the end of the 1970s is primarily attributed to changes in political reality, which called for a new conceptualization of the policy-making process (e.g. Kenis and Schneider 1991). Political reality had changed to the extent that, as a result of processes of modernization and an increase in welfare-political measures, extensive functional differentiation processes had emerged in modern states (Willke 1992; Luhmann 1981). These differentiation processes had two decisive consequences for political theory. First, the interaction between state and private actors in the policy-making process had to be conceptualized in new terms. Traditional state theory had viewed 'the state' as the policy-making entity, which was hierarchically superior to society and could therefore be clearly separated from society. Instead, it was now recognized that some of the state's coercive power had to be trimmed in order to be able to use the problem-solving abilities of functionally specialized private actors. As state actors increasingly came to depend on the voluntary contributions of private actors, the latter came to have a greater say in the policy-making process. Accordingly, policy making was understood as including both state and private actors which were linked with each other by interdependent relationships (Grimm 1993; Kenis and Schneider 1991: 34ff.; Offe 1987).

Second, 'the state' could no longer be viewed as a unitary actor. Instead, research began to take the 'political-administrative system' (PAS), defined as a multi-centred policy-making and implementation system, as its point of departure (Voigt 1995, 1993: 10).

The pluralist and liberal neo-corporatist analytical approaches which had prevailed in the scholarly literature up to the end of the 1970s proved to be inadequate models for the newly discovered complexity of the policy-making process. For both pluralism and liberal neo-corporatism assumed that the relationship between political-administrative actors, on the one hand, and private actors, on the other, could be described uniformly across issue areas. Pluralist models posit that actors within the PAS play a fairly weak role in the process of interest intermediation. The PAS is regarded as an 'arena' for competing private interests only (Smith 1993: 356; Mitchell 1991: 79ff.; Skocpol 1985: 4; Krasner 1984: 229–30). Conversely, liberal neo-corporatist analytical models are based on the assumption that the formulation and implementation of policy result primarily from 'cooperation between the interests of society and the interests of the state', with the PAS being attributed the decisive role in structuring this cooperation (Staeck 1997: 62–63; see also Jordan and Schubert 1992: 7). Pluralism and liberal neo-corporatism thus ignore the fact that, in modern societies, processes of interest intermediation can vary depending on the issue area (Jordan and Schubert 1992: 10; see also Gamble 1995: 525; Kenis and Schneider 1991: 36).[3]

In this context, the concept of the policy network was developed. It was intended to provide an analytical tool which, 'in conjunction with both different models of the distribution of power and different theories of the state' (Rhodes and Marsh 1992: 202), would be sufficiently flexible to account for the various forms of cooperation between actors within the PAS ('PAS' actors[4]) and private actors in policy-making processes (Dowding 1995; Rhodes and March 1992; Lehmbruch 1991: 122).

Definition

A social network is characterized by relatively stable patterns of interaction between actors, groups and organizations. It comprises formally autonomous but interdependent actors (Ortmann, Sydow and Windeler 1997: 350–1; Benz 1993: 168–9; Marin and Mayntz 1991: 15). In the context of political processes of interest intermediation, the network notion refers to interdependent relationships between PAS actors and private actors: 'policy making includes a large number of public and private actors from different levels and functional areas of government and society' (Jordan and Schubert 1992: 11, referring to Hanf 1978).

Interactions between private and PAS actors in the policy-making process occur as communication, coordination and cooperation (Staeck 1997: 57). *Communication* takes place in the form of hearings, consultations and the exchange of information. Division of labour, negotiating processes and exchange relationships are regarded as *coordination* and *cooperation*. *Division of labour* refers to the delegation of at least parts of public tasks to private actors. *Exchange arrangements* take place when 'one side [is given] influence on policy formulation and implementation in the network, while the other side gains information, political support and, possibly, relative control over those affected' (Staeck 1997: 58–9, our translation). In most cases, *bargaining processes* include exchange arrangements, but as there are also bargaining processes in which this is not the case (Mayntz 1993: 45–6), here bargaining processes are to be dealt with as an analytical category of their own.

Taking into account the research in the field of the new institution-alism that has been flourishing since the 1980s, it is also emphasized that policy networks are primarily formed by *organized* domestic actors (Marin and Mayntz 1991: 14, 17; see also Knoke *et al.* 1996: 3–4; Voigt 1995: 57; Mayntz 1992). This means that individual as well as collective unorganized actors are ignored. A domestic actor is regarded as or-ganized if he takes decisions at a collective level both with regard to the formation of his political preferences and concerning the deployment of resources for action (Scharpf 1997: 54ff.).

In sum, policy networks can be defined as a set of relationships among organized private and PAS actors which results from their interaction in the form of 'communication, coordination and cooperation' with a view to the formulation and implementation of policy (Staeck 1997: 57, our translation; see also Kenis and Schneider 1991: 41–2; Marin and Mayntz 1991: 16).

There is disagreement in the literature as to whether or not the policy network approach entails general assumptions about how domestic actors interact in the political decision-making process. Some authors argue that policy networks constitute a new form of political governance which can be contrasted with hierarchies and markets. In this view, policy networks refer to relationships characterized by symmetric inter-dependence (Kenis and Schneider 1991). Other authors emphasize instead that policy networks can include different kinds of governance, including hierarchy: 'While policy networks are predominantly infor-mal, decentralized and horizontal, they never operate completely outside power-dependence relations, i.e. outside asymmetric interdependencies' (Marin and Mayntz 1991: 15–16; see also Schubert 1995: 232; Jordan and Schubert 1992: 10; Waarden 1992a: 31). We agree with this latter position because the policy network concept should be kept wide enough to be able to account for empirical variation in policy making: policy-making resources may be distributed more or less (un)evenly within the network depending on the individual policy.

Aims of network analyses

When studying policy networks, various dependent variables (and thus also different points of departure) can be chosen for analysis. Two important types of network analysis can be distinguished. First, the network structure can be considered from a network participant's perspective. In this case, the analytical focus is on how the integration of this actor in the inter-organizational environment affects his behaviour. Second, the network structure in its entirety can be chosen as the unit of analysis. The aim of analysis is then to gain insights into what political outcomes such a network produces, or indeed prevents (Hanf and O'Toole 1992: 169–70). In doing so, the policy network concept can either refer to a specific form of political control, to be evaluated, for example, from the point of view of its efficiency or of the distributive justice it generates, or, as is done here, to a heuristic model of interest intermediation which presents politics as an interest-driven policy-making process (Staeck 1997: 64–5).

If policy networks are conceived of as a heuristic model of interest intermediation, it is necessary to define what role shall be accorded to the interaction of the network actors in the process of interest intermediation. While one type of such a model holds that actors' preferences can be taken as fixed during the process of interest intermediation, another type starts out from the assumption that actors' preferences are open to change while they interact with other actors. According to this latter model, the process of interest intermediation is assumed to involve cognitive processes such as persuasion or learning which may cause actors to modify their payoff structures. This view is characteristic especially for the network approaches in public policy research. By relying on game-theoretical formulations, highly differentiated models of strategic interaction between the network participants are developed and linked to specific policy outcomes (Scharpf 1997; Stokman 1995). However, such a dynamic conceptualization of actors' preferences would be incompatible with our general assumption of actors as substantially rational. On the basis of this premise, actors' preferences may change due to a modification of the objective constraints on action, but not as the result of cognitive processes. In our model developed in the sections below, we will therefore assume actors' preferences to be stable in the process of interest intermediation.

Finally, we need to decide how narrowly we want to define policy networks. Policy networks in the wider sense emerge in relation to an issue area as a whole (e.g. development aid, foreign trade, military defence) and can thus also be termed 'policy field networks'. In contrast, policy networks in the narrow sense arise in interactions 'related to a certain policy' (Pappi 1993: 92, our translation). For the analysis of foreign policy behaviour, policy field networks and policy networks can equally form the point of departure – depending on the qualities of the policy field under consideration. In the interest of analytical clarity, case studies will first examine whether foreign policy behaviour can be explained by a policy field network; if this is not possible, then the policy network will have to be determined and used as a basis for foreign policy analysis.

It should be emphasized that network analysis is not an actual theory of state behaviour, but 'rather a tool box for describing and measuring relational configurations and their structural characteristics' (Kenis and Schneider 1991: 44; see also Dowding 1995; Marsh and Rhodes 1992). However, if it is supplemented by theoretical assumptions (as is done in the following sections) network analysis allows for a theoretically informed empirical determination of those domestic interests which are most likely to shape German foreign policy behaviour (Daugbjerg and Marsh 1998; Marsh 1998; Peters 1998; Staeck 1997; Dowding and King 1995: 1; Héritier 1993a and 1993b).

A network conceptualization of domestic interests

Our network conceptualization of domestic interests proceeds in four steps. After domestic actors' foreign policy preferences have been derived from their basic interests, the dominant actors – those actors which are able to assert their preferences most successfully in the process of interest intermediation – will be identified. On the basis of the composition of the set of dominant actors, the policy network structure can then be established. Given the network structure and the preferences of the dominant actors, it is then possible to derive the domestic interests which are most likely to shape foreign policy behaviour.

As outlined above, foreign policy network analysis is only possible on the basis of additional utilitarian-liberal assumptions. Theoretical assumptions are needed both with regard to domestic actors' preferences and concerning the question of who are the dominant actors. The theoretical assumptions we will take as our point of departure in order to ascertain domestic actors' preferences build upon the resource dependency theory in organization theory. According to this approach, organizations above all strive for their survival. At the same time, however, many of those resources necessary for ensuring an organization's survival are controlled by actors in the environment of the organization. Therefore, the preferences of an organization can be explained primarily by investigating the resource dependencies of the organization. More precisely, it has to be determined on which external actors and in what way the respective organization depends for resources which are critical for its survival (Knyphausen-Aufseß 1997; Scott 1986: 228–35; Pfeffer and Salancik 1978).

We have chosen the resource dependency school as the theoretical basis for ascertaining domestic actors' preferences for two reasons. First, given our conceptualization of actors as organized actors, it is reasonable to try to make use of the findings of organization theory. Second, the core assumptions of the resource dependency theory render it as an organization theory particularly apt for the analysis of policy networks: it is based on the view of organizations as open organizations. Instead of assuming that the environment of organizations is abstract or unitary, resource dependency theory investigates the specific dependencies of an organization on other organizations in its environment. In addition, the relationships between an organization and its environment are conceptualized as interorganizational relationships characterized by interdependence (Schreyögg 1997: 481–2).

In order to determine who the dominant domestic actors in a foreign policy network are, additional theoretical assumptions are necessary. First, we need criteria for identifying the most assertive private actors and the most assertive PAS actors. Here, we will proceed from issue area-specific policy network research, which views domestic actors' level of 'structural mobilization' as the prime determinant of their overall assertiveness (Atkinson and Coleman 1989). However, we will extend this approach by taking domestic actors' level of 'situative mobilization' into account as well. Second, theoretical assumptions have to be developed about the interaction of the most assertive private and the most assertive PAS actors in the process of interest intermediation. Again, we will make use of issue area-specific policy network research, which posits that the most assertive PAS actors' level of 'autonomy' of the most assertive private actors is decisive for which actors will be the dominant actors within a given network. We will provide additional theoretical content to this concept by making use of the concept of 'administrative interest intermediation' (Lehmbruch 1991, 1987).

The concept of administrative interest intermediation starts out from the empirical observation that interest intermediation in contemporary industrialized countries increasingly occurs as interorganizational exchange between PAS actors and private actors.[5] This finding is explained by reference to mutual resource dependencies of PAS actors and private actors. According to the concept of administrative interest intermediation, domestic actors are rational actors who are involved in interorganizational exchange processes on the basis of a 'self-interested exchange calculus'. The autonomy of PAS actors from private actors then depends on PAS actors' level of resource dependency from private actors and on the level of institutionalization of private influence.

Our theoretical assumptions meet two criteria. On the one hand, they are sufficiently specific to capture major characteristics of the German political system adequately. At the same time, they are broad enough to allow for their application across issue areas of foreign policy.

Domestic actors' foreign policy preferences

Utilitarian liberalism proceeds from the fundamental assumption that actors are utility maximizing. It also assumes that actors have certain basic interests – first and foremost securing their own physical and social survival – and that in concrete decision-making situations, on the basis of individual utility maximization, they give concrete expression to those interests in terms of policy preferences. In the following, two methods for establishing actors' policy preferences will first be discussed. Having done that, we will then consider how the basic interests of domestic actors in Germany can be determined, and how they can be defined in order to allow foreign policy preferences to be deduced for specific foreign policy decisions.

Ascertaining preferences: the empirical-inductive and the theoretical-deductive approach

Preferences can be ascertained either theoretically-deductively or empirically-inductively. In the former method, actors' policy preferences are deduced logically from their theoretically assumed basic interests based on the concept of substantial rationality. In the latter approach, inferences about actors' preferences are drawn on the basis of actors' observed behaviour, actors' statements about their preferences or expert opinion about actors' foreign policy preferences.[6]

Generally, the theoretical-deductive approach should be preferred because the empirical-inductive method of ascertaining actors' foreign policy preferences poses various problems for the researcher. For example, there is a great danger of circular reasoning if an actor's behaviour is used as the basis for inferences about his fundamental preferences (Snidal 1985b: 40f.). If, instead, preferences are ascertained on the basis of actors' statements, there is a danger that an actor will not always reveal his true preferences.[7] The greatest disadvantage of inductive preference investigation, however, is that it does not offer any possibility of distinguishing between policy preferences determined by an individual's basic interests or by social norms, and therefore allows no distinction between the approaches of utilitarian liberalism and constructivism.

It should be noted that it can be difficult in certain issue areas to infer actors' preferences deductively: problems occur especially frequently in those issue areas which are at a distance from economic policy (Zürn 1997: 300). Of course, it is also possible that, in certain policy-making situations, various alternatives provide an equally high level of utility. In such a situation, an actor must be held to be indifferent and no preferences can be deduced from his basic interest.

If it is not possible, or possible only to a limited extent, to determine actors' preferences deductively, help can be sought in the empirical-inductive method, in particular by using the method of questioning experts (Zürn 1997: 300ff.).

Basic interests and preferences of domestic actors

All domestic actors require certain resources to safeguard their survival. These resources can be material or immaterial. By material resources we mean above all an actor's financial means, while the policy-making power he has at his disposal constitutes his immaterial resources. In sum, *domestic actors' basic interest is aimed at increasing their financial means (i.e. income, assets) and at extending their policy-making power.*

However, domestic actors differ as to whether policy-making power or financial means are considered decisive for safeguarding their survival. While the ability of actors of the PAS depends, in the first instance, on the allocation of policy-making power, private actors primarily seek to safeguard their survival by accumulating, or tapping into, their financial means.

In other words, the basic interest, shared by all domestic actors, in maximizing policy-making power and financial means must be defined differently for different groups of actors. In particular, attention should focus on domestic actors' dependence on that part of their domestic environment which controls essential resources and can therefore make them available or withhold them.

PAS actors

The survival of PAS actors depends on whether they can retain or strengthen their position in the political-administrative system. Three

classes of PAS actor can be distinguished: political, political-administrative and administrative actors. The position of all PAS actors depends
on the policy-making power vested in them and, in addition, on the
financial means at their disposal. Of course, safeguarding or gaining
policy-making power has priority over a gain in financial means.

The basic interests of political, political-administrative and administrative actors have to be determined separately, however, as they depend
on different actors in their domestic environments, who transfer policy-
making power and financial means to them or withhold them from
them.

1 **Political actors**   Political actors are those actors whose positions in
the PAS are legitimized by elections. In Germany, they include the
Chancellor, who is elected and can be dismissed by an absolute majority
of the *Bundestag*, as well as the members of the *Bundestag*, and the state
(*Länder*) governments represented in the *Bundesrat*.

Political actors are assumed to have three basic interests. First, in order
to extend their policy-making power, they seek to ensure their prospects
for re-election and second, to prevent the transfer of their policy-making
power to international institutions. In addition, they seek to increase
their financial means by increasing their organizational budget.

Political actors' most important basic interest is their interest in being
re-elected: 'Political leaders are utility-maximizers, who desire to remain
in power most of all. Their utility comes from remaining in office, not
from pursuing a particular ... policy' (Milner 1997: 86; see also Hall
1997: 178–80; Gwartney and Wagner 1988: 7f.; Stigler 1975: 125). The
more successful political actors are in satisfying the policy expectations
of their voters, the greater their electoral chances will be. As every voter
is a utility maximizer (Downs 1967), he votes for the candidate from
whom he expects the highest gain in individual utility.[8] It is therefore
assumed that political actors generally support the policy option that
most strongly increases their voters' utility. As explained below, voters
can anticipate gains in utility if the state of the overall economy
improves, if their partisan expectations are fulfilled and if the internal
coherence of the federal government is ensured. Accordingly, three types
of political actors' foreign policy preference resulting from their basic
interest in being re-elected can be distinguished: political actors will
support the foreign policy options which improve the performance of
the domestic economy, meet partisan objectives and contribute to
intra-governmental cohesion.

The most important foreign policy preference of political actors is to improve the performance of the domestic economy, i.e. to enhance economic growth and to lower inflation and unemployment. This preference is deduced from the 'economic voting' hypothesis, according to which the state of the domestic economy can serve as a *proxy* for individual utility: if the economy is flourishing, then most individuals will probably be well off. Therefore, voters are assumed primarily to be interested in a good performance of the domestic economy. As many empirical studies have confirmed, the positive development of the economy in fact increases the prospects for re-election of the incumbent political actors (Milner 1997: 34–5; Powell and Whitten 1993: 391; Gibowski 1991: 122–3, 128; Lewis-Beck 1988).

In order to apply the economic-voting hypothesis, it is crucial to know how far foreign policy behaviour contributes to Germany's economic prosperity and thus affects political actors' prospects for re-election. It is obvious that only a few areas of foreign policy, including especially foreign trade policy, have a direct and tangible impact on Germany's economic situation. In many other areas of German foreign policy, in contrast, political actors' interest in re-election is only marginally affected unless individual policies prove to be extremely costly and are linked, for instance, to an additional tax burden on the electorate. Whether and to what extent specific foreign policy preferences can be derived from political actors' interest in re-election will therefore depend on the individual policy's material cost structure. Another important qualification of the economic-voting hypothesis is the narrow time horizon of politicians. They will not focus on what would be good for society's prosperity in the long run but will worry primarily about the next election (Garrett and Lange 1996: 50). Therefore, political actors' interest in re-election will only be affected by a policy which can be expected to have a significant economic impact before the next election.

While a good performance of the domestic economy is voters' general interest, they may also hold more specific, partisan interests. In order to increase their prospects for re-election, political actors will strive to meet partisan objectives if they are voiced by their party's core constituencies[9]. It has to be kept in mind, however, that political actors will be primarily worried about the positive development of the domestic economy because this concerns the primary interest of all voters and is therefore most important in order to ensure their prospects for re-election.

Finally, political actors will support the foreign policy option which is most likely to contribute to intra-governmental cohesion. Voters will favour a stable and coherent government as, in case of frequent intra-governmental conflict, policy making may become blocked or at least inefficient.[10] Political actors' preference for maintaining intra-governmental coherence will usually be in line with their preferences for either a good performance of the domestic economy or the fulfilment of partisan expectations: in case of intra-governmental conflict, political actors will try to get the government to agree on the position that corresponds most closely with those preferences. Should neither of these two preferences be affected, political actors will urge for a consensus on the majority position within the government.[11]

In order to extend their policy-making power, political actors will not only strive to ensure their prospects for re-election, however. Especially in the foreign policy context, political actors' ability to retain or extend their policy-making power presupposes that their policy-making power is not curtailed by international institutions. In situations in which political actors' policy-making power is affected, a political actor will always prefer the option which prevents a transfer of his policy-making power to international institutions.

Conflicts may well emerge between a political actor's foreign policy preferences derived from his interest in re-election and his preferences resulting from his interest in preventing a transfer of policy-making power to international institutions. This is above all to be expected when the strengthening of an international or supranational organization is accompanied by a palpable increase in a society's welfare, and so exerts a positive influence on political actors' prospects for re-election. In this case, political actors will see an advantage in transferring power, especially if they are able to attribute the successes of policies to themselves and failures to the international institutions. Political actors' interest in re-election takes precedence over their interest in retaining power for, unlike the transfer of power to international institutions, re-election is an 'all or nothing' game for a political actor – if an election is lost, he will no longer have any policy-making power at all.

While political actors are primarily interested in retaining or extending their policy-making power, they are also interested in increasing their financial means by increasing their organization budgets. In order to increase their organization budgets, political actors will support the foreign policy option which entails additional responsibilities for them,

or which makes additional resources necessary for their existing responsibilities.

2 **Administrative actors**   Administrative actors are those actors whose
incumbency of positions in the PAS is not the result of an electoral
mandate but of the assignment of responsibility by political actors. These
include both state executive organs (e.g. the armed forces or the central
bank) and so-called 'quangos' [12] which, while performing governmental
tasks, do not have a public law status (in the area of development policy,
for example, these would include the *Kreditanstalt für Wiederaufbau*
and the *Deutsche Gesellschaft für technische Zusammenarbeit*).

As with political actors, the position and, finally, the survival of
administrative actors depend first and foremost on their having the
policy-making power they need to fulfil the tasks entrusted to them.
While financial means are equally necessary for their survival, the
granting of those resources is generally determined by the type and
scope of an administrative actor's policy-making power. The increase
in financial means at an administrative actor's disposal is therefore
secondary to the increase in his policy-making power.[13] In a concrete
foreign policy decision-making situation, therefore, an administrative
actor will favour the option which most clearly extends, or at least does
not reduce, his policy-making power or financial means. In the case of
a conflict between his interests in increasing his financial means and
his policy-making power, an administrative actor will prefer the option
which has the most favourable impact on his policy-making power.

In order to extend their policy-making power, administrative actors
hold two basic interests. First, and most importantly, they strive to
strengthen their policy-making power vis-à-vis international institutions.
Second, they wish to extend, or at least to retain, their significance as
executive organs for political actors.

Administrative actors are primarily at pains to prevent their policy-
making power from being taken over by international institutions as
the distribution of policy-making power between the national realm
and international institutions has an immediate impact on them. This
does not mean that administrative actors will always be opposed to
multilateral cooperation. However, they will only consent to cooperating
in those international bodies that operate under unanimity.

An indirect – and therefore secondary – influence on administrative
actors' policy-making power is exerted by political actors' estimation of
how successful administrative actors are in fulfilling the tasks assigned

to them: it can be assumed that the more successful administrative actors are in fulfilling the tasks entrusted to them, the more policy-making power and financial means political actors will allocate to them (Mueller 1989: 252; see also Niskanen 1971: 42). An administrative actor will therefore always choose the option which best contributes to fulfilling the organizational purpose stipulated, or at least supported, by political actors (Downs 1967: 7).

3 **Political-administrative actors** Federal ministers[14] are termed political-administrative actors because they occupy a role bridging the divide between the political and the administrative subsystems of the PAS. On the one hand, federal ministers can be compared to political actors in that they cannot take office without electoral support for the parties they represent in the federal government. At the same time, however, federal ministers are similar to administrative actors in that they depend on appointment by a political actor, the Federal Chancellor.[15]

As a result, political-administrative actors are assumed to hold the basic interests which were deduced for the administrative actors as well as those which were derived for the political actors: while they are interested in increasing their financial means, they are primarily interested in extending their policy-making power. In order to extend their policy-making power, they strive to retain their policy-making power vis-à-vis international institutions, to retain or extend their significance as executive organs for the programmatic decisions of political actors, and to secure their (i.e. their party's) prospects for re-election.

Should the political and administrative interests of political-administrative actors collide, their behaviour will be shaped by the interest which is most directly concerned. If both interests are equally strongly affected, political-administrative actors will favour the option which corresponds with their administrative interests. We accord primacy to political-administrative actors' administrative interests because these interests are linked more directly with their specific position in the PAS. If political-administrative actors maximize their prospects for re-election, this is a necessary, but not a sufficient, condition for their policy-making power to be upheld or extended. If they are successful in fulfilling their organizational purpose or in resisting the transfer of competences to international bodies, however, this will be more directly conducive to the position of their respective bureaucracy within the PAS, and will therefore affect their policy-making power more strongly.

Table 4.1 Basic interests and foreign policy preferences of PAS actors

	Basic interests	Specification of basic interests	Foreign policy preferences
Political actors	Extend policy-making power	Ensure prospects for re-election	Satisfy expectations of voters: • improve performance of the economy • meet partisan objectives • maintain intra-governmental cohesion
		Retain policy-making power vis-à-vis international institutions	Avoid transfer of policy-making power to international institutions
	Increase financial means	Increase organization budget	Take on new responsibilities or acquire additional resources for existing responsibilities
Administrative actors	Extend policy-making power	Retain policy-making power vis-à-vis international institutions	Avoid transfer of policy-making power to international institutions
		Extend, or at least retain, significance as executive organ for political actors	Fulfil the organizational purpose
	Increase financial means	Increase organization budget	Take on new responsibilities or acquire additional resources for existing responsibilities
Political-administrative actors	Extend policy-making power	Retain policy-making power vis-à-vis international institutions	Avoid transfer of policy-making power to international institutions
		Extend, or at least retain, significance as executive organ for the programmatic decisions of political actors	Fulfil the organizational purpose

		Satisfy expectations of voters:
		• improve perform-ance of the economy
	Ensure prospects for re-election	• meet partisan objectives
		• maintain intra-governmental cohesion
Increase financial means	Increase organization budget	Take on new responsibilities or acquire additional resources for existing responsibilities

Private actors
We distinguish between three types of private actor: companies, economic pressure groups and political advocacy groups. The survival of all
private actors depends primarily on their having sufficient financial
means. The basic interest of all private actors is therefore directed
towards increasing their income and assets.

However, private actors differ in terms of how they obtain and
increase their financial means: while companies obtain or increase their
financial means through their own economic activities, economic pressure groups and political advocacy groups motivate their members or
other domestic actors to make financial contributions. At the same time,
those domestic actors which make payments to economic pressure
groups may not be, and indeed often are not, the same as those who
give financial support to political advocacy groups. Therefore, this
section will investigate the basic interests and preferences of companies,
economic pressure groups and political advocacy groups separately.

1 **Companies** Companies safeguard their survival by earning their
financial means themselves. Their basic interest in increasing their
financial means is manifested in the augmentation of company profits.

German companies' profit opportunities are affected by German
foreign policy to the extent that it can influence both their export
opportunities abroad and the extent to which they have to face import
competition. This is not only true of foreign trade policy, but also of
other areas of foreign policy, from security policy to human rights policy
and development policy. In every pertinent foreign policy-making situation, companies will advocate the policy option offering them the best

prospects for profit from the point of view of their international competitiveness.

2 **Economic pressure groups**   Economic pressure groups are either industry and farmers' associations or trade unions. As both actors are mainly financed by their members, their basic interest is to increase membership contributions. Members will only continue to make contributions, or indeed increase them, if they gain a net benefit. This will be the case if an economic pressure group is successful in fulfilling its organizational purpose.

The organizational purpose of economic pressure groups basically consists in increasing the material gains of their members, or at least in improving their income-generating opportunities. The aim of industry and farmers' associations is to increase the profit opportunities of the industries or the incomes of farmers they represent. In contrast, material gains for union members depend on the improvement of employees' working conditions – i.e. the level of wages and the prospects for employment – in the industries represented by the union. Generally speaking, economic pressure groups support the foreign policy option which involves the highest prospects for material gains for the respective pressure group's members.

Economic interest groups are also interested in extending their policy-making power, for the more policy-making power they have, the more easily they will be able to fulfil their organizational purpose and, correspondingly, their prospects for increasing membership contributions will also be greater. The policy-making power of economic pressure groups will increase through the extension of the organizational mandate. However, the extension of its organizational mandate affects the fulfilment of an economic pressure group's organizational purpose less directly than the improvement of its members' prospects for material gains. Therefore, economic pressure groups' interest in getting more policy-making power will be secondary to their interest in achieving material gains for their members.

3 **Political advocacy groups**   Political advocacy groups are non-profit-oriented private organizations. Nonetheless, their survival, like that of economic pressure groups, depends on their having the financial means they need to survive. Unlike economic pressure groups, however, their financial means come from a variety of sources, the most important being membership contributions, donations by other private actors and

grants from actors in the PAS. Therefore, political advocacy groups' basic interest will consist in increasing donations, grants, and membership contributions.

Like economic pressure groups, political advocacy groups will only be able to increase their financial means if they are successful in fulfilling their respective organizational purpose. In contrast to economic pressure groups, however, the organizational purpose of political advocacy groups is not to achieve material or immaterial gains for their members. Instead, they seek to further goals which contribute to the common good, such as a reduction in pollution, an improvement in other people's living conditions, etc.[16] In foreign policy-making situations, therefore, political advocacy groups will advocate the option which is likely to generate the greatest immaterial or material gains as defined by their organizational purposes.

Table 4.2 Basic interests and foreign policy preferences of private actors

	Basic interest	*Actor-specific operationalization*	*Foreign policy preference(s)*
Companies	Increase financial means	Increase company profits	Provide the best opportunities for company profit, taking international competitiveness into account
Economic pressure groups	Increase financial means	Increase membership contributions	Fulfil the organizational purpose: • Increase members' opportunities for material gain • Extend the organizational mandate
Political advocacy groups	Increase financial means	Increase donations, grants and membership contributions	Fulfil the organizational purpose: • Increase immaterial or material gains as defined by the organizational purpose • Extend organizational mandate

Like economic pressure groups, political advocacy groups strive for more policy-making power, although their interest in achieving immaterial and material gains as defined by their organizational purpose always takes precedence.

Dominant actors

Dominant actors are those domestic actors who are capable of shaping German foreign policy behaviour with regard to a given issue. In order to determine who the dominant actors are, we will make use of the policy network concept which specifies the dominant domestic actors as those which are able to assert their preferences most successfully in the process of interest intermediation in a given foreign policy-making situation.[17] In order to identify the dominant domestic actors within a policy network, we need criteria for measuring their assertiveness. To some extent, we will be able to build upon the writings of Peter Katzenstein (1978) and Atkinson and Coleman (1989), who have developed a structural approach to ascertaining the dominant actors within policy networks. Peter Katzenstein was concerned with policy networks at the national level. He identified the extent of centralization or fragmentation in the respective state and society and the level of differentiation between the two as the decisive determinants of domestic actors' assertiveness within the policy network of a given state (1978: 311).

Michael Atkinson and William Coleman returned to this approach, but concluded that it was necessary to concretize the variables Katzenstein had identified for issue area-specific policy network research:

> In seeking to refine concepts appropriate to the sectoral level, the temptation is to borrow the language of strength and weakness employed so effectively at the level of whole states. Unfortunately ... it is not quite so simple. At the meso level, the matter of state strength cannot be settled by an appeal to constitutional norms, the embeddedness of the party system, recruitment practices or the degree of state centralization. Much greater attention must be paid to specific bureaucratic arrangements and to the relationships that the officials involved maintain with key societal actors ... we use the concepts ... that have proven so successful at the macro level, but redefine them in order to encompass the wider variety of sectoral institutions. (Atkinson and Coleman 1989: 49f.)

Accordingly, the authors concentrated on the level of private actors' structural mobilization, the degree of concentration of decision-making competence in the PAS and on the autonomy of PAS actors from private actors as determining factors of domestic actors' assertiveness in policy networks.

While Atkinson and Coleman's concept of issue area-specific policy networks will serve as the basis for our policy network model, we believe that two extensions are necessary. First, their approach is based on domestic actors' level of structural mobilization only as they try to identify patterns of policy making within an issue area (industrial policy). In contrast, we are concerned with analysing foreign policy making with regard to individual policies and need a more disaggregated model which allows for the consideration of policy-specific factors. Therefore, we will not only take domestic actors' structural level of mobilization but also their 'situative level of mobilization' into account. Second, while Atkinson and Coleman develop some criteria in order to measure PAS actors' autonomy from private actors, these criteria are not sufficiently specific for their unambiguous application in empirical studies. At the same time, as they admit themselves, they certainly do not provide an 'exhaustive list' of relevant criteria (Atkinson and Coleman 1989: 52). The problem is that their conceptualization of autonomy is not grounded in a theoretical framework which would enable us to infer under which circumstances a high or a low level of PAS actors' autonomy is to be expected. However, as we will show below, it is possible to provide such a theoretical basis by making use of the concept of 'administrative interest intermediation'.

We will determine who the dominant actors are in a foreign policy network as follows. First, we will identify those private and PAS actors which have at least a low level of both structural and situative mobilization. These actors are assumed to be sufficiently assertive to take part in the policy-making process and, accordingly, to form part of the policy network. They will be referred to as 'assertive actors'. Second, from among those, the 'most assertive private actors' and 'the most assertive PAS actors' will be identified. Finally, depending on the level of autonomy of the most assertive PAS actors from the most assertive private actors, it is possible to ascertain the dominant domestic actors within the policy network.

Assertive actors

Private actors
According to Atkinson and Coleman, a private actor's *level of structural mobilization* will be all the higher,

- the higher is his level of representation, i.e. the more individuals and legal entities affected by the respective policy he represents;

- the greater is the representation of individuals and legal entities concentrated in that actor, i.e. the less that actor has to compete with other organized private actors for the same members;

- the higher is his hierarchical level, i.e. the better he is in a position to make binding decisions for his members;

- the greater is that actor's capacity for generating technical and political information (Atkinson and Coleman 1989: 53).[18]

In sum, a private actor's overall level of structural mobilization is judged to be higher the higher the actor scores in the four dimensions listed above.

As stated above, however, we believe that a private actor's assertiveness does not only depend on his level of structural mobilization, but also on his level of *situative mobilization*. The decisive factor here is how intense an actor's policy preferences are (Goldmann 1988: 44, 52ff; Olson 1982: 34). We assume that a private actor's level of situative mobilization will be all the more intense the more a policy affects his basic interests. A private actor's level of situative mobilization will be low if his basic interests are only indirectly affected. If his basic interests are directly affected, his level of situative mobilization will be high.

PAS actors

PAS actors' prospects for asserting themselves can be ascertained similarly to those of private actors. First, the more decision-making competence a PAS actor has for a certain policy, the higher his level of structural mobilization will be (Atkinson and Coleman 1989: 51). A PAS actor's level of structural mobilization will be low if he has the right to participate in the decision-making. If he has the right to veto a decision, his level of structural mobilization will be high. Second, the extent to which PAS actors' basic interests are affected in a given policy-making situation also has to be considered and, accordingly, how highly mobilized they are *in situative terms*.

Most assertive actors

The most assertive private actors and the most assertive PAS actors have to be ascertained separately. However, in both cases we will apply the same two-step procedure. First, we will identify from among the assertive private actors or the assertive PAS actors those actors who are most strongly mobilized in situative terms. Second, from among those actors the most assertive private actors or PAS actors will be those who have the highest level of structural mobilization.

PAS actors' autonomy and the dominant actors
The extent to which PAS actors are autonomous from private actors is an indicator of how capable they are of asserting their interests over private actors' interests. The greater the most assertive PAS actors' autonomy is, the less capable of asserting their preferences the most assertive private actors will be. In order to ascertain the autonomy of the most assertive PAS actors from the most assertive private actors, we will make use of the concept of administrative interest intermediation.

First, the concept of administrative interest intermediation explains the interaction of PAS and private actors in the processes of interest intermediation on the basis of a self-interested exchange calculus of the actors involved. Private actors will get access to, and influence on, the policy-making process if they are able to deliver essential policy-making resources needed by the PAS actors in return. The most important policy-making resources are the provision of information and of legitimacy (Lehmbruch 1991: 130). Second, private actors' access to the policy-making process will be easier the more firmly their links with PAS actors are established. If patterns of influence have already been institutionalized, these give rise to an 'institutional inertia' which will continue to facilitate private actors' access to the policy-making process (Lehmbruch 1991: 127). In sum, *PAS actors' autonomy from private actors will be all the greater,*

- the less they depend on private actors' contributions in order to fulfil their organizational purpose (such as information and the provision of legitimacy);

- the less PAS actors' links with private actors are institutionalized (such as private actors' rights to be informed, consulted or to co-decide).

PAS actors are accorded a *high* level of autonomy if they score highly on both dimensions mentioned above. In this case, the most assertive PAS actors will be the dominant domestic actors. If, in contrast, the most assertive PAS actors' level of autonomy from the most assertive private actors is *low* with respect to both dimensions, the most assertive private actors will be the dominant actors.

It is also possible that both private and PAS actors are the dominant domestic actors. This is the case if at least one of the following two conditions is met. First, the most assertive PAS actor's level of autonomy from the most assertive private actors is *medium*. This will be the case if he scores medium with regard to both dimensions, or if he scores high on one dimension but only low or medium on the other. Alternatively, one of the most assertive private actors can dominate in dealings with one of the most assertive PAS actors and can therefore influence his behaviour decisively, but other most assertive PAS actors are not similarly dependent on this private actor and are therefore also able to assert their preferences.

Policy network structures

Once the dominant domestic actors have been identified, is is possible to describe the variety of network structures.

If the dominant domestic actor(s) belong(s) to the PAS only, we speak of a *policy network with PAS leadership*, as the PAS actors do not have to defer to private actors' preferences. If there is only one dominant PAS actor, he will assert his preferences directly (*concentrated PAS leadership*). If, in contrast, there are several dominant PAS actors, as is usual when policies involving more than one ministry are concerned, the policy pursued will reflect a compromise between several PAS actors (*decentralized PAS leadership*).

A network in which the dominant domestic actor(s) are only private actors is termed a *policy network with private leadership* because PAS actors will be unable to assert their preferences over those of the most assertive private actors. Here, too, one can distinguish between two

Table 4.3 Network typology for an analysis of German foreign policy

	High level of autonomy of PAS actors		Medium level of autonomy of PAS actors	Low level of autonomy of PAS actors
	One most assertive PAS actor	Several most assertive PAS actors	One or several most assertive PAS actors	One or several most assertive PAS actors
One most assertive private actor	Concentrated PAS leadership	Decentralized PAS leadership	Corporatist	Concentrated private leadership
Several most assertive private actors				Decentralized private leadership

classes of network depending on whether there are several dominant private actors who have to reach a compromise (*decentralized private leadership*), or whether one dominant private actor can be identified who can directly assert his preferences (*concentrated private leadership*).

If the dominant domestic actors are both private and PAS actors, private as well as PAS actors take part in the policy-making process and need to take into account each others' preferences, such a policy network shall be designated *corporatist*.[19]

The independent variable 'domestic interests'

Given the policy network structure and the foreign policy preferences of the dominant actors within the network, the 'domestic interests' shaping Germany's foreign policy behaviour can be ascertained. However, utilitarian liberalism will only allow for predictions about German foreign policy if pertinent domestic interests in Germany can be found to be sufficiently strong. This will be the case if:

- the dominant actor in a concentrated network has at least low-intensity preferences; or

- the majority of dominant actors in a decentralized or corporatist network have at least low-intensity preferences for the same option of foreign policy action.

If these requirements are not met, no prediction about German foreign policy will be possible on the basis of utilitarian liberalism. Instead, utilitarian liberalism assumes that society will be either split or indifferent with a view to choosing from among the various options for foreign policy action.

General features of foreign policy networks in Germany

Foreign policy networks in Germany differ depending on the issue area of foreign policy or the individual foreign policy concerned. In particular, domestic actors' level of situative mobilization cannot be established in general terms. However, recent research indicates that an analysis of the overall characteristics of a political system – 'macro variables' – may help to explain regularities of interest intermediation structures to be found across issue areas or policies (Daugbjerg and Marsh 1998; Lehmbruch 1991: 132ff.). In this section, we try to identify generalized features of policy networks in Germany which can serve as a reference point for case studies.

Many authors ascribe a high level of structural mobilization to Germany's private actors. Especially in comparison with other industrialized countries, Germany's private actors are said to enjoy a high level of representation and organization (Waarden 1993: 197; Katzenstein 1987: 23–4). However, recent empirical research has revealed that this general tendency is true only for some issue areas of German policy. Above all, it is in the economic issue areas (including agriculture) where private interests are highly mobilized. Private actors' level of structural mobilization is also high in issue areas of social welfare, industrial policy and health care. In contrast, private actors' level of structural mobilization is low in non-economic issue areas, such as constitutional and judicial affairs and defence (Sebaldt 1997: 79ff.; Lehmbruch 1994: 370–3). Therefore, a comparatively stronger participation of private actors can be expected in those issue areas of foreign policy in which Germany's economic prosperity is affected. In fact, private actors play a visible part in Germany's foreign trade policy (chapter 8).

A particularly striking feature of the German political-administrative system is its high level of fragmentation. In most cases, several PAS actors have a say in the policy-making process and are therefore structurally mobilized. This is due to two important factors.

First, Germany has always been governed by coalition governments. As a result of party rivalries between the coalition partners, coalition governments are often linked with greater potential for intragovernmental conflict than one-party Cabinets. At the same time, the coalition partners are highly dependent on each other for staying in power, and are therefore constrained to work out compromises. As a result, coalition governments are shaped by a pronounced diffusion of decision-making power within the federal government (Anderson 1999: 9; Kohler-Koch 1998: 290; Kaarbo 1996: 503ff.; Smith 1991: 53).

Second, Germany's federal structure accords an important role to the *Länder* governments in the policy-making process. To be sure, this is less true for foreign policy than for domestic policy. However, in those foreign policy issue areas which touch upon the domestic legislative competences of the *Länder*, and where national decision-making competence has been transferred to the international level, *Länder* rights to be consulted, informed or even to veto are pronounced. In particular, *Länder* interests come into play in those policies which are decided upon at the EU level, such as EU constitutional policy or foreign trade policy (see chapters 7 and 8).

To a certain extent, the fragmentation of the German PAS is reduced by the special position of the Chancellor. The Chancellor has the prerogative to propose the federal ministers to be appointed or dismissed by the federal President, to decide on Cabinet reshuffles and to set the general guidelines for the federal government's policy. His position vis-à-vis the federal ministers is further enhanced by the fact that the ministers cannot be dismissed by the *Bundestag*. In addition, the Chancellor can only be removed from office by a constructive vote of no confidence by the *Bundestag*, i.e. by electing a successor with the majority of the *Bundestag's* members. Of course, the Chancellor also has to take into account coalition dynamics and has to respect the specific policy autonomy of his ministers. In matters which directly touch upon the Chancellor's interest in re-election, however, the Chancellor is able to make use of his directive powers and to assume a superior position within the Cabinet (Helms 1996; Elgie 1995: 79ff.; King 1994; Smith 1991; Müller-Rommel 1988a: 152).

At the same time, Germany's PAS actors typically maintain stable and close working relationships with private actors. For this reason, Germany's political system has been described as sectoral corporatist, i.e. as characterized by issue area-specific policy networks based upon close communication, coordination and cooperation between PAS and private actors (Sebaldt 1997: 241ff.; Voigt 1995: 59ff.; Lehmbruch 1994: 370–1; Edinger 1993: 178ff.; Katzenstein 1987: 367). Contemporary research in sectoral corporatism offers a double explanation for this finding. First, sectoral corporatism is more likely to occur in societies which are characterized by a fragmented PAS because private actors then have more points of access to the PAS, and may be able to play public officials off against each other (Daugbjerg and Marsh 1998: 65–6; Waarden 1992b: 134). Second, the potential for sectoral corporatism is greater in those societies in which private actors are highly structurally mobilized. The reason is that public officials are interested in cooperation with private actors in order to get access to the political resources controlled by them. The higher a private actor's level of structural mobilization, the more political resources he can offer: as he represents a significant share of citizens, social groups or organizations in an issue area of public policy, he will be able to provide legitimacy for public policy. Due to a high level of organization, he is typically able to generate important information which public officials need in order to formulate effective policies. As a general rule, the higher a private actor's level of structural mobilization, the greater the PAS actors' willingness to share policy-making power with this actor will be (Streeck 1994: 17–18; Lehmbruch 1991: 129ff.). This latter proposition seems highly plausible for the German case as 'sectoral corporatism' is not equally pronounced across issue areas. Again, it is primarily the socio-economic sphere – in which private actors display a particularly high level of structural mobilization – where private actors have managed to get privileged access to the PAS (Lehmbruch 1994: 370–2).

The fragmentation of the German PAS, and the far-reaching entanglement of private actors with PAS actors in issue areas of economic policy, allow for several inferences about German foreign policy.

First, we can expect corporatist policy networks to prevail in issue areas of economic foreign policy. Due to the pronounced fragmentation of the German PAS, networks with private leadership will be less likely: even if a private actor is able to 'capture' one PAS actor, there will in most cases be other PAS actors that participate in the policy-making process and that do not directly depend on this private actor. When we look at recent research on German foreign trade policy, corporatist networks are in fact typical (see chapter 8).

Second, in non-economic issue areas of foreign policy, policy networks with PAS leadership will tend to dominate as private actors' access to the PAS is rather limited. At the same time, we will mostly find networks with decentralized PAS leadership since the dispersion of decision-making power within the German PAS renders networks with concentrated PAS leadership rather unlikely. Policy networks with decentralized PAS leadership are indeed the most frequently observed type of policy network, as for example, in German EU constitutional policy and security policy (see chapters 6 and 7).

Still, it has to be kept in mind that these general assessments are based on domestic actors' levels of structural mobilization only. Depending on the level of situative mobilization of domestic actors, network structures may differ for individual policies.

Post-unification Germany and gain-seeking foreign policy

The salient characteristic of utilitarian liberalism is the assumption that it is the interests of utility-maximizing domestic actors which shape a state's foreign policy behaviour. Each actor's basic interest is to achieve gains, which can either be material – in the form of an increase in financial means – or immaterial – in the form of an increase in policy-making power. From the point of view of utilitarian liberalism, German foreign policy is always geared to achieving gains for the dominant domestic actors, and can accordingly be labelled *gain-seeking policy*. From a utilitarian-liberal point of view, changes in German foreign policy will occur on two conditions: they will either result from changed foreign policy preferences on the part of the dominant actor(s) or from a changed composition of the set of dominant actors in a policy network. Only if at least one of these conditions is met, are changes in German foreign policy to be expected. Conversely, utilitarian liberalism expects continuity in German foreign policy if both the composition and the preferences of the dominant actors in a policy network remain constant.

German unification may have led to a change in German foreign policy by impacting on Germany's domestic interests. As is argued below, however, the impact of unification on German domestic interests was limited. Modifications of Germany's domestic interests due to unification are conceivable in three ways.

First, unification may have led to a decline of the level of structural mobilization of Germany's economic pressure groups. Such a decline could be expected if Germany's economic pressure groups had been unable to build up a similarly high level of representation and organization in East Germany as they enjoyed in West Germany. However, recent empirical research has shown that West Germany's economic interest groups were indeed successful in extending their organizational infrastructure to East Germany. The *Institutionentransfer* from West Germany to East Germany was not limited to political and administrative structures, but included the associational system as well (Kleinfeld 1999: 778; Lehmbruch 1996: 65; Schmid and Voelzkow 1996: 426–7). Overall, the representational monopoly of economic pressure groups in post-unification Germany is comparable to the time before unification.[20]

Second, unification may have led to changes of preferences of Germany's economic pressure groups. While economic pressure groups were able to maintain their structural integrity, empirical research has highlighted that, on matters of substance, members disagree more often than before unification (Kleinfeld 1999: 778; Lehmbruch 1994). The increasing disparity of interests is not surprising since socio-economic hetereogeneity in Germany has grown considerably since unification (Schmid and Voelzkow 1996: 427, 431). However, so far disagreements within economic interest groups have chiefly concerned domestic policy.[21]

Third, unification may have altered the preferences of both private and PAS actors as the financial burden of unification has diminished the room for manoeuvre of public finance. In fact, distributional conflicts have become stronger as financial resources have become increasingly scarce.[22] Especially with regard to those issues of foreign policy which affect the flow of financial resources from Germany to other countries and vice versa, foreign policy preferences of domestic actors have taken a different direction since 1990: generally, Germany's domestic actors have been less willing to make net contributions to international organizations or payments to other countries and have called for a reduction in both. This is evident, for instance, when we look at the position of domestic actors on Germany's net contributions to the EU budget (chapter 7) and the distribution of the EC's technology policy funding among the EC member states.[23]

In sum, unification did not significantly alter Germany's domestic interests and, therefore, from a utilitarian-liberal perspective it is to be expected that Germany will continue to pursue its gain-seeking foreign policy in the same form and intensity as hitherto.[24]

Notes

1   These two concepts are a reference to a volume edited by Peter Katzenstein *Between Power and Plenty. Foreign Economic Policies of Advanced Industrial States* (1978); see also Zürn (1997: 299), and Weede (1996: 7).

2   Therefore, we cannot make use of those agency-based utilitarian-liberal approaches in the literature which are based on an overall characterization of the structures of interest intermediation. Important examples are what are known as 'society centred' and 'state centred' analytical approaches (Ikenberry, Lake and Mastanduno 1988). While the former assign the state the role of an executive organ of private interests, in the latter private interests play only a subordinate role in the foreign policy-making process. In state-centred approaches, foreign policy is conceived of either as the result of conflicts of interest among state actors – if the state is fragmented – or the state, as a unitary actor, pursues a 'national interest' with its foreign policy, independently of private interests (Krasner 1978).

3   The need for issue area-specific political research had already been highlighted in the late 1960s. Rosenau (1966) called for the issue area-specific analysis of foreign policy. In a similar vein, Lowi (1972) pointed out that the character of the political problems present in a certain issue area determines the way in which domestic actors will try to solve those prob-

lems: 'policy determines politics' (Lowi 1972: 299). More recently, the issue area concept has proven useful for the analysis of international regimes (Mayer, Rittberger and Zürn 1993).

4 The term 'PAS actors' refers to all actors within the PAS – political, administrative and political-administrative actors (see p. 80ff.).

5 Originally, the concept of administrative interest intermediation was developed to describe the relationships between actors in the administrative subsystem of the PAS and private actors only. However, we will apply the concept to the relationships of all PAS actors with private actors.

6 Questioning experts is not necessarily an empirical-deductive way of ascertaining preferences because the experts asked may themselves define actors' preferences theoretically-deductively. However, as different experts scarcely investigate in the same way, and consequently a theoretical-deductive method of ascertaining preferences obeying well-defined criteria is not possible when questioning different experts, this method will here be included among the empirical-inductive methods.

7 For further criticism of the inductive method of defining preferences, see Snidal (1985b: 40ff).

8 It has been discussed at length in the literature whether a rational actor who weighs the cost of voting against the benefits to be gained from it will bother to vote at all. Assuming that the voter is rational, critics state that, as the probability that a certain voter will decide an election's outcome is practically zero, the expected benefit from casting his vote will be lower than his costs. He therefore will not vote. However, other discussions have shown that this argument relies on certain assumptions about the voter's utility function. A more detailed discussion of this 'paradox of voting' can be found in Mueller (1989: 349ff.).

9 By 'core constituencies' we mean those groups of voters which form the electoral base of the respective party.

10 Of course, the government's coherence will only be important for the core constituencies of Germany's federal political actors, the Chancellor and the members of the Bundestag.

11 The assumption that political actors will settle on the majority position within the Cabinet is based on the premise that no party represented in the government, as a rational utility-maximizing actor, has an option to leave the Cabinet. This question has been discussed at length in the literature on coalition governments. However, there has been no consensus on which of the coalition partners is in a better position to assert itself in the case of intra-governmental conflict. Some authors hold that it is typically the smaller coalition partner who has the better exit option (Kaarbo 1996: 504–5), while others contend that it is rather the bigger coalition partner who is able to set the terms of coalition policy making (King 1994: 154). Finally, some authors emphasize the mutual dependence of the coalition

partners instead (Smith 1991: 53). While we certainly cannot settle this argument here, we would like to emphasize that, in any case, a breakup of a coalition imposes significant costs on all coalition partners. Therefore, it seems highly implausible that coalition partners will leave a coalition on the grounds of a disagreement on a single issue. Instead, the costs of a breakup of the coalition can only be expected to outweigh the costs of maintaining it if major political issues are at stake, such as the domestic economy or the question of war and peace. If this is the case, however, utilitarian liberalism assumes that all actors within the Cabinet hold the same policy preferences due to their interest in re-election.

12 'Quasi non-governmental organizations'
13 Early studies of administrative actors generally provided a comprehensive list of the bureaucracy's aims. However, it is only possible to derive a clear order of preferences if the various aims form a hierarchical order (Downs 1967: 79–87). Unlike us, Niskanen (1971: 36–42) assumes that budget maximization is the prime aim of administrative actors. In contrast, policy-making power does not show up in his model; however, as policy-making power is the condition for administrative actors' existence, we hold that it is justified to assume that administrative actors' interest in preserving or extending policy-making power is more fundamental than their interest in increasing their financial means. See also Jackson's critique of Niskanen's model (1983: 131–5).
14 The term 'federal ministers' does not refer to individuals *per se*, but to them as representatives of their respective bureaucracies in the federal government.
15 Formally speaking, the federal President appoints and dismisses federal ministers on the proposal of the Chancellor, which is the latter's exclusive prerogative (art. 64).
16 It has to be conceded that the assumption that the members and supporters of political advocacy groups do not attach any expectations of material gain to their financial contributions or donations is not fully compatible with our fundamental assumption that all domestic actors are utility maximizers. If we follow the definition of utility set out above, then their utility is not increased as a result of their payments. Some authors have suggested that the notion of utility should be widened in order to account for altruism from a utilitarian-liberal point of view. They argue, for example, that individuals may support political advocacy groups in order to avoid social or psychological costs (Kirchgässner 1991: 45–65). However, this assumption is not congruent with our model of domestic actors as substantially rational and self-interested. We take political advocacy groups as an empirical fact of foreign policy making in Germany. While we cannot offer an explanation as to why individuals or corporations become members or supporters of political advocacy groups in the first

place, we can still account for their expectations towards political advocacy groups once they have made this decision. The latter aspect is the
one which is relevant for our model: we are concerned with the policy
preferences of existing political advocacy groups, rather than with predicting if and how new ones will come into existence.

17 It may seem surprising that network analysis, which starts from the
assumption that policy making is increasingly characterized by interdependence of domestic actors, should focus so much on 'dominance', i.e.
on power, within the network. However, as was outlined above, the network approach is not necessarily linked to the assumption of symmetric
interdependence. In a given policy network, some domestic actors may,
and usually do, control more political resources than others, and may
therefore be able to assume an asymmetric power position vis-a-vis other
actors within the network. At the same time, the concentration on 'dominant' actors does not preclude coalition formation and negotiation in the
policy-making process if political resources are distributed more evenly
within the network. (On the role of power within networks, see Kappelhoff
1995; Messner 1995: 233ff.; Crozier and Friedberg 1979.)

18 It should be noted that these criteria for determining the level of private
actors' structural mobilization are not undisputed in the literature. While
we suggest that large organizations have a head start in terms of mobilization (because they typically enjoy a greater level of representation and
are more capable of generating technical and political information) and
can therefore assert themselves over others, Olson (1982, 1971) argues that
the level of structural mobilization of organized private actors is all the
higher, the smaller is their size. Olson's argument proceeds from the
assumption that 'large groups, at least if they are composed of rational
individuals, will *not* act in their group interest' (Olson 1982: 18). In Olson's
view, small organizations represent private interests most effectively
because they are more homogeneous and in a better position to control
'free rider' effects (Olson 1982: 24f.). However, Olson's argument ignores
the fact that "'narrow' organizations, by competing for their shares of the
social product, usually attenuate each other's associational power' (Czada
1991: 265). Moreover, large-scale organizations can take advantage of 'scale
economies of associational action' and thus offer their members a great
many selective incentives for a low contribution (Czada 1991: 277). In
addition, it should be considered that, especially in the context of the
interest intermediation processes of foreign policy making, larger associations are better able to assert themselves than smaller ones, as they are
more likely to have the policy-making resources – e.g. information or the
procurement of legitimization – which PAS actors require (Czada 1991:
276ff.).

19 Of course, using 'corporatism' to describe a policy network is not the same

as characterizing the relationship between PAS actors and private actors in a political system as a whole. The concept of corporatism applied to political systems as a whole – what is known as 'macro-corporatism' – is concerned with cooperation between PAS actors and private actors on the national level. Macro-corporatism refers to the deliberate inclusion of antagonistic domestic interests in the policy making process. Typical examples of macro-corporatist policy-making are tripartite institutions, which are formed by actors from the PAS, unions and industry associations with reference to macro-economic problems (in Germany, for example, the former Konzertierte Aktion, or the attempts of the Kohl and Schröder governments to establish a Bündnis für Arbeit). According to macro-corporatism, tripartite institutions are formed because conflict solving and consensus formation on the national level are regarded as a precondition for effective macro-economic governance.

If, in contrast, a policy network is described as 'corporatist', this is based on the concept of 'meso-corporatism', which was developed to analyse cooperation between PAS actors and private actors in individual issue areas. According to meso-corporatism, those private actors who are especially highly mobilized in a structural and situative sense are granted privileged access to the policy-making process. (For the distinction between macro- and meso-corporatism, see Czada 1994; Cawson 1985; Lehmbruch 1984. For an explicit application of the meso-corporatism concept to policy networks, see Waarden 1992a: 40; Jordan and Schubert 1992: 22.)

20 For industry associations, see Henneberger 1996; for trade unions, see Fichter and Reister 1996; for agriculture, see Kretzschmar 1996.

21 One particularly controversial topic has been wage policy (Kleinfeld 1999: 772–3; Czada 1996: 353; Schmid and Voelzkow 1996: 431ff.; Wielgohs and Wiesenthal 1995: 310).

22 Interviews with officials of the Bundesministerium für Wirtschaft und Technologie (BMWT), the Foreign Office, and the Bundesministerium für Bildung und Forschung (BMBF), Bonn, September 1998.

23 Interview with an official of the BMBF, Bonn, September 1998.

24 Of course, German domestic interests may still have changed due to reasons which were not related to unification. However, this is an empirical question which is examined on a policy-specific basis.

5

Constructivist foreign policy theory

*Henning Boekle, Volker Rittberger
and Wolfgang Wagner*

Introduction

Since the early 1990s, constructivism has emerged as the major challenger of rationalist (i.e. both neorealist and utilitarian liberal) theorizing in International Relations. Like rationalism (or rational choice), constructivism is first of all a metatheory which has inspired theorizing in various fields, including change in the international system (Ruggie 1998) and communicative action (Risse 2000). Though research on foreign policy has become influenced by constructivist thinking, too, a testable and coherent foreign policy theory has been missing. The aim of this chapter is therefore to develop such a foreign policy theory on the basis of constructivist metatheory in order to render this way of theorizing applicable to the analysis of German foreign policy after unification. Constructivism starts from the assumption that actors follow a logic of appropriateness rather than a logic of consequentiality.

In contrast to many other constructivist studies, this chapter argues that social norms rather than other ideational factors are best suited to explain foreign policy and thus to serve as an independent variable. Within this framework, social norms are seen as the more influential the more they are shared among the units of a social system and the more precisely they distinguish between appropriate and inappropriate behaviour. Our discussion of socialization processes as the causal mechanism linking social norms and state behaviour makes clear that norms cannot exclusively be attributed to either the international or the societal level but interact in several ways. We therefore discuss two traditions of constructivist research that have so far remained largely separate from each other. Whereas transnational constructivism has focused exclusively on the impact of international norms on foreign policy behaviour,

societal constructivism has taken norms shared within domestic society
as most influential. Though the distinction between international and
societal norms is useful in analytical terms, it is theoretically artificial.
We therefore aim at integrating both research traditions into a single
constructivist theory of foreign policy. With a view to the derivation of
constructivist predictions about post-unification German foreign policy
and their empirical test based on several case studies, we have been
especially concerned with issues of operationalization and measurement. In order to formulate testable constructivist predictions, we
must be able to identify the social norms pertaining to our cases *ex
ante*. We have therefore paid considerable attention to indicators of
international and societal norms. We conclude with some reflections
about German foreign policy which, from a constructivist point of view,
is conceptualized as norm-consistent foreign policy.

The logic of appropriateness: social norms as independent variables

The point of departure for a constructivist theory of foreign policy is
its critique of the concept of utility-maximizing *homo oeconomicus* which
is at the core of neorealist and utilitarian-liberal analyses of foreign
policy (see chapters 3 and 4). According to this concept, ideas, values
or norms can only play a role as instruments for asserting and justifying
given interests. Constructivist theory of foreign policy, in contrast,
emphasizes the independent influence of these variables. According to
the constructivist view, actors' behaviour is guided by social norms,
defined as intersubjectively shared, value-based expectations of
appropriate behaviour.[1] The assumption of the independent influence
of social norms is incompatible with the concept of the rational,
utility-maximizing *homo oeconomicus*. This concept is replaced by an
actor concept described as *homo sociologicus* or *role player* (Hasenclever,
Mayer and Rittberger 1997: 155; Schaber and Ulbert 1994). In the
constructivist view, actors take decisions 'on the basis of norms and
rules on the background of subjective factors, historical-cultural
experience and institutional involvement' (Schaber and Ulbert 1994:
142, our translation). When faced with various alternative courses of
action, *homo oeconomicus* considers the anticipated consequences of his
action in order to choose the alternative which will maximize his
utility; *homo sociologicus*, in contrast, bases his action on a 'logic of
appropriateness', which takes intersubjectively shared, value-based

expectations of appropriate behaviour as its point of reference. The logic of appropriateness states that

> behaviors (beliefs as well as actions) are intentional but not willful. They involve fulfilling the obligations of a role in a situation, and so of trying to determine the imperatives of holding a position ... Within a logic of appropriateness, a sane person is one who is 'in touch with identity' in the sense of maintaining consistency between behavior and a conception of self in a social role. (March and Olsen 1989: 160–1; see also March and Olsen 1998: 311–12; Hasenclever, Mayer and Rittberger 1997: 155–7; Finnemore 1996a: 28–31)

Because of their immediate orientation to behaviour, social norms rather than other ideational variables are the appropriate independent variable of a constructivist theory of foreign policy. In contrast to rationalist models (e.g. Krasner 1999; Cortell and Davis 1996), norms are not a function of interests but precede them. The effect of social norms on behaviour cannot therefore be reduced to that of 'constraints' or 'incentives' in the sense that they increase or reduce the cost of certain modes of behaviour and thus have a merely *regulative* effect on actors' behaviour.[2] In the constructivist view, social norms also have a *constitutive* effect, i.e. they 'legitimize goals and thus define actors' interests' (Klotz 1995: 26).[3] By identifying certain goals as legitimate, norms act as 'motives' (Klotz 1995: 26). As 'motives', norms prescribe the goals towards which states legitimately strive. The 'motives' function ascribed to social norms by constructivists manifests itself in that states define their preferences in accordance with the goals that have been designated as legitimate.

Social norms are distinguished from other ideational variables by virtue of three characteristics: (1) immediate orientation to behaviour (see Finnemore 1996a: 22–3; Florini 1996: 164); (2) intersubjectivity (Finnemore 1996a: 22; Klotz 1995: 32); and (3) counterfactual validity (see Hasenclever, Mayer and Rittberger 1997: 164–5; Goertz and Diehl 1992: 638–9; Kratochwil and Ruggie 1986: 767–8).

The most important defining characteristic, *immediate orientation to behaviour*, distinguishes social norms from ideas, 'principled' and 'causal beliefs' as well as world views, and from identity and culture. World views are comprehensive conceptions of reality which generally include 'causal beliefs' and 'principled beliefs' while at the same time transcending them. Like 'culture' and 'identity', world views are too abstract for generating actual expectations of behaviour. Because of their immediate orientation to behaviour, social norms are best suited to explain foreign policy behaviour.

The second defining characteristic, *intersubjectivity*, distinguishes social norms from ideas, defined as 'beliefs held by individuals' (Goldstein and Keohane 1993: 3).[4] The influence of individual 'belief systems' is examined by cognitive approaches (see Little and Smith 1988). Although the proponents of cognitive theories do not dispute the social origins of individual beliefs and values, they regard the *individual* beliefs held by decision makers as exerting an independent influence on foreign policy behaviour. More or less explicitly, therefore, individual beliefs of decision makers are ascribed a great degree of autonomy vis-à-vis their social environment.[5] However, one objection to such explanations is that 'examining decision-making processes through individual motivation and cognition alone ignores the commonality of shared norms underlying dominant ideas or knowledge' (Klotz 1995: 32). Explanations which attribute a state's foreign policy behaviour to the 'belief systems' of individual policy makers are thus unsatisfactory in that they always raise the question of the social roots of individual beliefs without themselves being able to answer it. Cognitive approaches will therefore not be integrated into our constructivist theory of foreign policy.

Finally, the third defining characteristic is that social norms have *counterfactual validity* because they involve 'issues of justice and rights of a moral or ethical character' (Goertz and Diehl 1992: 638–9). Counterfactual validity distinguishes norms from non-value-based expectations of behaviour that result from consequentialist considerations, such as prudence. Because of their reference to values, norms possess a 'compliance pull' independent of interests (Hurrell 1993; Franck 1990). This 'compliance pull' does not necessarily cause uniform norm-compliant behaviour by actors within a given context of action. However, the existence of a norm does not have to be called into question if it is occasionally violated because, due to their reference to values, social norms possess counterfactual validity (see Hasenclever, Mayer and Rittberger 1997: 164–5; Goertz and Diehl 1992: 638–9; Kratochwil and Ruggie 1986: 767–8). Of course, the assumption of the counterfactual validity of norms must not be extended so far that any moral demand made at any time by any actor is uncritically ascribed the status of a social norm, despite the fact that it is largely ignored in practice. We therefore discuss criteria as to when an expectation of appropriate behaviour can be said to be a social 'norm' and thus an independent variable for an explanation of foreign policy behaviour.

The strength of norms: commonality and specificity

Critics of constructivist foreign policy theory point out that an actor is frequently confronted with many value-based expectations of appropriate behaviour, thus rendering difficult or arbitrary a distinction between relevant and irrelevant expectations of behaviour. Constructivists are therefore always at risk of 'explaining' foreign policy *ex post* by choosing that expectation of behaviour as an explanation which comes closest to the observed behaviour to be explained (Legro 1997: 33). However, criteria for determining the strength of social norms can be found in the constructivist literature, and these considerably increase the possibility of formulating predictions *ex ante*. In the constructivist view, the strength of a social norm (and thus the strength of its influence on foreign policy behaviour) depends on two properties: on its *commonality*, i.e. on how many members of a social system share a value-based expectation of behaviour; and on its *specificity*, i.e. on how precisely a norm distinguishes appropriate from inappropriate behaviour.

Commonality

From a constructivist point of view, social norms impact on behaviour when they reach a 'tipping point', i.e. when they are shared by a 'critical mass' of units within a social system. However, as Finnemore and Sikkink note, criteria for identifying how many members constitute such a 'critical mass' have not yet been developed, even though 'empirical studies suggest that norm tipping rarely occurs before one-third of the total states in the system adopt the norm' (Finnemore and Sikkink 1998: 901). However, we hold that, in order to make sound constructivist predictions about the foreign policy behaviour of individual states such as Germany, no less than the vast majority of actors within the pertinent social system should share an expectation of appropriate behaviour. Only then does it possess a sufficient level of commonality. Below this threshold, a constructivist prediction should not be formulated.

Specificity

From a constructivist perspective, the impact of a social norm depends not only on its commonality but also on its specificity (Legro 1997: 34). To a considerable extent, the precise meaning of norms depends on their *explication*, i.e. their formal expression; for instance, in written international conventions or domestic legislation (see Raymond 1997: 225; Franck 1990: 64 *et passim*). An unspecific expectation of behaviour does not rule out certain modes of behaviour as inappropriate, thus allowing for a wide range of behavioural options to be justified as appropriate and scarcely enabling the actors within a social system to determine when a norm has been violated (see Chayes and Chayes 1993: 188–92). Consequently, unspecific norms are unsuitable as a standard of appropriate behaviour and therefore as an independent variable for explaining foreign policy behaviour. In order to guide a state's foreign policy, a norm has to be sufficiently specific, i.e. at least some behavioural options have to be ruled out as clearly inappropriate.

Socialization processes as causal mechanisms

In constructivist foreign policy theory, the effect of social norms is attributed to *socialization processes*. In its original, sociological meaning, socialization is a 'process in which a person grows into the society and culture surrounding him and, by learning social norms and roles, becomes an independent, competent social being' (Weiß 1986: 269, our translation). In the course of this process, the actor 'acknowledges the institutionalized modes of thought and behaviour as correct, makes them – literally – "his own" and brings his interests and preferences into line with them' (Schimmelfennig 1994: 338, our translation; see also Müller 1993a).

However, the socialization process should not be conceived of as a one-way process to which the actor being socialized contributes no preconceptions of his own. Rather, the actor being socialized may well reflect on what he internalizes during the socialization process and may even modify its content (Schimmelfennig 1994: 339–40). As individuals are constantly confronted with new decision-making situations in the course of their lives, and hence need to learn new expectations of behaviour or reinterpret those that they have already internalized, socialization is never complete but is a continuous process (Parsons 1951: 208).[6]

Compared with the process of an individual's socialization into his social environment, the peculiar characteristic of the socialization process of foreign policy decision makers[7] is that two analytically distinct socialization processes occur simultaneously. Because foreign policy decision makers are at the interface of two social systems –

i.e. international society, on the one hand, and domestic society, on the other, they face two classes of socializing agent and, consequently, go through two different socialization processes. *Transnational socialization* signifies a process whereby government decision makers internalize international norms, i.e. value-based expectations of appropriate behaviour that are shared among states. *Societal socialization* refers to a process whereby government decision makers internalize societal norms, i.e. value-based expectations of appropriate behaviour that are shared by the citizens of their state.

Transnational socialization

Within *international society* (see p. 116f.), states are the constitutive units and therefore the most important socializing agents. The norms shared within international society are regarded by their constitutive members (i.e. states) as standards of appropriate behaviour. International organizations, in contrast, are not constitutive units of international society. However, they are significant as socializing agencies in that they are associations of states. In the transnational-constructivist view, international organizations are important as socializing agencies because they represent value communities made up of states (Keck and Sikkink 1998: 34). In the constructivist view, states acknowledge the expectations of appropriate behaviour formulated by international organizations as standards of appropriate behaviour if they regard themselves as part of the value community of the member states and seek recognition as an equal member by the other member states. Because international organizations represent value communities, their organs may function as 'teachers of norms' (Finnemore 1996a, b, 1993).

In recent years, transnational interactions among non-state actors have greatly increased, not least due to increasing economic interdependence and new technological developments in communications. Many authors view these developments as indicators of an emerging 'transnational civil society' in which expectations of appropriate behaviour relating to state actors' foreign policies may also be shared (see Rittberger, Schrade and Schwarzer 1999; Wapner 1996). *Transnational advocacy coalitions* are widely seen to represent the central actors of transnational civil society (see Boli and Thomas 1999; Keck and Sikkink 1998). By communicating expectations of appropriate behaviour, held by segments or the whole of transnational civil society, to both states and international organizations, these cross-border coalitions of societal actors play a twofold role in international society. On the one hand, they act as 'norm entrepreneurs' in that they develop further existing norms and help establish new ones (Finnemore and Sikkink 1998) and, on the other, they demand and verify compliance with existing norms (Keck and Sikkink 1998).[8] Accordingly, in tracing the processes leading to specific foreign policy decisions, the role of advocacy coalitions in propagating norms and fostering norm-consistent behaviour must be accorded appropriate consideration.

As constitutive entities of international society, states not only socialize but also are socialized because they are the primary addressees of internationally shared, value-based expectations of appropriate behaviour (Armstrong 1994: 16ff.). States acknowledge the norms of international society as standards of appropriate behaviour because their identity as states depends on their membership in international society (Armstrong 1994: 21, 24; Schimmelfennig 1994: 344). International norms which define collective goals and specify appropriate modes of behaviour for pursuing them have a socializing effect on states because states are constantly concerned with their reputation as recognized (i.e. norm compliant) members of international society.

The constructivist concept of reputation differs from the way reputation is understood in rationalist theories. In the latter, states are concerned with their reputation as reliable allies or partners in negotiations (see Mercer 1996; Chayes and Chayes 1993: 177; McElroy 1992: 46–53). Constructivists hold that states seek to preserve and consolidate their reputation as legitimate members of international society (Franck 1990: 191). The difference in these concepts of reputation thus affects the way in which states can be sanctioned. Constructivist theories emphasize immaterial or even symbolic sanctions aimed at states' status as legitimate members of international society, e.g., the cancelling of diplomatic, cultural or sports contacts (see Black 1999; Klotz 1999; Mangaliso 1999). In rationalist theories, in contrast, emphasis is placed on sanctions which have a negative effect on the pursuit of power or plenty (e.g. trade embargoes).

Societal socialization

Whereas rationalist approaches emphasize the importance of public pressure for the effect of societal norms on decision-makers' behaviour (Checkel 1997: 476–7; see also Raymond 1997: 216; Cortell and Davis 1996; McElroy 1992: 43–6), constructivist foreign policy theory regards processes of societal socialization as decisive for the effect of societal norms. Both society as a whole and its various groups are regarded as socializing agencies which address expectations of appropriate behaviour to the political decision makers. From a constructivist view, there are three ways in which societal expectations of appropriate behaviour impact on the behaviour of foreign policy decision makers. First, foreign policy decision makers have already internalized societal expectations of appropriate behaviour via the process of political socialization to which all the citizens of a state are subject. Second, before becoming representatives of their state in international society, politicians generally run through national political careers in the course of which they internalize more specific societal expectations of appropriate behaviour. Third and finally, decision makers behave consistently with societal expectations of appropriate behaviour because they wish to be recognized as representatives of their society in dealings with their international environment. If a government does not comply with the societal expectations of behaviour assigned to it, it runs the risk of losing its recognition by society as its legitimate representative.

Foreign policy decision makers are simultaneously subject to transnational and societal socialization processes. On the one hand, they are on the receiving end of expectations of appropriate behaviour assigned to them by international society. On the other, domestic society expects its representatives to abide by societally shared expectations of appropriate behaviour on the international level. If there are contradictory expectations of behaviour of sufficient commonality and specificity on the international and societal levels, then a constructivist prediction is just as impossible as when these expectations of behaviour are completely absent on both levels or do not reveal sufficient commonality and/or specificity. This is because the constructivist theory of foreign policy (yet) offers no criteria for determining whether international or societal norms have a stronger influence on foreign policy decision makers. If there are conflicting societal and international norms, any constructivist explanation is prone to criticism because it cannot be ruled out that actions are in fact guided by an interest with no normative basis and are justified only *ex post* by recourse to a norm which matches the behavioural option chosen.

By the same token, converging international and societal expectations of appropriate behaviour reinforce each other. Then, foreign policy decision makers comply with the expectations of behaviour assigned to them because of their self-understanding as both members of

international society and as representatives of their own society. Therefore, if there are the same expectations of appropriate behaviour on
both the international and the societal level, constructivist theory claims
that its explanation of foreign policy is particularly powerful. However,
an expectation of appropriate behaviour does not need to be present
simultaneously on both levels in order to allow for the expectation that
it guides foreign policy decision makers. If there is an expectation of
appropriate behaviour with sufficient commonality and specificity on
only one of the two levels, the degree of its internalization by foreign
policy decision makers (and thus its effect on their behaviour) will be
regarded as lower than if international and societal norms are congruent.
Nevertheless, in these cases there is no reason to reject the usefulness
of constructivist theory for explaining and predicting foreign policy
behaviour.

These considerations enable us to rank the predictive power of
constructivist foreign policy theory based on international and societal
norms (table 5.1). Constructivist theory claims high predictive power
when there are convergent expectations of appropriate behaviour of a
sufficient degree of commonality and specificity on both levels. Medium
predictive power exists if there is an expectation of appropriate behaviour with sufficient commonality and specificity on one level only.
When international and societal norms contradict each other, it is just
as impossible for constructivist foreign policy theory to make predictions as when norms with sufficient commonality and specificity are
lacking on either level.

Table 5.1 Predictive power of constructivist theory

International level	Societal level	Relationship	Predictive power
Norm present	Norm present	Convergent	++
Norm present	Norm absent	–	+
Norm absent	Norm present	–	+
Norm present	Norm present	Contradictory	–
Norm absent	Norm absent	–	–

Note: As already mentioned, a norm must have sufficient commonality and
specificity in order to be classified as 'present' for the purposes of this table.

Transnational and societal constructivism

In constructing a theory of foreign policy, we must ensure that independent and dependent variables are located on the same level of analysis. Thus international norms have to be transformed from a systemic into a unit-level variable. Since all norms address behavioural expectations to specific actors, they can, and must for our purposes, be reformulated as *expectations of appropriate behaviour addressed to Germany.*

Whereas the level-of-analysis problem may be taken into account this way, the co-determination of agents and structures has been regarded as posing more serious problems for constructivist (empirical) research. As elements of (social) structure, norms address behavioural claims to specific (corporate) actors[9]. At the same time, however, norms may emerge, alter or even decay through the activities of agents. Constructivists have devoted considerable attention to the question of the interaction between agents and structures, and have stressed the interdependence of the two. Indeed certain authors regard this *structurationist* view of 'agents and structures as mutually constituted or codetermined entities' (Wendt 1987: 350) as the defining characteristic of the constructivist research agenda (e.g. Wendt 1999: 1, 139; Checkel 1998: 326; Hopf 1998: 172). It would, however, be premature to conclude from the structurationist view of the agent–structure problem that it is impossible, within a research design, to distinguish analytically structural variables from agency variables and to examine their impact separately. Alexander Wendt, for example, states that

> neither state agents nor the domestic and international system structures which constitute them should be treated *always* as given or primitive units; theories of international relations should be capable of providing explanatory leverage on both. This does not mean that a particular research endeavor cannot take some things as primitive: scientific practice has to start somewhere. (Wendt 1987: 349, our emphasis; see also Dessler 1989: 443–4)

Since our aim here is to derive predictions about German foreign policy, i.e. a (corporate) actor's behaviour, we do not problematize the effects of German 'agency' on the (normative) social structures of international society. We merely seek to explain German foreign policy behaviour on the basis of those norms that are firmly embedded in these social structures. Hence we do not follow the full structurationist 'circle'.[10]

As our discussion of the various causal mechanisms has made clear, the independent variable 'social norms' can neither be attributed exclusively to the level of the international system nor to that of states and their societies. Rather, norms can be invoked by actors within and outside states and be expressed by either of them as expectations of appropriate behaviour addressed to a state's foreign policy decision makers. Especially prominent norms, such as the protection of human rights or the promotion of free trade, are widely shared both within states and on the level of international society. Whether research focuses primarily on the influence of international or societal norms depends above all on whether the aim is to investigate the similarity of foreign policies given different interests (see Finnemore 1996a) or differences in state behaviour given an identical systemic environment (see Ulbert 1997). For an analysis of continuity and change in German foreign policy, any decision to focus on either international or societal norms must appear arbitrary, especially as neither of these levels enjoys any theory-based primacy over the other. Moreover, focusing on either international or societal norms runs the risk of being blind to their mutually reinforcing or counteracting interrelation. After all, as interwoven but analytically discrete social systems, German society and international value communities such as the EU or the North Atlantic Alliance do not necessarily formulate the same expectations of appropriate behaviour concerning German foreign policy. Only when the two levels are separated *analytically*, is it possible to discover differences between the expectations of German society and those of other states, but also interactions between them.

Transnational constructivism

The concept of international society

Like neorealism, transnational constructivism [11] assumes that the foreign policy behaviour of states is first of all shaped by the characteristics of their international environment. However, while neorealism postulates that the *material* structure of the international system (the distribution of power among states) constrains actors' behaviour, transnational constructivism stresses the impact of the *immaterial* international structure (shared social constructions of reality, institutions, norms) on state behaviour (Wendt 1999: 1, 23–4; Finnemore 1996a: 15). Neorealism's concept of the international system is thus replaced in transnational constructivism by the concept of *international society* which, as a *social* system, constitutes the identities and preferences of its members and is reproduced by their practices (Wendt 1999, 1994, 1991; Ruggie 1998; Wendt and Duvall 1989). International society has originally been defined as 'a group of states, conscious of certain common interests and common values, conceiv[ing] themselves to be bound by a common set of rules in their relations with one another, and shar[ing] in the working of common institutions' (Bull 1977: 13). However, even though states are its *constitutive* units, international society also comprises a wide range of both intergovernmental and non-governmental actors which may play an important role in the creation and diffusion of international norms. The former may help define collective goals and direct expectations of appropriate behaviour to their member states (see Finnemore 1996a, b; McNeely 1995). The latter may work as links between states and transnational civil society, establishing and diffusing expectations of appropriate behaviour which relate to states' policies (see Keck and Sikkink 1998; Smith, Chatfield and Pagnucco 1997).[12]

The point of departure for transnational-constructivist arguments about the impact of international norms on state behaviour is the discovery that the practices of state actors within international society are characterized by a considerable degree of isomorphism (Finnemore 1996a: 6, 22; McNeely 1995: 2–3, 20; Meyer 1987: 46–50). Neorealists also assume some degree of isomorphism in state behaviour because all states need to secure their survival under anarchy by recourse to self-help (Waltz 1979: 93–7). However, if securing survival were the only motive for behaviour, states with different identities and preferences would only behave similarly in those areas that were of immediate concern to their survival, but not in other areas which played no role, or only a very negligible one, in guaranteeing their survival. Constructivism therefore attributes the isomorphous behaviour of states to the influence of international norms (Finnemore 1996a: 30).[13]

Like neorealism, transnational constructivism also assumes the absence of a superior coercive power on the international level. However, constructivists cite this absence as a further argument in favour of the effect of international norms because fear of punishment by such a power cannot account for the wide range of isomorphous state behaviour (see Wendt 1992). Furthermore, proponents of transnational constructivism point out that the complex interdependencies between actors and between issue areas of public policy often make it impossible that actors calculate the benefits they may gain from compliance with a certain norm. This does not imply that actors are assumed to behave irrationally. However, constructivism posits that rationality itself is in large part socially constructed and thus a result of shared understandings and expectations of appropriate behaviour (Hasenclever, Mayer and Rittberger 1997: 158–61; Hurrell 1993: 59). In the constructivist view, therefore, norm compliance is not, as in rationalist accounts of the impact of international norms, linked to states' 'demand' for norm-regulated international cooperation arising from self-regarding interests (see Keohane 1983). Rather, it is the 'supply' of expectations of appropriate behaviour within international society which leads to increasing isomorphism in state behaviour (Finnemore 1996a: 12; McNeely 1995: 12–13). The processes of standardizing the behaviour of state actors do not, however, occur globally and uniformly across all issue areas, but frequently within regional and/or functional *social subsystems* whose members subscribe to a commonly shared social construction of reality and to shared values (see Hurrell 1995). Such subsystems, conceived of by constructivists as value communities of like-minded states, define their member states' behavioural roles and thus also address expectations of appropriate behaviour to them (see Raymond 1997: 226). Therefore, norms which are institutionalized within these social subsystems must also be considered in a trans-national-constructivist analysis of foreign policy behaviour.

The role and significance of international institutions

Occasionally, there is confusion in the literature with regard to the conceptual difference between 'norms' and 'institutions'. For example, sovereignty has been described as both a norm and an institution (see Finnemore and Sikkink 1998: 891; Finnemore 1996a: 16). However, if we consider the definitions of norms and institutions that have become broadly accepted, the terms can be clearly distinguished from one another. While a norm is always a *single* value-based expectation, we can follow Zürn in defining a *social institution* as

> a permanent and consolidated pattern of behaviour of a specific number of actors in specific, recurring situations. The patterns of behaviour are based on a set of rules which define behavioural roles, give a meaning to activities and shape actors' expectations, thus themselves directing relationships between actors in the recurring situations. (Zürn 1992: 141, our translation)

Constructivists view the existence of social institutions on the international level as one of the central elements characterizing international society and distinguishing it from the neorealist concept of an anarchical international system in which interaction outcomes are determined solely by the international distribution of power (see Buzan 1993b: 330–6; Wendt and Duvall 1989). *International institutions* are social institutions which exist on the level of international society as a whole or of one of its subsystems, and constitute the roles and shape the behavioural patterns of their members.[14] As Zürn's definition shows, they represent sets of interrelated norms which, *as a whole*, constitute behavioural roles and give meaning to the concrete expectations of behaviour attributed to those roles. Consequently, sovereignty is clearly an institution consisting of a bundle of norms and giving meaning to them (see Finnemore and Sikkink 1998: 891).[15] By integrating interrelated norms into such norm sets which establish behavioural roles, institutions thus give a significance to individual norms which goes beyond that of constituting a certain goal of action or regulating behaviour. States meet the expectations of behaviour set by individual norms because they seek to perform the role ascribed to them by international institutions. By integrating norms into norm sets constituting behavioural roles, institutions also give permanence to individual norms because the redefinition of an individual norm's expectation of behaviour would require a redefinition of the entire behavioural role which the norm in question has helped to constitute (see Goldstein and Keohane 1993; Krasner 1983a, b).

Proponents of the transnational-constructivist research tradition interpret the political order of international society ('world polity', see McNeely 1995; Ruggie 1993; Meyer 1987) as a network of international institutions. The foundation of this order rests on the institution of sovereignty itself because it is through sovereignty that states as constitutive units of international society come into being. At the same time, the norms subsumed under the institution of sovereignty specify the basic parameters of legitimate state action. Above the level of this 'constitutional structure' of international society (Reus-Smit 1997), transnational constructivism locates specific international institutions, such as international organizations and regimes. *International organizations* are formal associations of states with tasks that are partly issue area specific and partly transcend issue areas. Unlike regimes, they can act as purposive collective actors made up of states (Rittberger and Zangl 1995: 26–7; Keohane 1989a: 3–4). Not least, their function is to formulate collective goals and to specify appropriate means for achieving them. In the emergence and communication of international norms, therefore, they play a central role which they in part also seek to fulfil by functionally integrating transnational advocacy coalitions, thus granting empowerment and legitimacy to such coalitions as actors in international society. *International regimes* are sets of principles, norms, rules and decision-making procedures which define the ends and means of action within specific issue areas of international relations and thus establish reciprocal reliability of expectation (Hasenclever, Mayer and Rittberger 1997; Krasner 1983b). From a transnational-constructivist view, the impact of norms embedded in specific international institutions on state behaviour stems from the deeper normative structure of the 'world polity' because international society is assumed to share the general expectation that the actions of its individual members match the shared expectations of appropriate behaviour addressed to them (see Hurrell 1993: 59).

When using internationally shared expectations of appropriate behaviour as a basis for deriving constructivist predictions about German foreign policy behaviour, reference will mainly be made to explicit and specific norms of both an international legal and non-legal nature which are embedded in issue area-specific international institutions (international regimes, international organizations). For they define the positive aims of state action and specify the means for their achievement, whereas norms which can be ascribed to 'constitutional structure' only define the properties a state must possess in order to be recognized as such, as well as the most fundamental standards of behaviour it should observe. Groups of states associated in certain organizations frequently only represent subsystems of international society. The value-based expectations of appropriate behaviour embedded in these organizations thus only pertain to their member states and not to international society as a whole (Raymond 1997: 226). When formulating constructivist expectations of behaviour for German foreign policy, Germany's membership or non-membership of these subsystems must therefore be considered. However, certain expectations of behaviour can also depend on characteristics of states other than membership in a social system. For example, the expectation to grant development aid to developing countries is obviously not directed to all members of international society but only to the industrially developed nations. This means that in identifying transnational-constructivist expectations about German foreign policy, certain characteristics of Germany as a country may also have to be considered in order to determine whether Germany is one of the addressees of the international norm from which the prediction is derived.

Societal constructivism

Societal constructivism stresses the dependence of foreign policy behaviour on the norms which are shared *within society*. Within this research tradition, some scholars have focused on the influence of norms that are shared by 'epistemic communities' or 'advocacy coalitions'; other scholars have emphasized the importance of (political) culture and (national) identity. Because 'culture' and 'identity' possess a higher level of commonality than norms shared by epistemic communities or advocacy coalitions, they are more important for a constructivist theory of foreign policy. We therefore draw on the research on (political) culture and (national) identity (see especially our discussion of indicators on p. 124ff.). However, we prefer a conceptualization of our independent variable as 'norms' instead of 'identity' or 'culture' for two reasons. First, we emphasize the close relationship between transnational and societal constructivism, i.e. between international and societal *norms*. Second, because of its immediate orientation to behaviour (see above), the concept of 'norms' is better suited for an analysis of a state's foreign policy *behaviour*. Though we focus on societal expectations of appropriate *foreign* policy behaviour, societal expectations of appropriate *domestic* policy behaviour may also become influential in contexts of foreign policy for which no norm specifically pertaining to foreign policy behaviour exists ('domestic analogy', see p. 123).

Deficiencies of expert- and advocacy-based approaches
Some scholars have paid attention to the impact of social norms that are shared by 'epistemic communities' (Haas 1992) or 'advocacy coalitions' (Sabatier 1993). These expert- and advocacy-based approaches have been particularly successful in analysing (foreign) policy in issue areas about which decision makers are insufficiently informed and thus dependent on expert advice. From a constructivist point of view, however, expert- and advocacy-based approaches have a major shortcoming because, by definition, the norms shared by groups of experts only possess a low level of commonality. As a consequence, constructivists regard them as less important than the norms that are shared by society as a whole. Moreover, constructivist theory has not established

criteria as to which social norm prevails whenever there are two or
more groups of experts holding competing expectations of appropriate
behaviour. Therefore, expert- and advocacy-based approaches are particularly susceptible to allegations of providing ex-post explanations
while ignoring other possible independent variables.

Because of these shortcomings of expert- and advocacy-based approaches, we will avoid singling out any societal subgroup as a bearer
of norms and instead focus on those norms that can be ascribed to the
'society' in its entirety.

Culture- and identity-based approaches

Another group of constructivist scholars has emphasized the importance
of '(national) identity' and '(political) culture' as explanatory variables.
In contrast to social norms, there are no commonly accepted definitions
of (political) culture and (national) identity (see Duffield 1999: 769).
Most scholars working in that field, however, highlight similar features
of both concepts. Most importantly, both identity and culture are widely
shared within a society (cf. Duffield 1998: 23). They are 'a property of
collectivities rather than of individuals' (Duffield 1998: 23). Culture and
identity are 'transmitted from one generation to the next through
mechanisms of socialization' (Berger 1998: 9). As a consequence, they
are stable over long periods of time (Banchoff 1999b: 270; Duffield
1999: 770; Berger 1998: 198; Risse-Kappen 1994: 209). Finally, both
'culture' and 'identity' are frequently conceptualized as comprehensive
concepts that include ideas, values or norms (Berger 1998: 9; Duffield
1998: 23).

(Political) culture and (national) identity are particularly suited to
explain general attitudes and broad patterns of (foreign policy) behaviour (Duffield 1998: 15). As a consequence, they have mostly been
applied to cross-national comparisons as well as to studies emphasizing
continuous patterns in a state's general approach to foreign policy. Risse
et al. (1999), for example, have used the concept of (national) identity
to explain differing general attitudes and preferences towards the Euro
in Germany, France and the UK. Other studies relying on the concepts
of culture and identity and stressing the underlying continuity of a
state's policy include Johnston's (1996) study of Chinese strategic culture
and Berger's (1998, 1996) work on Japanese and German security
policies. However, the concepts of (political) culture and (national)
identity are less suited for an analysis of foreign policy behaviour within
and across issue areas. As John Duffield (1998: 28) has pointed out,

political culture may be vague, incomplete or indeterminate. Similarly, Risse *et al.* 'do not assume that such broad constructs as national identities directly determine particular political behaviour and decisions' (1999: 157).

In order to present a coherent constructivist theory of foreign policy that is applicable to a wide range of specific cases, we have conceptualized the independent variable as 'social norms' rather than as 'culture' or 'identity' (see above). However, the research carried out by the scholars just mentioned has been of great importance for constructing *indicators* of societal norms (see below).

*The transfer of domestically valid norms to issue areas of foreign policy:
the domestic analogy*
Constructivists generally expect foreign policy to be shaped by value-based expectations of appropriate *foreign policy* behaviour. However, the value-based expectations of appropriate *domestic* policy shared by society can also impact on a state's foreign policy. Proponents of societal constructivism assume that foreign policy decision makers 'want their international environment to be ordered by the same values and principles as their domestic system' (Billing *et al.* 1993: 163). Of course, domestic policy-related, value-based expectations of appropriate behaviour will shape foreign policy only if there are no foreign policy norms with sufficient specificity and commonality because, by definition, the latter will always be more specific (and thus more influential) than the former.

Anne-Marie Burley (1993a), for example, has suggested that US foreign policy in the years immediately following World War II was aimed at transferring the domestic practices of the New Deal to the international level. According to Burley, the basic New Deal norm that the government should safeguard citizens' economic and social welfare by correcting market failure was shared by a large cross-section of US society. Thus, Burley argues, US politicians sought to comply with the expectation that they should seek to safeguard social welfare and correct market failure in structuring the international economic order as well. The norms of the New Deal, though originally only relating to the domestic sphere, thus also shaped US foreign policy. As this example[16] demonstrates, norms that have emerged for domestic policy and initially only claim validity for this sphere frequently possess a high degree of commonality and specificity and are therefore suitable for societal-constructivist explanations of foreign policy behaviour.

The identification of norms

In this section we construct and discuss various indicators of international norms, and societal norms. These indicators help us to identify systematically the value-based expectations of appropriate German foreign policy behaviour on the international and societal levels. The identification itself, i.e. the measurement of the independent variable, must be left to the application of constructivist foreign policy theory to our case studies (chapters 6 to 9).

Indicators of international norms

From the constructivist point of view, three indicators of international norms can be singled out as the most important, i.e. general international law, legal acts of international organizations and final acts of international conferences.

General international law

Like any law, international law can be understood as 'the expression of social and political values ... of a community' (Burley 1993b: 211). Although violations of international law are not normally punished, states' practices are by and large characterized by compliance with the law rather than by its violation (see Akehurst 1987: 2; Henkin 1968: 46). Constructivist authors conclude from this that a logic of appropriateness is at work in international society whose yardstick is not least provided by international law, i.e. the body of substantive and procedural norms which is regarded as legally binding by the constitutive units of international society.[17] As international society has no constitution equal to that of individual states, its 'legislation' in the form of international law is largely decentralized (see Coplin 1969: 144). In this process, art. 38 of the Statute of the ICJ has become the central procedural rule in that it names four authoritative sources of international law:

1 international treaties;

2 customary international law;

3 'the general principles of law recognized by civilized nations'; and

4 (as 'subsidiary means') judicial decisions and 'teachings of the most highly qualified publicists of the various nations'.

International treaties
International treaties are voluntary agreements between states whose prescriptions are regarded as legally binding. Because states enter voluntarily into treaty obligations, the commonality of international treaty-based norms can be ranked as high within the social system constituted by the state parties.[18] Treaty obligations frequently display a high degree of specificity as well because they are usually issue area specific. These legal documents are therefore especially useful for the identification of the norms of international society.

Customary international law
This body of legal norms is defined as

> those *rules of behaviour* that have so far been observed by the subjects of international law in their mutual transactions ... if this practice ('state practice') is joined by the conviction that there is a *legal duty* to comply with the objective rule (*opinio juris vel necessitatis*). (Seidl-Hohenveldern 1997: 99; italics in the original, our translation).[19]

Since customary international law requires both that it is recognized by states as law and that there is a match between value-based expectations of behaviour and actual behaviour (Byers 1999: 130), its norms can generally be assumed to possess a sufficient degree of commonality to allow for the formulation of constructivist predictions. Due to the exemplification of appropriate behaviour by states' repeated or even constant behavioural practice, the norms embedded in customary international law generally also present a sufficient degree of specificity.[20]

General principles of law
These are legal norms which are universally recognized in the domestic laws of 'civilized nations' and whose validity is extended to international relations in situations for which no treaty or customary legal norms exist (Seidl-Hohenveldern 1997: 108). Today, the term 'civilized nations' no longer refers to a restricted set of states (i.e. the Western nations) as such a restriction would violate the principle of the sovereign equality of states laid down in art. 2 (1) of the UN Charter. Hence, at least all UN member states today are regarded as 'civilized nations' (see Henkin 1995: 39–40). Thus the commonality of norms embedded in 'general principles of law' must today be regarded as sufficient. However, the specificity of such norms may vary considerably. Again, resort may be taken to UN General

Assembly resolutions – especially when they express their intent to state general principles of international law (see Szasz 1997: 31) – and judicial teachings and decisions in order to interpret the precise content of a norm which is embedded in such general principles.

Judicial decisions and teachings of the most highly qualified international lawyers

The formulation chosen in Art. 38 of the ICJ Statute with respect to this source of international law makes it clear that it is not a legal source in its own right but solely a 'subsidiary means' for the interpretation of international legal norms emanating from other legal sources (Graf Vitzthum 1997: 92). One problem when using this 'subsidiary means' is that interpretations by judges or scholars of international law are subjective legal opinions rather than intersubjectively shared expectations of appropriate behaviour. Nevertheless, judicial decisions and doctrines may be indispensable for the situation-specific interpretation of an international legal norm in order to arrive at a clear constructivist prediction because they usually make very concrete statements about the content of an expectation of behaviour and thus attach a great degree of specificity to it. Moreover, on the condition that states have submitted themselves to its jurisdiction, judicial decisions issued by the ICJ may contribute to the development of international law by setting precedents for subsequent state practice (Klein 1997: 351).

Legal acts of international organizations

Expectations of appropriate behaviour addressed to their member states are made explicit by international organizations in legal acts such as resolutions and regulations. Compared with the treaties through which international organizations are created, such legal acts are regarded in international legal science as 'secondary law of states' communities' (Seidl-Hohenveldern and Loibl 1996: 213–14, our translation). Even though legal acts issued by international organizations are thus a part of the body of international law, their legal force may differ considerably. Thus resolutions of the UN General Assembly are not legally binding on UN member states except when they deal with questions of membership and the UN budget. With regard to other issues, such resolutions only have the nature of 'recommendations' addressed to UN member states (see Joyner 1997: 440–6; Szasz 1997; 40–3, 46). Conversely, EU regulations are directly binding on all EU member states. From a constructivist perspective, however, international organizations are regarded as value communities (see Keck and Sikkink 1998: 34). Expect-ations of appropriate behaviour expressed in their legal acts thus always indicate *social* norms whose strength is not dependent on the extent to which they are *legally* binding but on the extent to which they are shared among member states and rule out certain modes of behaviour as inappropriate. The commonality of an expectation of appropriate behaviour expressed in a resolution can be inferred from the way in which the resolution was adopted. If it was adopted by a vast majority of member states, the commonality of the expectation of appropriate behaviour it expresses is sufficient to allow for the derivation of a constructivist prediction. Below this threshold, however, such documents cannot be seen as presenting a shared expectation of approp-riate behaviour. The specificity of the expectations of behaviour contained in these legal acts can also vary greatly, frequently declining at the expense of securing wide support. The specificity of expectations of appropriate behaviour expressed in resolutions must therefore be determined individually.

Final acts of international conferences
In recent years, international society has increasingly resorted to large international conferences in order to formulate common goals and adopt action programmes to achieve them (e.g. the Vienna World Human Rights Conference, the Peking World Women's Conference, the Copenhagen World Social Summit) (see in general Messner and Nuscheler 1996b; Rittberger 1995). The final acts of these conferences are neither international treaties nor legal acts of international organiz-ations but represent declarations of common political intent by the participating states.[21] With regard to the emergence of shared percep-tions of problems, the definition of common goals of international society and the specification of appropriate strategies for their achieve-ment, however, the significance of these acts cannot be neglected. In deriving constructivist predictions about foreign policy behaviour, therefore, account must be taken of the norms expressed in these documents. The final acts of such conferences are generally accepted without a vote or by consensus. This suggests that the commonality of the norms they contain should generally be sufficient. However, as with legal acts of international organizations, the expectations of behaviour that such acts contain frequently represent compromise formulae with only low specificity. Sometimes, however, world conferences confirm already existing norms. In these cases, the specificity of the expectations

of behaviour contained in such acts tends to be higher because an international consensus is established on the specific expectations of behaviour resulting from the confirmed norms.

Indicators of societal norms

In order to generate constructivist predictions about German foreign policy, the independent variable 'social norms' must also be operationalized and measured on the level of German society. As in research on political culture (which comprises the analysis of shared values and norms), this task can be achieved with both qualitative-interpretative and quantitative methods (Bergem 1993: 55). The interpretation of the constitutional and legal order, and the analysis of programmes and election platforms of political parties and of parliamentary debates draw on qualitative methods. Survey data analysis, on the other hand, represents the most common method in quantitative political culture research.

The constitutional and legal order of a society

Intersubjectively shared, value-based expectations of political decision makers' behaviour take on lasting influence when they are integrated into a society's institutional order. In institutionalized form, norms can have an impact even when no one genuinely believes in them as principled statements (Goldstein and Keohane 1993: 20). In modern societies, societal norms are institutionalized in the constitutional and legal order.[22] In judicial decisions, moreover, these legal provisions are constantly being adapted to new situations. In the sociology of law, it has been pointed out that, when the law is adapted by professional judges to changing conditions within the societal and international environment, the existing societal norms find their way into the legal order. As long as societal ideas do not conflict with the recognized principles of the legal order, a judge proceeds from dominant societal values (see Rehbinder 1993: 22) when applying legal norms. A complex interplay thus exists between societal norms and the constitutional and legal order. On the one hand, 'law consists of those parts of the social structure which have arrived at a particular consolidation' (Röhl 1987: 531, our translation) and integrates new developments only after some delay. On the other hand, the various references in legal texts to societal practice as a source of norms (e.g. 'in good faith') ensure that the constitutional and legal order remains tightly linked with societal norms.

A society's constitutional and legal order is therefore a valid indicator of societal norms. Furthermore, it is a suitable indicator because a society's constitutional and legal order is public and therefore easily accessible for the scholar.

In order to identify societally shared, value-based expectations of appropriate *foreign* policy behaviour by way of analysing the constitutional and legal order, a two-stage procedure is necessary. First, one must examine the norms relating to foreign policy in the constitutional and legal order, expressed in the German Basic Law (*Grundgesetz*), post-constitutional legislation and the rulings of the Federal Constitutional Court. It should not, however, be expected that the constitutional and legal order will set standards for all areas of foreign policy. As a second step, therefore, according to the domestic analogy (see p. 123), provisions must be identified in the constitutional and legal order which set standards for domestic policy and which can be presumed also to guide foreign policy decision makers in their interactions with the international environment.

Party programmes and election platforms

One of the tasks of political parties in a democratic system of governance is to articulate and aggregate policy expectations in society in order to include them in the processes of public policy making. Thus party programmes and election platforms are also suitable indicators of societally shared, value-based expectations of appropriate foreign policy behaviour (Jachtenfuchs, Diez and Jung 1997).[23] Although the programmatic work in parties is performed, above all, by party elites and active party members, the formulation of expectations of behaviour is still closely linked with the norms of society as a whole (see also Banchoff 1999b: 269). Programmatic documents in particular serve not only to bring party members to identify themselves with the party but also to present the party to outsiders, offering non-members the opportunity to identify themselves with the respective party's programme.[24] As parties are always competing for the electorate's support, their programmes aim at reflecting and articulating societal norms.

A party's relative showing at the polls can serve as a measure of the societal support for the value-based expectations of appropriate foreign policy behaviour articulated by that party. The programmes and platforms of splinter parties do not have this significance as indicators of expectations of behaviour shared by society as a whole. Whether a party has appreciable societal support for its platform can be seen from

whether it is represented in the *Bundestag* on the basis of that platform.
Under German electoral law, parties are represented in the *Bundestag*
if they either receive at least 5 per cent of the votes cast nationwide or
win the direct parliamentary mandate in each of three constituencies.
From the perspective of societal constructivism, this means that the
parties represented in the *Bundestag* articulate societal expectations of
behaviour which are shared either by at least 5 per cent of all voters or
by a regionally concentrated majority of the electorate.[25] In order to
have a sufficient level of commonality and to impact on German foreign
policy behaviour, a societal value-based expectation of appropriate
behaviour must at least be articulated by the two major parties, the
Christlich-Demokratische Union (Christian Democratic Union; CDU)
and the *Sozialdemokratische Partei Deutschlands* (Social Democratic
Party; SPD), that 'do not regard themselves as representing specific
sections of the population but attempt to appeal to all citizens' (Rudzio
1996: 139, our translation; see also Banchoff 1999b: 269).[26]

Parliamentary debates

Parliamentary debates are frequently used as an indicator of societal
norms (see Banchoff 1999b; Breuning 1997, 1995). Because of its 'highly
organized, programmatic debates', the *Bundestag* in particular is
regarded as the 'locus of the most important public clashes over state
policy' (Banchoff 1999b: 272). According to constructivism, representatives are to be seen as the 'mouthpiece' of societal norms rather
than as rational vote maximizers. Thus representatives' speeches can be
regarded as the expression of societally shared, value-based expectations
of appropriate foreign policy behaviour.

As indicators of societal norms, parliamentary debates, on the one
hand, and party programmes and election platforms, on the other,
are not independent of each other because, in both cases, the norms
are propagated by political parties. As members of the *Bundestag* are
generally subject to party discipline, it cannot be expected that the norms
they articulate will openly contradict the norms set out in their parties'
programmes. It is, however, plausible to assume that societal expectations of behaviour are formulated more specifically in *Bundestag*
debates than in party political programmes and election platforms
because speeches in *Bundestag* debates usually refer to specific policies
in actual situations. The indicator 'parliamentary debates' may therefore
be a more precise source of societally shared expectations of appropriate
behaviour than the indicator 'party programmes and election platforms'.

In *Bundestag* debates, members of the government also exercise their right to speak. However, the speeches of government members can be regarded as an indicator of societally shared expectations of behaviour only to a limited extent because they also express official government policy and are thus part of the dependent variable. Even so, it does not necessarily constitute circular reasoning when speeches of members of the government and the parliamentary parties supporting it are considered in identifying societal norms for explaining government policy. From a constructivist perspective, value-based expectations of appropriate behaviour which are only shared by the parties supporting the government do not possess sufficient commonality to have an impact on German foreign policy. Only if a value-based expectation of appropriate behaviour is shared by a major party apart from the parties supporting the government, or indeed by all parties represented in the *Bundestag*, does it possess a sufficient level of commonality and can thus be expected to shape German foreign policy.

Survey data

Approaches which assume societal influences on foreign policy have always been interested in analysing the role of public opinion (see e.g. Holsti 1996; Risse-Kappen 1991; Russett 1990). Most studies, however, assume that decision makers act according to a consequentialist logic, i.e. their interest in re-election (see Russett 1990: 10). Societal constructivism, in contrast, assumes that public opinion influences foreign policy because it expresses societally shared, value-based expectations of behaviour with which foreign policy decision makers, following a logic of appropriateness, seek to comply. Societal constructivism thus regards public opinion as an *indicator* of societal norms.

If a large sample is used,[27] standardized questioning of a representative cross-section of the population and statistical data analysis yield highly reliable results. Critics, while scarcely doubting the high degree of reliability of findings, nevertheless cast doubt on their validity as indicators of societal norms. Survey data are only valid if they indeed measure a stable disposition to behaviour and not non-committal, fleeting opinions (Groß 1995: 18).

In addition to some fundamental methodological objections to surveys in general (see Rohe 1994; Lijphart 1980), doubts have been voiced with regard to the possibility of employing survey data to measure societal attitudes towards *foreign* policy issues in particular. Most importantly, in comparison with domestic policy issues, public opinion with regard to foreign policy issues has been regarded as generally unstable and incoherent.[28] While empirical studies have put this proposition into perspective, even proponents of societally centred explanations of foreign policy behaviour concede that the mass public is often poorly informed (see Holsti 1992: 447). As a consequence, distortions through unavoidable 'instrumentation effects' are particularly strong (Groß 1995: 17; see also Dobler 1989: 10–11).

Taken together, survey data are a valid indicator of societal norms only if several conditions are met. First, the issue in question must be familiar to the interviewees. Second, instrumentation errors must be minimized, e.g. both questions and answers need to be worded very carefully. Finally, surveys must be conducted over a longer period of time (e.g. panel studies). Otherwise, volatile opinions instead of societal norms may be measured. In terms of research practice, however, these conditions will only rarely be fulfilled. Societal norms will therefore generally have to be identified using other indicators.

Post-unification Germany and norm-consistent foreign policy

The constructivist theory of foreign policy posits that the actions of foreign policy decision makers are shaped by social norms, defined as intersubjectively shared, value-based expectations of appropriate behaviour. From a constructivist perspective, the dependent variable 'German foreign policy behaviour' can thus be conceptualized as *norm-consistent foreign policy*.

Studies of German foreign policy inspired by constructivist theorizing have pointed at Germany's continued enmeshment in a network of international (normative) institutions and its unaltered societal norms (Banchoff 1999a, b; Berger 1998; Duffield 1998; Katzenstein 1997b; Anderson and Goodman 1993). From this, they infer that significant changes in Germany's foreign policy behaviour as predicted by neo-realism (see chapter 3) are not to be expected. In our view, however, the assumption that international and societal norms have remained unchanged in spite of the end of the Cold War and German unification is premature. In order to provide a well-founded constructivist explanation of German foreign policy, this assumption must be examined empirically. As the norms which are significant for foreign policy are firmly embedded in international and societal institutions, the assumption that rapid norm change is unlikely is plausible at first sight.

Nevertheless, profound changes such as the end of the Cold War and German unification represent unexpected shifts in context, even for firmly institutionalized norms, and may thus lead to their substantial alteration or modification (see Keohane and Nye 1993). As a consequence, the pattern of continuity and change displayed by norms may also vary across different issue areas and even across specific subjects within a single issue area. A general prediction about German foreign policy after unification must therefore confine itself to formulating the proposition that German foreign policy behaviour will change only if and when the norms pertaining to the issue in question have changed. More specific, substantive constructivist predictions will have to be formulated for the individual cases.

Notes

1 On definitions of social norms, see Finnemore and Sikkink 1998: 891; Legro 1997: 33; Finnemore 1996a: 22; Goldstein and Keohane 1993: 20; Parsons 1961: 120.

2 Constructivists also reject the view that ideas may only serve as focal points in the absence of unique equilibria or as 'road' maps when actors only have incomplete information (Goldstein and Keohane 1993: 11–26).

3 The distinction between a 'regulative' and a 'constitutive' effect of norms, which was first made by Rawls (1955), is not treated uniformly in the constructivist literature. Some authors regard regulative and constitutive norms as different categories. In their view, constitutive norms do not generate any specific expectations of behaviour because their function lies in the constitution of actors' identities, not in the regulation of their behaviour (e.g. Klotz 1995). Others hold that each norm has a regulative and a constitutive function because, as a 'motive', it constitutes a practice and hence constitutes a certain social role of the actor (e.g. Finnemore 1996a; Onuf 1989).

4 For their part, ideas can include values in the sense of 'principled beliefs held by individuals' as well as 'causal beliefs'.

5 One example of a cognitive account of German foreign policy is Thomas Banchoff's study of German EU policy after 1990 in which he ascribes the German federal government's policy of bringing about further European integration to 'Helmut Kohl's historical ideas' (Banchoff 1997: 66).

6 In sociology, there is a common distinction between primary and secondary socialization. Primary socialization takes place when a child grows into its family and society and is therefore completed when the child becomes an adult. Secondary socialization, in contrast, signifies the continuing

process of an actor's internalizing of standards of appropriate behaviour. Secondary socialization is particularly significant for constructivist foreign policy theory while primary socialization only plays a role with respect to the growing into international society of 'new' states, such as the newly independent former Soviet republics (Schimmelfennig 1994), or with respect to the way in which new political elites grow into their role as the government of a country following a change in that country's domestic political system (Armstrong 1994: 25ff.; 1993).

7　As with societal norms, it is the individual foreign policy decision makers who, as state representatives, internalize internationally shared expectations of appropriate behaviour. However, as the internationally shared expectations of behaviour to which foreign policy decision makers are subject are directed towards the state they represent, one generally speaks of states being socialized (see Checkel 1997: 477; Raymond 1997: 216; McElroy 1992: 40–3).

8　Studies on the activity and significance of transnational advocacy coalitions emphasize their role as a link between norms shared by the international society, by transnational civil society and by national societies. Transnational advocacy coalitions thus gain increasing importance in inverse proportion to the degree of receptiveness shown by governments to the expectations of behaviour that their social environments address to them. By appealing to internationally shared expectations of behaviour, transnational advocacy coalitions seek to mobilize international pressure in order to incite the government in question to modify its behaviour ('the boomerang pattern', see Keck and Sikkink 1998: 12–13; for the 'spiral model', see Risse and Sikkink 1999: 17–19).

9　What one views as 'structure' and 'agent' is highly dependent on which level of analysis one chooses. As Hendrik Spruyt notes, '[t]he individual can be embedded in the structure of a bureaucratic organization. That organization, taken as an agent with a particular corporate identity, is in turn embedded in a larger political structure, and so on' (Spruyt 1994: 14).

10　The practicability of empirical tests of the structurationist model in a single and coherent research design is questionable (see Checkel 1998: 340–2). In applying constructivist theory to empirical studies, most authors have applied reduction to either structure or agents. At best, they have sought to do justice to the structurationist claim by combining case studies with a focus on either structure or agency. Thus, for example, in her case studies on the impact of norms of state science bureaucracies, the law of war and the World Bank's definition of development, Martha Finnemore explicitly begins by demonstrating the impact of social structure (norms) on agency before reverting her perspective and demonstrating the impact of agency on normative shifts in the social structure (see Finnemore 1996a: 24f.).

11 To a significant extent, transnational constructivism has its origins in a research tradition known as 'reflexive institutionalism' (Schaber and Ulbert 1994; Keohane 1989c) or 'sociological institutionalism' (Finnemore 1996a, b). While the affinity of this research tradition with constructivism results from the fact that it is also based on the fundamental assumption of the social construction of reality, the label 'transnational' is justified by its assumptions about the processes of, and the actors involved in, the creation and diffusion of international norms. The 'classical' definition of transnational relations assumes the non-state constitution of at least one of the interaction partners (Risse-Kappen 1995a: 3; Keohane and Nye 1972: xii). Following other authors (e.g. McNeely 1995), we are using this term in order to underline the fact that participation in processes in which international norms are constituted and communicated is not necessarily restricted to governmental actors alone.

12 Of course, transnational civil society actors may also seek to achieve certain goals independent of states. Wapner (1996) calls these independent actions and interactions within transnational civil society 'world civic politics'.

13 Finnemore (1996a) has demonstrated the isomorphism of state behaviour with regard to the establishment of state scientific bureaucracies or to the treatment of wounded combatants in wars. Other case studies on the institutionalization of education (Meyer et al. 1979) or the establishment of women's franchise (Ramirez and Weiss 1979) have arrived at the same result.

14 For a definition of social institutions, see also Hall and Taylor (1996: 938). For a definition of international institutions, see McNeely (1995: 19), Keohane (1989a: 162–3) and Young (1989: 5–6).

15 In a recent study which, however, seeks to refute the constructivist claim about the impact of international norms on state behaviour by recourse to power-related arguments, Stephen Krasner has even distinguished four types of sovereignty, each establishing different norm sets (Krasner 1999: ch. 1).

16 Further examples can be found in Noël and Thérien 1995, Katzenstein 1993, and Lumsdaine 1993, as well as in the vast literature on the democratic peace (e.g. Weart 1994; Russett 1993).

17 This 'sociological' definition of law, which has been proposed, for instance, by Hart (1961), differs from both naturalist and positivist definitions, which derive the legal nature of norms either from requirements of natural law or from enforcement and sanctioning of certain modes of behaviour (see Arend 1996: 290–2).

18 Of course, the law of international treaties allows the state parties to exclude certain treaty obligations or to modify their content by means of reservations. However, such reservations must not run contrary to the overall intent of the treaty (Akehurst 1987: 129–31).

19   Using customary international law as an indicator of international norms
     may raise the danger of post-hoc explanations of state behaviour if the
     existence and substance of a norm of international customary law, which
     is taken to have caused a certain mode of behaviour, is inferred from that
     behaviour itself and from its rhetorical justification (see Byers 1999: 136).
     However, since we posit that a norm of customary international law must
     also have a sufficient degree of commonality in order to be regarded as
     influential on state behaviour, we can overcome this danger of post-hoc
     explanation.

20   There are, of course, norms whose status as customary international law
     is disputed. Here, other indicators, especially the literature on international
     law and legal acts of international organizations (e.g. UN General Assembly
     resolutions), which claim the status of customary law for a specific norm,
     may provide guidance for its interpretation (cf. Seidl-Hohenveldern 1997:
     104; Seidl-Hohenveldern and Loibl 1996: 217–18; Akehurst 1987: 215–16).

21   However, certain international conferences serve to negotiate and adopt
     international treaties. This applies for example to the UN Conference on
     the Law of the Sea (1958, 1960, 1973–82) and the Rome Diplomatic
     Conference which finalized and adopted the statute of the International
     Criminal Court (ICC) in 1998.

22   The degree of significance accorded to the legal codification of societal
     norms varies from society to society. The FRG is regarded as one of the
     states in which societal norms are legally codified to a great extent (see
     Bulmer 1997: 67–8; Katzenstein 1993: 276; Johnson 1978).

23   Critics of constructivist reasoning may object that party programmes and
     election platforms can also serve as indicators of societal interests. To be
     sure, it is difficult, if not occasionally impossible, to distinguish value-based
     expectations of behaviour, on the one hand, and interest-based demands,
     on the other, when analysing these documents. However, it is important
     to note that we use party programmes and election platforms as valid
     indicators of societal norms only if at least the two major parties share the
     same value-based expectation of appropriate behaviour. This threshold
     makes it more difficult to confuse societal norms with societal interests.
     This also applies to the analysis of parliamentary debates (see p. 130).

24   Societal constructivism thus views parties as being primarily marked by
     having programmes and members. From the perspective of utilitarian
     liberalism, in contrast, it would be appropriate to regard parties primarily
     as competitors, their programmes having no intrinsic value but serving
     solely as instruments to maximize votes (for a distinction between the two
     types of party see Klingemann and Volkens 1997: 519).

25   For an analysis of societal norms following unification, it is interesting to
     note that the *Partei des Demokratischen Sozialismus* (Party of Democratic
     Socialism; PDS) has become established as a regional party in the new

federal states (*Länder*) because this means that there are societally shared expectations with regard to German policy specific to the new *Länder*, supported by a relative majority concentrated there. Precisely because the PDS represents constituents that only entered the political stage as a result of unification, the PDS and its programmes and platforms should in any case be considered for the purpose of identifying societal norms.

26 Empirical studies have found a remarkably high degree of correlation between election platforms and a government's actual behaviour (Klingemann, Hofferbert and Budge 1994, and for Germany, Hofferbert and Klingemann 1990). These studies also emphasize the disproportionately great influence of the *Freie Demokratische Partei* (Free Democratic Party; FDP) in formulating German foreign policy. As an indicator of social norms, however, the FDP platforms have the same status as other small parties, such as *Bündnis 90/Die Grünen*.

27 The minimum number of respondents should be 2000 (Wildenmann 1992: 67).

28 The most prominent proponents of this view have been Walter Lippmann and Gabriel Almond (see the discussion in Holsti 1996).

Part III
Case studies

6

German security policy within NATO

Rainer Baumann

Introduction [1]

Ever since the creation of the *Bundeswehr* in 1955, membership of
NATO has been at the heart of (West) Germany's security policy. After
German unification and the end of the East–West conflict, the question
arose as to whether Germany would distance itself from the alliance.
In this chapter, we will look at Germany's foreign policy behaviour in
NATO. No claim is made to cover German security policy as a whole.
Issues not primarily linked to NATO (such as non-proliferation policy)
will not be included, and it will be necessary to make a case selection.

There is a substantial body of literature on post-unification Germany's
security policy in and for Europe. Most authors highlight multilateralism
and an aversion to the use of military force as key characteristics of
German security policy. Wolfgang Schlör (1993) found that Germany's
participation and integration in NATO have remained a core element
of its security policy. Reinhard Wolf (1996) and Hans Giessmann (1999)
point to a continued German embeddedness in security institutions such
as NATO, and Gunther Hellmann (1997) observes a policy of self-binding
in this respect. In the most comprehensive study on this issue to date,
John Duffield (1999, 1998, 1994) argues that Germany's (re)turn to
power politics in security policy, as expected by realists (see Layne 1993;
Waltz 1993; Mearsheimer 1990), has been prevented by its integration
in international institutions and by a domestic political culture that calls
for a low profile in military affairs. Also focusing on political culture,
Thomas Berger (1998, 1996) argues that deeply rooted anti-militarist
sentiments in German society shape security policy. Both Berger and
Duffield note that Germany has adapted its position on out-of-area
operations without giving up its caution concerning the use of force.

Axel Sauder (1995) contrasts Germany's multilateralist orientation in security policy with the more autonomy-oriented security policy of France. He argues that the different policies are based on different conceptions of European security: centring on integration in the German case and on sovereignty in the case of France. Knut Kirste (1998) and Nina Philippi (1997) study German participation in out-of-area operations. They stress that post-unification Germany's behaviour fits that of a civilian power (see Kirste and Maull 1996; Maull 1990) well. Alexander Siedschlag (1995) shows that, in an incremental process, Germany has begun to embrace the idea of participating in multilateral non-defence operations (see also Bach 1999: 119–75). Finally, Michael Berndt (1997) argues that Germany pursues a military policy that secures political influence on Germany's allies in order to achieve its (economic) national interests. Hence most authors stress continuity in post-unification Germany's security policy. They see only modest adaptations to a changed international environment.

This chapter builds on the work of other authors, but it also adds new aspects to the literature. First, the predictions of competing foreign policy theories will be developed and tested systematically. While German security policy within NATO has already been analysed from different theoretical viewpoints (e.g. Hellmann 1997; Wolf 1996), this study has an even stronger theoretical focus. Second, we shall get a more comprehensive account of Germany's foreign policy *behaviour* in this issue area than is provided by most studies. Many of the studies mentioned have a strong focus on decision makers' declarations on German security policy, or on wider political discourses. In concentrating on actual policy behaviour, the present study complements this body of analysis.

The following issues can be identified as the universe of cases: integration in NATO's military structures; troop size and military spending (burden sharing in the alliance); participation in non-Article–5 operations;[2] cooperation with NATO partners on armaments policy; policy concerning NATO's Eastern enlargement; policy concerning NATO's role in the field of cooperative security; and policy regarding a European Security and Defence Identity. From these, (1) the integration of the *Bundeswehr* in NATO's military structures and German participation in NATO's out-of-area operations were selected for further study. These cases fulfil the three criteria for case selection discussed in chapter 10. First, they allow for a meaningful comparison of German policy in the 1980s and 1990s. Second, for both cases the formulation of a neorealist prediction is feasible. Finally, integration in NATO and participation in NATO-led out-of-area operations have been among the most important issues concerning Germany's security policy within NATO. Integration in NATO's military structures has always been at the heart of the cooperation within the alliance, while the growing importance of NATO-led out-of-area operations has been among the most striking changes of the alliance after the end of the East–West conflict (see Theiler 1997: 106–10). Before we turn to the cases, some clarifications are needed on how to study German security policy within NATO from the viewpoint of different foreign policy theories.

Theories of foreign policy and German security policy within NATO

Neorealism

From a neorealist perspective, states primarily safeguard their security in the anarchic international system. Neorealism claims high explanatory power for security policy. The two cases of German NATO policy should thus be easy cases for the two variants of neorealist foreign policy theory.

According to *neorealism*, NATO is an alliance founded to balance the threat posed by the Soviet Union. After the breakup of the Warsaw Pact and of the Soviet Union itself, NATO members' readiness to cooperate should begin to vanish (see Hellmann and Wolf 1993). Germany, which was constrained by its integration in the alliance to an especially high degree, and whose power position has been strengthened after unification, is expected to be among the driving forces of this dissolution process. It has become less necessary for Germany to coordinate its security policy with other NATO states and to follow the lead of the US (Mearsheimer 1990: 6). Germany will especially display more autonomy-seeking policy vis-à-vis other NATO members. Even neorealism does not expect an immediate and full German retreat from NATO. It does, however expect German NATO policy to become more unilateral and less cooperative than during the time before unification.

Modified neorealism concurs in that NATO was founded to counter the Soviet threat. Yet, according to this variant of neorealist theory of foreign policy, it is also important that the alliance offers substantial opportunities to exert influence on the other members,[3] especially for the more powerful NATO states. As post-unification Germany has not only gained in power but is also facing substantially reduced security pressures, the influence to be kept or gained from continuing actively to participate in NATO is not of secondary importance compared with the autonomy resulting from loosening ties with NATO. Modified neorealism thus expects post-unification Germany to accept some autonomy losses in return for substantial gains in influence on other NATO states.

Utilitarian liberalism

According to the utilitarian-liberal theory of foreign policy, Germany's security policy in NATO will qualify as gain-seeking policy, serving the interests of the dominant domestic actors. A striking feature of decision making on most issues of NATO policy is the lack of assertive private actors (see Müller-Rommel 1988b: 308–14).[4] Soldiers' organizations such as the Deutsche Bundeswehrverband usually lobby for their position on topics such as military spending or soldiers' social benefits, but on other issues they are not situatively mobilized. The military industry has good contacts with procurement officials at the Defence Ministry (see Gose 1997) without obtaining substantial influence on issues other than military procurement. Organized groups within the peace movement, such as the Deutsche Friedensgesellschaft-Vereinigte Kriegs-dienstgegnerInnen, lack both situative and structural mobilization. They have hardly any influence on the decision-making processes (see Cooper 1997). Overall, the PAS actors do not depend on private actors in fulfilment of their tasks. They enjoy a high level of autonomy vis-à-vis private actors. In both cases analysed below, the network is characterized by PAS leadership both before and after unification.

Consequently, in analysing the policy networks in this case study, we concentrate on political, political-administrative and administrative actors. The political actors are the Chancellor[5] and the members of the *Bundestag*. The *Länder* governments represented in the *Bundesrat* do not have competences in security policy. The *Bundeswehr* is an administrative actor, while the Ministers of Foreign Affairs, of Defence and of Finance are political-administrative actors. If the Chancellor, who possesses the *Richtlinienkompetenz*, is highly situatively mobilized, the network is marked by concentrated PAS leadership. When the Chancellor's situative mobilization is low, there will be decentralized PAS leadership, since the network will comprise several most assertive PAS actors.

The actors' preferences have to be determined on a case-specific basis. As a general tendency, utilitarian liberalism expects political actors to try to minimize the risks and costs of defence. They will usually prefer a multilateral German security policy in NATO, with Germany keeping a low profile. Administrative and political-administrative actors are expected to strive for keeping and enhancing their own competences. To the extent that integration and a low profile in NATO curtail such competences, their preferences will counter those of political actors. Utilitarian liberalism expects German security policy in NATO to be characterized by this conflict among PAS actors.

Constructivism

Constructivist foreign policy theory offers a different view of Germany's NATO policy than the rationalist theories discussed above. According to this theory, post-unification Germany will pursue a NATO policy consistent with pertinent international and societal norms.

International norms: As a community of democratic states with common values (see Risse-Kappen 1996, 1995b), NATO serves as an institutional frame through which international norms are addressed at member states. Member states are expected to cooperate within NATO on security issues. In order to identify international norms of sufficient commonality and specificity, we have to keep in mind that, first, general international law, e.g. the prohibition of the use of force (UN Charter art. 2 para. 4) or the principle *pacta sunt servanda*, sets a general frame of appropriate behaviour for all states. International treaties that Germany has ratified, such as the Washington Treaty of 1949, provide more focused prescriptions of appropriate behaviour within NATO. Finally, decisions taken and documents adopted by the North Atlantic Council and other NATO organs, e.g. NATO's Strategic Concepts of 1991 and 1999, indicate more precisely what behaviour is expected from member states.

Societal norms: According to constructivism, German NATO policy will also be consistent with the norms of German society. Some scholars argue that the antimilitarist sentiments established in the 'old' FRG manifest themselves in a preference for avoiding unilateral steps and for military restraint (see Berger 1998: 193–201; Duffield 1998: 237–40). General normative guidelines for German NATO policy, as found in the Basic Law, point in the direction of a non-aggressive and cooperative security policy. German armed forces may be used for purposes other than defence only if this is explicitly stipulated by the Basic Law (art. 87a para. 2 GG). The preparation of an aggressive war is unconstitutional (art. 26 para. 1 GG), whereas the basic principles of international public law are a part of German law (art. 25 GG). Germany may participate in a system of collective security that serves the maintenance of peace (art. 24 para. 2 GG). While such participation is not mandatory, the inclusion of such a clause in the Basic Law indicates that Germany is expected to pursue a multilateralist security policy. While NATO is more a system of collective self-defence than a system of collective security, the German Federal Constitutional Court has ruled that institutions such as NATO and the WEU may also be seen as systems of collective security if they serve the maintenance of peace (Entscheidungen des Bunderverfassungsgerichts (BVerfGE) 90, 351; see also Randelzhofer 1994, paras 18–20). Since the legal framework will often not be very specific in prescribing German security policy behaviour, it will be necessary to study the programmes and platforms of the political parties. As we shall see, there is a broad consensus among the parties on the issues analysed in this study.

Case 1: integration of the *Bundeswehr* in NATO's military structure

Case description and dependent variable

NATO differs from ordinary alliances in having an integrated command structure and in comprising a set of organs for planning, research and administration. Forces of member states are assigned to NATO and may be put under full NATO command in case of crisis or war. Some units, especially naval forces, have even been put under full NATO command during peacetime. For several decades, there have also been multinational units. It must be noted, though, that several changes in NATO's strategy and force posture took place beginning in 1990. During the East–West conflict, NATO forces were oriented towards repelling a massive Soviet attack. They had a high level of readiness and were mainly stationed at the Eastern front line. National corps of the member states covered small sections so that, in case of an attack, the forces of several members would inevitably be drawn into conflict. In its Strategic Concept of 1991, NATO stressed that this threat had given way to diverse risks and instabilities. It decided to establish a new force posture based on main defence forces with a much lower level of military readiness, immediate and rapid reaction forces, and augmentation forces, to be provided mainly by the US and not to be regularly stationed in Europe. Also, it was agreed to rely more on multinational units (see Tuschhoff 1994: 365–73).

Created as an 'alliance army' (*Bündnisarmee*) within NATO (see Haftendorn 1986: 149–56), the *Bundeswehr* had always been integrated in NATO's military structure to an especially high degree. With the entry into force of the Two-plus-Four Treaty in 1990, Germany gained back its full sovereignty in military affairs. Yet, art. 5 para. 1 of this Treaty stipulated that *Bundeswehr* forces to be stationed in the new *Länder* must not be assigned to NATO until the complete removal of Soviet/Russian forces from German territory by the end of 1994. For the first time the FRG was in possession of combat forces not integrated in NATO structures. A number of defence experts foresaw a trend in German defence policy towards renationalization (Tuschhoff 1994: 384–6; Young 1992a: 24–7; Nerlich 1991: 308; Orden 1991: 353).

Germany's policy concerning the integration of the Bundeswehr *in NATO's military structures* is thus the dependent variable. We will look at three different indicators of military integration. First, we evaluate the assignation of German forces to NATO on a three-point scale: Germany can have military units not assigned to the alliance, it can have its armed forces fully assigned to NATO, or it can put them under even stricter NATO control. As a second indicator we have chosen the participation of German armed forces in multinational units: Germany can be reluctant to participate in such units, it can integrate some of its armed forces in multinational units, or it can strive to integrate a major part of its armed forces in multinational units. An increased German participation in multinational units after unification does not automatically count as a strengthening of military integration because multinational units have assumed a greater role in NATO's post-Cold War strategy and military structures. Finally, we assess military integration in NATO by looking at Germany's national capacities for military planning, command and control: Germany can abstain from acquiring such capacities and rely entirely on NATO structures, it can create capacities for participation in multilateral military operations, or it can create capacities necessary for unilateral operations.

Independent variables and predictions

Neorealism
Due to the Allied special rights and responsibilities concerning Berlin
and Germany as a whole (see Haftendorn and Riecke 1996), and
especially due to being threatened by the Soviet Union, from a neorealist
perspective the 'old' FRG had no choice but to integrate its armed forces
in NATO's military structures. With the end of the Cold War and the
demise of Soviet (later Russian) power, the need for such a policy
declined.
   Renationalizing armed forces and military capacities yields significant
autonomy gains for post-unification Germany, but a strong presence in
NATO's military structures is also a source of influence on other member
states (see Millotat 1996: 59; Bundesminister der Verteidigung (BMVg)
1994: 88). By following a policy of renationalization, Germany would
suffer substantial losses of influence. Assigning forces to NATO implies
that, in case of crisis or war, these forces will not remain under national
command. Assignation restricts a state's autonomy, but it is also a source
of influence within the alliance. For instance, a strong presence in NATO's
military structure facilitates obtaining command posts, as well as shaping
decisions about common equipment of NATO forces (Tuschhoff 1994:
384). Concerning multinational units, the situation is similar. If forces
are integrated in multinational units, it becomes harder to use them
autonomously (Hallerbach 1991: 23). Yet the state gains some control
over the use of the forces of the other participating state(s), and it
enhances its overall presence in the alliance (see Tuschhoff 1994: 382–4).
Thus, concerning assignation of armed forces to NATO and participation
in multinational units, post-unification Germany is confronted with a
trade-off between autonomy and influence. Establishing national capacities for military planning, command and control, however, enhances
Germany's abilities for independent action without leading to substantial
influence losses within NATO. Nor would Germany, from a neorealist
perspective, gain influence among NATO states by refraining from
acquiring such capacities.
   According to *neorealism*, when confronted with a trade-off between
autonomy and influence, post-unification Germany will clearly prefer
autonomy. It will have no interest in maintaining or strengthening the
military structure of NATO. Rather, it will use its enhanced power
position to enlarge its space for independent action and to prevent
further autonomy losses. Neorealism expects that post-unification

Germany, pursuing an autonomy-seeking policy, will strive for lowering its integration in the military structures of NATO.

As its power position has improved, post-unification Germany will reduce the integration of the *Bundeswehr* in NATO's military structures, and it will strengthen its national military capacities.

According to *modified neorealism*, in light of drastically reduced security pressures, post-unification Germany will accept some autonomy losses in return for substantial influence gains. Thus Germany will not reduce its military integration in NATO structures. Rather, it will pursue an influence-seeking policy by keeping its forces assigned to NATO and by readily participating in multinational units. When strengthening its national military structures does not lead to substantial influence losses within NATO, as with regard to national capacities for planning, command and control, modified neorealism expects that post-unification Germany will pursue an autonomy-seeking policy.

As its power position has improved and its exposure to security pressures has decreased, post-unification Germany will continue to integrate the *Bundeswehr* in NATO's military structures. It will strengthen its national capacities for military planing, command and control as long as it does not weaken this integration.

Utilitarian liberalism
The policy network comprises the Chancellor and the *Bundestag* as political actors, the Ministers of Foreign Affairs, of Defence and of Finance as political-administrative actors, and the *Bundeswehr* as an administrative actor. The fundamental interest of the political actors is to get re-elected and, to a lesser extent, to enhance their competences. Military renationalization would require increased military spending.[6] To cover these expenses, tax increases or cuts in social spending (measures unpopular with the electorate) would be necessary. Political actors will thus prefer keeping Germany militarily integrated in NATO, so that Germany can keep its costs of defense low by externalizing some of them on its NATO partners. Neither for the members of the *Bundestag* nor for the Chancellor this preference would be countered by substantial gains in competences resulting from military renationalization. The position of the members of the *Bundestag* would not be strengthened if Germany lowered its level of military integration, as most of the policy in this field is executive in nature. While military integration in NATO creates some limitations on the Chancellor's

independent decision-making competences, they are not nearly as important to the Chancellor as enhancing his prospects for re-election. It follows that the Chancellor and the members of the *Bundestag* will favour keeping *Bundeswehr* forces assigned to NATO, as well as participating in multinational units (which links forces of NATO partners to the defence of Germany). Since they want to eschew Germany's entanglement in costly military operations, they will oppose the creation of national capacities for the planning and conduct of military operations.

The political-administrative actors will have divergent preferences. The Foreign Minister will prefer to keep Germany's integration in NATO's military structures for four reasons. First, it strengthens Germany's position in NATO's political bodies, in which Germany is mainly represented by diplomats from the Foreign Office. Second, it helps to maintain Germany's good relations with its Western partners, which is of key importance for the work of the Foreign Minister to be seen as successful. Third, lowering the level of this integration would not result in any additional competences or funds for the Foreign Minister. Finally, the Foreign Minister's interest in re-election converges with his administrative interests. The Minister of Finance, like the political actors, will oppose any policy that would make increased defence spending necessary. In contrast, the Minister of Defence will favour renationalization. His administrative interest in renationalization will dominate his political interest in continued military integration. Integrating German armed forces in NATO opens up possibilities for co-decision making for the Defence Minister, but this is more than countered by the prospects of reducing the level of integration in NATO's military structures. Accompanied by the appropriation of necessary additional funds, renationalization would result in more opportunities for independent decision making for the Defence Minister.

The preferences of the *Bundeswehr* will fully converge with those of the Defence Minister. While keeping the German armed forces integrated in NATO structures offers some career opportunities for the officer corps of the *Bundeswehr*, reducing the level of integration in NATO's military structures results in a vast amount of additional competences for the *Bundeswehr*, as national military structures would have to be built up.

The only actors favouring a reduced level of military integration in NATO and strengthened national military structures are the Defence Minister and the *Bundeswehr*. They will not assert themselves against a coalition comprising the Chancellor, the Foreign Minister, the Minister of Finance and the members of the *Bundestag*, since the Chancellor will be highly situatively mobilized. He will be the dominant actor in a network characterized by concentrated PAS leadership.

As there have been constant domestic interests in favour of the integration of the *Bundeswehr* in NATO's military structures, post-unification Germany will continue to integrate the *Bundeswehr* in NATO's military structures without strengthening its national military capacities.

Constructivism

From a constructivist perspective, the integration of the *Bundeswehr* in NATO's military structures has had a normative basis, both in Germany's international environment and in German society. These value-based expectations prescribing appropriate German security policy behaviour have not been altered by unification and the end of the East–West conflict.

International norms: NATO members are not only expected to offer mutual military assistance in case of an unprovoked attack by third countries, but also to cooperate within the institution's military structures during peacetime. In 1954, in a decision that became part of the Paris Treaties (reprinted in: *Europa Archiv* 1954: 713–16), the North Atlantic Council ruled that all forces of NATO member states stationed on the territory of the Supreme Allied Commander Europe (SACEUR) should be assigned to NATO. The FRG has been fully subject to the norm of assigning armed forces to NATO and of cooperating in the alliance's military structures. The norm has sufficient specificity: only the active participation in NATO's military structures counts as appropriate behaviour. It also has sufficient commonality, since it is based on a unanimous decision and addressed to all NATO members.

NATO has not only had the function of collective self-defence (i.e. security *for* Germany). For Germany's Western neighbours, NATO's function of providing security *from* Germany has been equally important (Haftendorn 1986: 36–7). From the outset, the *Bundeswehr* was not to be an ordinary national army but the West German contribution to the common defence of the Western allies. After the failure of the European Defence Community, the integration of the *Bundeswehr* in NATO was agreed upon in the Paris Treaties of 1954. Hence, while the norm to assign troops to NATO and to cooperate in its military structures has addressed all members, it has always had a special weight in the case of Germany. This has not been altered by German unification and the end of the East–West conflict. Since the Soviet Union/Russia did not tolerate NATO troops in East Germany until all Soviet/Russian forces had withdrawn from there (see Baumann and Kerski 1994), the Western powers accepted non-integrated German armed forces, at least for some years, in order to obtain Soviet consent for German unification. The norm for Germany to assign its troops to NATO has not been weakened: art. 5 para. 3 of the Two-plus-Four Treaty explicitly mentions that, after the complete Soviet withdrawal, the German forces in East Germany may be integrated in alliance structures.

While the basic norm to integrate the armed forces in NATO's military structures has remained constant, some changes have occurred on the NATO level as to what form this integration should take. In its Strategic Concept of 1991, NATO decided that multinational units should become more important in the alliance. Thus, for post-unification Germany, strengthening its participation in multinational units is the appropriate behaviour in order to fulfil the norm of integration in NATO's military structure. Also, NATO called for the creation of mobile and flexible reaction forces and of procedures that allow the deployment of NATO forces for crisis management purposes (see Varwick and Woyke 1999: 85–8). In the case of Germany, this requires that at least some national capacities for command and control are created (Young 1992b: 315–16).

Societal norms: The norm to conduct defence policy within NATO and to maintain the *Bundeswehr* as an alliance army has also become embedded in German society. While the Basic Law is not specific in this respect, an analysis of the programmes and platforms of the political parties reveals that the CDU, Christlich-Soziale Union (Christian Social Union; CSU), SPD and FDP, both before and after unification, have concurred that Germany should remain integrated in NATO and be a reliable alliance partner (sufficient commonality).[7] The Greens and, after unification, the PDS have called for radical demilitarization.[8] The norm has sufficient specificity, since the pertinent passages in the programmes and platforms clearly rule out the policy options leaning towards renationalization.

Keeping the *Bundeswehr* integrated in NATO's military structures and eschewing military renationalization was the appropriate behaviour for Germany in the 1980s and the 1990s, in line with both international and societal norms. The only change was that, after 1990, an international norm evolved for Germany to strengthen its national planning, command and control capacities to be able to contribute to crisis management efforts. Constructivism's prediction is unequivocal:

> As there have been international and societal norms that Germany should integrate its armed forces in NATO's military structures, post-unification Germany will continue to integrate the *Bundeswehr* in NATO's military structures. It will strengthen its national military capacities only in accordance with NATO norms.

German foreign policy behaviour

Before unification, the *Bundeswehr* was highly integrated in NATO's military structures: all West German combat troops were assigned to NATO and the *Bundeswehr* participated in several multinational units. In addition, Germany was completely lacking the capacities necessary for unilateral military operations. Post-unification Germany has continued the integration of its armed forces in NATO, both with regard to assignation and to participation in multinational units. Concerning capacities for military operations, it has departed from its pre-unification policy. Yet the reforms in this field were modest, and aimed at making the *Bundeswehr* fit for new tasks within NATO (see Sauder 1995: 264) rather than being a first step towards renationalization. Germany has established some planning and command structures, but it has not created a general staff or any similar body. Let us look at Germany's foreign policy behaviour in greater detail.

Assignation of armed forces
The 'old' FRG was the only NATO member state whose entire combat forces were assigned to NATO (Sauder 1995: 265). The German air force had, by and large, already been put under full NATO command in peacetime (BMVg 1985: 113). Post-unification Germany has maintained this complete NATO assignation. As mentioned above, due to the Two-plus-Four Treaty, the German forces in the new *Länder*, at first, were not allowed to be assigned to NATO. As soon as it was possible, on 1 January 1995, Germany assigned these forces to the alliance.[9] East German air force units and the swimming units of the naval forces were soon put under full NATO command, as their counterparts in the Western part of the country had always been (*NZZ*,

4 February 1995). Hence a major part of the German air and naval force has not only been assigned to NATO but has even been placed under NATO command during peacetime, just as before unification (Vad and Meyers 1996: 34–6).

Participation in multinational units
Germany's dedication to military integration has also been underlined by its participation in multinational units, both before and after unification. No other NATO country has been engaged in so many multinational units as Germany after unification (see *IHT*, 9 December 1997).

In the 1980s, when NATO had a few such units (see Hallerbach 1991: 22–3), the FRG contributed to several of them. It was represented in three intervention forces put under full NATO command (the Allied Command Europe Mobile Force (AMF), Standing Navel Force Atlantic (STANAVFORLANT) and the Standing Naval Force Channel) as well as in NATO's early warning unit , the Airborne Warning and Control System (AWACS) (Langen 1992: 667–8; BMVg 1985: 75). West Germany and Denmark cooperated in the binational corps LANDJUT established in 1970 (Whitford and Young 1997: 46).

Since unification, Germany has continued to integrate forces in multinational units (see Sauder 1995: 267–8). It has contributed a brigade to the AMF (Bundespresseamt 1995: 17–18) and a division to the new Allied Command Europe Rapid Reaction Corps (ARRC), which has been commanded by a British general. Germany was interested in obtaining this command post, but lost out to the UK (Vad and Meyers 1996: 33; Schlör 1993: 58–9). Also, Germany has taken part in the Multinational Division Central, which can be integrated in the ARRC (Bundespresseamt 1995: 18). Furthermore, it has collaborated in several bi- and multinational corps. Most of these have integrated staffs. The only corps with national staffs are the two US–German corps (operational since 1993), because of US reluctance to put troops under foreign command.[10] The German–Dutch Corps, created in 1994, has an integrated staff, whose competences were further strengthened in 1997 (*Die Welt*, 7 October 1997). The formation of the Eurocorps was initiated by France and Germany in 1991, building on the French–German brigade established in the late 1980s (see Klein 1990). It can be put under NATO (as well as WEU) command. Unlike the corps as such, the German forces within it are assigned to NATO. Operational since 1995, the corps has an integrated staff and consists of forces from Belgium, France, Germany, Spain, and Luxembourg (Bundespresseamt

1995: 20). The Multinational Corps North East, comprising Danish, German and Polish forces, has been operational since September 1999, after Polish forces were integrated in LANDJUT (see Vad and Meyers 1996: 34). The German air force has continued to participate in AWACS. The *Bundeswehr* has continued to participate in three standing naval units of NATO (Langen 1992: 667–8).

National capacities for planning, command and control

Before unification, the *Bundeswehr* did not have a general staff. The Inspector General of the *Bundeswehr* was not a commanding officer in the traditional sense, but the senior military adviser to the Minister of Defence. This structure was established to secure strict civilian control of the military. The 'old' FRG had no wartime-operational control over its armed forces (Young 1992b: 316) and thus no national capacities to conduct military operations.

In the 1990s, Germany largely kept this structure. Nevertheless, it changed the force posture of the *Bundeswehr* in accordance with NATO's changed strategy,[11] which puts greater emphasis on conflict management. Germany also created some command structures necessary for participation in military conflict management. Command structures were strengthened by creating a new body for the army, the *Heeresführungskommando* in Koblenz in 1994. For the first time in its history, the *Bundeswehr* now has something like a national command agency. It assumes command functions in case of German participation in multilateral military operations (*NZZ*, 23 March 1994: 5), but it lacks the central function of a general staff, i.e. full command. Similar agencies were created for the air force and for the navy, but there is still no command agency responsible for the *Bundeswehr* as a whole. The second major change was the establishment of the *Führungszentrum der Bundeswehr* within the Ministry of Defence in 1995. This is a permanent body[12] to assist the Minister in the course of multilateral military operations by processing information and assuming diverse planning tasks. Officials of the Defence Ministry stress that the *Führungszentrum* neither commands any troops (Rosenbauer 1997: 17) nor resembles a general staff (Weidemaier 1995: 42). There are no plans for a further upgrading of this agency (interview at the Ministry of Defence, Bonn, June 1998). Former Defence Minister Volker Rühe called the creation of a general staff unnecessary (*Der Stern*, 16 February 1995). Hence some national capacities for planning, command and control have been established, but only to enable the *Bundeswehr* to take part in multilateral military operations (see Young 1996).

Concerning the structure and equipment of the military forces, the situation is similar. Priority has been given to the equipment of the Crisis Reaction Forces (BMVg 1994: 103). Since 1997, the first platoon of the *Kommando Spezialkräfte* (the Commando Special Forces of the *Bundeswehr*) has been operational, an elite force for tasks such as evacuating soldiers or civilians from dangerous spots (*Süddeutsche Zeitung (SZ)*, 13 September 1997: 6). Still, the *Bundeswehr* lacks important assets necessary to conduct unilateral operations, especially with regard to intelligence and transport. In this area, some developments and acquisitions have been planned, modest in scope (see Gordon 1996: 263–4) and in cooperation with NATO partners, such as France or the UK.[13] Germany does not intend to achieve the ability to conduct unilateral operations (interview at the Ministry of Defence, Bonn, June 1998; see also BMVg 1999: 24, 167).

Summary
German foreign policy behaviour concerning integration of the *Bundeswehr* in NATO's military structures has been marked by a high degree of continuity, underlined by its willingness to assign armed forces to NATO and to participate in multinational units. By creating some national capacities for planning, command and control necessary for participation in multilateral military operations, Germany has departed from its pre-unification policy behaviour. Since Germany has not created structures that allow full national wartime command of armed forces, however, these changes have been modest in scope. The expectations of defense experts that post-unification Germany will strive for military renationalization (see p. 147) have turned out to be unfounded so far.

Test of predictions
As we will see, the empirical analysis of this case lends most support to the constructivist foreign policy theory. The prediction of neorealism is fully disconfirmed. Modified neorealism and utilitarian liberalism receive substantial support in the covariance analysis. Yet only constructivism can fully account for post-unification Germany's foreign policy behaviour. A look at further observable implications provides additional

support for constructivism as opposed to modified neorealism and utilitarian liberalism.

Covariance analysis

The prediction of *neorealism* receives little empirical support. Neorealism predicts that post-unification Germany will keep at least some of its troops free of NATO assignation whereas, in fact, Germany even re-assigned its forces in East Germany as soon as possible. It further predicts that Germany will eschew participation in multinational units, but it turned out that the country has participated in a great number of such units. Finally, neorealism expects that post-unification Germany will build up national capacities for planning, command and control in order to be able to conduct unilateral military operations. Germany's steps in this direction not only fell short of enabling full national wartime command of German armed forces. More importantly, they aimed at keeping the integration of the *Bundeswehr* in NATO's military structures and increasing its ability to take part in multilateral operations. Obviously, autonomy seeking has not been an important factor underlying post-unification Germany's policy in this case. Consequently, with its strong emphasis on autonomy seeking, neorealism does not provide a satisfactory prediction.

Modified neorealism fares much better. Post-unification Germany's readiness to maintain the assignation of its forces to NATO is in accordance with modified neorealism. The same holds for its participation in multinational units. However, in contrast to modified neorealist expectations, Germany has not created strong national capacities, such as a general staff that allows full national wartime command of forces. It has only acquired modest capacities for participation in multilateral operations. Stronger national capacities in this field would have enhanced German autonomy without leading to loss of influence. Thus Germany's restraint remains a puzzle for modified neorealism.

Like modified neorealism, *utilitarian liberalism* correctly predicts full assignation of forces and participation in multinational units. It is also in accordance with utilitarian liberalism that Germany has not created capacities for unilateral military operations. Yet post-unification Germany's readiness to prepare the *Bundeswehr* for participation in multilateral operations contradicts the liberal contention that the Chancellor (supported by the *Bundestag* and most political-administrative actors) will opt against the creation of capacities facilitating such participation.

Constructivism receives most empirical support in this case. It correctly predicts Germany's policy with regard to assignation and multinational units. Moreover, it can best account for Germany's modest steps towards creating national capacities for planning, command and control. The theory predicts that post-unification Germany will strengthen its capacities in this field in line with NATO expectations. Germany has done just that: by establishing the *Führungszentrum* and the command agencies for the army, the navy and the air force, as well as by providing the Crisis Reaction Forces with better equipment than the Main Defence Forces, Germany has responded to these expectations. This has not weakened but strengthened Germany's military integration in NATO.

Further observable implications
Scrutinizing further observable implications in this case raises doubts about the explanatory power of modified neorealism and utilitarian liberalism, and it lends further support to constructivism.

According to *modified neorealism*, Germany accepts the integration of its armed forces in NATO structures in return for influence on its NATO partners. This implies that Germany will actively pursue opportunities to enhance its influence. Command posts are an important intra-organizational resource in this respect. From a modified neorealist perspective, post-unification Germany can be expected to strive for more command posts, for instance in multinational units. This, however, has hardly been the case. To be sure, Germany was interested in obtaining the important command of the ARRC. Also, some German officials have occasionally claimed that, due to the country's important military contributions, especially in NATO's Central Region, additional command posts for German officers were warranted (see Kuebart 1991: 506). In general, however, post-unification Germany has taken a low-key approach towards claiming command posts. In the Eurocorps, the Dutch–German Corps and the new Multinational Corps North East, in which command posts alternate between the participating countries, Germany agreed that one of its partner countries first obtained the post of the corps commander (see *NZZ*, 23 April 1994: 3). In 1994, it turned down the offer to obtain a prestigious naval command post, the command of STANAVFORLANT (*Der Spiegel*, 17 January 1994). Unlike France, which has made its return to NATO's military structures contingent upon obtaining the supreme command of Allied Forces Southern Europe (see Yost 1998: 215–16), post-unification Germany has abstained from making such claims. Overall, it has hardly tried to link its military integration to intra-organizational resources.[14] Consequently, while modified neorealism correctly predicted Germany's foreign policy behaviour concerning both assignation and participation in multinational units, there are strong indications that this behaviour was not guided by the goal of influence seeking, as expected by modified neorealism.

Utilitarian liberalism is disconfirmed in a similar fashion. According to this theory, the process of policy formulation on matters of military integration after unification will be characterized by a conflict of interests between actors favouring continued integration (the Chancellor, the *Bundestag* and the Ministers of Foreign Affairs and of Finance) and actors favouring military renationalization (the Minister of Defence and the *Bundeswehr*). In fact, neither of the two latter actors has shown any reservations about Germany's continued military integration in NATO structures.[15] In publications by the Ministry of Defence, it is stressed instead that the *Bundeswehr* must remain integrated in the North Atlantic alliance (BMVg 1999: 19; BMVg 1994: 50).

From the viewpoint of *constructivism*, Germany pursues a policy of continued military integration because, in light of both international and societal norms, it views it as appropriate. If this perspective is correct, Germany should have a genuine preference for military integration rather than seeing it as a means of enhancing its control of intra-organizational resources or for the reduction of costs. Public statements of German government officials suggest that this is in fact the case. In these statements, the notion that Germany's armed forces should remain integrated in NATO often appears to be an unquestioned assumption.[16] Also, when asked in confidential interviews about the rationale behind Germany's continued readiness to keep the *Bundeswehr* in NATO's military structures, government officials viewed the fact that it helps to maintain the integration within the alliance as a sufficient reason for pursuing this policy,[17] or they admitted that they could not even think of a serious alternative.[18] These statements illustrate that integration in the North Atlantic alliance has become an integral part of German security policy. This stands in contrast to modified neorealism's and utilitarian liberalism's expectation of instrumental cooperation within NATO, but it is in accordance with the constructivist argument that both international and societal norms have shaped Germany's identity so that maintaining the military integration of its armed forces in NATO has become a genuine German preference.

Case 2: participation in out-of-area operations

Case description and dependent variable

NATO was created as a system of collective defence. The core of the Washington Treaty of 1949 is Article 5, stipulating that an attack on any member of the alliance is to be treated as an attack on all. While the question of non-Article–5, i.e. 'out of area' operations of NATO countries has repeatedly been the source of differences among NATO states since the founding of the alliance (see Stuart and Tow 1990; Bentinck 1986), prior to the 1990s it was of secondary importance. Since the end of the East–West conflict, however, this question has become a central topic among NATO states. In 1994, NATO declared its readiness to conduct such out-of-area operations based on a mandate by the UN or the OSCE (Bulletin des Presse- und Informationsamtes der Bundesregierung 3/1994: 20–1).

Germany's participation in non-Article–5, i.e. non-defence operations, is the dependent variable. It must be noted that, during the East–West conflict, there were no NATO-led operations in the strict technical sense. Non-defence operations in which NATO countries cooperated without carrying them out within the framework of NATO's command structure may be used for comparison, however. The following non-defence operations will serve as points of observation. Before unification: the military actions taken against Iran in the Persian Gulf (1987) and the fundamental decision of the Federal Security Council on the question of German participation in the out-of-area operations of 1982. After unification: the monitoring and enforcement of UN-mandated sanctions against (former) Yugoslavia (1992–96); the Implementation Force (IFOR) (1995–96); the Stabilization Force (SFOR) (since 1996); the strikes against Iraq (1998); the air strikes against the Federal Republic of Yugoslavia (FRY) in the Kosovo conflict (1998–99); and the Kosovo Force (KFOR) (since 1999). An analysis of Germany's foreign policy behaviour in the Gulf War of 1990/91, which took place in a transition period during and immediately after German unification, will also be included here. Yet this point of observation will not be used for the test of predictions, since it does not clearly fall in the time period after unification and neither neorealist nor constructivist predictions could be formulated for this instance.

In every instance, Germany's contribution to the out-of-area operation will be coded by means of a simple scale: Germany fully participates with combat troops; it participates with non-combat troops only; it restricts its role to financial or logistical support; or it fully abstains from participating.

Independent variables and predictions

As we shall see, all predictions in this case are conditional, since all theories expect post-unification Germany to participate in an out-of-area operation if certain conditions are met.

Neorealism

From a neorealist perspective, two aspects are central with regard to a state's readiness to participate in non-defence operations: the readiness to use military force and the readiness to cooperate with other states in such an endeavour. Both variants of neorealist foreign policy theory expect post-unification Germany to be more willing than the 'old' FRG to use military force. Using force against another country is the strongest form of influence-seeking policy. Due to its enhanced power position, *ceteris paribus*, Germany will resort to the use of force more often than before unification. Neorealism and modified neorealism do not expect powerful states to use force whenever possible, however. Rather, states conduct autonomy- and influence-seeking policies in order to safeguard their security. If a conflict has no or only remote repercussions for Germany's security, both variants of neorealist foreign policy theory expect Germany not to intervene in that conflict – neither unilaterally nor in concert with other NATO states. Neorealism and modified neorealism both expect post-unification Germany to show an increased willingness to use military force only if its security is affected. Germany's security is affected directly when it faces an attack on its territory or when it is at least threatened by such an attack. When violent conflicts threaten to escalate into bigger wars, especially in regions close to Germany, this also has a negative impact on German security. Then we may speak of indirect repercussions for German security. The impact of a conflict on German security will be operationalized by looking at its geographical proximity. Conflicts in Europe have more of an impact on German security than conflicts further away.

With regard to the willingness to cooperate with alliance partners, the two variants of neorealist foreign policy theory diverge. If Germany participates in non-defence operations with other NATO states, it can co-decide on the planning and conduct of the operation, which translates into substantial influence on the other NATO states. At the same time, Germany will be bound by the joint decisions, and it may have to subordinate some of its armed forces to the command of non-German officers. This would imply autonomy losses for Germany.

From the perspective of *neorealism*, post-unification Germany will be reluctant to concede more than the necessary minimum of command power over its own armed forces to agents of other states unless its survival is directly endangered. This will hardly be the case in non-Article–5 operations. Germany will not participate in an operation where German troops are put under the direct command of a non-German officer. It will prefer ad-hoc coalitions with other NATO states to relying on the highly institutionalized NATO structures.

> As its power position has improved, post-unification Germany will participate with combat troops in out-of-area operations in ad-hoc coalitions together with other NATO states, if its security is affected and if its armed forces deployed in the operation remain under German command.

From the perspective of *modified neorealism*, too, Germany will only participate in non-defence operations if its security is affected.[19] Due to its substantially reduced security pressures, however, it will accept the autonomy loss stemming from participating in a NATO-led operation in order to obtain the substantial amount of influence that such participation entails. If Germany decides to participate in an operation, it will prefer full participation with combat troops since only that will enable it to exert the desired influence on the conduct of the operation.

> As its power position has improved and its exposure to security pressures has decreased, post-unification Germany will participate with combat troops in out-of-area operations together with other NATO states, if its security is affected.

Utilitarian liberalism

As in case 1, both before and since unification, the policy network comprises the Chancellor and the *Bundestag* as political actors, the Ministers of Foreign Affairs, of Defence and of Finance as political-administrative actors, and the *Bundeswehr* as an administrative actor.

Both the Chancellor and the members of the *Bundestag*, whose authorization is necessary for out-of-area deployments of German soldiers,[20] will be reluctant to allow German troops to participate in out-of-area operations of its NATO partners. Nor would the electorate receive substantial material benefits from such German participation. Instead, political actors who support the participation of the *Bundeswehr* in a NATO-led operation would endanger their prospects of re-election. First, large operations of that kind entail substantial financial costs. Second, any out-of-area operation, and especially when combat troops are involved, risks even graver costs, i.e. the loss of soldiers' lives. Political actors have a strong preference for avoiding being held responsible for such costs and for the deaths of German soldiers. When both the financial costs and the risk of German casualties are low, however, the interests of the Chancellor and of the members of the *Bundestag* in re-election will not be affected, and they will thus not be situatively mobilized. Also, they recognize that NATO allies could be angered by what they perceive to be German free-rider behaviour of having them conduct out-of-area operations that are in the common interest; in the long run, it could endanger the desired protection that Germany receives through NATO. Therefore, the Chancellor and the members of the *Bundestag* will not object to some logistical or financial support to Germany's NATO partners in case of any multilateral out-of-area operation.

Political-administrative actors share this political interest, but they all have overriding administrative interests. The Foreign Minister seeks to maintain good relations with Germany's main partners, above all the US and France. Also, he does not want to be sidelined in international crisis management. The opportunities for the Foreign Minister to play a role in such instances are much higher if Germany contributes troops to an international military force deployed in connection with this crisis. Therefore, the Foreign Minister will support German participation in out-of-area operations of its NATO partners. The Minister of Defence and the *Bundeswehr* will adopt the same position, if for somewhat different reasons. For a long time, the central task of the German armed forces was to contribute to deterring the perceived massive Soviet threat. With the end of the East–West conflict, German unification and the breakup of the Soviet Union, the need for such deterrence has greatly diminished. In order to keep as much of their funds and their competences as possible, the Defence Minister and the *Bundeswehr* are in need of new, additional tasks. The participation of *Bundeswehr* forces in NATO-led out-of-area interventions would thus perfectly fit the organizational interests of these two actors. It follows that, after unification, the Defence Minister and the *Bundeswehr* will support German participation in out-of-area operations of NATO countries more strongly than during the time before unification. Since this question directly affects the fundamental interests of these two actors, their situative mobilization will be high. The Minister of Finance, finally, will oppose any German commitments that place additional burdens on the federal budget. With respect to smaller out-of-area operations or smaller German contributions to an out-of-area operation, the situative mobilization of the Minister of Finance will be low, however.

We conclude that the Ministers of Foreign Affairs and of Defence as well as the *Bundeswehr* will favour contributing German troops to the out-of-area operations of NATO partners. Since the consent of both the Chancellor and (a majority of) the *Bundestag* will be needed, they will only assert themselves when the political actors have no strong preferences, i.e. when the financial costs are moderate and the risk of German casualties is small. Utilitarian liberalism expects that post-unification Germany will continue to refrain from participating in non-defence operations of NATO states, except for low-level contributions to non-combat operations. Risks will be low, when no German ground troops are sent into a hostile environment or when naval or air forces are engaged in smaller operations against a weak opponent at best. Costs can be regarded as low, when the operation can be paid from the regular defense budget without additional appropriation of funds.

> As there have been constant domestic interests against the participation of German armed forces in out-of-area operations, post-unification Germany will continue to refrain from participating with troops in out-of-area operations with other NATO states, unless they entail low casualty risks and financial costs.

Constructivism

Constructivism expects German participation in out-of-area operations consistent with international or societal norms. After unification and the end of the East–West conflict, norms at both levels have evolved that call for German participation in such operations together with NATO partners, if they have a firm international legal basis. These expectations are value based, as the out-of-area operations are to serve humanitarian concerns or the maintenance or restitution of peace.

International norms: During the East–West conflict, despite repeated

US calls for more military support from NATO partners in conflicts around the globe, there was no commonly shared expectation within NATO that states contribute troops to non-Article–5 operations (see Stuart and Tow 1990). After the end of the East–West conflict, operations for collective peace enforcement, in accordance with chapter VII of the UN Charter, as well as operations for peacekeeping, have gained in importance. While at first there was a considerable increase in UN peacekeeping operations, the growing difficulties the UN was facing with violent intra-state conflicts soon led to the acknowledgement of the importance of regional organizations in this respect (see Boutros-Ghali 1995). NATO began to embrace the idea of conducting such operations. In its Strategic Concept of 1991, it pointed to new risks to security and decided to create crisis reaction forces (Bulletin des Presse-und Informationsamtes der Bundesregierung 2/92). In May 1992, at the Ministerial Meeting of the Defence Planning Committee and the Nuclear Planning Group, NATO declared its readiness to contribute to peace-keeping operations under the auspices of the Conference on Security and Cooperation in Europe (CSCE) (Bulletin des Presse- und Informa-tionsamtes der Bundesregierung 57/92). At its Brussels summit in 1994, it stated its willingness to conduct out-of-area operations on the basis of a mandate by the UN or the CSCE (Bulletin des Presse- und Informationsamtes der Bundesregierung 3/1994: 20–1). The new Strategic Concept of 1999 lists crisis management as one of the tasks of the alliance. NATO is ready to undertake 'peacekeeping and other operations under the authority of the UN Security Council or the responsibility of the OSCE' (NATO Press Release NAC-S(99)65, para. 31). It is said that 'the combined military forces of the alliance must be prepared to contribute to conflict prevention and to conduct non-Article 5 crisis response operations' (NATO Press Release NAC-S(99)65, para. 41). In this document, NATO also points to its 'common values of democracy, human rights, and the rule of law' (NATO Press Release NAC-S(99)65, para. 6) as the basis of its purposes and tasks. As all NATO decisions indicating the existence of a norm for NATO members to take part in NATO-led military operations have been reached with German participation and consent, there may be a risk of making a circular argument. Germany was not a *demandeur* in this area, however. It has been exposed to the expectations articulated by other NATO partners to become ready for participation in non-Article–5 operations.[21] Thus it is methodologically defensible to view these NATO decisions not as a consequence of German policy within NATO (dependent variable) but as an indicator of a NATO-wide international norm that can shape the behaviour of the German decision makers (independent variable).

Hence the international norm addressed at Germany has changed significantly. Unlike before unification, Germany is now expected to make substantial contributions to those non-defence operations of its NATO partners that are in accordance with international law. This norm has attained sufficient commonality. The norm is also of sufficient specificity, although it cannot be said whether a substantial contribution with non-combat troops suffices or whether only participation with combat troops counts as norm-consistent policy.

Societal norms have changed, too. While the constitutional provisions have not been altered, the debate about the constitutionality of German participation in multilateral out-of-area operations in the first half of the 1990s resulted in significant changes of the commonly shared interpretation of these provisions. Before unification, the opinion that the Basic Law, particularly art. 87a para. 2, prohibits any use of force by the *Bundeswehr* for purposes other than individual or collective self-defence was common among legal scholars and predominant among politicians. In the 1980s, no party represented in the *Bundestag* opted for legitimizing the participation of the *Bundeswehr* in multilateral out-of-area operations. The SPD, FDP and Green Party were strictly opposed to it (see SPD 1989: 183; Die Grünen 1987; FDP 1980: 8). Therefore, before unification a widely shared expectation existed in German society that *Bundeswehr* troops should abstain from participating in armed conflicts for purposes other than self-defence. This position, which was later labelled the 'culture of restraint', emanated from the conclusions that Germans had reached in light of the disastrous consequences of German aggression and militarism earlier in the century (see Berger 1998: 55–86; 1996: 329–31).

After the end of the East–West conflict, fuelled by the Gulf War of 1990/91 and the growing importance of UN peacekeeping operations, this normative consensus broke up and a political debate on the issue began (see Bach 1999: 119–75; Duffield 1998: 173–221; Markovits and Reich 1997: 137–49). In this debate, the constitutional question of whether Germany was permitted to participate in out-of-area operations was mixed up with the political question of whether it should do so. In its decision of 12 July 1994 (BVerfGE 90: 286), the Federal Constitutional Court settled the first question: the *Bundeswehr* may participate in out-of-area operations conducted within the framework of a system of collective security if the *Bundestag* gives its authorization. It is important to note that the Court explicitly supported the contention that NATO is a system of collective security (BVerfGE 90: 351). It puts art. 24 para. 2 GG on at least an equal footing with art. 87a para. 2 GG. Still, constitutional limits to deployments of German troops in out-of-area operations remain: German participation within a collective security system must serve the maintenance of peace (art. 24 para. 2 GG); the fundamental rules of international law are part of German federal law (art. 25 GG); and preparation of a war of aggression is unconstitutional (art. 26 para. 1 GG). These provisions prescribe a general value-based orientation of German security policy (see Dalvi 1998). Of course, the legality of German participation in NATO-led out-of-area operations does not imply that the Basic Law calls for such participation. To find out whether a new societal norm has evolved that calls for German participation in NATO-led operations under certain circumstances, we have to examine the programmatic positions of the political parties.

The parties have taken up the distinction between peacekeeping and peace enforcement. In the period since 1990, a broad consensus has emerged that the *Bundeswehr* should participate in multilateral out-of-area operations with a strong peacekeeping character. The CDU and CSU soon demanded that Germany, as a member of the transatlantic community, participates in both forms of multilateral out-of-area operations (CDU 1998: chap 25; CDU 1994: 92, 52; CSU 1993: 132; CSU 1992: 8). The FDP at first only called for participation in peacekeeping operations. It did not support combat operations before 1994 (FDP 1994: 131; FDP 1990: 29). In SPD programmes the idea of *Bundeswehr* participation in peace-keeping and humanitarian operations is also embraced (SPD 1994), but support for German participation in NATO-led operations that entail the use of force cannot be found before 1998. Even then, the party resorted to the imprecise term 'peace missions' (SPD 1998: 45). The programmes of the Green Party indicate opposition to German participation in operations in which force is to be used (Bündnis 90/Die Grünen 1998; 1994a: 55–6). Notably, by 1998, the party had opened up for German participation in peacekeeping operations (Bündnis 90/Die Grünen 1998: 7). The PDS, finally, has consistently opposed any *Bundeswehr* deployment outside German territory (PDS 1998: ch. 4; 1994; 1993: 23). All parties supporting German participation in out-of-area operations have emphasized the need for a

firm international legal basis, such as a mandate from the UN Security
Council (see SPD 1998: 46; CDU 1994: 92; FDP 1994: 131).

We can derive several conclusions. First, a broad consensus did not
emerge before 1994. Since then, the norm that Germany should contribute troops to multilateral peacekeeping operations has gained
sufficient commonality. Second, there is no societal norm calling for
German participation in multilateral combat operations. One of the two
large parties, the SPD, has been openly against, or at least not explicitly
in favour of, such participation. Its support for the participation in an
operation such as SFOR, which is technically a combat operation but
could also be seen as 'robust peacekeeping', demonstrates that the crucial
point is not whether an operation falls under chapter VII of the UN
charter. Rather, the operation needs to have a strong peacekeeping
character for German participation to be consistent with societal norms.
Finally, the party programmes indicate that Germany should only
contribute troops to an operation with a firm international legal basis,
for instance a mandate from the UN Security Council. Overall, a societal
norm has evolved to participate with *Bundeswehr* units in non-Article–5
operations that are authorized by the Security Council or the OSCE
and have a strong peacekeeping character.

Due to changed international and societal norms, post-unification
Germany is expected to participate in the non-Article–5 operations of
NATO. Two qualifications must be kept in mind, however. First, on
both the societal and the international level, a strong reference is made
to international law. Germany is expected to participate in NATO-led
operations that have a firm legal basis. Second, the norms do not call
for German contributions with combat troops. The societal consensus
only goes so far as supporting the contribution of troops that have
largely peacekeeping tasks. The international norm is not specific
enough. It cannot be said that limiting its contributions to non-combat
troops would be inappropriate for Germany as a member of the North
Atlantic community.

> As pertinent norms have evolved on both the international and the
> societal level, post-unification Germany will participate with *Bundes-*
> *wehr* troops in out-of-area operations together with other NATO states,
> if the operation has a firm international legal basis and a strong
> peacekeeping character.

German foreign policy behaviour

Before unification
Before unification, West Germany restricted its participation in out-of-area operations with other NATO states to logistical assistance. It was not ready to contribute troops.

This position had already been taken in November 1982, when the Federal Security Council stressed that the Basic Law, in particular art. 87a para. 2 GG, forbids any deployment of the *Bundeswehr* 'out of area'.[22] West Germany expressed its willingness to provide logistical support to its alliance partners in such cases, if necessary. This had been spelled out in the Wartime-Host-Nation-Support Agreement between the West German and US governments in April 1982 (see Deiseroth 1985), which provided that, in the case of a deployment of US forces outside the territory of NATO, West Germany offered the US the use of military bases in Germany and to close military gaps caused by the transfer of US forces to the crisis area.

The West German position was put to the test in the Persian Gulf in 1987. The US, following a Kuwaiti request, sought to protect oil tankers from attacks by Iranian forces. Among other things, US naval and air forces escorted Kuwaiti ships. This led to several skirmishes in the Gulf region. In July 1987, the US called upon its NATO partners, the FRG among them, to provide military assistance. The German government was asked to send several ships for the purposes of military protection of tankers as well as mine sweeping in the Persian Gulf (Gross Stein 1988/89: 158). It rejected this demand, arguing that art. 87a para. 2 GG did not allow such a step. It merely sent three ships to the Mediterranean from October to mid-December 1987 to temporarily replace ships of its NATO partners that had been dispatched to the crisis region. No German ships were sent to the Gulf (Schubert, Bahr and Krell 1988: 220).

After unification
After unification, Germany's foreign policy behaviour gradually changed towards a greater willingness to participate fully in out-of-area operations.

Persian Gulf (1990–91)
The question of cooperation among the NATO allies also played an important role in the Gulf War. The crisis following Iraq's invasion of

Kuwait took place as the Two-plus-Four talks on German unification reached the final stages. In August 1990, a few weeks after the invasion, the German federal government decided that, for constitutional reasons, Germany would not contribute armed forces to a military operation in the Gulf region (Kaiser and Becher 1992: 15). As opposed to most of its NATO partners, Germany did not send troops to the Gulf up to the end of the war (see Stichworte zur Sicherheitspolitik 1/91: 33). German forces temporarily took over some functions of units of NATO allies that were sent to the Gulf, and Germany provided logistical support to US, British and Dutch forces (Kaiser and Becher 1992: 40–1, 46–7). In addition, it paid about 18 billion DM to allies participating in the war (most of it to the US) as well as to states in the region which were financially affected by the crisis (Kaiser and Becher 1992: 47–8). After the Gulf War was over, Germany agreed to send some mine-sweeping personnel to the region (Kaiser and Becher 1992: 41–5).

Former Yugoslavia (1992–96)
In connection with the war in Bosnia-Hercegovina (see Gow 1997; Calic 1996), NATO countries took military measures to monitor or enforce resolutions by the UN Security Council. In 1991, the Security Council imposed an arms embargo on Yugoslavia (S/RES 713 of 25 September 1991). In the following year, these measures were extended to general and mandatory economic sanctions against Serbia and Montenegro (S/RES/757 of 30 May 1992). Both NATO and the WEU sent naval forces to the Adriatic in July 1992, in order to monitor the embargo, which in June 1993 were officially combined into 'Operation Sharp Guard'. It lasted until the termination of the sanctions by the Security Council on 1 October 1996 (S/RES 1074).[23] Although the operation was nominally a joint NATO–WEU endeavour, it relied heavily on NATO assets (see Siedschlag 1995: 44; interview at the WEU, Brussels, February 1999). It fell short of a military intervention as requested by the government of Bosnia-Hercegovina. From July 1992 on, Germany participated in this operation with a destroyer and three reconnaissance planes (*IHT*, 16 July 1992: 1). Transport planes of the *Bundeswehr* also took part in the international airlift to Sarajevo. From February 1994 on, German air force personnel participated in NATO's AWACS operations to monitor the no-fly zone over Bosnia-Hercegovina established by the Security Council (S/RES 781 of 9 October 1992). At the same time that NATO was threatening Serb forces around Sarajevo with air strikes, the German government was stressing that AWACS would in

no way be involved in such strikes (*Frankfurter Allgemeine Zeitung* (*FAZ*), 12 February 1994). On 22 July 1994, the *Bundestag* gave its consent to German participation in the AWACS operation and the measures to monitor the embargo (*NZZ*, 24/25 July 1994: 3).[24] Again, no *Bundeswehr* soldiers took part in combat operations. NATO's air strikes in support of the United Nations Protection Force in 1994 and 1995 were based on S/RES 836 of 4 June 1993 and S/RES 844 of 18 June 1993. Unlike other member states, Germany did not contribute fighter planes.

Bosnia-Hercegovina (IFOR, 1995–96)

After the signing of the Dayton Accord to end the war in Bosnia-Hercegovina, the NATO-led IFOR, to be stationed in Bosnia, was given the task of monitoring compliance with the Accord and of providing a secure environment for civil reconstruction. The deployment was authorized by the UN Security Council (S/RES 1031) on 15 December 1995. In addition to NATO countries, Russia, Arab states and others participated in IFOR which comprised a total of about 60,000 soldiers. The operation took place under the supreme command of SACEUR. The field commander was a US officer. IFOR was divided into three sectors commanded by US, British and French officers. Germany agreed to participate in IFOR with up to 4,000 soldiers.[25] They were non-combat troops that provided, *inter alia*, transport and medical assistance to the troops of other participating countries (*SZ*, 7 December 1995, reprinted in: Stichworte zur Sicherheitspolitik 1/96: 12–14). Their headquarters was not in Bosnia itself but in Croatia.

Bosnia-Hercegovina (SFOR, since 1996)

After the mandate for IFOR had run out in late 1996, a smaller force, based on S/RES 1088, with basically the same tasks took its place. SFOR's mandate at first lasted eighteen months until 19 June 1998, but was then extended without time limit (S/RES 1174 of 15 July 1998). SFOR comprises some 35,000 soldiers. Germany has kept the size of its contingent at about 3,000. More importantly, the German troops have been regular combat troops stationed in Bosnia-Hercegovina. The major part of this German contingent is part of a French–German unit commanded by a German officer. Together with Spanish, Italian and other French forces it belongs to the Multinational Force South East, commanded by a French general (with a German as chief of staff). Due to its quantitatively and qualitatively upgraded contribution in comparison to IFOR, Germany demanded a high-ranking post in SFOR's overall command stucture. The allies accepted this request: Germany was given the post of the chief of staff of SFOR (*NZZ*, 12 December 1996: 3).[26]

Iraq (1998)

Since the Gulf War of 1990/91, there have been tensions between Iraq and Western states, especially the US and UK. The government of Saddam Hussein has repeatedly been accused of not fulfilling its obligations under S/RES 687 of 3 April 1991. In early 1998, the situation was about to escalate. A US-led coalition threatened Iraq with air strikes and cruise missile attacks ('Operation Desert Thunder') unless Iraq began to cooperate fully with the inspectors of the Special Commission. This operation was averted by the successful negotiations of UN Secretary-General Kofi Annan. Seven NATO countries offered military forces for this planned operation (*SZ*, 21/22 February 1998: 6). Germany was not among them, but the German government offered support to the US forces by granting the use of US military bases in Germany for the conduct of the operation (*NZZ*, 9 February 1998). In November and December 1998, the situation escalated again, leading to a series of attacks on Iraqi targets, carried out mostly by US and British forces. The legality of the raids is controversial. Whereas the US claims that, based on S/RES 687 and S/RES 688, the international community may use force against Iraq in case of Iraqi non-compliance with the terms of the cease-fire of 1991, this is not explicated in the pursuant resolutions, and some states do not share the US interpretation (see Johnstone 1994: 37–41). Germany did not participate in this operation.

Former Republic of Yugoslavia (1998–99)[27]

When the deliberations among NATO states about how to end the hostilities in Kosovo began in early 1998, Germany was among the states that did not rule out a NATO-led intervention. The UN Security Council called upon the Serb authorities to end the atrocities against ethnic Albanians and to remove most of their forces from Kosovo. The pertinent resolutions did not authorize the threat or use of military force against the FRY in case of its non-compliance, since this Western request met with serious Russian and Chinese reservations (S/RES 1160 of 31 March 1998; S/RES 1199 of 23 September 1998). As the crisis escalated again in the autumn of 1998, NATO nevertheless threatened the FRY with air strikes. Germany was ready to contribute fighter planes to these strikes. In October, it seemed that the use of force could be averted, as Yugoslav President Milosevic agreed to comply with S/RES 1199 and to admit the deployment of the OSCE-led Kosovo Verification Mission (KVM), a monitoring force of 2,000 unarmed observers. Unarmed planes of NATO states also participated in the monitoring, while an armed, NATO-led 'Extraction Force' was stationed in neighbouring Macedonia in order to rescue the KVM, if necessary. The UN Security Council approved of the agreement (S/RES 1203 of 24 October 1998). On 19 November 1998, the *Bundestag* gave its consent to German participation in the Extraction Force with 250 men with a very broad majority (*SZ*, 20 November 1998: 6). As it became apparent that the FRY still did not fully comply with the Security Council resolutions, NATO states, at the initiative of the US, again threatened to conduct air strikes against the FRY in early 1999. After the trilateral Rambouillet negotiations (see Weller 1999) between the Contact Group [28] and representatives of the FRY and of the Kosovars in February and March 1999 had failed, NATO carried out its threat. On 24 March 1999, it began to inflict air strikes on Serbia and Montenegro. The air strikes were not authorized by a UN Security Council resolution. The *Bundestag* had given its approval to full German participation in this operation beforehand.

Kosovo (KFOR, since 1999)

After eleven weeks of air strikes, the Western countries got the Yugoslav government as well as representatives of the Kosovars to sign an agreement that, among other things, foresees the stationing of a NATO-led Kosovo Force. The deployment of KFOR was authorized by the UN Security Council on 10 June 1999 (S/RES/1244). Similar to the case of IFOR and SFOR, five sectors have been established. Deviating from the NATO-led forces in Bosnia-Hercegovina, however, Germany took over the command in one of these sectors, and in September 1999 it assumed the field command of KFOR. With up to 8,500 soldiers (Stichworte zur Sicherheitspolitik 6/99: 56), the German contribution is among the biggest of all countries.

Summary

German foreign policy behaviour has changed profoundly, as table 6.1 illustrates.

Table 6.1 German participation in out-of-area operations with other
NATO countries

Before unification	After unification						
Persian Gulf 1987	Persian Gulf 1990/91	FRY 1992–95 (IFOR) 1995–96	Bosnia (IFOR) 1995–96	Bosnia (SFOR) since 1996	Iraq 1998	Kosovo 1998–99	Kosovo (KFOR) since 1999
Support only	Support only	Non-combat troops	Non-combat troops	Combat troops	No partici-pation	Combat troops	Combat troops

Step by step, post-unification Germany has given up its reservations
about participating in out-of-area operations. Up to the Gulf War, it
did not provide more than logistical and financial support to its allies.
In the military operations against the former Yugoslavia in the early
1990s, Germany participated with non-combat air force personnel, with
the proviso that they would not take part in combat missions. IFOR
marked the first time that Germany sent ground troops, but restrictions
on the German contribution (no combat troops; stationed in Croatia)
were not given up until SFOR. The recent Kosovo war has been another
step. For the first time, the FRG has contributed combat troops deliberately to use force against another state.

Test of predictions

Covariance analysis
In order to determine the predictive power of the foreign policy theories,
we have to check for every point of observation in the period after
unification whether the conditions for participation spelled out by the
theories were present. There are four conditions altogether: that German
security is affected by the crisis (neorealism, modified neorealism); that
Germany can keep command of its armed forces (neorealism); that the
out-of-area operation rests on a firm international legal basis (constructivism); and that the risks and costs of participation are low (utilitarian
liberalism).

German security was affected in all out-of-area operations carried
out in the Balkans. While it was not directly threatened by these wars,
they had the potential of leading to a bigger war in Europe by spilling
over to neighbouring countries. In contrast, the crisis emerging from

the conflict between Western states and Iraq in 1998 hardly affected German security.

Also, in all operations in the Balkans, Germany had to, or would have had to, give up command power over its armed forces to a high degree, since these operations were carried out within the military structures of NATO. The strikes against Iraq in 1998 were carried out by an ad-hoc coalition of NATO partners. It is not clear to what extent Germany would have had to have handed over the direct command of *Bundeswehr* forces.

Risks and costs were low in only two instances: the monitoring and reconnaissance operations against the FRY in the early 1990s and the brief attacks on Iraq in 1998, whose military potential had already been curbed in the Gulf War. In all other out-of-area operations, the risks and costs of participation were substantial. In the cases of IFOR and SFOR, ground troops were sent to an area where a war had taken place that had cost some 200,000 lives. KFOR has been deployed to a province marked by grave ethnic conflict between Albanians and Serbs. The air strikes against Serbia and Montenegro, finally, were a massive, open-ended air campaign. The danger that it would take longer than a few days (as it did), that it would escalate into a bigger war and that NATO would suffer a significant number of casualties (both of which turned out not to happen) could not be ruled out.

Most of the out-of-area operations studied here had a firm international legal basis, because they were authorized by the UN Security Council acting under chapter VII of the UN Charter. The two exceptions are the strikes in the Persian Gulf and the air strikes against Serbia and Montenegro in the Kosovo conflict. Concerning the Persian Gulf operation, the argument that the use of force was legitimized by two UN Security Council resolutions is contested. In the absence of an authorization by the Security Council, the legal basis of the air strikes on the FRY in the Kosovo War was questionable (see Cassese 1999; Ipsen 1999; Simma 1999).

This translates into different theoretical expectations for each point of observation (table 6.2).

Table 6.2 Theoretical expectations for German participation
in out-of-area operations

Point of observation	Neorealism (German security/command power)	Modified neorealism (German security)	Utilitarian liberalism (risks and costs)	Constructivism (firm international legal basis)
FRY, 1992–95	(Yes/no) No participation	(Yes) Combat troops	(Low) Non-combat troops	(Yes) Non-combat troops
Bosnia (IFOR), 1995–96	(Yes/no) No participation	(Yes) Combat troops	(High) Support only	(Yes) Non-combat troops
Bosnia (SFOR), since 1996	(Yes/no) No participation	(Yes) Combat troops	(High) Support only	(Yes) Non-combat troops
Iraq, 1998	(No/unclear) No participation	(No) No participation	(Low) Non-combat troops	(No) No participation
Kosovo, 1998–99	(Yes/no) No participation	(Yes) Combat troops	(High) Support only	(No) No participation
Kosovo (KFOR), since 1999	(Yes/no) No participation	(Yes) Combat troops	(High) Support only	(Yes) Non-combat troops

On this basis, we can now determine which of the theories provides the best predictions. The result of the covariance analysis is presented in table 6.3.

Modified neorealism and constructivism get much more empirical support in this case than neorealism and utilitarian liberalism. *Modified neorealism* fares especially well concerning Germany's full participation in the NATO-led non-defence operations in the Balkans since 1996. Germany's restraint up to IFOR provides a puzzle for modified neorealism, however. In these instances, Germany was restrained by something modified neorealism cannot account for.

For *constructivism*, the fact that post-unification Germany has gradually increased the scope of its participation in out-of-area operations does not come as a surprise, because it is at least roughly in line with the gradual change of the pertinent international and societal norms. From a constructivist perspective, the German decision makers tried to satisfy the growing expectations of Germany's international environment, but they were also bound by domestic norms that would change only slowly. Nevertheless, the theory has a hard time explaining Germany's participation in the air strikes against Serbia and Montenegro.

Table 6.3 Case-specific predictive power of the foreign policy theories

Point of observation	German participation	Neorealism	Modified neorealism	Utilitarian liberalism	Constructivism
			Predictive power of the theories (theoretical expectation)		
FRY, 1992–95	Non-combat troops	None (No participation)	Some (Combat troops)	High (Non-combat troops)	High (Non-combat troops)
Bosnia, 1995–96 (IFOR)	Non-combat troops	None (No participation)	Some (Combat troops)	None (Support only)	High (Non-combat troops)
Bosnia, since 1996 (SFOR)	Combat troops	None (No participation)	High (Combat troops)	None (Support only)	Some (Non-combat troops)
Iraq, 1998	No participation	High (No participation)	High (No participation)	None (Non-combat troops)	High (No participation)
FRY, 1998–99	Combat troops	None (No participation)	High (Combat troops)	None (Support only)	None (No participation)
Kosovo, since 1999 (KFOR)	Combat troops	None (No participation)	High (Combat troops)	None (Support only)	Some (Non-combat troops)
(Overall: high/some/none)		1/0/5	4/2/0	1/0/5	3/2/1

Note: The predictive power is coded as high if the theory predicts the foreign policy behaviour. If it at least correctly predicts whether Germany participates with troops (combat or non-combat) or whether it does not participate with troops (support only or no participation), it will be coded as having some predictive power.

The importance of observing international law is stressed both at the societal level and in Germany's international environment. Still, Germany has participated in a combat operation that may have violated one of the core elements of international law, i.e. art. 2 para. 4 of the UN Charter. Even if we accept that, in the Kosovo conflict, Germany acted in line with a norm calling for humanitarian intervention,[29] it would remain a puzzle for constructivism why Germany has given priority to such a norm over one of the cornerstones of the international order, even more so because German participation does not rest on an established societal normative consensus.

Further observable implications
The covariance analysis shows that overall the best prediction is offered by modified neorealism, but constructivism also has substantial predictive power. As in case 1, a closer inspection of some of the decisions taken by the German government, and a search for the rationale underlying them, will provide us with some additional insight. This analysis further supports modified neorealism, whereas doubts are raised about constructivism.

In line with *modified-neorealist* expectations, the more post-unification Germany contributed to NATO-led out-of-area operations in the Balkans, the more influential posts in connection with these operations it received. After the relative enlargement of the German contribution from IFOR to SFOR, Germany was given a high-ranking staff post in the SFOR command chain. In the KFOR operation, the *Bundeswehr* has been given the command and control of one of KFOR's five sectors and, in autumn 1999, a German general assumed the field command of KFOR. More importantly, Germany actively demanded such additional posts and status improvements. Due to its growing readiness to participate in out-of-area operations, Germany's influence on political aspects of crisis management has grown since the early 1990s.[30]

The major weakness of the *constructivist* explanation in this case lies in the timing between the change of norms and the change of foreign policy behaviour, at least with regard to societal norms. Several times, the federal government went beyond the domestic normative consensus, most notably in the instances of participating with combat troops in SFOR and the war against the FRY. It is very plausible to assume that such steps have themselves shaped the development of the societal norm since the German public got used to engagements of the *Bundeswehr* step by step. This implies that, to some extent, the policy of the German government has been based on a deliberate strategy to accustom the German people gradually to out-of-area operations of the *Bundeswehr*.[31] Apparently, for German decision makers the domestic norms operated as constraints they could not fully ignore but nevertheless tried to overcome slowly.

While this analysis cannot fully settle the question of what has mainly guided Germany in its remarkable foreign policy change concerning the participation in multilateral out-of-area operations, there is sufficient ground to state that modified neorealism provides the most adequate explanation of post-unification Germany's foreign policy behaviour in this case.

Conclusion

Summary of empirical findings

Two central aspects of Germany's security policy within and vis-à-vis NATO have been analysed in this chapter: Germany's military integration in NATO and German participation in multilateral non-Article–5 operations of NATO countries. A lot of continuity can be found in post-unification Germany's policy compared with that of the 'old' FRG. Germany has not embarked on any renationalization of defense policy. It has kept its military forces within NATO, and it has been very active in strengthening multilateral structures, e.g. multinational forces. At the same time, the development of post-unification Germany's growing readiness to participate in non-Article–5 missions of NATO marks a profound change in its foreign policy behaviour. Step by step the country has pushed back the limits of its participation in multilateral out-of-area operations. In the air strikes against Serbia and Montenegro, German armed forces took part in combat operations even without a UN mandate, something that would have been unthinkable a few years earlier. Of course, this development could also be described as continuity in Germany's efforts to be a reliable partner of its NATO allies, but it is more accurate to say that cooperation with its NATO partners and military restraint have been important goals of Germany's security policy, both before and after unification. Before unification, these two goals hardly ever collided, due to the low salience of the out-of-area issue. After unification, it has become more and more apparent that Gemany prefers to compromise its tradition of military restraint rather than weakening its reputation as a reliable partner within NATO.

Thus this study finds continuity in German foreign policy as far as military integration is concerned, and change regarding participation in non-defence operations.

Evaluation of theories

Besides studying two central aspects of Germany's security policy within NATO, the second purpose of this chapter has been to examine which of the foreign policy theories can best predict and explain German security policy within NATO. The findings are summarized in table 6.4.

Table 6.4 Summary of empirical findings and explanatory power
of theories

Case	Continuity/ change	Neorealism	Modified neorealism	Utilitarian liberalism	Constructivism
Integration in NATO structures	Continuity	Disconfirmed	Mostly confirmed but puzzling further observables	Mostly confirmed but puzzling further observables	Confirmed
Participation in out-of-area operations	Change	Disconfirmed	Mostly confirmed	Disconfirmed	Mostly confirmed but puzzling further observables

The clearest finding is that *neorealism* completely fails in both cases.
It neither predicts post-unification Germany's willingness to continue
its integration in NATO nor its growing readiness to participate in
multilateral non-defense operations carried out by utilizing NATO's
command structure. The insistence on the priority of autonomy seeking
has proven to be misleading about the direction of German security
policy within NATO.

Modified neorealism gets considerably more empirical support. It
rightly predicts both post-unification Germany's staying in NATO's
military structure and its willingness to participate in NATO-led non-
defence operations. In both cases, there are inconsistencies between the
modified-neorealist expectation and the empirical evidence, to be sure.
According to the theory, post-unification Germany should have been
more active in establishing a general staff. Also, modified neorealism
cannot account for the restraint Germany showed in participating in
NATO-led operations up to the mid 1990s. Yet Germany has lived up
to modified neorealism's predictions to a greater degree since 1996. It
can thus be argued that there has merely been a greater time lag between
the enhancement of the German power position and the change of
German foreign policy behaviour than predicted by modified neorealism. Overall, modified neorealism provides fairly good predictions
in both cases.

For *utilitarian liberalism*, the results are mixed at best. It correctly
predicts Germany's continued integration in NATO's military structures
although the creation of capacities for command and control that enable
Germany to take part in out-of-area operations counter utilitarian-
liberal expectations. This deficiency manifests itself much more clearly

in the second case. Utilitarian liberalism cannot account for post-unification Germany's turn towards taking part in NATO-led out-of-area operations.

Constructivist foreign policy theory gets full empirical support in the case of military integration. Post-unification Germany's growing willingness to participate in non-Article–5 operations of NATO can also be explained by constructivism. Yet we found in this case that societal norms have only a constraining effect on German foreign policy behaviour. To a significant extent the German foreign policy behaviour preceded the establishment of the societal norm, whereas constructivist foreign policy theory would have expected it to be vice versa. Unlike modified neorealism, which in this case only suffers a time-lag problem, constructivism expects the timing to be completely different from what was actually the case. Also, Germany's full participation in the air strikes against FRY, which had a doubtful legal basis, does not confirm constructivist foreign policy theory. Nevertheless, German NATO policy overall provides considerable empirical support for constructivism.

Two of the four theories considered, neorealism and utilitarian liberalism, are of limited help in explaining post-unification Germany's security policy in NATO, whereas the other two theories, modified neorealism and constructivism, offer much better explanations. Apparently, the German desire to live up to international and societal expectations was more present in case 1, whereas the goal of securing influence within the alliance was especially important in case 2. However, it is safe to conclude that overall both constructivism and modified neorealism provide important insights in German security policy within NATO since unification.

Contribution to the state of the art

It could be argued that these findings are more important for constructivism, since cases from the field of security policy must be seen as easy cases for any neorealist foreign policy theory. At the same time, in light of the existing literature, it may be the good predictive power of modified neorealism that is more noteworthy. As mentioned above, many students of German security policy within NATO have argued that factors such as Germany's political culture or its embeddedness in the transatlantic community have shaped German security policy. The present study adds further evidence to this body of literature. At the same time, the fact that much of German NATO policy can also be explained by modified neorealism has rarely been noticed to date. In much of the existing literature, German security policy is seen as confounding neorealism (Duffield 1999, 1998; Berger 1998, 1996; Hellmann 1997; Wolf 1996). This study indicates that the distinction between a neorealist and a modified-neorealist foreign policy theory is an important innovation because it helps to shed light on German security policy within NATO.

Notes

1   Protocols of the interviews conducted for this case study are available from the author.

2   Non-Article–5 operations are non-defence operations that are usually referred to as 'out-of-area operations'. Of course, out-of-area operations also include operations that have no connection with NATO. Such operations are not included here. Still, for matters of simplicity, I will use the terms interchangeably in this chapter.

3   For an analysis of how the FRG turned power into influence in NATO in the 1950s and 1960s, see Tuschhoff (1999).

4   This judgement was shared by several members of parliament and policy experts at the *Bundestag*. Lobby groups were seen as important only with regard to some specific issues, such as conscientious objection or the campaign against landmines (interviews at the *Bundestag*, Bonn, June 1998).

5   The Federal Security Council, a Cabinet committee that prepares decisions and consults on important questions of security policy, is also headed by the Chancellor.

6   A comparison of the military spending of the FRG and of France, which has not participated in NATO's military structures since 1966 and has developed its own nuclear deterrent, supports this contention. France has consistently spent higher shares of its GDP on defense than the FRG. In the 1980s, for instance, France annually spent between 3.7 and 4.1 per cent of its GDP on defense. West Germany's defence expenditure ranged from 2.8 to 3.4 per cent (SIPRI 1991: 174).

7   For the period before unification, see CSU 1976: 70; CDU 1978: 202; FDP 1980: 8; CDU/CSU 1987: 9, 12; FDP 1987: 8; SPD 1987: 43. For the period after unification, see CSU 1993: 126; CDU 1994: 92; FDP 1994: 121; SPD 1998: 45.

8   See Die Grünen 1983: 6; 1987: 26; Bündnis 90/Die Grünen 1994: 55; PDS 1993: 23. The Greens have by now conceded that leaving NATO would raise international concerns about a German *Sonderweg* (1998).

9   The order of the Defence Minister is reprinted in Bulletin des Presse- und
    Informationsamtes der Bundesregierung 1/95: 3; see also *Neue Zürcher
    Zeitung* (*NZZ*), 4 February 1995.
10 Interviews at the Ministry of Defence and Foreign Office, Bonn, June 1998.
11 Based on the Defense Policy Guidelines of 1992 (BMVg 1992; see also
    Young 1995), the White Paper of 1994 (BMVg 1994) and new Conceptual
    Guidelines of the same year (BMVg 1995), it was decided to create crisis
    reaction forces of about 50,000 troops, along with the main defence forces.
12 In early *Bundeswehr* engagements in UN peacekeeping operations the Min-
    istry resorted to ad-hoc task forces. In 1993, a coordination staff was
    created. One year later, after the experience in Somalia (UN Operation in
    Somalia II (UNOSOM), this body was not deemed sufficient either, event-
    ually leading to the establishment of the *Führungszentrum*.
13 For instance, plans have been made to create a joint reconnaissance satellite
    system, as well as to develop a new transport vehicle and a new transport
    air plane (*Bonner Generalanzeiger*, 30 April 1998).
14 In confidential interviews, government officials stressed that Germany was
    not striving for more command posts and that the reason for its partici-
    pation in multinational units was not the enhancement of German
    influence on NATO partners (interviews at the Foreign Office and the
    Ministry of Defence, Bonn, June 1998).
15 Interviews at the Ministry of Defence and the Foreign Office, Bonn, June
    1998.
16 Numerous speeches by representatives of the German government can be
    cited in support of this point. For example, see the speech by Minister of
    Defence Volker Rühe at the Deutsche Atlantische Gesellschaft on 11 May
    1995 (Bulletin des Presse- und Informationsamtes der Bundesregierung
    40/1995: 345–8), and the speeches by Chancellor Helmut Kohl before the
    Bundestag on 27 October 1995 (Bulletin des Presse- und Information-
    samtes der Bundesregierung 88/1995: 853–5) and at the 34th Munich
    Conference on Security Policy on 7 February 1998 (Bulletin des Presse-
    und Informationsamtes der Bundesregierung 15/1998: 169–73).
17 Interview at the Ministry of Defence, Bonn, June 1998.
18 Interview at the Foreign Office, Bonn, June 1998.
19 From a modified neorealist perspective, the substantial reduction of se-
    curity pressures on Germany implies that post-unification Germany hardly
    faces direct threats to its security, but there may still be wars that have
    indirect repercussions for German security.
20 This at least has been the case since the Federal Constitutional Court's
    decision in 1994 (BverfGE 90: 286).
21 Interviews at the Ministry of Defence and the Foreign Office, Bonn, June
    1998.
22 Already in 1966, the federal government had turned down a request by

the US to send troops to Vietnam by referring to constitutional constraints (*SZ*, 4 August 1997: 7).

23 Factual information about this operation is available at http://www. nato. int/ifor/general/shrp-grd. htm.

24 The German federal government had first sent the forces without the consent of the *Bundestag*. After the decision by the Federal Constitutional Court, which ruled that the approval of the *Bundestag* was mandatory, the government deemed it necessary to get formal parliamentary approval.

25 In fact, the German contingent comprised about 3,000 soldiers, 2,700 of whom were army personnel (BMVg, PrMitt, 15 August 1996, reprinted in: Stichworte zur Sicherheitspolitik 9/96: 23–5).

26 Interview at NATO HQ, Brussels, February 1999.

27 On the historical background of the Kosovo conflict, see Malcolm 1998; Bartl 1997.

28 The Contact Group comprises the US, Russia, France, the UK, Germany and Italy. The Rambouillet talks grew out of a US initiative. The US wanted the talks to be held under the auspices of NATO, but the Europeans insisted on conducting the negotiations within the framework of the Contact Group (interview at NATO HQ, Brussels, February 1999). For the full text of the Rambouillet agreement, see http://jurist.law.pitt.edu/ramb.htm.

29 This would imply that the NATO air strikes can be seen as a 'just war'. As shown by Peter Mayer (1999), this contention is not without problems.

30 Interview with a German diplomat at NATO HQ, Brussels, February 1999.

31 Interview at the Bundestag, Bonn, June 1998.

7

German EU constitutional foreign policy

Wolfgang Wagner

Introduction [1]

In EU politics two dimensions can be distinguished: regulative politics and constitutive or constitutional politics (see Anderson 1999: 6 and *passim*). Though the EU is not a state (and is unlikely to become one in the forseeable future), EU primary law has been regarded as the EU's constitution (see, among others, Weiler 1999; Mancini 1991; Stein 1981). In formal terms, the EU constitution refers to those provisions with the highest-ranking legal status. With regard to its contents, the EU constitution refers to the establishment of organs; the distribution of competences between organs and between the EU and the member states; the decision-making procedures for EU legislation, administration and adjudication; and the rights and duties of member states as well as the protection of citizen rights (see, among others, Jachtenfuchs 1999: 97ff.; Preuss 1995: 43–4; Bieber 1991: 393–4). In the process of European integration constitutional politics has been 'largely coextensive with the high politics surrounding periodic "grand bargains"' (Anderson 1999: 6). In contrast to regulative politics, supranational and societal actors have played only a minor role in constitutional politics, which has been dominated by the member states (see Gehring 1997: 130).

In the period of concern (the 1980s and 1990s), constitutional policy issues have been negotiated during the intergovernmental conferences (IGCs) on the Single European Act (SEA) in 1985/86, on the Treaty of Maastricht in 1990/91 and on the Treaty of Amsterdam in 1996/97. These Treaty amendments were followed by negotiations on the EU financial constitution, i.e. on the size of member states' financial contributions to the EU budget and the distribution of EU expenditures across policy areas and among member states. These negotiations have taken place at various summits of the European Council, particularly in March 1988 in Brussels, in December 1992 in Edinburgh and in March 1999 in Berlin. From the perspective of the member states, negotiating the EU's constitution has been an important part of their foreign policies which may be termed 'EU constitutional foreign policy'.

In contrast to regulative politics, constitutional politics is less influenced by issue-specific considerations. As a consequence, Germany's EU constitutional foreign policy is particularly suited to answer the question of whether post-unification Germany has continued a policy of furthering European integration. The universe of cases of EU constitutional politics comprises, first, cases of (re-)allocating competences between the EU and its member states; second, cases of changing decision-making procedures; and, third, cases of changing the rights and duties of the member states. In the realm of EU constitutional politics, issue-specific variables are most important in the first set of cases because Germany's policy on allocating decision-making powers in a certain issue area (e.g. monetary politics) is likely to reflect issue-specific considerations (e.g. implications for inflation and exchange rate stability). Therefore, this case study focuses on cases of the second and third category. The extension of QMV in the Council to further issue areas (case 1) and the strengthening of the EP's legislative powers (case 2) are important constitutional issues of the second category, while the member states' financial (net) contributions to the EU budget (case 3) is a prominent issue of the third category. Each of these issues has been negotiated before as well as after unification and is therefore suited to comparing pre-unification and post-unification Germany's behaviour.

Germany's post-unification EU policy has attracted considerable scholarly attention. While some observers have regarded continuity to be the dominant feature of post-unification Germany's EU policy (Staack 2000; Bulmer, Jeffery and Paterson 1998; Kohler-Koch 1998; Katzenstein 1997b), others have noted significant changes ranging from new preferences in specific areas of regulative politics (Anderson 1999) to the underlying aims of the integration process (Maurer and Grunert 1998; Hort 1997). In the area of constitutional politics, post-unification Germany has been expected or perceived to have put greater emphasis on its unilateral freedom of action (Frenkler 1998; Wernicke 1998; Janning 1996b: 36–7; Deubner 1995: 11).

Theories of foreign policy and EU constitutional foreign policy

Neorealism

From a neorealist perspective, international organizations, including the EU, are instruments of power politics at the disposal of the powerful member states (see Rittberger and Zangl 1995: 74). The EU has offered Germany opportunities to influence the policies of its partners, most importantly to have them relinquish privileges harming Germany or accept obligations benefiting Germany. In turn, however, Germany itself has had to consent to limit its freedom of unilateral action. As a consequence of Germany's improved power position, neorealists expect Germany to step up its pursuit of power politics, i.e. to intensify autonomy-seeking as well as influence-seeking behaviour.

In EU constitutional politics, a member state's autonomy may be constrained by limitations on its sovereignty. As Andrew Moravcsik has pointed out,

> [c]onstraints on sovereignty can be imposed in two ways: pooling or delegation of authoritative decision-making. Sovereignty is *pooled* when governments agree to decide future matters by voting procedures other than unanimity ... Sovereignty is *delegated* when supranational actors are permitted to take certain autonomous decisions, without an intervening interstate vote or unilateral veto. (1998: 67)

Because both pooling and delegating of sovereignty constrain a member state's autonomy, Germany may increase its autonomy by opposing any further *pooling* as well as *delegation* of sovereignty. In terms of a member state's influence, however, pooling and delegation differ in their effect. Delegation does not enhance a member state's control over the other member states because decision-making power is then *transferred* to an independent body. Though the actual independence of a supranational actor has to be examined individually, the exercise of control over any supranational actor is generally seen as limited and costly (Pollack 1997). When sovereignty is pooled, however, it 'is not transferred to a supra-national body because the crucial decisionmaking role is taken by an interstate body' (Keohane and Hoffmann 1991: 8). In other words, when sovereignty is pooled member states may obtain concessions from their partners, i.e. exert influence on them. Thus the pooling of sovereignty actually brings about an increase in a member state's influence.

From a *neorealist* point of view, post-unification Germany is expected not to transfer any further sovereignty to the EU, i.e. to oppose any further pooling or delegation. From a *modified neorealist* perspective, post-unification Germany is prepared to sustain autonomy losses if substantial gains in influence can thereby be achieved because dramatically decreased security pressures after the end of the Cold War allow Germany to pay less attention to safeguarding its autonomy. Modified neorealism therefore expects post-unification Germany to oppose any further delegation of sovereignty but to accept the further pooling of sovereignty whenever substantial influence gains can thereby be achieved without suffering dramatic losses of autonomy.

Utilitarian liberalism

The most striking feature of the German EU constitutional policy network (for an overview see Bulmer, Jeffery and Paterson 1998: 26–42; Goetz 1996) is the absence of private actors. Though companies, economic pressure groups and political advocacy groups play, of course, a prominent role in EU regulative politics, none of them is significantly involved in EU constitutional policy making (see Moravcsik 1997b: 226; Gaddum 1994: 214; Bulmer and Paterson 1987:26).[2] Thus German EU constitutional policy is made in a network with PAS leadership.

Because each minister has a say on those issues of Germany's EU constitutional policy which come under his jurisdiction, the ministers are part of the policy network. In questions of major importance, however, ministerial autonomy may be trumped by the Chancellor, who has a high level of structural mobilization because of his *Richtlinienkompetenz* and because intergovernmental negotiations on constitutional questions are concluded in the European Council comprising the heads of state or government. Whether the Chancellor or a minister is situatively mobilized depends on the constitutional issue at stake and has to be examined on a case-by-case basis.

A peculiar German feature of EU constitutional policy making is the powerful position of the *Länder* governments mainly acting through the *Bundesrat*. In return for approving the transfer of competences to the EU, the *Länder* governments obtained improved institutionalized participation in EU constitutional policy making (see Laufer and Münch 1997: 237). While the *Länder* governments were not structurally mobilized during the 1980s, they had a high level of structural mobilization in the 1990s. During the negotiations on the SEA, the *Länder* governments had not been granted access to German EU constitutional policy-making. A few years later, however, they were allowed to nominate two representatives to participate in the German delegation for the Maastricht Treaty negotiations which gave them an immediate influence on German constitutional policy (see Clostermeyer 1992: 177; Borchmann 1994: 110). The participatory rights of the *Länder* governments were extended even further by the new Basic Law art. 23 and subsequent legislation (see Hrbek 1997: 15; Goetz 1996: 26). Now, the federal government is legally obliged to take the *Länder* governments' position into account (see Lang 1997; Oschatz and Risse 1995).

The participatory rights of the *Bundestag* have lagged behind those of the *Länder* governments (Lang 1997; Goetz 1996). Though the *Bundestag* must approve changes in the EU constitution, its immediate influence on German policy during the negotiations on the EU constitution has been rather limited. During the negotiations of both the SEA and the Maastricht Treaty, the *Bundestag* was merely kept informed. Since the Basic Law amendment of 1993, the federal government is obliged thoroughly to inform the *Bundestag* at the earliest possible time and to consider its statements during negotiations. For the entire period under consideration, the *Bundestag* has had only a low level of structural mobilization.

Because of the absence of private actors and the plurality of assertive actors of the PAS, the German EU constitutional policy network is best characterized as a network with decentralized PAS leadership. With regard to institutional issues (as in case 1 and case 2), the PAS actors' basic interest in retaining their decision-making power *vis-à-vis* international institutions is affected. Whereas citizens' voting behaviour has not been affected by institutional issues, the political actors' basic interest in enhancing their prospects of re-election is affected when budgetary questions are at stake. Thus in case 3, the Federal Chancellor and members of the *Bundestag* will have a high level of situative mobilization (see p. 211f.). As a consequence, actors of the political *and* administrative system will dominate the network in case 1 and case 2, whereas political actors will be the dominant actors in case 3.

Constructivism

International norms: From a constructivist perspective, the EU is regarded as a value community (see Schimmelfennig 1998). The preambles to the Treaty Establishing the European Community (TEC), the SEA and the Treaty on European Union (TEU) as well as various European

Council documents, express the community's basic constitutional principles which guide the general direction of EU constitutional development. Moreover, ECJ rulings interpreting the basic constitutional principles may serve as a further indicator of European norms. Of course, the actual extent of member states' consensus when signing documents such as treaties or communiqués representing hard bargain compromises has also to be considered.

On several occasions, the EU member states have committed themselves to advancing European integration. Beginning with the Treaty of Rome, they agreed to pursue an 'ever closer union among the peoples of Europe' (preamble). This pledge has remained unchanged by the Maastricht and Amsterdam Treaties. The commitment to an ever closer union has been supplemented by the 1983 Solemn Declaration ('resolved to continue the work begun ... and to create a united Europe') and the preamble to the SEA. These documents indicate that there is a norm shared among the original member states, and accepted by those joining later, that member states shall contribute to the formation of an ever closer union. Because this norm clearly precludes some behavioural alternatives (e.g. the renationalization of competences or the weakening, let alone abolition, of Community organs), it is specific enough to guide member state policy. Still, case-specific norms remain to be examined.

Societal norms: Scholars in a societal constructivist tradition have emphasized that European norms resonate well with Germany's Europeanized identity (see Banchoff 1999b; Katzenstein 1997b; Goetz 1996). In its preamble as well as in its new art. 23, the Basic Law commits Germany to contributing to a united Europe (Oppermann and Classen 1993). However, though the EU has received the status of a state goal (Scholz 1996: 35), the provisions of the Basic Law have remained unspecific in terms of concrete EU constitutional policies. The programmes and election platforms of political parties elected to the *Bundestag* also indicate a societal norm that European integration shall be advanced[3] (see also Jachtenfuchs 1999). Whether party programmes and election platforms indicate sufficiently specific value-based expectations about appropriate German EU constitutional policy has to be examined on a case-by-case basis.

The societal norm that Germany shall contribute to furthering European integration converges with the European norm that Germany shall contribute to an ever closer union. On a general level, constructivists expect Germany to pursue a norm-consistent EU constitutional foreign policy, i.e. to contribute to furthering European integration. In order to derive case-specific constructivist predictions about German EU constitutional foreign policy behaviour, issue-specific norms remain to be examined.

Case 1: extension of QMV in the Council

Case description and dependent variable

The Council representing member states' governments is the most important organ in EU decision making. With only few exceptions, the Council decides by either unanimity or qualified majority. When decisions are taken by qualified majority, the member states' votes are weighed according to the size of their population, ranging from two votes for Luxembourg to ten votes for the four biggest member states including Germany. For any decision to be taken about 71 per cent of all votes is required, though the exact number of votes has been changing due to the accession of new member states. Because decisions are generally taken faster under QMV, the extension of QMV strengthens the Council, which can then act more efficiently.

Germany's behaviour during the negotiations on an extension of QMV is this case's dependent variable (a return from QMV to unanimity has never been negotiated). Germany's behaviour comprises agenda setting as well as its actual stance in the negotiations on an extension of QMV. In the opening stages of each negotiation, agenda setting, i.e. general statements on whether and to what extent QMV should be extended, can be observed. During the later stages of an IGC, the negotiations focus on the extension of QMV to specific articles in the TEC/TEU.

Usually, the Commission and the Presidency suggest specific articles to which an extension of QMV is proposed, whereas the member states mainly contribute listings of those articles on which they prefer unanimity. Though each of these issue area-specific discussions could be treated as a case on its own, it is the overall policy on extending QMV that is of interest here. While Germany's issue area-specific policy may further confirm or disconfirm the predictions below, the most important piece of evidence is Germany's *overall* policy on extending QMV, i.e. its agenda-setting behaviour and the total number of issue areas (Treaty articles) for which Germany accepted QMV. Germany's behaviour may be more or less supportive of an extension of QMV. At one extreme, it may actively push for an extension of QMV without claiming any significant exception. At the other extreme, Germany may actively oppose any further extension of QMV. On the middle ground, Germany may advocate a general extension of QMV while insisting on a more or less comprehensive list of exceptions from that general rule. Germany's behaviour was observable during the IGCs in 1985, 1990/91 and 1996/97 when the extension of QMV was one of the most important issues. Post-unification Germany's behaviour during the negotiations in 1991 and 1996/97 can well be compared with pre-unification Germany's behaviour in 1985.

Independent variables and predictions

Neorealism
In the Council 'states give up autonomy for well-guaranteed access and influence' (Wessels 1991: 137). By increasing the Council's capacity to act, the introduction and extension of QMV both augments a member state's influence on its partners and exacerbates its own loss of autonomy. Even if no formal vote is taken, member states are compelled to avoid isolation and to look for compromises (Teasdale 1996). According to Hayes-Renshaw and Wallace,

> [t]he early acceptance of majority voting reassured the participating countries that a difficult country, especially a difficult large country, could be outvoted and bound by a majority vote. In the early days of the EC the possibility of thus binding in Germany was not a trivial concern. (1997: 44)

From a *neorealist* point of view, a more powerful Germany can be expected to be less willing to accept the loss of autonomy that an extension of QMV brings about. Neorealism therefore predicts:

> As its power position has improved, post-unification Germany will increase its opposition against a further extension of QMV in the Council of the EU.

In contrast, *modified neorealism* emphasizes that the extension of QMV increases Germany's capacity to influence the other member states' behaviour and may enable Germany to elicit concessions from other member states beneficial to Germany. From a modified neorealist perspective, the decrease of security pressures after the end of the Cold War is expected to lead to a change in Germany's overall policy on the extension of QMV. Whereas Germany is expected to oppose an extension of QMV in the 1980s because of the high security pressures during the Cold War, it is expected to support the extension of QMV in the 1990s because, in view of decreased security pressures, it prefers substantial influence over autonomy.

An extension of QMV in the Council is likely to yield substantial gains in influence for Germany in those issue areas in which Germany is unlikely to be outvoted, i.e. in which it holds preferences close to the European median position (Moravcsik 1998: 486). Germany is thus expected to oppose QMV in those issue areas in which Germany aims at maintaining extreme positions and to support QMV in those issue areas in which it holds preferences close to the European median position. Whether Germany's issue-specific policy concurs to such a pattern will further confirm or disconfirm the hypothesis of modified neorealism. The modified neorealist prediction, however, only addresses Germany's overall policy on extending QMV in the Council:

> As its power position has improved and its exposure to security pressures has decreased, post-unification Germany will no longer oppose but support an extension of QMV in the Council.

Utilitarian liberalism
Ministers that are represented in the Council are directly affected by any change in the Council's decision-making procedures. With the introduction of QMV, ministers have to look for compromises and may face difficulties in defending particular interests. Thus whenever QMV applies to policy issues covered by a minister's portfolio, his basic interest in retaining his decision-making power is directly affected. As a consequence, ministers have a highly pronounced preference for unanimity in the Council, i.e. against the extension of QMV into their respective portfolios (see also Gaddum 1994: 263). Since 1993, the same has held true for the *Länder* governments whenever QMV is extended to issue areas that are within the exclusive jurisdiction of the *Länder* because they may then represent Germany in the Council. Thus the *Länder* governments are expected to have highly pronounced preferences against QMV in the areas of culture, education and environment, as well as justice and home affairs. Because proposals to extend QMV to these issue areas was particularly prominent during the negotiations on the Amsterdam Treaty the *Länder* governments' level of situative mobilization in 1996/97 is expected to be high and their preference

against an extension of QMV highly pronounced. Before the *Länder* governments were granted the right of representing Germany in the Council their basic interest in retaining their decision-making power was affected only indirectly. During the negotiations in 1985 and 1990/91 the *Länder* governments therefore had only a low-intensity preference against an extension of QMV.

Changes in the Council's decision-making procedures hardly affect the *Bundestag*'s basic interest in retaining its decision-making power because the *Bundestag* may influence Council decisions only indirectly, i.e. by scrutinizing the federal government's policies. To the extent that the *Bundestag* does hold a preference, however, it can be assumed to have a preference against QMV because the possibility of outvoting the German government would diminish its influence on Council decisions even further. Finally, the extension of QMV has no significant impact on the economic performance of a member state nor on citizens' voting decisions and therefore leaves the political actors' interest in re-election unaffected.

Germany's policy on extending QMV has been made in a policy network with decentralized PAS leadership. Because of their high level of situative mobilization, the ministers and, after 1993, the *Länder* governments, have been the dominant actors in that network. Because both ministers and *Länder* governments prefer unanimity over QMV, the following utilitarian-liberal expectation can be derived:

> Because Germany's domestic interests have been opposed to an extension of QMV in the Council, post-unification Germany will continue to oppose an extension of QMV.

Constructivism
International norms: The TEC stipulates that decisions are taken by (simple) majority lest a provision explicitly states the contrary. Thereby, majority voting is established as the general rule and unanimity as an exception to this rule (see Gaddum 1994: 193). In Maastricht, the member states have again committed themselves 'to enhance further the efficient functioning of the institutions' (preamble to the TEU), which must be read as a commitment to the extension of QMV (Hilf and Pache 1995a: 7). In the late 1960s, however, the so-called 'Luxembourg Compromise'[4] had made it clear that not all member states endorsed QMV. To the present day, a few member states have remained reluctant to support a further extension of QMV. However, the

proponents of QMV have been in the majority. Though the norm does not fully determine the degree to which QMV should be extended and allows for exceptions from QMV, it precludes some behavioural alternatives (e.g. adherence to the status quo) as inappropriate. In sum, on the European level, the norm to extend QMV possesses sufficient commonality and specificity to guide German policy.

Societal norms: An analysis of election platforms and parliamentary debates reveals that there has been a consensus among the CDU/CSU, SPD and FDP that QMV should be extended to further issue areas. Pertinent statements were made during the federal election campaigns in 1980 (CDU/CSU 1980: 11; FDP 1980: 17), 1983 (FDP 1983: 17) and 1998 (SPD 1998: 74; FDP 1998: 96). More importantly, representatives of the CDU/CSU, SPD and FDP asked for an extension of QMV in the *Bundestag* on the occasion of the Milan European Council (which launched the IGC leading to the SEA) and the final stages of the Amsterdam negotiations.[5] Though neither the Greens nor the PDS have joined that consensus, the norm has had a sufficient level of commonality. Like the European norm, the societal norm is sufficiently specific to guide German policy.

On the issue of QMV, European and societal expectations about appropriate German behaviour converge. On both the European and societal level we find a widely (though not universally) accepted and sufficiently specific norm that Germany shall support an extension of QMV to further issue areas. Therefore, the constructivist prediction reads as follows:

> As there has been a norm that Germany shall support the extension of QMV in the Council on both the European and the societal level, post-unification Germany will continue to support an extension of QMV in the Council to further issue areas.

German foreign policy behaviour

German behaviour before and during the IGC on the SEA 1985
The 'Luxembourg Compromise' had been accepted in spite of opposition from Germany (Gaddum 1994: 197). In the course of the early 1980s, the German government pleaded that the Council should resume the practice provided for by the Treaty, i.e. majority voting as the general rule and reference to 'national interests' as an exception.[6] In the Dooge Committee that had been set up in 1984 to propose institutional

reforms, Germany advocated QMV for Common Market provisions, particularly arts 100 and 57 (2) (Gaddum 1994: 249). In 1985, notwithstanding the German use of the 'veto' in the Agricultural Council, the Federal Republic supported the convening of an IGC to re-launch European integration. During the subsequent negotiations, several ministers, especially the Minister of Finance and the Minister of the Interior, aimed at securing unanimity in matters covered by their respective portfolios. Eventually, the federal government supported QMV for the approximation of laws (new arts. 100a and 100b), for implementing decisions relating to the European Regional Development Fund (ERDF) (new art. 130e) and of Research and Development (R&D) programmes (new art. 130k-m) and accepted QMV for health standards (art. 118a). The German government opposed QMV for indirect taxation (art. 99), for R&D framework programmes (art. 130i), for social security for migrant workers (art. 51), for the organization of the professions (art. 57 para. 2) and for environmental standards (art. 130s).[7] As regards provisions for the organization of professions, Germany was the only member state to insist on unanimity and therefore effectively imposed a veto. In opposing QMV for indirect taxation, Germany was supported by the UK, Ireland and the Netherlands (Corbett 1987: 245). With regard to environmental and health standards, Germany was joined by other rich member states that feared a lowering of standards. A German proposal that the government with the highest standards be accorded a veto was rejected (Moravcsik 1998: 366). However, the Commission was instructed to 'take as a base a high level of protection' (art. 100 para. 3). Moreover, member states were granted the right to maintain higher standards if deemed necessary (art. 100 para. 4).

German behaviour before and during the IGC on the Maastricht Treaty, 1990/91
In 1990/91, Germany 'maintained its traditional support for the [principle] of QMV' (Moravcsik 1998: 391). Only a few days before the opening of the IGC on Political Union, Chancellor Kohl and French President Mitterand sent a joint letter to the Italian Presidency of the Council suggesting that '[w]ithin the Council, voting at qualified majority should be the rule for Community matters. Exceptions to this rule should only apply to a restricted number of sectors and cases listed in the treaty'.[8]

A few months later, the German delegation introduced a list of issue areas for which it favoured unanimity.[9] In addition to a range of constitutional provisions,[10] the list included the organization of professions (art. 57 para. 2), indirect taxation (art. 99), the approximation of laws (art. 100) and further measures to attain one of the Community's objectives (art. 235). During the negotiations, Germany furthermore insisted on unanimity as regards R&D framework programmes (art. 130i) and parts of environmental policy (art. 130s para. 2). With regard to new EU competences, Germany favoured unanimity for culture (art. 128) and industrial policy (art. 130). It advocated QMV in the areas of social policy (except social security), of asylum and immigration (see Henson 1992: 247; Lange and Malhan 1995: 139; *FAZ*, 29 May 1991) and for CFSP-implementing measures. Germany supported the extension of QMV to a broad range of policies, including health (new art. 129), consumer protection (new art. 129a), trans-European networks (new art. 129d) and general environmental policy (art. 130s). Furthermore, Germany endorsed QMV for vocational training (art. 129), for agreements with third states and organizations (art. 228) and for several provisions of EMU.

German behaviour before and during the IGC on the Amsterdam Treaty, 1996/97

During the so-called 'Maastricht II' -negotiations, Germany maintained its position of having QMV as a general rule in EC non-constitutional decision making.[11] The German government was even prepared to accept QMV on a range of constitutional provisions, including some on which Germany had explicitly insisted on unanimity during the Maastricht negotiations.[12] Changes also occurred in the realm of regulative policies. In contrast to 1990/91, Germany accepted QMV for the approximation of laws (art. 100) as well as for the adoption of R&D framework programmes (art. 130i). With regard to new Community competences introduced by the Amsterdam Treaty, Germany accepted that the better part would be decided by QMV.[13] For employment policy Germany preferred unanimity but accepted QMV towards the end of the negotiations. However, the German government insisted on unanimity for new areas of the common commercial policy (services and intellectual property; art. 133 (5)). With regard to policies outside the TEC, i.e. in the second and third pillars, Germany pushed for an extension of QMV in the CFSP. Towards the end of the negotiations, however, Germany no longer accepted the automatic transition to QMV with regard to asylum and immigration policies.

Summary

After unification, Germany continued its policy of supporting the extension of QMV in the Council. In each of the negotiations Germany helped to set the agenda for an extension of QMV. As table 7.1 shows, Germany endorsed the general extension of QMV to an ever broader range of Treaty provisions while insisting on numerous exceptions in each of the three IGSs.

The list of Treaty provisions on which Germany preferred unanimity has, by and large, remained unchanged and included indirect taxation, parts of environmental policy, social security and the organization of professions. Changes have taken place in both directions, i.e. Germany agreed to QMV on legislation in areas where it had previously insisted on unanimity (e.g. R&D framework programmes) and vice versa (e.g. asylum and immigration). Taken together, these changes have been balanced. Thus Germany's policy on extending QMV has been characterized by continuity.

This finding deviates from the studies by Frenkler (1998) and Maurer and Grunert (1998). These authors have taken Germany's last-minute opposition to extending QMV to asylum and immigration policy in Amsterdam as evidence of a policy change. However, by focusing on that widely publicized episode they do not give full weight to the complete picture, which also includes changes in the opposite direction (e.g. R&D framework programmes). Moreover, whereas Frenkler and Maurer and Grunert (implicitly) compare Germany's reluctant policy on QMV extension in Amsterdam with Germany's behaviour in Maastricht, the SEA negotiations are better suited for comparing post-unification Germany's with pre-unification Germany's behaviour. Compared with its behaviour in 1985, Germany's behaviour in 1996/97 is clearly marked by continuity.

Table 7.1 Germany's policy on extending QMV in the Council

	Important provisions on which Germany endorsed QMV	Important provisions on which Germany insisted on unanimity
1985 (SEA)	• Mutual recognition of formal qualifications (art. 57 para. 1) • Transport (art. 84) • Approximation of laws (new arts. 100a and 100b) • Implementing decisions relating to the ERDF (art. 130e) • R&D (art. 130k-m) • Health standards (new art. 118a)	• Organization of professions (art. 57 para. 2) • Indirect taxation (art. 99) • R&D framework programmes (art. 130i) • Social security for migrant workers (art. 51) • Environmental standards (new art. 130s)
1991 (Maastricht)	• Visa (art. 100c) • EMU (art. 103 para. 5; art. 104a para. 2; art. 104b para. 2; art. 104c para. 14, sub-para. 3; art. 105a para. 2) • Education (art. 126) • Vocational training (art. 127) • Health (art. 129) • Consumer protection (art. 129a) • Trans-European networks (art. 129d) • General environmental policy (art. 130s) • Development policy (art. 130w) • Social policy (protocol) • Agreements with third states or organizations (art. 228) • Implementing measures in Justice and Home Affairs (to be determined unanimously) • Implementing measures in CFSP (to be determined unanimously)	• Organization of professions (art. 57 para. 2) • Indirect taxation (art. 99) • Approximation of laws (art. 100) • Culture (art. 128) • Industrial policy (art. 130) • R&D framework programmes (art. 130i) • Parts of environmental policy (art. 130s para. 2) • Further measures to attain one of the Community objectives (art. 235) • Constitutional provisions

1996/97 (Amsterdam)	• Approximation of laws (art. 94)	• Indirect taxation (art. 93)
	• R&D framework programmes (art. 166)	• Culture (art. 151)
		• Industrial policy (art. 157)
	• Customs cooperation (new art. 135)	• Common commercial policy (services and intellectual property, art 184 new para. 5)
	• Fight against fraud (new art. 280)	• Immigration and asylum (art. 67)
	• Protection of data (new art. 286)	• Several constitutional provisions
	• Employment (new art. 128)	
	• CFSP common actions (art. 23)	

Note: The Amsterdam Treaty changed the numerical order of the Treaty articles.

Test of predictions

Covariance analysis

The predictions of both *neorealism* and *utilitarian liberalism* that post-unification Germany will oppose an extension of QMV are not supported by the empirical evidence. Though post-unification Germany did oppose the extension of QMV to a number of issue areas it advocated it in general and endorsed it for a considerable number of policies.

Utilitarian liberalism, however, has been successful in predicting actors' preferences. As predicted by the theory, ministers have a highly pronounced preference for preventing the extension of QMV to issue areas under their jurisdiction. Particularly strong opposition came from the Minister of the Interior and the Minister of Finance. As regards the *Länder* governments, utilitarian liberalism predicts a preference against the extension of QMV that was of low intensity in 1985 and 1991 and was highly pronounced in 1997. This again is supported by the empirical evidence:[14] *Bundesrat* resolutions concerning the IGCs in 1985 and 1990/91 did not mention voting procedures in the Council. Yet even though the *Länder* governments unanimously adopted a resolution in 1995 that advocated QMV to become the general rule in EU law making, they eventually asked for unanimity in a range of policies, including aspects of economic and monetary union, indirect taxes (art. 99), culture (art. 128), parts of environmental policy (art. 130 (2)), immigration and asylum policy, further measures to attain one of the Community's objectives (art. 235) and constitutional issues. However, utilitarian liberalism has not been successful in predicting the preference of the *Bundestag*. According to utilitarian liberalism, the *Bundestag* is expected to have a preference against extending QMV with low intensity. This prediction is not supported by the empirical evidence.[15] In 1985, after the European Council's decision to convene an IGC, the *Bundestag* asked the federal government to pull its weight in favour of having QMV included in the negotiations. On the eve of, as well as during, the 1996 IGC, the *Bundestag* again expressed its preference for an extension of QMV.

While the neorealist and utilitarian-liberal predictions were both disconfirmed, both *modified neorealism* and *constructivism* correctly predicted that post-unification Germany would support an extension of QMV. However, the modified neorealist prediction that Germany would oppose the extension of QMV before unification is not supported by the empirical evidence. As pointed out above, Germany had already supported the extension of QMV during the negotiations on the SEA.

Further observable implications
As mentioned above, *modified neorealism* can be further tested by examining whether or not Germany supports QMV in issue areas in which it holds preferences close to the European median position and opposes QMV in issue areas in which it aims at maintaining extreme positions. However, Germany's opposition to QMV with regard to the organization of professions (art. 57 para. 2) is the only observation that clearly confirms that prediction because it is indeed the peculiar *Handwerksordnung* that Germany seeks to preserve. However, Germany opposed QMV for a broad range of issue areas in which it hardly holds extreme preferences, e.g. indirect taxation (art. 99), industrial policy (art. 130), environmental policy (art. 130s), and asylum and immigration policy. Furthermore, Germany even advocated QMV for CFSP at the very time (1991) that it held extreme preferences (i.e. the recognition of Slovenia and Croatia). Taken together, modified neorealism is further disconfirmed when Germany's issue area-specific preferences are taken into account.

The only theory that has not been refuted so far is *constructivism*. Of course, Germany's insistence on unanimity for a range of issue areas does not point to the impact of a norm which stipulates that QMV shall be extended. However, the constructivist prediction is not disconfirmed by Germany's exemption of issue areas from an extension of QMV because the norm to extend QMV does allow for exceptions. Unfortunately, it is not possible to generate constructivist predictions about Germany's issue area-specific policy on extending QMV because the shared expectations among EU member states and within German society are not specific enough. Taken together, German policy on that issue can therefore be explained most adequately as *norm-consistent foreign policy*.

Case 2: strengthening the EP's legislative powers

Case description and dependent variable

The EU is the only international organization with a Parliament whose members have been directly elected. Since 1975 the EP has had considerable powers in drawing up the annual budget. In the realm of legislation, however, the EP was initially granted only a consultative role. The introduction of legislative powers became an issue after the first direct elections had taken place in 1979. Since then the strengthening of the EP's legislative powers has been on the agenda of intergovernmental negotiations (for an overview see Corbett, Jacobs and Shackleton 1995: 188–223).

During the negotiations on the SEA, discussions focused on the introduction of a cooperation procedure that would entitle the EP to reject the Council's legislative proposals (see Corbett, Jacobs and Shackleton 1995: 197ff.). Any rejection by the EP, however, could be overruled by an unanimous common position of the Council. Not surprisingly, the EP asked for a modification of this procedure that would put it on an equal footing with the Council. That demand was one of the major issues in the IGC of 1990/91. The Maastricht Treaty then introduced the so-called 'co-decision procedure' that granted the EP a third reading and established a conciliation committee in case the Council's common position was rejected by Parliament. In 1996/97, modifications of existing procedures, especially of co-decision, were an issue of only minor importance. The negotiations focused on the extension of the co-decision procedure to further areas of EU policy making.

Germany's behaviour towards the issue of strengthening the EP's legislative powers is the dependent variable in this case. As in the previous case, Germany's behaviour comprises agenda setting as well as its actual stance in the negotiations on granting the EP more legislative powers.

Here, Germany's behaviour can vary between strong reluctance and outright support: at one extreme, it may actively promote a strengthening of the EP's legislative powers and accept new legislative procedures and their application to a wider range of policies; at the other extreme, Germany may actively oppose any further strengthening of the EP's legislative powers, either by rejecting new procedures or by insisting on the status quo.

Independent variables and predictions

Neorealism

By strengthening the EP's legislative powers, the EU member states delegate sovereignty to a supranational organ. As students of principal–agent models have pointed out, delegating sovereignty to the EP differs from delegating sovereignty to other supranational organs (e.g. the Commission) in some important respects. Most importantly, the consequences of increasing the EP's legislative powers on the substance of EU legislation have been regarded as highly uncertain (Moravcsik 1998: 487). Furthermore, the member states have only few mechanisms available to control the Parliament, which therefore enjoys a particularly high level of autonomy (Pollack 1997: 101). Because unanimity is required to change the EU's constitutive treaties, and because the Members of the EP have been directly elected, it is extremely difficult for the member states to take back delegated sovereignty from the Parliament. Taken together, by strengthening the EP member states limit their decision-making power in an incalculable and irreversible way (Jachtenfuchs 1999: 329). Put in neorealist language: the strengthening of the EP's legislative powers involves a loss of autonomy for every member state without bringing about significant gains in any member state's influence. As a consequence, both *neorealism* and *modified neorealism* arrive at the following prediction:

> As its power position has improved, post-unification Germany will increase its opposition against a strengthening of the EP's legislative powers.

Utilitarian liberalism

The EP's legislative powers are strengthened at the expense of the Council. Wherever the cooperation and co-decision procedures apply, the Council's capacity to act has been limited. Thus the German federal ministers' basic interest in retaining their decision-making power is directly affected by a strengthening of the EP's legislative powers. Therefore, ministers will have a strong preference against any further increase in the EP's legislative powers.

Because in 1993, the *Länder* governments acquired the right of representation in the Council in certain issue areas, they subsequently developed a preference similar to those of the federal ministers, i.e. a strong preference against any further increase of the EP's legislative powers. Before 1993, however, the *Länder* governments' influence was mediated by the federal ministers. Therefore, during the negotiations on the SEA and the Maastricht Treaty, the *Länder* governments had only a low level of situative mobilization. The same holds true for the *Bundestag* for the entire period under consideration because the *Bundestag*'s influence has always been mediated by the federal government's representatives in the Council. Finally, a strengthening of the EP has not had an impact on the prospects of the German economy nor on the voting behaviour of German citizens. Thus the political actors' interest in re-election has not been affected. The decentralized PAS-led policy network has been dominated by actors holding a strong preference against a strengthening of the EP's legislative powers (i.e. federal ministers and, after 1993, *Länder* governments). The following utilitarian-liberal expectation can therefore be derived:

> Because Germany's domestic interests have been opposed to a strengthening of the EP's legislative powers, post-unification Germany will continue to oppose a strengthening of the EP's legislative powers.

Constructivism

International norms
Parliamentary democracy has become a fundamental constitutional principle of the EU (see also Hilf and Pache 1995b:7; Huber 1992: 350). On several occasions, the member states have committed themselves to implement this principle, i.e. to further advance parliamentary democracy on the level of the EU. The heads of state or government have acknowledged that, for the democratic people of Europe, 'the European Parliament, elected by universal suffrage, is an indispensable means of expression' (Stuttgart Solemn Declaration of 1983). They have expressed their determination 'to work together to promote democracy' (preamble to the SEA, 1985) and have voiced their desire 'to enhance further the

democratic and efficient functioning of the institutions' (preamble to the TEU, 1991). The ECJ also contributed to the recognition of parliamentary democracy as an EU constitutional principle by declaring that 'the people should take part in the exercise of power through the intermediary of a representative assembly'.[16] At the same time, however, it is clear that some member states do not support the strengthening of the EP. Denmark, the UK and, to a lesser degree, Portugal, Ireland and France share the notion that democratic legitimacy can only be claimed by the Council, whose members are accountable to their national Parliaments (see Corbett 1993). Still, the norm that the EP's legislative powers shall be strengthened possesses a sufficient degree of commonality because the strengthening of the EP is considered appropriate by a majority of member states and because this majority view is endorsed by the ECJ. The norm has a sufficient degree of specificity as well: while member states may choose between a range of behavioural alternatives which are equally appropriate, some behavioural alternatives (such as a strengthening of the Council at the expense of the EP) are clearly ruled out as inappropriate.

Societal norms

Several indicators point to a societal norm that Germany shall contribute to the strengthening of the EP. To begin with, the Federal Constitutional Court has ruled that a strengthened EP is an indispensable element of the EU constitution. According to the Court's Maastricht ruling of 1993 it is 'decisive … that the democratic bases of the Union are built up in step with integration', though primarily 'democratic legitimation comes about through the feed-back of the actions of the European institutions into the parliaments of the Member States'.[17] As an analysis of party programmes and election platforms shows, an all-party consensus on the desired strengthening of the EP emerged in the course of the 1990s.[18] Before unification, only the Greens had not picked up the issue in their party programme or in any of their election platforms. This development can also be observed in parliamentary debates.[19] Finally, survey data gathered by *Eurobarometer* twice a year have demonstrated that the strengthening of the EP has traditionally been popular with the German public.[20] Interestingly, after unification the level of support in the East German *Länder* was even higher than in the West.

The existence of a strong societal norm to strengthen the EP in Germany has been explained by reference to Germany's federal constitution, which is based on the notion that every layer of decision making has to have its own parliamentary legitimation. Based on a domestic analogy, this domestic constitutional principle is applied to the multi-layered system of the EU (Wagner 1999). The societal norm to strengthen the EP has a sufficient degree of specificity because some behavioural alternatives (e.g. opposition to proposals for moderately strengthening the EP) are clearly ruled out.

On the strengthening of the EP, European and societal norms converge: both the majority of EU member states and German society expect Germany to contribute to the strengthening of the EP's legislative powers. The constructivist prediction thus reads as follows:

> As there has been a norm on both the European and the domestic level that Germany shall contribute to the strengthening of the EP, post-unification Germany will continue to support the strengthening of the EP's legislative powers.

German foreign policy behaviour

German behaviour before and during the IGC on the SEA, 1985
During the negotiations on the SEA, Germany presented its own proposal to strengthen the EP's legislative powers. The initiative provided for a conciliation committee in case of differing positions between Council and EP but left the ultimate decision-making power with the Council (Gaddum 1994: 264–5). The proposal was criticized as being insufficient,[21] especially in comparison to an Italian initiative that would give the EP an even better standing (see *NZZ*, 23 October 1985). On its own estimate, the German delegation was among the modest supporters of a strengthened EP.[22] However, many delegations regarded the Italian proposal as a tactical move (Corbett 1987: 257). Germany has therefore been counted among those member states that strongly supported a strengthening of the EP and its legislative powers (Moravcsik 1998: 366–7). The cooperation procedure eventually introduced by the SEA has much in common with the German proposal.

German behaviour before and during the IGC on the Maastricht Treaty, 1990/91
In their joint initiative for an IGC on political union, Chancellor Kohl and French President Mitterrand mention as their first objective to 'strengthen the democratic legitimation of the union'.[23] In their second

joint letter later that year, Kohl and Mitterrand specified that 'current procedures could be strengthened in the direction of co-decision making for the European Parliament for acts that are truly legislative in nature'.[24] A joint declaration by Foreign Minister Genscher and his Italian counterpart De Michelis was exclusively concerned with the strengthening of the EP. The two foreign ministers proposed that the EP may initiate legislation, play a stronger role in appointing the members of the Commission and be put on an equal footing in legislative affairs with the Council. German behaviour during the negotiations has been reported to be very supportive of strengthening the EP's legislative powers (see Staack 2000: 387, 419; Moravcsik 1998: 455; Nicoll and Salmon 1994: 228; Corbett 1993: 58; Wolf 1992: 313). Compared with its policy in 1985, Germany increased its efforts to strengthen the EP's legislative powers.

German behaviour before and during the IGC on the Amsterdam Treaty, 1996/97

In a series of declarations, the German government announced its support for a further strengthening of the EP's legislative powers. For example, in a government statement of November 1994, the strengthening of the EP's competences is mentioned as a central German policy goal.[25] In a striking contrast to the Maastricht negotiations, however, a strengthening of the EP is included in some but not all governmental statements on German EU constitutional policy.[26] Moreover, some statements refer to the desired strengthening of the EP along with an improved participation of the national Parliaments.[27] During the negotiations themselves, however, none of the German actors involved in EU constitutional policy making opposed any move to strengthen the legislative powers of the EP. Some ministers' opposition to the extension of co-decision to their respective portfolios was rather directed at the introduction of QMV that co-decision inevitably brings about. Observers of the negotiations cannot recall any instance of Germany opposing moves to strengthen the EP and see Germany as among the strongest supporters of the EP.[28]

Summary

In each of the IGCs, Germany supported a strengthening of the EP's legislative powers. While the German efforts reached a peak during the Maastricht Treaty negotiations, they have been strong in the entire period under consideration. Even when its proposals were topped by others (as was the case in 1985), Germany never opposed any measure to strengthen the EP's legislative powers. Moreover, Germany's general statements in favour of strengthening the EP increased the pressure on the more reluctant member states to go along with a further strengthening of the EP. Clearly, Germany's behaviour in that case has been marked by continuity – an observation widely shared in the pertinent scholarly literature (see Anderson 1999: 45; Jachtenfuchs 1999: 313; Moravcsik and Nicolaïdis 1999: 71–2).

Test of predictions

Covariance analysis
This finding clearly contradicts the *neorealist* and *utilitarian-liberal* predictions that post-unification Germany will oppose a strengthening of the EP's legislative powers. Only *constructivism* correctly predicts that post-unification Germany will continue to push for a strengthening of the EP's legislative powers.

Further observable observations
The analysis of actor preferences further disconfirms *utilitarian liberalism*. The theory predicts that the federal ministers and, after 1993, the *Länder* governments have strong preferences against a strengthening of the EP's legislative powers. As regards the *Bundestag*, utilitarian liberalism holds that it was not mobilized at all. However, the strengthening of the EP has been a prominent position of the *Bundestag*. The issue was prominent in resolutions on the SEA as well as on the IGC 1996.[29] The governments of the *Länder* also continuously expressed their preference for a strengthening of the EP.[30] What is more, the intensity of that preference increased, contrary to utilitarian liberalism's prediction.

Though *constructivism* cannot account for the varying strength of support in 1991 and 1996/97, it clearly offers the best explanation of post-unification Germany's policy. The result of this analysis, i.e. that norms rather than domestic interests explain Germany's policy on strengthening the EP, concurs with recent research on this matter (see Moravcsik 1998: 468; Jachtenfuchs 1999: 345; Wagner 1999: 435).

Case 3: Germany's financial contribution to the EU budget

Case description and dependent variable

The financial constitution of the EU determines the size as well as the general composition of the budget, i.e. to what extent certain types of revenue may be raised and to which tasks expenditure is allocated. Since 1988, the structure of revenues and their allocation to various policy areas have been codified in a so-called 'financial perspective' that covers a number of years.[31] As a rule, these financial perspectives have resulted from intense interstate bargaining after agreement had been reached on questions of policy. Thus the 'Delors packages' were negotiated in 1987/88 (Delors I) and in 1992 (Delors II), i.e. after the SEA and the Maastricht Treaty, respectively. Soon after the Amsterdam Treaty was signed in 1997 the Commission again introduced a proposal on future financing arrangements ('Agenda 2000' or 'Santer I').[32]

A particular feature of the EU financial constitution is its system of so-called 'own resources' that was established in 1970. The Community then was authorized to dispose of customs duties, agricultural levies and member states' budgetary contributions based on a harmonized VAT base. In 1988, a fourth own resource was introduced based on member states' GNP. The willingness of German governments to endorse increased EU expenditure and their readiness to shoulder a disproportional budgetary burden indicate Germany's commitment to European integration. Germany's behaviour during the 1980s, when the British rebate and the Delors I package were negotiated, can well be compared with Germany's behaviour after unification. The 1992 negotiations on Delors II were still embedded in the context of German unification (i.e. of Kohl's promise in 1990 that unification would not imply increased costs for the other member states) (see Weidenfeld 1998: 412). Thus German policy during the Agenda 2000 negotiations may be perceived as the more important observation point for answering the question of whether Germany has revised its European policy after unification.

The dependent variable in this case is *Germany's behaviour during the negotiations over the member states' net contributions to the EU budget.* Germany's behaviour comprises statements of its policy on member state net contributions as well as its actual stance in the negotiations about member states' net contributions. At one extreme, Germany may readily accept an increase in its net contributions to the EU budget. At the other extreme, Germany may insist on a reduction of its net payments. Though this case focuses on Germany's *net* contributions, Germany's policy on its *gross* contributions, as well as the kind of budgetary reform Germany has been proposing, may yield further observations which may confirm or disconfirm the theories under consideration. Table 7.2 shows the development of Germany's contributions to, and receipts from, the EU budget.

Table 7.2 German contributions to, and receipts from, the EU budget

Year	Gross contributions (m. ECU)	Net contributions (m. ECU)	Share in contributions	Share in receipts	Ratio of share in receipts to share in contributions
1981	5,057.1	2,554.8	28.1	16.1	57.3
1982	5,698.5	3,171.7	26.9	14	52
1983	6,472.1	2,646.8	28.1	17.7	63
1984	7,052.4	3,033.1	28.4	16.7	58.8
1985	7,504.3	3,319.3	28.8	16.9	58.7
1986	8,730.2	3,741.8	26.2	16.4	62.6
1987	9,384.6	4,842.8	26.5	14.7	55.5
1988	11,534.9	6,107.2	28.2	15	53.2
1989	11,110.4	6,530.6	25.1	12.8	51
1990	10,357.5	5,550.4	25	12.9	51.6
1991	15,394.2	8,796.8	29.1	12.3	42.3
1992	16,997.5	9,697.6	30.2	12.5	41.4
1993	19,076.4	11,830.3	29.8	11.3	37.9
1994	21,366.3	13,637.1	33.3	12.8	38.4
1995	21,324.1	13,431	31.4	12.5	39.8
1996	20,766.9	10,894.9	29.2	13.6	46.6
1997	21,217.3	11,228.1	28.2	13.1	46.5
1998	20,632.9	10,465.7	25.1	13.3	53

Source: EU Court of Auditors, *Annual Reports*.

Independent variables and predictions

Neorealism
From a *neorealist* point of view, the EU financial constitution commits member states to transfer resources which they can thereafter no longer

spend autonomously. Thus the higher a member state's gross contribu-tions, the bigger is, *ceteris paribus*, its loss of autonomy. The severity of a member state's loss of autonomy, however, depends on the balance of (gross) contributions and the payments received from the EU budget. The more a member state's share in EU expenditure exceeds its share in financing the budget, the less it suffers a severe loss of autonomy because the other member states effectively transfer resources via the EU budget. Conversely, a member state's loss of autonomy is the more severe the more its payments to the EU exceed its receipts.

From a *modified neorealist* perspective, it has to be discussed whether a member state's influence on EU policies increases with the size of its financial contributions, i.e. whether Germany may use its net payments as side-payments to elicit concessions from other member states (see Carrubba 1997; Paterson 1996: 168). The independent powers of the Commission, of the ECJ and of the EP, however, make the translation of financial commitments into bargaining power in regulative politics very difficult. As a result, Germany cannot gain substantial influence on EU policy making by increasing its (net) payments to the EU budget.[33] Therefore, neorealism and modified neorealism both arrive at the following prediction:

> As its power position has improved, post-unification Germany will increase its efforts to achieve a reduction in its net payments to the EU.

Utilitarian liberalism
In contrast to the previous cases, financial resources instead of decision-making powers have been at stake during the negotiations on the EU financial constitution. Moreover, the size of Germany's net contribution to the EU budget affects the political actors' basic interest in being re-elected.

Because Germany's contributions to the EU budget are federal pay-ments (Bundesministerium der Finanzen 1997: 51), the *Länder* governments are affected only marginally[34] and therefore are not situ-atively mobilized. In contrast, the basic interest of those actors responsible for the federal budget in safeguarding their control over financial resources is directly affected. Thus the Minister of Finance and the *Bundestag* have been highly situatively mobilized during the entire period under consideration, their preference against any increase in Germany's EU contributions intensified still further after unification due to the fiscal burden of German unification, on the one hand, and the expanding size of German contributions (mainly due to the growing Community budget), on the other.

In addition, Germany's net contributions directly affect the political actors' basic interest in being re-elected. Many government policies designed to further the domestic economy are inhibited by budgetary constraints which are aggravated by increased German net contributions to the EU budget. Furthermore, political actors use parts of the federal budget to satisfy the interests of core constituencies, e.g. by financing regional infrastructure projects, and granting sectoral subsidies or social benefits. Thus the Chancellor and the members of the *Bundestag* have also had a high level of situative mobilization, which again intensified after unification. The decentralized PAS-led EU constitutional policy network has been dominated by actors with an increasingly strong preference for reduced German net contributions. The utilitarian-liberal prediction therefore reads as follows:

> Because Germany's domestic interests in reducing Germany's net contributions to the EU have intensified after unification, post-unification Germany will increase its efforts to achieve a reduction in German net contributions to the EU budget.

Constructivism

International norms

The fundamental norm regarding member states' contributions to the Community budget has been that the size of each state's contribution shall depend on its capacity to pay. In the early days of the Community, issues of equity and fairness were not very prominent (due to the rather small size of the budget) (Laffan 1997: 48). Nevertheless, the principle of *juste retour*, i.e. of balanced contributions and receipts, was never seriously considered as a basis for financing the Community (Reister 1975: 27). In the 1970s and 1980s, the Community's fundamental contributionary norm became specified. With the accession of the UK, however, member states also engaged in a long dispute about appropriate contributions.

The most important specification of the basic contributionary norm was that the capacity to pay can best be measured by a member state's national income converted at current exchange rates into a common currency. The GNP resource which was (re-)established in 1988 was explicitly designed to bring a member state's contribution better into line with its capacity to pay. The relative importance of the GNP resource has increased ever since. At the same time, VAT contributions have been continuously cut back after a consensus had emerged that they disproportionately burdened the less prosperous states. For more than a decade, a member state's GNP has been regarded as the best indicator of that state's capacity to pay.

Soon after its accession to the Community in 1973, the UK brought the issue of appropriate financial contributions to the Community agenda (for the British budgetary problem see Taylor 1983; George 1998). By arguing that British contributions were too high, British politicians contested the then Community consensus. The British argued for the principle of *juste retour*, i.e. to have contributions to the EU budget in line with receipts from Brussels. Thus the British approach was centred on the concept of net payments. It has been widely criticized as '*non-communautaire*', particularly because it ignored non-quantifiable advantages of membership (European Commission 1998; European Parliament 1997; Keohane and Hoffmann 1991: 14).

Eventually, however, at the Fontainebleau European Council in 1984, the member states agreed to institutionalize a rebate for the UK. In the final communiqué, they acknowledged that no member state should be required to sustain a 'budgetary burden which is excessive in relation to its relative prosperity' (quoted in Moravcsik 1991: 57). Moravcsik has interpreted the Fontainebleau agreement as a generalization of the principle of *juste retour* (1991: 57). This interpretation, however, is not convincing (see Wallace 1999: 158). The rebate was explicitly designed for the UK only, and a general application was not intended.[35] Furthermore, member states continued to regard the rebate as *non-communautaire* (Laffan 1997: 54; Keohane and Hoffmann 1991: 14).[36] Finally, the Fontainebleau communiqué also states that expenditure is the most important instrument to address the problem of budgetary imbalances. Thus a reform of the budget on the expenditure side is considered an appropriate approach towards correcting member states' budgetary imbalances. In sum, the British rebate should be understood as an exception to the fundamental contributionary norm based on the capacity to pay.

As any other member state, too, Germany has been expected by the community of member states to contribute to the EU budget according to its capacity to pay, i.e. according to the relative size of its GNP.[37] If Germany considers its net payments to be too high, it is expected to advocate a reform of Community policies and expenditure in order to mitigate budgetary imbalances. Germany is expected not to claim a rebate for itself due to the *non-communautaire* nature of that measure. These value-based expectations about appropriate German policy have been shared by a majority of member states (the UK being a dissenter) and, therefore, have a sufficient level of commonality. Furthermore, this European norm possesses a high degree of specificity because it provides for a clear-cut distinction between appropriate reform efforts on the expenditure side and inappropriate efforts on the revenue side.

Societal norms

An analysis of party programmes and election platforms points to the increasingly controversial nature of Germany's EU contributions in German domestic politics. The first election platform to mention EU finances was the joint election platform of the CDU and CSU in 1987. In a rather vague fashion, the platform asked all member states to bear a fair share of the budget (CDU/CSU 1987: 13). In the context of the late 1980s, this can be read as abolishing the British rebate and reducing Germany's burden. In its Berlin programme of 1989, the SPD advocated the opposite position and asked for financial transfers between rich and poor member states (SPD 1989: 36). After the FDP had picked up the issue again in 1994 (1994: 127), EU finances were mentioned by the SPD, CDU, FDP and Greens in the 1998 campaign (CDU/CSU 1998: 29; FDP 1998: 98; Bündnis 90/Die Grünen 1998: 140; SPD 1998: 75). Except for the Greens, who criticized the 'unfortunate discussion about Germany as a paymaster', the parties asked for a fairer financing system or for reduced German net contributions. A reading of party programmes and election platforms indicates that a societal norm enjoining the federal government to seek a reduction of German net contributions emerged in the course of the 1990s. An analysis of parliamentary debates, by and large, supports that finding.[38] In spite of the dissenting position of the Greens, the norm has possessed sufficient levels of commonality and specificity to guide German behaviour. The acceptance of a further aggravation of Germany's net position, for example, is clearly ruled out as inappropriate.

   With respect to Germany's net contributions there is a societal norm that Germany shall aim at lowering its net payments to the EU budget. On the European level, however, no shared expectation about appropriate German net contributions exists. The European norm that Germany shall accept *gross* budgetary contributions in line with its capacity to pay, as well as the European norm that Germany shall strive for a reform of expenditure in case of a budgetary imbalance, may inform Germany's behaviour during the negotiations but they cannot guide German policy on its net contributions. Whether German behaviour concurs with these European norms may further confirm or disconfirm the constructivist foreign policy theory. The constructivist prediction, however, will only address Germany's behaviour regarding its net contributions:

> Because a societal norm that Germany shall increase its efforts to achieve a reduction of its net payments to the EU emerged in the course of the 1990s, post-unification Germany will increase its efforts to achieve a reduction of its net payments.

German foreign policy behaviour

German behaviour during the negotiations on the EC financial constitution in the 1980s

The issue of Germany's budgetary (im)balance with the EC entered the domestic agenda in 1973 when Hans Apel, the then parliamentary State Secretary in the Foreign Office, announced that Germany was not the Community's paymaster (see Bulmer and Paterson 1987: 67–8). During the negotiations on the British rebate, the federal government and the German public alike became increasingly sensitive to issues of budgetary balances. The Minister of Finance favoured a limitation of EC expenditure by reforming the Common Agricultural Policy (CAP) and an opening of the abatement mechanism to all member states with excessive budgetary imbalances.

The compromise on reducing British contributions reached in 1980 was made possible only because, in the crucial meeting, the then parliamentary State Secretary in the Foreign Office, Klaus von Dohnanyi, unilaterally accepted an increase in German contributions (see May 1984: 377). As a response to that, Finance Minister Matthöfer successfully urged the Cabinet to accept the goal of reducing German net payments as the government's official policy. In March 1984, Germany blocked an agreement on the size of the British rebate by suddenly refusing to pay Germany's share of any sum larger than ECU 1 billion (Moravcsik 1991: 56). A solution was reached at the Fontainebleau European Council a few months later when Germany's share in re-financing the British rebate was cut down to two-thirds.

In 1987/88, during the negotiations on Delors I, the Southern member states established a linkage between an increase of structural funds and the implementation of the Single Market. This implied an aggravation of Germany's net position since Germany would have to increase its contributions to the EU budget without benefiting from these funds itself. In a coalition with the UK, Germany tried to keep the EC budget as small as possible. However, in contrast to the UK, Germany did not support a reform of the CAP as a way of reducing its budgetary imbalance (Dinan 1994: 152). In the meantime, the Community had begun to face a severe financial crisis, which was resolved during the German Presidency in 1988. The resulting package – a budgetary ceiling of 1.2 per cent of the Community GNP, increased structural funds and a reform of the CAP – was seen as a remarkable success, a major part of which was attributed to the German willingness to shoulder an even greater financial burden (see Laffan and Shackleton 1996: 87; Shackleton 1990).

German behaviour before and during the negotiations on Delors II
The negotiations on Delors II took place in 1992 and were concluded at the Edinburgh European Council on 11/12 December. During these negotiations, budgetary questions were 'intimately and inextricably linked with a series of non-budgetary issues' (Shackleton 1993: 11), including EU enlargement and subsidiarity. The centre piece of the package proposed by Delors in February 1992 was an increase in overall expenditure from 1.2 to 1.37 per cent of Community GNP. Germany pulled its weight for smaller budgetary growth and rejected the Commission proposal (Schmuck 1993: 33–4). However, the German delegation was reminded of Chancellor Kohl's promise in 1990 that German unification would under no circumstances take place at the expense of the less prosperous member states (see Weidenfeld 1998: 412). Eventually, the member states agreed on maintaining the current expenditure ceiling for two more years and to let it rise to 1.27 per cent of the Community GNP until 1999. Expenditure on structural policy was significantly raised and a new cohesion fund was set up. Though Germany succeeded in drawing the five new *Länder* into the structural fund's first-priority funding, Delors II aggravated Germany's net position even further. According to observers, the agreement was 'secured in large measure by the willingness of Chancellor Kohl and the German government to bear the burden of the increase as the budget's largest contributor' (Laffan and Shackleton 1996: 87).

German behaviour before and during the negotiations on Santer I
Soon after the Edinburgh European Council, German politicians took up the issue of Germany's budgetary imbalance and increasingly demanded a reform of the EU finances. Initially, the government sought to increase German receipts from Brussels as a means of improving the budgetary balance.[39] After the Commission had published its proposal for a new financial perspective from 2000 to 2006 in 1997 and a report on the operation of the own resources system in 1998,[40] public discussion focused on these documents ('Agenda 2000' or 'Santer I').

In the course of the Agenda 2000 negotiations, the German government abandoned its policy of increasing receipts from Brussels. Instead, Finance Minister Waigel put forward the model of a modified correction mechanism which was officially presented in March 1998. The so-called 'capping model' (*Kappungsmodell*; see Stark 1997) acknowledges the wealthier member states' obligation to contribute disproportionately to the budget. However, the model aims at setting a ceiling on any member state's net payments defined in relation to GNP. In addition, Germany advocated a stabilization of overall expenditure, a reduction of the British rebate and a phasing out of the VAT resource. At the same time, however, Germany opposed any CAP reform (and thus reduction of expenditure) that met with the disapproval of German farmers.

Over the course of the negotiations, Germany became more assertive in asking for reduced net payments. At a meeting of the Council of Economic and Finance Ministers on 23 March 1998, Finance Minister Waigel threatened to block decisions on other policies unless a correction mechanism was agreed upon (see *Le Figaro* 23 March 1998; *Tageszeitung*, 23 March 1998).

The policy goal of improving the budgetary balance was further pursued by the new government of Gerhard Schröder, which took office in October 1998. In December 1998, Chancellor Schröder announced in a rather harsh fashion the end of Germany's ability and willingness to solve EU crises with financial contributions.[41] At the same time, the new government put more emphasis than its predecessor on agricultural reform as a possible way to soften Germany's net burden.[42]

During the preparations for the Berlin European Council on 24/25 March 1999, it became clear that VAT revenues would further lose significance, which would benefit all member states except Italy and Belgium. The German Presidency kept the capping mechanism in the negotiating box until the final bargaining stages at the Berlin European Council. During these negotiations, however, the German government clearly preferred reaching agreement over achieving a comprehensive reduction of German net payments.[43] Despite a concerted effort by Germany, Austria, Sweden and the Netherlands, the capping model did not carry the day. As a substitute, however, the four countries were granted a reduced share in (re-)financing the British rebate. In the German case, this reduction will amount to about 400 million Euro per annum after 2002. The Berlin European Council also agreed to cut the VAT resource to 50 per cent of its present size in two stages. After 2004, this reform will reduce Germany's gross contributions by another 300 million Euro per annum. The largest improvement of Germany's net position resulted from the expenditure side. The budgetary ceiling was kept at 1.27 per cent of the Community GNP. What is more, Germany attained an overall stabilization of EU expenditure in real terms. As a consequence, envisaged EU expenditure amounts to only 1 per cent of the Community GNP at the end of the new financial period. Because member states agreed to reduce the number of regions eligible for structural funds, Germany's share in receipts from these funds will increase, with the new *Länder* still among those regions with the highest funding priority. Taken together, Germany achieved a modest improvement of its net position. When the reforms have been ratified and enacted in 2002 Germany's net payments are expected to decrease from 0.54 per cent (in 1999) to 0.42 per cent of its GNP (Jessen 1999: 173).

Summary

In the second half of the 1990s, Germany stepped up its efforts to achieve a reduction of its EU net payments. Compared with its pre-unification policy, Germany became both more active and more assertive during the negotiations on the Santer I package. Germany's attempt to obtain a rebate, the development of a reform proposal (the capping mechanism) and the building of coalitions in support of it demonstrated a heightened level of activity. By threatening to veto the entire package unless the issue of net payments was properly addressed, Finance Minister Waigel displayed a formerly unknown German assertiveness on that issue. During the final bargaining stage, however, post-unification Germany continued to forgo a large decrease of its net payments in order to secure an overall agreement and thereby further progress in European integration.

Test of predictions

Covariance analysis

Post-unification Germany's increased efforts to negotiate a reduction of its net contributions to the EU budget was predicted by all three foreign policy theories. Because of the linkage between German unification and the negotiations on Delors II (see p. 216) an earlier effort by the German government to reduce its net contribution could not be expected. Thus further observable implications have to be considered in order to confirm or disconfirm the three foreign policy theories in this case.

Further observable implications

The analysis of European norms made it clear that Germany was expected to advocate a reform of expenditure in order to improve its budgetary balance. Clearly, this has not been the case. Though the Schröder government re-emphasized a reform of the CAP in order to improve the German net position, it continued to demand a rebate. Thereby the German government consciously disregarded European norms holding that expenditure instead of revenue should be the focus of any reform proposal. *Constructivism* is further invalidated by the timing of the norm change. As pointed out above, a societal norm that Germany shall negotiate a reduction of its net payments emerged *after* unification had aggravated budgetary constraints domestically. This timing weakens the constructivist claim that norms are not ex-post rationalizations of interests but have an independent impact on behaviour.

From a *neorealist* point of view, Germany can be expected to strive for a reduction of its net payments by all means available. In particular, however, Germany can be expected to prefer reduced contributions over increased receipts because the former preserves autonomy whereas the latter does not. The capping mechanism proposed by Germany concurs with this expectation and further confirms neorealism. Moreover, neorealism expects Germany to be assertive when asking for reduced net payments. Finance Minister Waigel's threat to block the entire Santer I package is in line with this expectation and further confirms neorealism.

Utilitarian liberalism is supported by a remarkable record of predicting the preferences of PAS actors: both Chancellors Kohl and Schröder as well as the *Bundestag* have shown great efforts to reduce German net contributions after unification. In 1985, a *Bundestag* resolution that asked the government to pull its weight for a German rebate (BT-Drs 10/4185, p. 3) was supported only by the CDU/CSU and FDP. In 1992, all parliamentary parties asked the government to oppose the Delors II package because of the proposed increase in overall spending. Furthermore, the *Bundestag* wanted the British rebate to be abolished (BT-Drs 12/3664). On the eve of the 1999 Berlin summit, the *Bundestag* asked for a real stabilization of expenditure and a fairer system of burden sharing (BT-Drs 14/514 and 14/550). As regards the Minister of Finance, the author's interviews have revealed a highly pronounced preference for a reduction in German net contributions, as has been predicted by utilitarian-liberal theory. Given the fact that German contributions to the EU budget are federal payments, the highly pronounced preference of the *Länder* governments remains puzzling from a utilitarian-liberal perspective, though it does not contradict utilitarian-liberal expectations. In contrast to the negotiations of 1988 and 1992, the *Länder* governments expressed a highly pronounced preference for reduced German EU contributions during the negotiations on the Agenda 2000. The *Länder* governments called for a new way of calculating member states' capacity to pay based on per-capita income and purchasing power parities [44] and criticized the federal government's capping mechanism for neglecting issues of fairness.

Taken together, both neorealism and utilitarian liberalism are confirmed by the congruence between predicted and observed behaviour, as well as by some further observable implications. Though the available evidence clearly disconfirms the constructivist prediction, it does not allow discrimination between the impact of Germany's improved power position, on the one hand, and of domestic interests in reduced net payments, on the other. Thus both neorealism and utilitarian liberalism can claim to offer a plausible explanation of post-unification Germany's policy on EU financial contributions.

Conclusion

Summary of empirical findings

This chapter has examined post-unification Germany's EU constitutional foreign policy on three issues, i.e. the extension of QMV in the Council, the strengthening of the EP's legislative powers and the contributions to the EU budget. Though these three cases can only give an incomplete picture of post-unification Germany's EU constitutional policy, they are particularly suited to uncover changes in Germany's integration policy after unification. Each case is concerned with Germany's *general* (as opposed to issue specific) commitment to furthering European integration.

The empirical analyses have revealed that post-unification Germany's EU constitutional policy has features of both continuity and change. Whereas a policy change has taken place on the issue of financial contributions, post-unification Germany has continued its policy on institutional issues, i.e. on extending QMV in the Council and on strengthening the EP's legislative powers.

Evaluation of theories

In each case, three theories have competed for an explanation of post-unification Germany's foreign policy behaviour. Whereas in the first two cases only one theory has offered an accurate prediction, case 3 has turned out to be overdetermined, i.e. Germany's policy has been correctly predicted by two different theories.

Germany's policy on institutional issues has best been predicted by *constructivism*. At first glance, this finding does not fit in the state of the art about Germany's policy on the extension of QMV. Andrew Moravcsik, for example, has argued that member states are concerned with making credible commitments rather than being moved by federalist ideology when institutional choices, including the extension of QMV, are at stake (1998: 485ff.). Following Moravcsik, those member states with preferences close to the median European position are likely to support QMV in order to achieve their policy aims. However, Moravcsik has been concerned with predicting member states' positions on QMV in specific issue areas: 'Although the credible commitments view best explains the delegation and pooling of *specific* and *precise* powers, it leaves unexplained patterns of support for more *general* institutional commitments' (Moravcsik 1998: 488). Furthermore, the likely effect of QMV on policies may be clear in the realm of economic policies but it is much harder to determine in non-economic issue areas for which constitutional ideas may thus become influential (Jachtenfuchs 1999: 329). Therefore, the findings of this study may best be seen as adding insights about general institutional choice to Moravcsik's research on issue-specific institutional choice.

In the case of the strengthening of the EP's legislative powers, only constructivism delivered a valid prediction. This finding confirms recent research on member state preferences (see Jachtenfuchs 1999; Wagner 1999; Moravcsik 1998): according to Andrew Moravcsik, 'patterns of support for general institutional provisions reflect federalist ideology' which, for Moravcsik, is 'clearest in support for the European Parliament' (1998: 489). Here the German behaviour 'appears to reflect public and parliamentary ideology' (1998: 488). Similarly, Markus Jachtenfuchs has argued that ideas best explain member states' preferences with regard to the EP (1999: 345). Both scholars hold that the consequences of delegating powers to the EP are highly uncertain so that actors cannot derive their preferences from (material) interests.

In contrast to Germany's institutional policy, its policy on its contributions to the EU budget cannot be explained by constructivism. German decision makers have consciously disregarded European norms and have not followed a logic of appropriateness, as predicted by constructivism, but a logic of consequentiality. It has remained an open question, however, whether material gains or autonomy gains motivated the German government to increase its efforts to achieve reduced net payments to the EU. Both *neorealism* and *utilitarian liberalism* correctly predicted post-unification Germany's behaviour and can therefore offer plausible explanations. Because theory-led analyses of member states' contribution policies have been missing from the scholarly literature, this finding cannot be related to any state of the art.

Germany's EU constitutional policy should have been an easy case for *neorealism* because constitutional issues are closely linked to the distribution of power, to the delegation of sovereignty and to (financial) burden sharing. However, neorealism's record has been rather poor. The general neorealist prediction that Germany will step up its pursuit of power politics has been substantiated in only one case, namely Germany's policy on its contributions to the EU budget. This concurs with Simon Bulmer's observation that 'the realist school is of greatest value where member states act in a competitive manner with the European Community, such as in arguments about contributions to the EC budget' (1991: 71).

By paying additional attention to the low security pressures on post-unification Germany, *modified neorealism* derived a prediction distinct from neorealism in one case. Whereas neorealism expected Germany to oppose any further extension of QMV in the Council, modified neorealism correctly predicted continued German support for such a reform. Thus in the realm of EU constitutional policy the modification of neorealism has enhanced its explanatory power. However, modified neorealism's prediction turned out to be less accurate than the constructivist one. Taken together, the neorealist theories of foreign policy have only modestly contributed to an explanation of post-unification Germany's EU constitutional policy.

Constructivism has turned out to have a high predictive capacity for Germany's policy on institutional issues, though it cannot explain Germany's contribution policy. Still, constructivism has been the most successful theory in explaining post-unification Germany's EU constitutional policy. This finding fits well with a growing body of literature which has emphasized the importance of 'ideational' factors in Germany's EU policy. The better part of that literature, however, has been concerned with tracing Germany's EU policy to an Europeanized identity (Anderson 1999; Risse *et al.* 1999; Katzenstein 1997b), i.e. to an ideational variable with rather unspecific implications for state behaviour in a given issue area. In contrast, this case study has tried to identify issue-specific norms which can be expected to guide German policy.

Utilitarian liberalism's record is similar to that of neorealism. On institutional issues, utilitarian liberalism has failed to offer an empirically confirmed explanation. On the issue of financial contributions, the utilitarian-liberal prediction concurs with the empirical finding, though the available evidence does not allow discrimination between power politics and gain-seeking policy.

Overall, no one theory has been able to present a comprehensive explanation of Germany's EU constitutional policy (see table 7.3). The pattern of the theories' explanatory power points to a division of labour between constructivism, on the one hand, and the 'rationalist' theories, i.e. neorealism and utilitarian liberalism, on the other. According to that division of (explanatory) labour, norms become an important explanatory variable if distributional consequences from alternative actions are difficult to calculate. When distributional consequences are obvious, as in the negotiations on financial contributions, rationalist theories can correctly predict state behaviour. Whenever distributional consequences are uncertain, e.g. when decision making power is pooled or delegated, decision-makers follow a logic of appropriateness rather than a logic of consequentiality.

Table 7.3 Summary of empirical findings and explanatory power
of theories

Case	Continuity/ change	Neorealism	Utilitarian Liberalism	Constructivism
Extension of QMV	Continuity	Disconfirmed Modified neorealism: correct prediction but puzzling further observables	Disconfirmed	Confirmed
Strengthening of EP	Continuity	Disconfirmed	Disconfirmed	Confirmed
Net contributions to EU budget	Change	Disconfirmed	Confirmed	Correct prediction but puzzling further observables

Contribution to the state of the art

This chapter has contributed to the study of Germany's EU policy in
several ways.

In terms of describing post-unification Germany's EU constitutional
policy, this chapter has presented additional empirical data. Whereas
this chapter could build on a growing body of literature that describes
Germany's policy during the intergovernmental negotiations on the
SEA, as well as on the Maastricht and Amsterdam Treaties, a state of
the art on Germany's policy regarding its financial contributions was
virtually non-existent. Due to the ongoing negotiations, information
could be obtained by conducting a large number of interviews. The
description of Germany's behaviour during the negotiations on the
Santer I package adds to the available data about post-unification
Germany's EU policy.

For one case, this chapter has offered an alternative interpretation of
Germany's policy in terms of continuity versus change. Whereas Germany's insistence on unanimity for some provisions in Amsterdam has
frequently been regarded as signalling a change in post-unification
Germany's EU policy, this chapter has shown that Germany's behaviour
in Amsterdam was in line with its pre-unification policy.

As regards an overall assessment of post-unification Germany's EU
policy in terms of continuity and change, this chapter has arrived at a

complex picture. Whereas Germany's policy on institutional issues has been marked by continuity, it's policy on its financial contributions changed markedly in the second half of the 1990s. This finding is consistent with many other studies which conclude that 'since 1990 a complex pattern of continuity and change in Germany's European policies has emerged' (Anderson 1999: 2). This study did not confirm the thesis that post-unification Germany has put greater emphasis on keeping (or increasing) its room for unilateral policy, as some observers have argued (Frenkler 1998; Wernicke 1998; Janning 1996b: 36–7; Deubner 1995: 11). Germany's policy on extending QMV in the Council and on strengthening the EP's legislative powers point in the opposite direction.

Finally, concerning the explanatory power of neorealism, constructivism and utilitarian liberalism, each theory can claim to contribute to the explanation of Germany's EU constitutional policy. With accurate predictions in two cases (and some additional evidence), however, constructivism clearly fared best. By reaching this conclusion this case study adds further evidence to the growing body of literature that emphasizes the importance of norms (and other ideational variables) for the study of Germany's EU policy (see, among others, Anderson 1999; Risse *et al.* 1999; Bulmer, Jeffery and Paterson 1998; Katzenstein 1997b).

Notes

1 Protocols of the interviews conducted for this case study are available from the author.

2 This is not to say that private actors are not concerned with constitutional issues. Quite the opposite: private actors such as trade unions and industry associations have frequently expressed their views on constitutional issues. However, they are not part of the German EU constitutional policy network because their level of situative mobilization is too low.

3 See SPD 1959: 165; 1980: 15; 1987: 42; 1989: 13; 1990: 22; 1998: 72; CDU 1978: 200; 1994: 85; CDU/CSU 1980: 11; 1983: 12; 1987: 13; 1994: 48; FDP 1983: 16; 1987: 8; 1994: 126; 1997: 44; 1998: 95; Bündnis 90/Die Grünen 1994a: 56; 1998: 137; PDS 1998: 51.

4 The Luxembourg Compromise is a short declaration by the EC foreign ministers of January 1966 which 'maintained the principle of majority voting but acknowledged that "when very important issues are at stake, discussions must be continued until unanimous agreement is reached"' (Dinan 1998: 332).

5 See the speeches by MP Vogel (SPD), MP Rumpf (FDP) and MP Hellwig (CDU) on 27 June 1985 (PlPr. 10/149) and by MP Rudolf Seiters, MP Gero Pfennig (both CDU) and MP Heidemarie Wieczorek-Zeul (SPD) on 11 June 1997 (PlPr. 13/180).

6 See the speech by Foreign Minister Genscher to the EP on 19 November 1981, quoted in Auswärtiges Amt 1995: 482. See also Gaddum 1994: 208–9.

7 See Corbett 1987: 245; Kirchner 1992: 46; *Frankfurter Rundschau*, 4 July 1985; *General-Anzeiger*, 19 and 23 October 1985; *Die Welt*, 13 November 1985; *FAZ* 12 December 1985.

8 Text of the letter addressed to Andreotti by Kohl and Mitterand of 6 December 1990, in Laursen and Vanhoonacker 1992: 313–14, quote p. 314.

9 CONF-UP 1805/91 of 6 May 1991. The list is only concerned with existing Community policies. It therefore does not deal with either new Community policies or policies in the second and third pillars.

10 The constitutional issues included provisions on electing the EP (art. 138 (3)); on the composition of the Commission (art. 157 (1)) and the ECJ (art. 165 (4)); on the number of advocates-general (art. 166); on the number and the appointment of members of the Economic and Social Council (art. 194); on own ressources (art. 201); and on the rules governing the languages of the institutions (art. 217), the accession of new member states (art. 237) and association agreements with third states and international organizations (art. 238).

11 See the German government's declaration on current issues of European policy (Bulletin des Presse- und Informationsamt der Bundesregierung, no. 51 of 26 June 1995) and the joint letter of Chancellor Kohl and French President Chirac to the President of the European Council, John Bruton of Ireland (Bulletin des Presse- und Informationsamt der Bundesregierung, no. 102 of 9 December 1996).

12 See the German delegation, non-paper of 2 June 1997. For decisions on the number of members of the Commission (art. 157), of judges on the ECJ (art. 165) and of advocates-general (art. 166), Germany had advocated unanimity in 1991 and accepted QMV in 1997. Compared with a proposal on the extension of QMV tabled by the Dutch Presidency, the German list was more comprehensive regarding constitutional provisions, with the exception of art. 151 (2) (appointment of the Council's Secretary-General) that was only listed by the Dutch.

13 Altogether, the Amsterdam Treaty extends QMV to sixteen articles, eleven of which were newly introduced by the Amsterdam Treaty (Nentwich and Falkner 1997). The new policies include customs cooperation (art. 135), fight against fraud (art. 280) and protection of data (art. 286).

14 See Bundesrat-Drucksachen 31/86, 50/86, 150/86, 600/86, 220/90, 550/90, 252/91, 680/91, 810/92, 169/95 and 667/95, as well as conclusions from

German EU constitutional foreign policy

227

the conferences of the *Länder* ministers for European Affairs on 24 January 1996 and 25 June 1997 (unpublished documents).

15 See *Bundestag* resolutions of 23 October 1985, 6 December 1995 and 11 June 1997 (Drs. 10/4088, 13/3040, 13/3247 and 13/7901).

16 The so-called 'Isoglucose Ruling' of 1980 (case C–138/79), quoted in Corbett, Jacobs and Shackleton 1995: 191. See also Zuleeg 1993 and 1982: 26.

17 BVerfGE 89, 155; English quote taken from Winkelmann 1994: 753.

18 See SPD 1980: 15; 1987: 43; 1990: 22 and 1998: 74; CDU/CSU 1980: 11; 1987: 13; 1990: 19; 1994: 49 and 1998: 29; CDU/CSU: 1980: 11; 1987: 13 and 1994: 49; FDP 1980: 17; 1983: 17; 1987: 8; 1990: 22; 1994: 126; Bündnis 90/Die Grünen: 1994b: 57; 1998: 138; PDS: 1993: 24.

19 See *Bundestag* debates of 27 June 1985 (PlPr. 10/149), of 17 October 1991 (PlPr. 12/50), of 6 November 1991 (12/53) and of 11 June 1997 (PlPr. 13/180).

20 As the tables below show, before unification (1983–89), an average of 47.2 per cent of those Germans questioned would 'personally like the European Parliament to play a more important part than it does now'. After unification (1991–98) the number dropped slightly to an average of 44.6 per cent. The average number of Germans favouring a less important role for the EP was 13.1 per cent before and 13.7 per cent after unification (see *Eurobarometer* No. 19 (1983) ff.).

Before unification

	1/83 %	2/83 %	1/84 %	2/84 %	1/85 %	2/85 %	1/86 %	2/86 %	1/87 %	2/87 %	1/88 %	2/88 %	1/89 %	2/89 %	Average %
More important role	49	57	44	55	49	51	52	46	39	46	42	41	41	49	47.2
Same role	17	12	20	18	20	16	16	18	19	20	21	24	23	19	18.8
Less important role	11	10	10	12	11	14	13	12	15	15	14	16	15	15	13.1
Don't know	23	21	26	15	20	19	19	24	27	19	23	19	21	17	20.9

After unification

	1/91 %	2/91 %	1/92 %	2/92 %	1/93 %	2/94 %	1/95 %	2/95 %	1/97 %	2/97 %	1/98 %	2/98 %	Average %
More important role	60	53	51	53	47	44	43	41	37	30	37	39	44.6
Same role	15	16	16	13	19	24	18	25	22	29	27	25	20.8
Less important role	10	10	12	14	16	12	17	15	19	15	12	13	13.7
Don't know	15	22	21	20	19	20	21	20	21	26	24	23	21

Source: *Eurobarometer* (question was not put in 2/93, 1/94, 1/96 and 2/96).

21 Among the critics were German MEPs and the German Europa-Union (see *Die Zeit*, 18 October 1985; *FAZ*, 28 October 1985).

22 Foreign Office State Secretary Ruhfus according to the *Generalanzeiger* (Bonn) of 23 October 1985.

23 Joint letter by German Chancellor Kohl and French President Mitterrand to the Irish Presidency of 19 April 1990, quoted in Laursen and Vanhoonacker 1992: 276.

24 Joint letter by Chancellor Kohl and President Mitterrand to the Italian Presidency of 6 December 1990, quoted in Laursen and Vanhoonacker 1992: 313.

25 Cf. Bulletin des Presse- und Informationsamtes der Bundesregierung, No. 108, 24 November 1994.

26 Among the prominent statements on German EU constitutional policy that omit any reference to a strengthened EP are the agreement establishing the coalition between the CDU, CSU and FDP of 11 November 1994 and the statement on preparing the European Council in Cannes of 26 June 1995 (Bulletin des Presse- und Informationsamt der Bundesregierung No. 51, 26 June 1995).

27 See Joint letter by Chancellor Kohl and French President Chirac of 6 December 1995 and governmental statement on the Madrid European Council of 7 December 1995.

28 Author's interviews with Elmar Brok, MEP on 15 October 1998; with Richard Corbett, MEP on 14 October 1998; and with Axel Schäfer, MEP on 27 October 1998, as well as with members of the European Commission.

29 See Drs 10/4088, 12/3896, 13/3040, 13/3247 and 13/7901.

30 See Bundesrat-Drucksachen 279/89, 220/90, 680/91, 500/92, 169/95 and 667/95.

31 See the Interinstitutional Agreement on Budgetary Discipline and Improvement of the Budgetary Procedure (*Official Journal*(*OJ*) *L 185*, 15 July 1988) and Interinstitutional Agreement on Budgetary Discipline and Improvement of the Budgetary Procedure (*OJ, C 331*, 29 October 1993).

32 COM (97) 2000 fin.

33 This is also the perception held in the Foreign Office and the Ministry of Finance (author's interviews with officials of the Foreign Office and the Ministry of Finance in Bonn, May 1999).

34 Any change in the size of Germany's EU contributions slightly changes the *Länder* share of VAT revenues (Clostermeyer 1997: 147).

35 See Council Decision 85/257/EEC, Euratom of 7 May 1985, On the System of the Communities' Own Resources, *OJ*, L 128, 14 May 1985; and Council Decision 88/376/EEC, Euratom of 24 June 1988, On the System of the Communities' Own Resources, *OJ*, L 185, 15 July 1988.

36 The author's interviews in the Federal Ministry of Finance revealed that, in Germany, even advocates of a general abatement mechanism consider

that proposal as *non-communautaire* though justifiable in the light of the persisting British rebate.

37 Germany's contributions are roughly in line with its capacity to pay. The British rebate is largely responsible for the fact that, with the exception of the UK, all member states' contributions slightly exceed their GNP-based capacity to pay.

38 The *Bundestag* has discussed the system of own resources in various contexts, such as the federal budget and, more recently, the Agenda 2000 (see the debates on 1 December 1983 (PlPr. 10/40), 31 March 1995 (PlPr. 13/32), 11 December 1997 (PlPr. 13/210) and 10 December 1998 (PlPr. 14/14)). As compared with the election platforms, the size of the German contribution has received more acceptance and criticism has focused more on Community expenditure.

39 Agreement establishing the coalition between the CDU, CSU and FDP, Bonn, 11 November 1994.

40 European Commission, *Financing the European Union*, COM (98) 0560.

41 See especially Schröder's speeches at a Social Democratic convention in Saarbrücken on 8 December 1998 (www.spd.de/kampa/konferenz/reden/schroeder.htm, December 1998) and in the *Bundestag* on 12 December 1998.

42 See *Aufbruch und Erneuerung. Deutschlands Weg ins 21. Jahrhundert*. Agreement establishing the coalition between the SPD and Bündnis 90/Die Grünen, Bonn, 20 October 1998 (www.spd.de/politik/koalition/index.htm, November 1998).

43 Author's interviews with officials of the German Foreign Office, the Federal Ministry of Finance and the Directorate-General XIX (Budgets) of the Commission of the European Communities, May 1999.

44 See 'Finanzbeziehungen der Bundesrepublik Deutschland zur Europäischen Union', Report of the working group of state finance ministries to the conference of finance ministers, June 1997, Bundesrat-Drs 904/97, 28 November 1997, and 'Memorandum der Bayerischen Staatsregierung zu den Vorschlägen der Europäischen Kommission in der "Agenda 2000"', 16 September 1997.

8

German foreign trade policy within the EU and GATT

Corinna Freund

Introduction [1]

A country's foreign trade encompasses its export and import relations with other countries. Foreign trade policy can be described as the 'sum of all public measures taken in order to influence foreign trade' (*Gabler Wirtschaftslexikon* 1998). These measures may be directed towards the liberalization of markets, but may also aim at the protection of certain sectors of the domestic economy (Winter 1994: 33; Koch 1992: 134).

The most distinguishing general feature of German foreign trade policy is its multilateral character (Kirste 1998: 317ff.). First, and most importantly, Germany's scope for unilateral action in foreign trade policy is severely circumscribed by the fact that the competences for autonomous as well as for contractual foreign trade policy have been transferred to the EC since 1970.[2] Second the multilateral character of Germany's foreign trade policy is deepened by its membership in GATT and the World Trade Organization (WTO). Much of Germany's foreign trade policy is shaped by regular multilateral negotiations which take place in the GATT/WTO framework. Both the EC and Germany are legally committed not to contravene existing GATT/WTO obligations (Hilf 1986: 21).

Due to the importance of multilateral relations for Germany's foreign trade policy, the issue of international trade cooperation is the key aspect for investigation. In order to explain German foreign trade policy, we need to establish under which conditions and in which form Germany is willing to cooperate with other countries in trade affairs. The central role of international trade cooperation for Germany is also the focus of the contemporary literature on Germany's foreign trade policy. There is a broad consensus that Germany's foreign trade policy can generally be characterized as free trade oriented and as supportive of multilateral rules for international trade. However, it has not yet been examined whether this overall tendency of Germany's foreign trade policy behaviour has remained unchanged after unification. This shortcoming of the literature on German foreign trade policy is addressed by this case study, which investigates to what extent post-unification Germany's foreign trade policy has been marked by change or continuity.

Another topic which has not received sufficient attention in research on German foreign trade policy is the theory-led explanation of Germany's pro-liberal and multilateral stance with regard to foreign trade. In general, this overall tendency of German foreign trade policy is attributed to both strong domestic interests in open international markets and to a free trade norm rooted in the societal norm of a market economy. At the same time, domestic interests are believed to take precedence over societal norms in the case of conflict: it is emphasized that there are some issue areas of foreign trade policy in which Germany displays a highly protectionist behaviour, such as in agriculture, steel, coal mining and shipbuilding. This contradiction, it is argued, can be explained by looking at the specific configuration of domestic interests: while the general outward orientation of the German economy makes trade liberalization profitable for Germany's domestic actors in most cases, in some sectors, protectionist interests may prevail (Kirste 1998: 314ff.; Molsberger and Duijm 1997; Ragnitz 1996: 64ff.; Rode 1996: 174ff.; Donges 1995: 66ff.; Hayes 1993: 74ff.; Howell and Hume 1992: 156ff.; Weiss 1989: 625).

So far, however, it has not been tested whether Germany's power position, its domestic interests or societal and international norms can best explain Germany's foreign trade policy behaviour. This is what this case study sets out to do. Case 1 concentrates on Germany's foreign trade policy behaviour with regard to a highly salient issue of multilateral trade liberalization, i.e. trade in agriculture. Case 2 analyses the German position in an instance of regional trade liberalization which is partially at the expense of third countries, i.e. the liberalization of public procurement in the telecommunications sector of the EC. These two cases were selected because, from a larger set of cases, they best fulfil the following three criteria. First, they allow for the formulation of a neorealist prediction. Second, each of them deals with a subject matter that has not changed in substance over the course of unification and can therefore be taken as an indicator of change or continuity in Germany's foreign trade policy. Third, they concern issues that were subject to a major controversy within the EC in which Germany took a clear stance. In that way, it is possible actually to single out Germany's behaviour despite the transfer of national decision-making competence to the Community level. At the same time, it can be ensured that the respective issues were important to Germany and that they can thus be taken as representative of Germany's foreign trade policy behaviour.

The two cases of German foreign trade policy behaviour will be investigated below. In the next section, I will outline in more general terms what kind of German foreign trade policy behaviour with regard to international cooperation on trade liberalization is to be expected from the vantage point of three competing foreign policy theories: neorealism, utilitarian liberalism and constructivism.

Foreign policy theories and German foreign trade policy

Neorealism

Neorealism assumes that Germany will strive for enhancing its autonomy and influence but will favour autonomy over influence if the two are at odds. International cooperation on trade liberalization is an example of a conflict between autonomy and influence maximization: On the one hand, an agreement on trade liberalization gives Germany the opportunity to enhance its influence on other states' foreign trade policy. At the same time, however, Germany's own autonomy will be circumscribed. As Germany is assumed to be subject to high security pressures, neorealism argues, Germany cannot afford any loss of autonomy. Yet trade liberalization involves a severe loss of autonomy, as it not only implies a limit to Germany's freedom of action, but may also lay the ground for greater international interdependence, of which other countries may take advantage. At the same time, trading partners may, in the future, use their gains from trade liberalization in order to threaten Germany's security. According to neorealism, therefore, states will generally oppose international cooperation on trade liberalization (Gowa 1994: 46ff.). As its power position has improved after unification, neorealism predicts that Germany will resist trade liberalization even more strongly after unification.

Modified neorealism holds that Germany was confronted with high security pressures before unification, but has faced a declining level of threat since then. Modified neorealism infers that Germany will no longer accord primacy to gains in autonomy after unification. Instead,

Germany will be prepared to give up autonomy in return for substantial gains in influence and may therefore support international cooperation on trade liberalization. However, substantial gains in influence for Germany can only be expected if trade liberalization enhances the vulnerability of Germany's trading partners (by means of the rise of asymmetric interdependence to Germany's advantage). The achievement of relative gains is the precondition for Germany's assent to international trade liberalization after unification; absolute gains alone will not be sufficient. In order to derive modified neorealism's expectation about Germany's stance towards trade liberalization after unification, therefore, it is necessary to establish on a case-specific basis whether Germany is able to realize relative gains from trade liberalization.

Utilitarian liberalism

Germany's foreign trade policy making is composed of various sub-sectoral policy networks. Thus utilitarian-liberal predictions about Germany's foreign trade policy after unification have to be derived on a case-specific basis. It is possible, though, to describe some overall characteristics of the German foreign trade policy-making process and to give an idea of the general foreign trade policy orientations of those domestic actors that frequently take part in that process.

To begin with, decision-making competence with regard to Germany's foreign trade policy is highly fragmented. In most cases, several ministers are involved in the policy-making process. Even though the Federal Minister of Economics (BMWi) has the overall responsibility for Germany's foreign trade policy, many foreign trade policy decisions affect the responsibilities of other federal ministers as well (Westerhoff 1998: 104ff.; Hayes 1993: 78ff.; Howell and Hume 1992: 153ff.). A special role in the settlement of inter-ministerial conflicts occasionally involves the Federal Chancellor, as art. 65 of the Basic Law confers on him the power to give policy guidelines to the Cabinet. However, the Chancellor only makes use of his *Richtlinienkompetenz* if trade policy issues will impact on his prospects for re-election.

The fragmentation of foreign trade decision-making competence within the PAS is increased by the federal constitution of Germany. Since 1986, the German government has had to take the positions of the *Länder* governments represented in the *Bundesrat* into account if trade matters that involve essential *Länder* interests are negotiated within the EC. The actual influence of the *Länder* thus varies from topic to topic, depending on the extent of their domestic competence in the respective area of economic policy (Fischer 1999; Blume and Rex 1998; Lang 1997; Welck 1991: 35ff.).

Another distinguishing feature of Germany's foreign trade policy, as compared with other issue areas of German foreign policy, is the frequent inclusion of private actors in the policy-making process. As private actors involved in German foreign trade policy are typically well organized and enjoy a high level of representation, they are often in a position to provide useful information and advice for public policy makers and may help to legitimize foreign trade policies. Many of them have therefore found privileged access to ministers and to the Chancellor. The same is true for large individual corporations, which frequently try to lobby public actors independently of industry associations. Due to their important role for the development of the German economy, they have typically managed to establish close exchange relationships with the Chancellor and several ministers (Koopmann, Kreienbaum and Borrmann 1997: 46ff.; Hayes 1993: 81ff.; Howell and Hume 1992: 150ff.; Beyme 1989: 144ff.; Weiss 1989: 625).[3]

As PAS actors in Germany's foreign trade policy networks typically only have a medium level of autonomy *vis-à-vis* private actors, and decision-making competence is highly dispersed within the PAS, Germany's foreign trade policy is characterized by corporatist networks which include a variety of private and PAS actors. With regard to the general foreign trade policy orientations of Germany's domestic actors, utilitarian liberalism holds that, for many of them, the support of trade liberalization, and especially of multilateral trade liberalization, is a priority. Due to the pronounced trade dependence of the German economy, many domestic actors hold strong preferences for open world markets. Multilateral trading rules are of particular significance since the German economy is to a large degree composed of small and medium companies . As these companies do not have much bargaining power in direct negotiations with foreign governments on market access, the advantage they derive from multilateral liberalization is considerable. For large German companies, multilateral trade liberalization is equally important for other reasons. They operate increasingly on a multinational scale. In order to exploit the advantages of transnational production, multilateral trade liberalization is clearly more effective than bilateral bargaining.

According to utilitarian liberalism, multilateral trade liberalization is typically the priority of the Minister of Economics (as he is in charge of ensuring a good performance of the German industry), the German Chancellor (because of his interest in re-election) and for umbrella industry associations such as the Bundesverband der Deutschen Industrie (BDI) and Deutscher Industrie- und Handelstag (DIHT) (since the majority of their members have high stakes in foreign trade). In general, the Foreign Minister will also support multilateral trade liberalization as it is conducive to stabilizing Germany's overall relations with its trading partners. In sum, utilitarian liberalism holds that it is possible to identify a strong free trade coalition in many of Germany's foreign trade policy networks (Kirste 1998: 315, 322; Ragnitz 1996: 64ff.; Hayes 1993: 74ff.; Howell and Hume 1992: 166ff.).[4]

However, not all domestic actors benefit from trade liberalization. For instance, those private economic actors that gear their activities primarily towards the domestic market do not gain from trade liberalization but instead face import competition. Similarly, trade liberalization does not pay off for private economic actors that are not sufficiently competitive on an international scale. They can be assumed to favour tariff protection and export subsidies instead. In some foreign trade policy issue areas, such as in agriculture, those private actors who expect economic losses from foreign trade liberalization are assertive and have also found access to the most assertive PAS actors. They may then be able to push successfully for a rather protectionist foreign trade policy (Howell and Hume 1992: 181ff.).

Constructivism

Looking at *international norms*, the free trade norm certainly plays a prominent role within the normative frameworks of both the EC and the WTO. As we will see below, however, the respective stipulations are not sufficiently specific. With regard to agricultural trade liberalization, it is possible to deduce a value-based expectation about appropriate German behaviour from EC norms.

The subject matter of trade liberalization forms the core of the GATT regime. According to one important principle underlying the GATT, free world trade is conducive to the welfare of all nations. Therefore, the removal of all trade barriers is declared to be the long-term goal of the GATT (Seitz and Windfuhr 1989: 50ff, 66ff.). Contrary to the general free trade norm, however, another GATT norm stipulates that exceptions to this norm are legitimate under certain conditions (Müller

1993b: 58; Finlayson and Zacher 1981: 570).[5] A hierarchy of norms could be a way of solving the conflict between liberal and protectionist trade norms in the GATT. However, such a hierarchy does not exist. Instead, from its inception the GATT has tried to achieve multilateral trade liberalization while leaving member states scope for national adjustment. In order to describe this compromise, John G. Ruggie has coined the term 'embedded liberalism'.[6] Consequently, the GATT does not demand unconditional trade liberalization from its members, but is based on the expectation shared by its members that international negotiations will eventually lead to further trade liberalization – despite the consideration for national sensitivities. To this end, the GATT has developed the practice of multilateral rounds on trade liberalization (Gerke 1994: 4; Müller 1993b: 58; Ipsen and Haltern 1991: 14ff.). As the GATT leaves the outcome of negotiations on further trade liberalization to its members, it does not stipulate any specific concessions on trade issues that so far have not been dealt with in the GATT. As both case 1 and case 2 deal with trade issues that had not previously been regulated by the GATT framework, it is not possible to deduce an expectation about appropriate foreign trade policy behaviour of Germany on the basis of GATT norms concerning those subject matters.

General norms of the EC on foreign trade are formulated in art. 110f. of the TEC. In art. 110, the EC declares its intention 'to contribute to the gradual removal of impediments to international trade and of tariff barriers'. Similar provisions are found in the preamble to the TEC and in arts. 2 and 3 of the TEC. According to several rulings of the ECJ, however, art. 110 leaves considerable discretionary powers to the EC (Neumann and Welge 1996: 629; Nicolaysen 1996: 477–8; Reuter 1995: 51ff.). In particular, the EC is not obliged to apply Common Market trading standards to trade with third countries (ECJ ruling 1976, 811). In general, art. 110 is seen as a dynamic stipulation, i.e. as a matter of political interpretation (ECJ rulings C–897/73, C–907/73 and C–1493/87).

EC norms are more specific with regard to agricultural trade, however. EC member states share a norm according to which domestic agricultural markets shall be protected from foreign competition. This can be concluded from an analysis of art. 39f. of the TEC. According to this article, the CAP is to achieve an adequate standard of living for European farmers, a stabilization of the common agricultural market and inland supply with food. Even though these stipulations do not directly pertain to foreign trade in agriculture, the implicitly protectionist character of the CAP is evident. For instance, all agricultural market orders have to meet three criteria in order to conform to the CAP's overall goals: 'unity of markets', 'financial solidarity' and 'Community preference'. With regard to foreign trade in agriculture, the principle of Community preference is of particular significance. It states that agricultural market orders of the EC have to give Common Market consumers incentives to favour the Community's agricultural products over agricultural products from third countries. While the exact scope of the principle of Community preference is unclear, it is obvious that the functioning of the Community's agricultural markets is accorded primacy over agricultural trade relations with third countries (Koester 1996: 142ff.; Nicolaysen 1996: 401ff.; Ahner 1996: 847, 850). According to the ECJ's rulings, the EC's agricultural policy goals stated in art. 39f. of the TEC take precedence over the EC's general free trade norm stated in art. 110 of the TEC in cases of conflict (Nicolaysen 1996: 403).

The *societal norms* with regard to international cooperation on trade liberalization indicate an issue area-specific split: while there is an overall norm in Germany to promote free trade, protectionist norms prevail with regard to the agricultural sector.

The general free trade norm forms part of, but is not sufficiently specific in, the Basic Law or the Foreign Trade Act (*Außenwirtschaftsgesetz*).[7] In contrast, indications of a free trade norm in the election platforms and party programmes of Germany's political parties reveal that the norm has a sufficient degree of both commonality and specificity. From 1980 on, the CDU, the CSU, the FDP and the SPD agree that Germany should support free trade. They argue that economic growth is desirable and that open world markets contribute to economic growth. Therefore, free trade is seen as beneficial not only for Germany, but for all trading partners. Possible adjustment problems of individual economic sectors, for example, are not considered a legitimate justification of trade barriers. At the same time, the idea of regional trading blocs is rejected. Instead, Germany should strive for worldwide trade liberalization in order to ensure world market access for all trading partners.[8] Many authors have argued that the German free trade norm is rooted in Germany's identity as a 'trading state' (Kirste 1998: 315; Bellers 1990: 43).

In striking contrast to the general free trade norm, the societal norms about Germany's foreign trade behaviour with regard to agricultural trade are highly protectionist. This is already evident in the Agriculture

Act (*Landwirtschaftsgesetz*) of 1955. According to art. 1 of this Act, the German government is obliged to protect the domestic agricultural sector by means of tax, credit, price and trade policies. The goal of German agricultural policy is not only to ensure the overall survival of the agricultural sector of the economy, but also to offset the existing natural and economic disadvantages farmers have to cope with (Gaddum 1994: 118; Gabriel 1993: 140; Schönweiß 1984: 20f.). The programmes and platforms of Germany's political parties point in the same direction. From 1980 on, the CDU, CSU and SPD express their convictions that the agricultural sector should not be exposed to un-fettered foreign competition. They reason that the agricultural sector cannot be regarded as just another branch of the domestic economy but that it is a vital component of domestic society and needs to be protected as such. In particular, Germany's typical small family farms are believed to make a unique contribution to the 'cultural landscape' of rural areas. In the view of all three parties, the survival of German agriculture needs to be ensured by public measures such as domestic price support and tariff protection.[9] In sum, we can identify a societal norm of sufficient commonality that Germany should strive to ensure the survival of its agricultural sector and an adequate income for its farmers, if necessary also on the basis of protectionist trade measures. This norm can be accorded a sufficient level of specificity: while we do not know which specific level of protection will be regarded as appropriate, we can assume that Germany will at least oppose agricultural trade liberalization measures which would entail severe income losses for German farmers.

Case 1: the conflict between the EC and the US about trade in agriculture in the GATT Uruguay round

Case description and dependent variable

At the beginning of the 1980s, a major shift occurred in EC–US agricultural trade relations: Whereas the EC trade balance in EC–US agricultural trade had been negative since the formation of the EEC, from 1984 on an EC surplus began to emerge which was growing constantly. This development was worrisome for the US as it already had to cope with a growing overall trade deficit and the EC was its most important export market for agricultural products. Further sales problems were caused by a general drop in demand for agricultural products on international agricultural markets since the beginning of the 1980s. The US was particularly annoyed by the fact that the growth of EC shares in international agricultural trade was not caused by shifting comparative advantages but was largely due to an increase of domestic support and export subsidies for the EC's farmers.[10] Even though the US provided heavy subsidies to its agricultural sector, too, from the mid-1980s it began actively to pursue the liberalization of agricultural markets. It reckoned that the liberalization of agricultural markets would help US agriculture to improve its world market share as it was more competitive than that of the EC.

In the period considered in this case study, the conflict over the liberalization of agricultural trade was dealt with in the Uruguay round of the GATT. According to US plans, international trade in agriculture, which so far had been largely exempted from the GATT discipline, should now be subjected to GATT regulation. This would lead, so the US hoped, to a far-reaching liberalization of international agricultural markets with regard to market access, domestic support and export subsidies. The EC, however, initially rejected these requests (Patterson 1997: 135ff.; Erdmann-Keefer 1991: 5ff.; Ipsen and Haltern 1991: 74ff.; Seitz and Windfuhr 1989: 38ff.).

How widely the respective stances of the US and the EC differed could be seen at the beginning of the Uruguay round. From 1987 on, the US called for a complete elimination of all agricultural subsidies by the year 2000, whereas the EC took the position that subsidies should be frozen at existing levels. The negotiations became deadlocked in 1990, and even temporarily collapsed at the end of that year. After the breakdown of the negotiations, the US' pressure on the EC intensified. The US made it clear that, without an agreement on agricultural liberalization, there would be no agreement on trade liberalization at all, and it stayed firm on this issue linkage until the end of the negotiations. In November 1992, the EC and the US concluded the 'Blair House agreement' which paved the way for a breakthrough in the agricultural negotiations in late 1993 (Vahl 1997: 91ff., 133ff., 166ff., 231, 240ff.; Woolcock and Hodges 1996: 310, 316ff.; Reblin 1993: 244ff.).[11]

In the view of many observers, the internal reform of the CAP, which the EC adopted in May 1992, was a prerequisite for the GATT agreement on agricultural trade liberalization. The main idea of the MacSharry reform was to combine radical price reductions[12] and compulsory set-aside schemes [13] with direct compensatory aid payments [14] to farmers. It represented a radical departure from the Community's traditional high-price policy which had been the major stumbling block to the kind of agricultural trade liberalization under discussion during the Uruguay round: without a reduction of domestic prices, a lowering of trade barriers and subsidized exports would have been virtually inconceivable (Anderson 1997: 96; Patterson 1997: 152ff.; Rieger 1996: 110ff.).[15]

The dependent variable in this case is *Germany's behaviour concerning the stance that the EC shall take towards the US demands for agricultural trade liberalization in the Uruguay round*. The German position on several proposals made in the Uruguay round will be examined. More specifically, it will be investigated whether Germany supported or opposed proposals which were aimed at making progress in the negotiations on agricultural trade liberalization. I shall consider the following important junctures during the negotiations:

• The conflict within the EC Council on the Community's proposal for the negotiations on the Mid Term Review of the Uruguay round in 1988.

• The disagreement within the EC Council on the definition of its position for the qualifying date of 15 October 1990.

• The dissent within the EC Council on its stance with regard to the compromise proposal for the agricultural negotiations made by GATT Director-General Dunkel at the end of 1991.

• The consultations of the EC Council in 1993 on the approval or disapproval of the Blair House agreement, which had been concluded between the EC Commission and the US delegation in November 1992.

Independent variables and predictions

Neorealism
The liberalization of agricultural trade which the US tries to achieve in the Uruguay round would yield a loss of autonomy for Germany. At the same time, Germany cannot expect to obtain any gains in influence. As a result, both neorealism and modified neorealism predict that Germany will oppose agricultural trade liberalization throughout the Uruguay round.

Losses of autonomy would result from the fact that any agreement on the liberalization of agricultural trade implies additional obligations for action for Germany. What is more, the removal of trade barriers could lead to increased international interdependence and provide economic gains to the US which it could eventually use against Germany. The liberalization of agricultural trade cannot be expected to bring about any gains in influence for Germany, as the US' agricultural production structure is more competitive than that of the EC. The dominance of the EC on international agricultural markets does not correspond to its actual international competitiveness but is mainly the result of export subsidies and domestic support measures. As the US proposals for agricultural market liberalization are directly targeted at the elimination, or at least the restriction, of exactly these agricultural policy tools, the EC – and Germany – would most likely lose international market share to the US. With the lowering of trade barriers, European – and German – agricultural producers would also face increasing import competition from US producers on the Community's agricultural market. On the whole, Germany would have to fear relative economic losses (Zangl 1999: 127ff.; Ipsen and Haltern 1991: 77).

The fact that the US puts increasing pressure on the EC (and thus on Germany) from 1991 on will have no impact on Germany's behaviour. On the contrary, Germany will be even more reluctant to submit to American demands after unification, as it has become more powerful. Both variants of neorealist foreign policy theory agree that in those situations in which Germany cannot expect gains in influence from cooperation with the US, Germany will refuse such a cooperation even more strongly than before unification. The MacSharry reform will not alter Germany's calculation of the prospective economic costs of agricultural trade liberalization either, as it does not affect the prospects of relative economic losses of Germany *vis-à-vis* the US.

As its power position has improved, post-unification Germany will step up its opposition, within the EC Council, against the liberalization of agricultural trade.

Utilitarian liberalism

Most assertive private actors
Two types of private actor can be distinguished in the present case. First, there are those private actors who are affected by the proposed liberalization of agricultural trade. In this respect, the DBV has to be considered. Second, those private actors have to be taken into account

whose interests are concerned by the issue linkage between the liberalization of agricultural trade and the successful conclusion of the Uruguay
round as a whole which the US established after 1990. Here, the industry
associations, the BDI and the DIHT, as well as the umbrella organization
of industrial trade unions, the (Deutscher Gewerkschaftsbund (DGB)),
have to be investigated.

As will be described below, utilitarian liberalism holds that, until
1990, the DBV will be the most assertive private actor. It is expected
to hold preferences with high intensity against the liberalization of
agricultural trade. From 1991 on, the industry associations, which are
assumed strongly to support the liberalization of agricultural trade, are
expected to be the most assertive private actors.

The *DBV*'s basic interest is to improve farmers' incomes. However,
the proposals for the liberalization of international trade in agriculture
which were discussed in the Uruguay round aimed at the lowering of
tariff barriers to foreign competition and at the reduction of both export
subsidies and domestic support measures. If those proposals were put
into practice, the incomes of German farmers would most likely
decrease. For this reason, the DBV is expected to oppose the liberalization of agricultural trade called for by the US. The DBV will hold
preferences with high intensity until mid-1991. However, after the
MacSharry plan has been put forward in July 1991, the DBV is held to
be only weakly mobilized. While the liberalization of agricultural trade
under discussion would certainly not help to raise the incomes of
German farmers (as it would allow for more international competition
and would reduce export subsidies), the immediate losses of income
would be limited due to the direct income tranfers provided for by the
MacSharry plan.

The basic interest of Germany's *industry associations* is to raise German industry's profits.[16] Due to the fact that German industry is highly
dependent on foreign trade, the industry associations are expected to
favour concessions on agricultural trade in exchange for progress in the
liberalization of trade in manufactures (Gabriel 1993: 88). Consequently,
the BDI and DIHT are held to support the liberalization of agricultural
markets. However, the industry associations' situative level of mobilization will only be high if Germany's trading partners impose a *quid pro
quo* between progress in the negotiations on agricultural market
liberalization and trade concessions in the industrial sector. This will
be the case in the years from 1991 to 1994, when the US makes it clear
that a substantial liberalization of the Community agricultural markets

will be the precondition for the success of the Uruguay round as a whole.[17] Thus it can be concluded that the situative level of mobilization of Germany's industry associations will be low until 1990, but will rise to a high level from 1991 on.

The basic interest of the *DGB* is to raise its members' incomes and to improve their general working conditions. As the DGB represents employees in the industrial and services sector of the German economy, the DGB is expected to be interested in the successful conclusion of the Uruguay round: Since the further liberalization of industrial trade and trade in services is likely to increase the sales opportunities of Germany's companies, working conditions could improve as well. As this is only an indirect connection with the DGB's basic interest, however, the DGB's level of situative mobilization is expected to be low throughout the Uruguay round.

Most assertive PAS actors
As will be shown below, the Chancellor can be expected to be the most assertive PAS actor throughout the Uruguay round, as he will be strongly mobilized in both situative and structural terms. He will oppose the liberalization of agricultural trade liberalization before 1990, but will support it from 1991 on.

Political actors Political actors in the present case are the *Länder* governments represented in the *Bundesrat* and the Chancellor. The decision-making competence of the *Bundesrat* follows from the fact that the CAP touches upon essential interests of Germany's *Länder* (Welck 1991: 42; Schönweiß 1984: 17ff.). The *Länder* governments are also able to exert a considerable influence on the position of the BML by means of the conferences of the ministers of agriculture which take place twice a year.[18] The *Bundestag* does not have decision-making competence in this case, as agricultural trade policy lies within the exclusive competence of the Community. The EC Council decides on the mandate for, and adopts the results of, the negotiations of the EC Commission with the Community's trading partners with qualified majority; a formal ratification of trade agreements by the EC member states is not required (Neumann and Welge 1996: 638).

Political actors' level of situative mobilization is expected to be high as their basic interest in re-election is directly affected throughout the Uruguay round.

Until 1990, political actors' basic interest in re-election is held to be

directly affected because their interest in meeting partisan objectives is
concerned. At this time, the MacSharry plan has not yet been put
forward, and Germany's political actors are expected to worry that their
electoral support could decline due to the prospective economic losses
for Germany's farmers and the German food-processing industry.[19] The
interests of the agricultural sector are expected to be of particular
significance for the Chancellor and for CDU/CSU *Länder* governments,
as farmers are traditionally some of the most loyal voters for the
CDU/CSU (Patterson 1997: 147ff.; Schiller 1997: 466; Gabriel 1993: 93;
Haungs 1992). It is true that the relative importance of farmers' votes
for the election of the CDU and CSU has declined since the early 1980s
(Gluchowski and Wilamowitz-Moellendorff 1997: 197ff.; Patterson
1997: 157; Gabriel 1993: 92). However, the economic situation of
farmers continues to be an important determinant of political actors'
prospects for re-election as it not only influences the voting behaviour
of the farmers themselves, but also that of the voters in rural areas in
general: the economic situation of the farming sector is an important
determinant of the overall political mood and economic confidence of
the rural population.[20] Until 1990, therefore, Germany's political actors
are expected strongly to oppose the liberalization of agricultural trade.

From 1991 on, political actors' basic interest in re-election is held to
be directly affected as their interest in improving the performance of the
overall economy is concerned. After the breakdown of the agricultural
negotiations at the end of 1990, the US makes it explicit that it will link
its consent to the successful conclusion of the Uruguay round to concessions of the EC in the negotiations on agricultural trade. Thus the
protectionist position of the Community in the negotiations on agriculture turns out to seriously endanger the overall success of the Uruguay
round. Due to the pronounced export dependency of the German
economy, such an outcome would be detrimental to the performance
of the overall economy. As political actors' interest in improving the
performance of the economy is assumed to take precedence over their
interest in meeting partisan objectives, the further liberalization of trade
in manufactures and services is expected to be political actors' foremost
goal in this situation.[21] They are therefore expected to be willing to make
concessions in the agricultural negotiations in order to prevent a collapse
of the Uruguay round negotiations. In addition, the MacSharry plan has
been put forward by the Commission. It promises to dampen the negative
economic effects on Germany's agricultural sector considerably. From
1991 on, therefore, Germany's political actors are expected to support

a more conciliatory attitude of the EC towards US demands for a liberalization of agricultural markets.

Administrative and political-administrative actors   Formally, the ultimate responsibility for the approval of the negotiation mandates and results lies with the EC's foreign ministers constituting the General Affairs Council of the EC. In practice, however, the General Affairs Council consults with all the other Councils involved (Nicolaysen 1996: 514; Woolcock and Hodges 1996: 305). Therefore, the Minister of Agriculture, the Minister of Economics and the Foreign Minister have to be taken into account as political-administrative actors. In any case, however, they will be less assertive than the Chancellor, who is expected to be strongly mobilized in both situative and structural terms. Therefore, political-administrative actors will not be considered in more detail in this case.

Dominant actors and policy network structure
The Chancellor's level of autonomy from both the DBV and the industry associations is medium. On the one hand, the relationships between the Chancellor and both the DBV and the industry associations are characterized by a considerable degree of resource dependency: the Chancellor is interested in making use of the great capacity of both organizations to collect political and technical information. In addition, both organizations have a large membership and, respectively, reach many potential voters. Therefore, their cooperation is very helpful with regard to providing public support for the Chancellor's policy. On the other hand, however, the DBV's and the industry associations' rights to be informed or consulted by the Chancellor are only weakly institutionalized (Brösse 1999: 98ff.; Howell and Hume 1992: 161).[22]

Accordingly, the policy network structure will be corporatist during the whole period under consideration. Until 1990, the network is expected to be dominated by the Chancellor and the DBV. From 1991, the Chancellor and the industry associations are expected to be the dominant actors within the network.

Until 1990, all dominant network actors – the Chancellor and the DBV – are expected to oppose the liberalization of agricultural trade. From 1991 on, all dominant network actors – the Chancellor and the industry associations – are held to support agricultural market liberalization:

As Germany's domestic interests have changed from opposing the

liberalization of agricultural trade to supporting it, post-unification
Germany will no longer oppose, but instead support, within the EC
Council, the liberalization of agricultural trade.

Constructivism
International norms impacting on Germany's behaviour can be derived
from the TEC.[23] As was outlined on pp. 236–7, EC member states share
a norm according to which the domestic agricultural market shall be
protected from foreign competition. The norm has sufficient specificity,
since at least the Community's agricultural markets have to be shielded
off from any foreign competition which would seriously endanger them.
As was pointed out earlier, the liberalization of agricultural trade called
for by the US would in fact be incompatible with the structure of the
CAP as it exists until mid 1991. We can therefore predict that Germany
will oppose the US demands for agricultural trade liberalization in the
EC Council until mid 1991.

In July 1991, the situation changes. At this point, the Commission
puts forward the MacSharry plan for the reform of the CAP, which is
adopted by the Council – with minor changes – in May 1992 (Patterson
1997: 152ff.). Considering the EC norms identified above, the Mac-
Sharry plan is significant insofar as the EC member states, for the first
time, have a realistic perspective of achieving an agreement with the
US on agricultural trade that would be in line with the CAP. At the
same time, the MacSharry reform is likely to become accepted within
the EC, since internal problems of the CAP, in particular huge agricultural budget deficits, make a reform of the price support system quite
urgent (Patterson 1997: 154ff.; Rieger 1996: 115ff.). An assent to the
US proposals would therefore no longer call the CAP as such into
question. Domestic support could still be upheld, now primarily in the
form of direct income transfers. In sum, the MacSharry reform provides
the EC member states with a new behavioural alternative which would
allow the EC to agree to the US demands for agricultural trade liberalization without violating the EC norm of the protection of the
Community's agricultural sector. However, the norm does not stipulate
that the EC shall agree to international agricultural trade liberalization,
even under the provisions of the MacSharry reform of the CAP. As was
illustrated on p. 236, the EC's general free trade norm entailed in art.
110 of the TEC is not sufficiently specific either. Therefore, it is not
possible to derive a prediction about Germany's stance towards agricultural trade liberalization for the period after mid-1991.

Turning to *societal norms*, there is a norm of agricultural protection-ism shared within German society according to which Germany is supposed to ensure the survival of its agricultural sector and an adequate income for its farmers (see pp. 237–8). Given the structure of the CAP as it exists before the MacSharry plan has been published, severe losses of income for Germany's farmers would result from the agricultural trade liberalization called for by the US. The liberalization measures would reduce domestic prices, increase lower-priced foreign competi-tion from third countries and diminish the competitiveness of German farmers abroad. According to the societal norm of agricultural protec-tionism, therefore, Germany can be expected to oppose US plans for agricultural trade liberalization until July 1991. At the same time, however, the federal government is supposed to support free trade due to a general free trade norm described on p. 237. There is no indicator of a hierarchy between these two conflicting norms within German society. In fact, before 1990 this conflict of norms is not discussed in either party programmes or parliamentary debates. Until then, however, the incompatibility between the two norms was never as obvious as it was during the Uruguay round. Parliamentary debates indicate that, in 1990, when the conflict of societal norms had become more imminent, German society began to discuss explicitly the relationship between these two norms. Even then, however, the SPD and CDU/CSU emphas-ized that Germany would have to do justice to *both* societal norms during the negotiations on agricultural trade liberalization.[24] Therefore, it is not possible to derive a value-based expectation about appropriate German behaviour from societal norms until July 1991.

As is the case on the EC level, the MacSharry plan is also an important turning point on the domestic level insofar as it extends the range of norm-consistent alternatives of behaviour. The consent to US demands for agricultural trade liberalization would no longer call the protection of the German farming sector into question and would therefore no longer violate the domestic norm of agricultural protec-tion.[25] All farmers are certain to be compensated for the income losses which would result from price cuts. The domestic norm of agricultural protection certainly does not stipulate that Germany necessarily has to consent to agricultural trade liberalization under these conditions. However, such a behaviour would no longer be inappropriate. At the same time, the free trade imperative of Germany is much stronger and more unconditional than that of the EC. According to the societal free trade norm, Germany is clearly expected to support agricultural trade liberalization. In sum, the analysis of international and societal norms leads to the prediction:

As societal norms stipulate that Germany shall support free trade, post-unification Germany will no longer oppose but support the liberalization of agricultural trade within the EC Council after July 1991.

German foreign policy behaviour

Until 1990, Germany strongly opposed the liberalization of agricultural trade. This was evident by the end of 1988, when the negotiations between the EC and the US were already bogged down. While the US stayed firm on its demand of July 1987 that all agricultural subsidies should be abolished by the year 2000, the EC stuck to its position that subsidies should be frozen at existing levels. Great Britain and the Netherlands tried to get the EC to agree on a more accommodating stance for the so-called 'mid term review' of the negotiations, which was scheduled for November 1988. Specifically, they proposed to move closer to the compromise put forward by the Cairns Group[26] that called for the 'progressive and substantial' reduction of all forms of agricultural subsidy. In this way, they argued, the US could be isolated in holding on to an extreme position. Together with France, Spain, Ireland and Greece, however, Germany came out against this proposal.

Germany's intransigent policy was confirmed in September 1990. The Uruguay round was scheduled to be completed in December 1990, but the transatlantic conflict about agriculture was still unresolved. The US and the EC agreed to reconsider their respective positions and to come up with new proposals until 15 October. Germany, however, with the support of France, Ireland and the Mediterranean member states, blocked any decision of the Community until a special meeting of the European Council at the end of October. This meant that the Community, for the first time, was not able to agree in time on a joint position. When the EC finally submitted a proposal in November 1990, it was not of much use for making progress in the agricultural negotiations: not only was the EC's position un-obliging, but at the same time France, Germany and Ireland made no secret of their reservations about the proposal. As the Commission's credibility was undermined, the EC's negotiation partners did not take the new proposal as a serious offer and the negotiations broke down at the end of 1990 (Vahl 1997: 91ff., 133ff.; Woolcock and Hodges 1996: 310, 314ff.; Reblin 1993: 244ff.; *Agence Europe*, 19 November 1988).[27]

One year later, however, a major shift occurred in Germany's position on the negotiations on agriculture. Germany now began strongly to support the liberalization of trade in agriculture. This became evident when the EC discussed the Draft Final Act for the completion of the Uruguay round which GATT Director-General Dunkel had presented in November 1991. Together with Great Britain, Germany took the position that the Commission should begin negotiations on the basis of the Dunkel draft without considering the opposition of France and Ireland. This was a clear break with the consensual approach that the EC had so far taken in the negotiations.

Germany's interest in a successful conclusion of the negotiations on agricultural trade was obvious again in 1993, when in March, July and September of that year the EC discussed the adoption of the Blair House agreement. The Blair House agreement had been negotiated between the Commission and the US delegation in November 1992. It contained the EC's consent to a limitation of oil-seed plantings and guaranteed minimum levels of oil-seed imports and to a reduction in farm subsidies. At the beginning of 1993, it was still uncertain whether or not the Council would actually approve the Blair House agreement, as France voiced strong objections. Beforehand, the Council had agreed that the significance of the Uruguay round necessitated the Council to take its vote not by qualified majority but by consensus. Therefore, France's approval of the Blair House agreement, was essential. It was Germany, together with the Belgian presidency of the Council, that put most effort into convincing France to give up its opposition against the Blair House agreement which France finally did in September 1993 (Vahl 1997: 166, 231, 240ff.; Woolcock and Hodges 1996: 316ff.; Devuyst 1995: 451ff.; Reblin 1993: 255).[28]

Test of predictions

Covariance analysis

The *neorealist* prediction for the present case does not hold. Contrary to neorealism's expectation, post-unification Germany did not step up its opposition to the liberalization of agricultural trade but instead revised its position and supported the liberalization of agricultural markets for the first time. Both *utilitarian liberalism* and *constructivism* predict correctly that Germany will oppose the liberalization of agricultural trade until 1990, but will support it from 1991 on.

Further observable implications
In order to be able to determine whether constructivism or utilitarian liberalism gives a more accurate explanation of German foreign policy in the present case, it is necessary to consider further observable implications. However, as will be shown below, those do not yield any evidence for the superior explanatory power of one of the two theories, either. Instead, it seems that the determining factors identified by *both* theories were decisive for Germany's behaviour.

Utilitarian liberalism is confirmed in that the experts interviewed emphasized the crucial role of the Chancellor for Germany's stance towards the agricultural negotiations between the EC and the US. Until the end of 1990, the Chancellor supported the protectionist position of the Minister of Agriculture, notwithstanding the opposition of the Minister of Economics and the Foreign Minister. At this time, he mainly feared electoral losses in rural areas, while not expecting the Uruguay round to fail as a whole. After the breakdown of the negotiations in 1990 and in light of the issue linkage imposed by the US, the Chancellor revised his position. In view of the economic costs that would have resulted from a failure of the Uruguay round, the Chancellor shifted to a more accommodating position of the EC in the negotiations on agriculture. He asserted this preference against the strong opposition of the Minister of Agriculture. The experts also confirmed the utilitarian-liberal expectation that the industry associations' situative level of mobilization rose considerably after 1990 and that their intensified pressure on the Chancellor was strongly conducive to the Chancellor's change of preference. The MacSharry reform was described as a vital precondition for the shift of the Chancellor's position insofar as it helped to reduce the risk of electoral losses in the rural areas.[29]

The *constructivist* explanation of Germany's behaviour turned out to be equally plausible. The experts interviewed agreed that the societal norm of agricultural protection was very important for Germany's intransigent policy until 1990. In their view, Germany's support for agricultural trade liberalization was only possible on the basis of the MacSharry plan, as it allowed Germany to do justice both to its conviction that adequate domestic support for Germany's farmers would have to be upheld and to its free trade orientation.[30]

It is true that, in one respect, the explanatory power of utilitarian liberalism is stronger than that of constructivism because the former can account much better than the latter for the impact of exogenous factors on Germany's behaviour in the present case. From a utilitarian-liberal vantage point, both the issue linkage imposed by the US and the MacSharry reform caused domestic actors to reassess their cost–benefit calculations of an agreement on agricultural trade liberalization. From a constructivist perspective, the MacSharry reform widened the range of appropriate modes of behaviour which conform with both the norm of agricultural protection and the free trade norm. However, constructivism cannot capture theoretically why there was a change of German behaviour without a change of either international or societal norms.

Case 2: the conflict between the EC and the US about the liberalization of public procurement in the telecommunications sector of the EC Common Market

Case description and dependent variable

Since the early 1980s, trade conflicts in the telecommunications sector have gained increasing prominence in transatlantic trade relations. This development has resulted from increasing technological innovation and political deregulation which have turned the telecommunications sector into one of the major growth markets of the industrialized economies. At the same time, as telecommunications is viewed as a key industry, its development has important repercussions for the performance of the overall economy (Voeth 1996: 26ff., 52ff.; Freytag 1995: 9–10; Karunaratne 1993: 99).

One particularly contentious issue in EC–US trade relations has been the liberalization of public procurement in the telecommunications sector of the Community's Common Market. While the US had abolished monopolistic structures of its telecommunications sector in the early 1980s, public monopolies in the EC were still untouched at this time. As a result, EC-based producers enjoyed improved access to the US telecommunications markets, whereas companies based in the US were unable to extend their shares of the European markets which were virtually shielded off by public procurement monopolies. As a consequence, an American deficit in transatlantic trade in telecommunications began to build up which, in 1987, already amounted to 2 billion

US dollars anually. The US called for the deregulation of public procurement in the EC's telecommunications sector. In 1986, it threatened to impose trade sanctions on the EC if it continued to ignore the American demands (Voeth 1996: 67; Woolcock 1992: 85–6; Howell and Hume 1992: 192ff.).

As part of the completion of the Common Market the EC in fact agreed on the liberalization of public procurement in its telecommunications sector. On 17 September 1990, the Council adopted the 'utilities directive', which aimed at the liberalization of public procurement in the four 'excluded sectors' (water, energy, transport and telecommunications).[31] These sectors had so far been exempted from the application of EC rules requiring openness in bidding on public procurement contracts. However, producers from third countries could not expect to benefit fully from these deregulation measures, as art. 29 of the directive provides for the discrimination of bidders from third countries under certain conditions. Specifically, bids from companies based in third countries, which are less than 50 per cent of EC origin, may be disregarded by the purchasing entity. If they are considered, offers that do meet the local content criterion have to be accorded a 3 per cent price preference (Bogdandy and Wernicke 1993: 218ff.; Schwok 1991: 87).

In the 1990s, the US repeatedly called for the unconditional withdrawal of the third-country provisions, which the EC refused to do (Harnisch 1996: 131–2; Bogdandy and Wernicke 1993: 216–17; Großmann 1993: 166). The US protest has to be seen in the context of its more general fears at the time that the creation of the Community's Common Market could be linked with new barriers to entry for third countries and could therefore lead to the emergence of a 'Fortress Europe' (Christe 1995: 50ff.).[32]

The utilities directive came into force in January 1993 (Bogdandy and Wernicke 1993: 216; OJ no. 297, 29 October 1990, 1–3). As a reaction, the US decided in February 1993 that bids of EC-based companies for public contracts in the area of telecommunications, energy and water would no longer be considered until the EC revoked the third-country provisions. The EC responded by announcing retaliatory measures (Bogdandy and Wernicke 1993; Europäische Zeitsche für Wirtschaftsrecht (EuZW) 15/1993: 460).

In April 1993, the EC and the US agreed on a 'Memorandum of Understanding', which stipulated the suspension of the third-country provisions for the electronics sector. After further American trade sanctions, this agreement was extended to the other sectors covered by the utilities directive – with the exception of the telecommunications sector. To this day, therefore, public procurement in telecommunications remains a matter of dispute in US–EC trade relations (Harnisch 1996: 132; Schomaker and Detken 1996: 548; Winter 1994: 84–5). However, the conflict about the utilities directive has lost much of its prominence since the early 1990s for two reasons. First, fears that the EC Common Market programme could lead to the emergence of a 'Fortress Europe' have proved to be exaggerated. Secondly, due to the increasing privatization of the EC's telecommunications sector, the significance of public procurement has declined considerably.[33]

The dependent variable in the present case is *Germany's behaviour with regard to the opening of public procurement in the EC telecommunications sector for third-country producers, especially for US-based companies.* From 1988 on, this question was primarily discussed with reference to the third-country provisions of the EC's utilities directive. Specifically, therefore, it will be investigated *whether Germany opposed or supported the third-country provisions.* The following situations will be taken as points of observation:

- The consultations of the EC Council on the third-country provisions of the utilities directive from 1988 to 1990.

- The EC's reaction to the imposition of American trade sanctions in February 1993.

Independent variables and predictions

Neorealism
Like all trade liberalization measures, the opening of public procurement in the telecommunications sector of the EC to bidders from third countries would imply a loss of autonomy for Germany. At the same time, it is not expected to yield gains in influence for Germany as it would face relative economic losses vis-à-vis the US.

This assessment results from several considerations. First, in the time span considered, public procurement in telecommunications plays a considerably smaller role in the US than in the EC. Second, the growth potential of the American telecommunications market is considerably lower than that of the EC's telecommunications sector. Therefore, Germany's gains from free access to public procurement in the American telecommunications sector would be comparatively small (Bogdandy and Wernicke 1993: 219; Großmann 1993: 167). At the same time, American producers are likely to take away market share from German producers in the Common Market as the competitiveness of US companies in the telecommunications sector is at least equal to that of German companies.[34] In sum, the third-country provisions allow Germany to avoid economic losses relative to the US.

As the liberalization of public procurement in the telecommunications sector of the Common Market would imply a loss of autonomy and would yield no gains in influence for Germany, and Germany has grown more powerful with unification, *neorealism* and *modified neorealism* agree on the following prediction:

> As Germany's power position has improved, post-unification Germany will step up its support for the EC's third-country provisions concerning public procurement in the telecommunications sector.

Utilitarian liberalism

Most assertive private actors
First, we have to identify those private actors who are affected by the *opening* of public procurement in telecommunications for American producers. These are the producers of telecommunications goods and services and the employees of those companies. The employees are organized in the German Metalworkers' Union (Industriegewerkschaft Metall (IGM)) while the producers are members of the association of the electrical and electronics industry, ZVEI. Large producers such as Siemens and Alcatel do not depend on ZVEI for the lobbying of PAS actors. Instead, they also try to influence the political decision-making process by means of their own direct, informal channels of communication with PAS actors (Grande 1989: 298).[35]

Second, those private actors have to be considered whose interests are affected by the *conflict* between the EC and the US about public procurement in the telecommunications sector. In this respect, the companies in those branches of the German economy which would become targets of US trade sanctions have to be examined. They are organized in Germany's umbrella industry associations, the BDI and DIHT.

As will be shown below, until 1992 the large corporations are expected to be the most assertive private actors. From 1993 on, the industry associations are held to be the most assertive.

As it is not possible to identify a unitary preference for either ZVEI or the IGM, neither of them is expected to be situatively mobilized. The reason is that both organizations have a large and highly heterogenous membership; in particular, they represent employers (or employees) from both multinationally active companies and companies which concentrate on the domestic market.

From the early 1980s on, those companies which operate on a multinational scale have faced the situation that technological change opens up new market opportunities while the domestic market alone is no longer sufficient to allow for the amortization of the growing costs in R & D. For this reason, it can be expected that the securing of export opportunities has gained increasing importance for multinationally active companies. The US market in particular plays a key role for the export activities of Germany's large producers such as Siemens and Alcatel. Therefore, they can be assumed to be strongly interested in avoiding American trade reprisals in the telecommunications sector. At the same time, Germany's large corporations can be expected to be afraid of falling victim to the third-country provisions themselves, as a large share of the components they use comes from third countries. In sum, the large corporations represented in ZVEI and the IGM are held to have a clear preference for doing away with the third-country provisions. Conversely, the producers which focus on the domestic market are assumed to be primarily interested in keeping the import competition for public procurement contracts as weak as possible. Thus they are expected to consider the third-country provisions in a positive light (Voeth 1996: 63ff.; Woolcock 1992: 78–9; Grande 1989: 86ff., 301ff.).[36]

It is then possible to accord a clear preference to Germany's *large telecommunications corporations* such as Siemens and Alcatel. They are expected strongly to oppose the third-country provisions with high intensity, as their basic interest – the maximization of profits – is held to be directly affected throughout the time span under consideration. First, the US not only constantly calls for the liberalization of public procurement in the EC's telecommunications sector, but also links this demand with direct threats of trade sanctions against German producers from the mid-1980s. Second, from the beginning of the EC's deliberations about the utilities directive in 1988, Germany's large corporations are expected to fear losing opportunities for access to the EC Common Market, should the third-country provisions of the utilities directive come into force (Voeth 1996: 67; Woolcock 1992: 85–6). The large corporations' level of structural mobilization, however, must be judged to be low. While the large corporations appear as a homogeneous group of producers with a common interest, they do not have a joint organizational base. Even though the large corporations have a great capacity for generating technical and political information,[37] in terms of organizational properties, i.e. the level of representation, concentration and hierarchy, therefore, the large corporations' level of structural mobilization is low.

As the *BDI and DIHT* represent the interests of companies from many different branches of industry, they are expected to be mobilized with regard to foreign trade matters when these affect the overall performance of German industry. This is the case from 1993 on. Then the US imposes trade sanctions which discriminate not only against telecommunications producers but against any EC-based company in bidding for public procurement contracts in the US in the areas of telecommunications, energy and water. In order to forestall these measures, the industry associations can be expected strongly to oppose the third-country provisions from 1993 on. The industry associations are judged to have a high level of structural mobilization as well: both the BDI and DIHT enjoy a high level of representation and hierarchy and their capacity for generating technical and political information is excellent. As the competences of the BDI and DIHT partially overlap, their level of concentration is slightly lower. In the present case, however, this aspect is not important since both associations share the same preference (Howell and Hume 1992: 160ff.).

Most assertive PAS actors
Until 1992, the Minister of Posts and Telecommunications and the Minister of Economics, both of whom are expected to hold strong preferences against the third-country provisions, are held to be the most assertive PAS actors. From 1993, the Chancellor, who is also assumed strongly to oppose the third-country provisions, is expected to be the most assertive actor within the PAS.

Political actors   The only political actor to be considered in the present case is the Chancellor, as he is the only political actor with decision-making competence in the case of the utilities directive. Neither the *Länder* governments nor the *Bundestag* participate in the Community's decision-making process about the directive: the *Bundestag* has the right to information and is allowed to give non-binding recommendations, while the *Bundesrat* merely has to be kept informed by the federal government.[38]

In the present case, no particular partisan interests of CDU, CSU or FDP voters can be identified. Until 1992, the fundamental interest of voters in economic growth is not expected to be affected either. It is true that Germany's largest telecommunications firms are assumed to fear that the third-country provisions of the utilities directive may reduce their sales potential. However, since the utilities directive has not yet been implemented, the eventual impact on the telecommunications industry and the German economy as a whole cannot be determined at this time. In addition, the probability and the extent of US trade sanctions are also still unclear. In 1993, however, the situation changes substantially. At this point, the US imposes trade sanctions and those measures discriminate not only against telecommunciations companies but also against other important branches of German industry. In this situation, the third-country provisions are likely to have negative repercussions on the overall performance of the German economy. In sum, the Chancellor's interest in re-election is expected not to be affected until 1992, but is held to be directly impacted on from 1993 on.

Political-administrative and administrative actors   No administrative actors are affected in the present case.[39] Political-administrative actors to be considered are the Minister of Posts and Telecommunications, the Minister of Economics and the Foreign Minister.

From the viewpoint of the *Minister of Posts and Telecommunications*, the third-country provisions curtail his decision-making power as they contain explicit provisions for the treatment of third countries in the public procurement process. In addition, the third-country provisions may conflict with the Minister's interest in procurement at the lowest possible costs in order to fulfil his organizational purpose. He is therefore expected strongly to oppose the third-country provisions. The same is true for the *Minister of Economics*, as German companies at least potentially have to face significant economic losses because of the third-country provisions.

The *Foreign Minister* is confronted with a conflict with the US, one of Germany's most important international allies and trading partners. In order to avoid possible trade conflicts and a deterioration in US–German relations, the Foreign Minister can be expected to oppose the third-country provisions. However, this is only true for the period until 1990, when the EC Council agrees on the utilities directive. Afterwards, the preferences of the Foreign Minister are unclear. On the one hand, the conflict with the US is not resolved. It even intensifies afterwards. In this situation, Germany could only accommodate the American objections by calling the Community's utilities directive into question. This would be possible either by delaying the incorporation of the utilities directive into domestic law or by demanding a reconsideration of the third-country provisions by the Council. Such a stance, however, would certainly lead to conflicts with Germany's EC partners. Therefore, it is not possible to infer theoretically whether the Foreign Minister will give priority to German–American or to German–Community relations, and thus it is not feasible to identify the Foreign Minister's position after 1990 deductively. Instead, an inductive approach has to be taken. The experts interviewed on this topic agreed that, from 1993 on, the Foreign Minister gave priority to Germany's commitment to Community law and urged the federal government to incorporate the utilities directive into domestic law immediately. They said that the Foreign Minister was only weakly mobilized until 1993, but strongly mobilized afterwards.[40]

The Foreign Minister, the Minister of Economics, and the Minister of Posts and Telecommunications have a low level of structural mobilization.

Dominant actors and policy network structure
Throughout the period of concern, the policy network structure can be characterized as corporatist. However, the composition of the dominant actors within the network changes in 1993. Until 1992, the dominant actors are the large telecommunications corporations and the Minister of Economics. From 1993 on, the Chancellor and the industry associations are the dominant actors within the network.

As outlined above, until 1992 the Minister of Posts and Telecommunications and the Minister of Economics are the most assertive PAS actors. The Minister of Posts and Telecommunications does not belong to the group of dominant actors within the policy network, however, as he is judged to have only a low level of autonomy of the most assertive private actors, the large telecommunications corporations. The Minister of Posts and Telecommunications' level of autonomy is only low because of the strong entanglement of the Minister's operative body, DBP Telekom, with the large producers. As DBP Telekom has only few R&D capacities of its own, a close exchange relationship has come into existence in which the companies make significant contributions in

R&D and get public contracts in return. As a consequence of this mutual resource dependency, the large companies' rights to be consulted and their co-decision rights are well institutionalized in formal consultation agreements, joint working groups and advisory bodies (Voeth 1996; Grande 1989: 52ff.). In contrast, the Minister of Economics' level of autonomy from the large telecommunications corporations is judged to be medium: by providing important information, the large telecommunications corporations are able to shape the position of the Minister of Economics to a considerable degree. However, the links between the large corporations and the Minister of Economics are only weakly institutionalized in a formal sense.[41]

As was argued above, for the period from 1993 on the Chancellor is held to be the most assertive PAS actor and the industry associations are the most assertive private actors. As was outlined in case 1, the Chancellor's autonomy from the industry associations is judged to be medium. Accordingly, the Chancellor and the industry associations are the dominant actors within the policy network from 1993 on.

Throughout the period of concern, all dominant domestic actors are expected strongly to oppose the third-country provisions. Even though the composition of the dominant actors with the policy network changes in 1993, Germany's domestic interests are held to remain constant:

> As Germany's domestic interests continue to be opposed to the third-country provisions of the EC's utilities directive after unification, post-unification Germany will continue its resistance to the EC's third-country provisions concerning public procurement in the telecommunications sector.

Constructivism

International norms
As was outlined on p. 236, it is not possible to infer an expectation about appropriate behaviour for the dealings with third countries from norms pertaining to the Common Market (Nicolaysen 1996: 233). As far as WTO norms are concerned, GATT does not prohibit preferential national procurement policies: according to art. III 8a of GATT, public procurement is exempted from the general rule of national treatment. In addition, art. III 8b of GATT even allows for public procurement contracts as subsidies to state-owned companies (Bogdandy and Wernicke 1993: 220f.; Ellger 1992: 206). The General Agreement on Trade

in Services (GATS) agreement, which was negotiated in the Uruguay round, does not contain norms pertaining to public procurement in the telecommunications sector. Explicitly, GATS stipulates that WTO member states may reduce international competition in their services markets by giving special privileges to state-owned companies. At the same time, GATS does not specify any conditions for the legitimacy of public monopolies (Ellger 1992: 211). The 'Agreement on Government Procurement', which was initially agreed in the Tokyo round and further developed in the Uruguay round, does not provide for specific liberalization measures either, but mainly seeks to establish public procurement as an area of trade regulation. Services are completely exempted from the government procurement code (Hauser and Schanz 1995: 9; Bogdandy and Wernicke 1993: 221).

Societal norms
In contrast to the EC and GATT normative frameworks, the free trade imperative is much more specific within German society. As described on p. 237, the party programmes and election platforms of Germany's political parties contain a value-based expectation according to which the German government shall support free trade. Contrary to the agricultural sector dealt with in case 1, this general free trade norm is not called into question by any norm stipulating that the protection of the domestic telecommunications sector or of German public procurement is appropriate. Since the third-country provisions of the utilities directive constitute a new barrier to import competition, it can be expected that Germany will oppose the third-country provisions:

> As societal norms stipulate that Germany shall support free trade, Germany will continue its resistance to the EC's third-country provisions concerning public procurement in the telecommunications sector.

German foreign policy behaviour

From the beginning of the EC's deliberations about the utilities directive in 1988, Germany clearly stood up against the third-country provisions.

This was already evident in 1988–90 when the EC Council discussed the Commission's draft for the utilities directive. Germany insisted that bidders from EC countries should not be given preferential treatment.

Because of Germany's resistance (and the opposition of the Netherlands and Great Britain), the negotiations on the utilities directive temporarily broke down in December 1989. In 1990, the Council adopted a compromise version of the utilities directive, in which the local content criterion as well as the preference for Community products had been curtailed significantly (Scherpenberg 1992: 131–2; Woolcock 1992: 78–9; Woolcock, Hodges and Schreiber 1991: 39).[42]

Germany's strong opposition to the third-country provisions was obvious again in 1993. Immediately after the utilities directive had come into force in January 1993, the US government imposed trade sanctions on the EC to which the EC responded by adopting retaliatory measures. In June 1993, however, Germany declared that it would refrain from giving preferential treatment to Community bidders when deciding upon the allocation of public procurement contracts in the tele-communications sector. Germany's position was strongly criticized by the EC Commission and by France (*EuZW*, 17/1993, 525; *EuZW*, 15/1993, 460).[43] Notwithstanding this criticism, Germany delayed the implementation of the utilities directive into national law until 1997.[44]

Test of predictions

Covariance analysis
Neorealism's prediction that Germany will be in favour of the third-country provisions and would even step up its support after unification was disconfirmed by the empirical findings. In contrast, *constructivism* and *utilitarian liberalism* correctly predict that Germany will oppose the third-country provisions throughout the period under consideration.

Further observable implications
Both constructivism and utilitarian liberalism are also confirmed by some further observable implications. On the grounds of the empirical evidence, it is not possible to discriminate between constructivism and utilitarian liberalism in terms of their explanatory power.

Constructivism is confirmed by the observation of experts that the PAS actors who participated in the decision-making process – the Minister of Economics, the Foreign Minister, the Minister of Posts and Telecommunications, and the Chancellor – referred primarily to Germany's general free trade norm as the reason for their objection to the third country provisions. Constructivism gets additional support from the fact that even though Germany finally implemented the utilities directive in 1997, to this day it does not apply the provisions in practice. Instead, Germany makes use of the discretionary powers provided for by the directive: according to the utilities directive, the third-country provisions are only obligatory in those cases where the allocation of a public procurement contract depends on the price criterion only. By relying on the criterion on the overall economy[45] of an offer instead, Germany has found a way to evade the third-country provisions. Given the fact that the third-country provisions have not been the subject of a major trade controversy in the latter half of the 1990s, Germany's continued reluctance to apply them renders the value-based account of Germany's behaviour even more plausible.

According to the experts interviewed, the *utilitarian-liberal* explanation of Germany's behaviour is accurate as well. They agreed that the large telecommunications companies, and later on the industry associations, successfully exerted pressure on the political and administrative actors. In 1993, when the US imposed trade sanctions on the EC, the danger of overall damage to the German economy was reportedly an important cause of the increasing mobilization of the Chancellor. It should be admitted, though, that the threat of US trade sanctions apparently influenced the PAS actors' position much earlier than utilitarian liberalism predicted. The experts argued that the PAS actors had been worried since the beginning of the EC's deliberations on the utilities directive that the third-country provisions could confirm the general impression on the part of the US that the Common Market programme would be linked with the emergence of a 'Fortress Europe' and could thus lead to an overall deterioration of Germany's foreign trade relations with the US.[46]

Conclusion

Summary of empirical findings

This chapter has examined post-unification Germany's foreign trade policy. More precisely, it has sought to ascertain Germany's posture towards international cooperation on trade liberalization. As the findings of both cases indicate, post-unification Germany supported trade liberalization. Moreover, Germany did not want to limit trade liberalization to the EC Common Market, but favoured a multilateral approach instead. In case 1, Germany gave up its resistance to the multilateral liberalization of trade in agriculture and, eventually, acquiesced to the demands of the US. In case 2, Germany rejected the proposals of some EC member states to link intra-EC trade liberalization with new barriers to entry for companies based in third countries. Instead, Germany urged equal access for all trading partners to public procurement contracts in the EC's telecommunications sector.

Post-unification Germany's foreign trade policy has been even more in favour of trade liberalization than before unification. With regard to the third-country provisions for public procurement in the tele-communications sector, Germany had already taken a clear pro-liberal stance before unification. However, before unification Germany had resisted the liberalization of agricultural trade which it has supported in the post-unification period.

Evaluation of foreign policy theories

In view of the empirical findings, *neorealism* fails completely in predicting German foreign trade policy behaviour. According to both neorealism and *modified neorealism*, Germany is expected to step up its opposition to trade liberalization after unification. In fact, however, post-unification Germany clearly supports trade liberalization in both cases.

Foreign trade policy is a hard case for neorealist foreign policy theory in general. Both neorealism and modified neorealism neglect the fact that foreign trade relations are characterized by strong international interdependence. According to neorealism, states will always refuse to cooperate with other countries on trade liberalization. Modified neorealism assumes that states will consent to international trade liberalization only if they expect to get substantial gains in influence in return, i.e. if trade liberalization yields relative economic gains vis-à-vis other countries. Due to the high level of international trade dependence (especially in the German case), however, this premise is highly implausible. Since trading partners have plenty of opportunities to impose trade sanctions or other retaliatory measures, the strive for relative gains is not very promising. Instead, an orientation of actors on achieving absolute gains is encouraged. In addition, due to the assumption of a unitary national interest, both neorealism and modified neorealism have problems accounting for the fact that foreign trade policy making involves a variety of domestic actors with competing interests.

Both *utilitarian liberalism* and *constructivism* have turned out to be very powerful in explaining post-unification Germany's foreign trade policy behaviour. Both theories predict correctly that post-unification Germany will support the liberalization of agricultural trade and will resist the discrimination of third-country-based companies in the bidding for public contracts in the EC's telecommunications sector. At the same time, both theories are also confirmed by further observable implications. On the basis of the empirical evidence, it is not possible to discriminate between utilitarian liberalism and constructivism in terms of explantory power. Thus Germany's foreign trade policy in the post-unification period can best be described as both gain-seeking and norm-consistent policy (table 8.1).

Table 8.1 Summary of empirical findings and explanatory power of theories

Case	Continuity/ change	Neorealism	Utilitarian liberalism	Constructivism
Liberalization of trade in agriculture within GATT	Change	Disconfirmed	Confirmed	Confirmed
Liberalization of public procurement in the EC telecommuni- cations sector vis-à-vis third countries	Continuity	Disconfirmed	Confirmed	Confirmed

Contribution to the state of the art

This chapter has confirmed the state of the art on German foreign trade policy in two ways. First, the theoretical findings of this case study are consistent with other analyses of German foreign trade policy in the sense that they point to the importance of both societal norms and domestic interests and to the insignificance of a country's (changing) power position in this issue area of German foreign policy. Second, just like many other studies of German foreign trade policy, this chapter has highlighted multilateral trade liberalization as the overriding objective of German foreign trade policy (Kirste 1998: 314ff.; Molsberger and Duijm 1997; Ragnitz 1996: 64–5; Rode 1996: 174ff.; Donges 1995: 66ff.; Hayes 1993: 74ff.; Howell and Hume 1992: 156–7; Weiss 1989: 625).

It has been examined whether or not German foreign trade policy has changed in the post-unification period. This case study has revealed that Germany's commitment to multilateral trade liberalization seems to have become even stronger since unification as Germany supported foreign trade liberalization in an issue area in which it displayed a highly protectionist behaviour before unification. This case study has also added to the literature on German foreign trade policy, as it has developed a constructivist explanation of German foreign trade policy behaviour with respect to two foreign trade policy issues: agricultural trade liberalization in the Uruguay round and the liberalization of public procurement within the telecommunications sector of the EC's Common Market. To date, the pertinent literature has had a strong utilitarian-liberal bias. While most of these studies were not explicitly theory guided, they started out from an analysis of German domestic interests without taking societal norms into consideration.

This shortcoming of the literature on these two issues of German foreign trade policy reflects a more general weakness of the existing literature on German foreign trade policy. So far, it has not actually been tested whether either constructivism or utilitarian liberalism may claim to have more explanatory power for German foreign trade policy. As mentioned earlier, Germany's deviation from the free trade norm in some issue areas of foreign trade policy has been primarily attributed to the overriding importance of domestic interests. However, as could be shown in the case of agricultural trade, protectionist behaviour of Germany may also be the result of protectionist societal norms rather than of protectionist domestic interests only.

In contrast to the judgement of most analysts of German foreign trade policy, the findings presented here do not accord primacy to domestic interests. Instead, Germany's foreign trade policy behaviour can be explained both by societal norms and by domestic interests. It must be admitted, however, that in both cases norms and domestic interests are highly congruent. Under these circumstances, it is next to impossible to discriminate between the respective explanatory power of the two theories.

Notes

1 Protocols of the interviews conducted for this case study are available from the author.
2 It is true that the Community competence in foreign trade matters is not complete in all issue areas (for details, see Jansen 1996: 530ff.; Neumann

and Welge 1996: 629ff.; Nicolaysen 1996: 487ff.; Bourgeois 1995; Winter 1994: 149ff.). But even when competences are shared, the Commission and the member states are committed (by art. 116 of the TEC) to cooperate closely in order to ensure a coherent stance of the EC (Siebert and Svindland 1992: 120ff.). The completion of the Common Market has further contributed to the loss of national competence, as national segmentations or markets have become ineffective (Nicolaysen 1996: 496ff.; Langhammer 1993: 3ff.; Duijm and Winter 1992: 376ff.).

3   Interviews with officials of the Foreign Office, 9 and 10 September 1998; and the BWMi, Bonn, 8 September 1998.

4   Interview with an official of the Foreign Office, Bonn, 10 September 1998.

5   This principle is manifest in numerous GATT norms that accord a special status to developing countries, customs unions and free trade areas; allow for exceptions in special circumstances (e.g. the concept of 'historic preferences', the 'Grandfather Clause' and temporary opting-out clauses); and, finally, exempt certain sectors (e.g. textiles and agriculture) (Ipsen and Haltern 1991: 24, 30ff.).

6   For the concept of 'embedded liberalism', see Ruggie 1994, 1983.

7   On the free trade norm in the Basic Law, see Reuter 1995: 260ff.; Bogdandy 1991: 138; Petersmann 1989: 58; Grosser 1985. On its status in the Foreign Trade Act, see Reuter 1995: 256; Bogdandy 1991: 139ff.; Bellers 1990: 245.

8   CDU 1994: 7, 96; CDU/CSU 1994: 53; CSU 1993: 57; CDU 1990: 22; CDU/CSU 1983: 13; CDU 1978: 205; SPD 1998: 15; SPD 1994; SPD 1989; SPD 1987: 14; SPD 1983: 402; SPD 1959: 155f., FDP 1997: 27; FDP 1994: 31f., 135; FDP 1990: 24; FDP 1987: 9; FDP 1983: 19, 23.

9   CDU 1998: 25f.; CDU 1994: 59f.; CSU 1993: 76f., 81; CDU 1990: 10; CSU 1990: 32; CDU/CSU 1987: 26f.; CDU/CSU 1983: 6f.; CDU/CSU 1980: 15; CDU 1978: 179; SPD 1994: 9; SPD 1989: 38; SPD 1987: 22f.; SPD 1959: 158.

10 The massive overvaluation of the US dollar since the early 1980s may also have played a minor role (see interviews with an official of the Permanent Representation of Germany at the EC (PR), Economics Department, Brussels, 10 October 1998; with a former official of Directorate-General (DG) VI of the EC Commission, Brussels, 26 October 1998, and a representative of the Deutscher Bauernverband (DBV), Brussels, 7 October 1998).

11 Interviews with an official of the Foreign Office, Bonn, 10 September 1998; with a research associate of DGAP, Bonn, 23 September 1998; with an official of the Bundesministerium für Ernährung, Landwirtschaft und Forsten (BML), Bonn, 9 September 1998; with an official of the PR, Economics Department, Brussels, 22 October 1998; and with a former official of DG VI, Brussels, 26 October 1998.

12 Reduction of grain prices by 30 per cent within three years and of beef prices by 15 per cent within three years (Rieger 1996: 115).

13 All farmers with holdings above a certain size were required to set aside 15 per cent of their arable land in order to be eligible for transfer payments (Rieger 1996: 115).

14 Farmers can obtain compensatory direct income payments if they grow eligible produce (i.e. those agricultural products most strongly affected by the agreed price reductions, such as grain, pulses, oil-seed and feed maize) (Rieger 1996: 115).

15 Interviews with an official of the Foreign Office, Bonn, 10 September 1998; with a research associate of the DGAP, Bonn, 23 September 1998; with an official of the BML, Bonn, 23 September 1998; with an official of the PR, Economics Department, Brussels, 22 October 1998; and with a former official of the DG VI of the EC Commission, Brussels, 26 October 1998.

16 In general, it would be reasonable to deduce the political preferences that result from this fundamental interest separately for the two industry associations. The DIHT coordinates the political activities of the German Chambers of Industry and Commerce, which reflect mainly regional concerns, whereas the BDI is the umbrella organization of industry assocations in Germany and thus voices the specific interests of different industrial sectors (Brösse 1999: 98ff.; Hayes 1993: 81). With regard to the negotiations on agricultural trade liberalization in the Uruguay round, however, the preferences of both groups can be expected to coincide, as the maximization of profits for the majority of the members of both associations depends to a large degree on open international markets for industrial products.

17 See note 11.

18 Interviews with a research associate of the DGAP, Bonn, 23 September 1998; with a member of the parliamentary group of the CDU at the *Bundestag*, Bonn, 23 September 1998; and with a representative of the DBV, Brussels, 7 October 1998.

19 Interviews with an official of the BML, Bonn, 23 September 1998; with an official of the BMWi, Bonn, 25 September 1998; and with a representative of the Zentralverband der Elektrotechnik und Elektrotechnikindustrie (ZVEI) e. V. (the German electrical and electronic manufacturers' association), Frankfurt a.M., 30 September 1998.

20 Interviews with a former official of DG VI of the EC Commission, Brussels, 26 October 1998; and with an official of the BMWi, Bonn, 25 September 1998.

21 In case of a failure of the Uruguay round negotiations, the World Bank predicted losses of economic welfare of about 4 per cent of the world's GNP per year. At the same time, it expected annual welfare gains of over 5,000 billion US dollars (20 per cent of the world's GNP) for the next ten

years, should the Uruguay round succeed. These estimates were of particular significance for Germany, as one-third of Germany's GNP goes into exports (Oppermann and Beise 1993: 4ff.).

22 Interviews with officials of the Foreign Office and the BMWi, Bonn, September 1998.

23 We will not consider GATT norms, as trade in agriculture was largely exempted from GATT regulation before the Uruguay round. It was one of the intentions of the Uruguay round to limit the special status of the agricultural sector in the GATT by means of a reduction of the impediments to agricultural trade and by its inclusion in the general GATT rules (Seitz and Windfuhr 1989: 127). The present case, therefore, does not concern GATT member states' compliance with existing norms and rules, but the development of new regulations. As was explained on pp. 235–6, it is not possible to deduce an expectation about appropriate German agricultural trade policy behaviour from GATT rules under these conditions.

24 From 1990, the SPD and CDU/CSU agreed that some reduction of agricultural protectionism would be necessary in order to respond to the imbalances and the surplus production on international agricultural markets. At the same time, both parties emphasized that agricultural market liberalization should not undermine the fundamentals of the CAP, as the existence of German farmers would then be endangered. Every effort should be made to ensure the overall success of the Uruguay round. However, only such a compromise in the negotiations on agricultural trade liberalization would be acceptable which would meet Germany's goals both with regard to the agricultural sector of the Common Market and to international trade in general (Deutscher Bundestag, PlPr 11/195, 9 February 1990, 15051D–15062C; PlPr 12/67, 12 December 1991, 5753A–5769C).

25 In May 1992, the SPD and CDU in fact agreed that the MacSharry reform was an acceptable basis for an agreement with the US. (Deutscher Bundestag, PlPr 12/112, 14 October 1992, 9545B–9558D).

26 The Cairns Group consists of fourteen agricultural-producing states, including Australia, Canada, New Zealand and several Latin American states.

27 Interviews with an official of the Foreign Office, Bonn, 10 September 1998; with an official of the BML, Bonn, 23 September 1998; with a representative of the DBV, Brussels, 7 September 1998; and with an official of the PR, Economics Department, Brussels, 22 October 1998.

28 Interviews with an official of the Foreign Office, Bonn, 10 September 1998; and with an official of the BML, Bonn, 23 September 1998; with a representative of the DBV, Brussels, 7 September 1998; with an official of the PR, Economics Department, Brussels, 22 October 1998.

29 Interviews with an official of the Foreign Office, Bonn, 10 September 1998; with a research associate of the DGAP, Bonn, 23 September 1998; with an

official of the BML, Bonn, 23 September 1998; with a representative of the DBV, Brussels, 7 October 1998; and with an official of the PR, Economics Department, Brussels, 22 October 1998; with a former official of DG VI of the EC Commission, Brussels, 26 October 1998.

30 Interviews with an official of the Foreign Office, Bonn, 10 September 1998; and with an official of the BML, 23 September 1998; with a member of the CDU parliamentary group, 23 September 1998; with a former official of DG VI of the EC Commission, Brussels, 23 October 1998.

31 Directive 90/531/EC, in: *OJ* no. 297, 29 October 1990: 1ff.

32 Interviews with an official of the BMWi, Bonn, 8 September 1998; with an official of the Foreign Office, Bonn, 10 September 1998; and with a former official of the Federal Ministry for Posts and Telecommunications, Bonn, 23 November 1998.

33 Interviews with an official of the BMWi, Bonn, 8 September 1998; and with a former official of the Federal Ministry of Posts and Telecommunications, Bonn, 23 November 1998.

34 Interview with a former official of the Federal Ministry of Posts and Telecommunications, Bonn, 23 November 1998.

35 Interviews with an official of the BMWi, Bonn, 8 September 1998; and with a representative of ZVEI, Frankfurt a. M., 30 September 1998.

36 Interview with a representative of the BDI, Cologne, 28 September 1998.

37 Interview with an official of the BMWi, Bonn, 8 September 1998.

38 Interview with a former official of the Federal Ministry of Posts and Telecommunications, Bonn, 23 November 1998.

39 At first sight, DBP Telekom, the administrative body providing for postal and telecommunications services, may be regarded as an administrative actor concerned. However, as the present case deals with public procurement, it does not make sense to treat DBP Telekom as separate from the Minister of Posts and Telecommunications. In this policy area, DBP Telekom's role is reduced to that of an executive organ of the Ministry of Posts and Telecommunications. All general decisions about public procurement are dealt with by the Ministry itself, and while DBP Telekom is certainly kept informed by the Ministry, it does not have the right actually to participate in the decision-making process (interview with a former official of the Federal Ministry of Posts and Telecommunications, Bonn, 23 November 1998).

40 Interviews with a former official of the Federal Ministry of Posts and Telecommunications, Bonn, 23 November 1998; and with an official of the Foreign Office, Bonn, 10 September 1998.

41 Interview with an official of the BMWi, Bonn, 8 September 1998.

42 Interviews with an official of the BMWi, Bonn, 8 September 1998; with an official of the Foreign Office, Bonn, 10 September 1998; and with a

former official of the Federal Ministry of Posts and Telecommunications, Bonn, 23 November 1998.
43 Interviews with an official of the BMWi, Bonn, 8 September 1998; with an official of the EC Commission, Brussels, 13 October 1998; and with a former official of the Federal Ministry of Posts and Telecommunications, Bonn, 23 November 1998.
44 Bundesanzeiger, no. 163a, 2 September 1997. For details, see Jestaedt *et al.* 1999: 123f.
45 In order to determine the overall economy of an offer, the purchasing entity may take several factors into consideration, such as delivery time and operating costs (Frank 2000: 202).
46 Interviews with an official of the BMWi, Bonn, 8 September 1998; with an official of the Foreign Office, Bonn, 10 September 1998; with a representative of BDI, Cologne, 28 September 1998; with a representative of the ZVEI, Frankfurt a. M., 30 September 1998; and with a former official of the Federal Ministry of Posts and Telecommunications, Bonn, 23 November 1998.

9

German foreign human rights policy within the UN

Henning Boekle

Introduction [1]

Human rights are rights to which all human beings are entitled by virtue of their being human (Donnelly 1989: 1; Vincent 1986: 101). As they address the 'relationship between rulers and ruled' (Krasner 1993b: 140), human rights are principally a domestic issue. However, they became institutionalized internationally after World War II (see Forsythe 1991), and many states have integrated human rights concerns into their foreign policies (cf. Gillies 1996; Baehr 1994; Sikkink 1993).

Foreign human rights policy may manifest itself in different ways. States may, or may not, enter into treaty-based human rights regimes; they may promote new, or the strengthening of existing, international human rights standards; they may support or oppose the establishment of new, or the strengthening of existing, international human rights institutions; and they may or may not react to violations of human rights in other countries by means of 'quiet diplomacy', public *démarches* or even by imposing sanctions. Out of this universe of cases of German foreign human rights policy, this study is devoted to one case which is of major importance in the issue area and allows for both the formulation of neorealist predictions and a comparison of German foreign policy behaviour before and after unification. Germany's membership in treaty-based human rights regimes is excluded because, even though 'a state's participation in international human rights regimes rests on national foreign policy decisions' (Donnelly 1989: 229), it hardly involves foreign policy decision making beyond the voluntary act of accession, as a government merely succumbs to international scrutiny of its domestic practices of rule (Kamminga 1992: 185).[2] Germany's policy towards international human rights norm setting will not be considered either because neorealism offers no theoretical guidance as to which specific human rights norms, if any, a state will promote (see Krasner 1995, 1993b). Due to the dramatic changes caused by the end of the Cold War, German policy within the Council of Europe and the CSCE/OSCE will also be excluded.[3] And finally, German reactions to human rights violations of other governments are not considered because a choice of 'target countries' for analysis of Germany's bilateral human rights policy would be prone to selection bias. This problem is aggravated by the fact that German foreign human rights policy, like that of most other Western states, almost exclusively focused on human rights violations in the communist world prior to the end of the Cold War, whereas violations in other countries were hardly addressed at all before 1989/90 (see Rauch 1998). Therefore, Germany's pre- and post-unification foreign policy behaviour with regard to reactions to other governments' human rights violations cannot be compared.

Thus *German policy towards the establishment and strengthening of UN human rights institutions* represents the case to be analysed in this chapter. It is a significant part of German foreign human rights policy because the UN human rights institutions based on the UN Charter and subsequent legal documents issued by UN political bodies are of major importance in the issue area of international human rights. Moreover, an institutional strengthening of the UN human rights machinery has been a continuous theme in German foreign human rights policy, thus allowing for a comparison of German behaviour before and after unification. Of course, analysis of one case cannot provide us with a full understanding of German foreign human rights policy. However, it can enhance our understanding of the basic factors shaping German foreign human rights policy and of continuity and change therein.

Whereas there are numerous studies of US foreign human rights policy (e.g. Forsythe 1995a, 1990; Mower 1987; Carleton and Stohl 1985) and some comparative ones (e.g. Forsythe 2000; Gillies 1996; Egeland 1988), human rights is an underresearched issue of German foreign policy and is at best cursorily considered in cross-country studies (e.g. Baehr 1994: 121–7; Kamminga 1992: 25–34). The few available studies on Germany's foreign human rights policy generally acknowledge that German foreign policy displays a commitment to international human rights norms and institutions (Baehr 1994: 126–7; Tomuschat 1987: 172–3). In particular, Germany has been at the forefront of norm-setting efforts against torture and the death penalty (Weyel 1997: 152; Baehr 1994: 126; Tomuschat 1991: 6). However, Germany's pre-unification foreign human rights policy is seen to have been strongly shaped by the Cold War (Rauch 1998: 66), and economic interests are also held frequently to outweigh human rights concerns in German foreign policy vis-à-vis countries in which human rights are violated (Deile 1999; Maier 1997; Thun 1993). It is widely agreed that the end of the Cold War has opened up new opportunities and challenges for German foreign human rights policy (Rauch 1998: 64; Baehr 1994: 121; Tomuschat 1991: 6). The question of continuity or change in Germany's foreign human rights policy, however, is only occasionally addressed empirically. Baehr (1994: 125) holds that '[t]he basic tenets of West German foreign [human rights] policy have been continued' whereas Rauch (1998: 66–70) observes that post-unification Germany has stepped up its human rights-related efforts (see also Deile 1999: 203).

No study has yet provided a thorough, theory-based analysis of German foreign human rights policy. This chapter provides such a theory-guided analysis of continuity and change in German foreign human rights policy in the chosen case. Before turning to the case, the next section outlines neorealism's, utilitarian liberalism's and constructivism's general expectations about post-unification Germany's foreign human rights policy.

Theories of foreign policy and German foreign human rights policy

Neorealism

Thus far, little has been written about foreign human rights policy from a *neorealist* perspective.[4] Neorealists agree that in the anarchical international system, states subordinate issues concerning the relationship between rulers and ruled to the pursuit of autonomy and influence. The implications of neorealism for explanations of German foreign human rights policy differ fundamentally according to whether international interference with the relationship between rulers and ruled within Germany or German policy towards this relationship in other countries is concerned. While neorealism maintains that states subordinate issues of the relationship between rulers and ruled in other countries to the pursuit of influence on their international environment, states are held to seek to maintain or even to expand their autonomy from interference by international human rights institutions with their own domestic practices of rule.

Foreign human rights policy has an interventionist dimension as it makes domestic practices of rule an international issue (Kühnhardt 1991: 300). Hence, even though the issue area of human rights is at best loosely linked with security and thus represents a 'hard case' for neorealist foreign policy theory, it is closely linked with sovereignty (see Krasner 1999, 1993b). As autonomy implies sovereignty, neorealism expects that states strive to prevent international interference with their domestic affairs. The stronger a state's power position in the international system, the more that state will withstand international interference in its domestic practices of rule. Neorealism hence predicts that, due to its power increase, post-unification Germany will increase its opposition to international human rights institutions imposing restraints on its autonomy. *Modified neorealism* holds that Germany, faced with reduced security pressures, will accept restraints on its autonomy in exchange for substantial gains in influence on other states. This is the case whenever sovereignty is pooled in human rights institutions which can interfere with states' domestic affairs. If sovereignty is delegated, in contrast, both neorealism and modified neorealism predict that Germany will oppose the strengthening of such institutions because no influence gain would accompany an autonomy loss. The strengthening of UN human rights institutions will therefore be assessed as to whether decision-making power is pooled in, or delegated to, these institutions (p. 280).

Utilitarian liberalism

The German foreign human rights policy network comprises private, political and political-administrative actors. Administrative actors are absent because no specialized public agency for implementing foreign human rights policy exists.

Private actors in the German foreign human rights policy network are of two kinds. Human rights Non-Governmental Organizations (NGOs) as *political advocacy groups* are interested in fulfilling their organizational purposes, i.e. in promoting the international protection of human rights. In general, therefore, they are highly mobilized in situative terms with regard to issues of German foreign human rights policy (see Deile 1998: 110–13). Their degree of structural mobilization has increased since 1993 when a Human Rights Forum (Forum Menschenrechte, FMR) was founded as an umbrella organization of German human rights NGOs, churches, trade unions and political foundations (see Lottje 1998). In contrast to human rights advocacy groups, *companies* and *economic pressure groups* are interested in economic gains. They are thus situatively mobilized only if foreign human rights policy actions endanger their business prospects. However, this is likely to happen only if economically important countries retaliate against Germany for criticisms of their domestic human rights record or similar serious encroachments on their sovereignty based on, or justified by, human rights grounds.

Political actors are assumed to be interested in enhancing their prospects of re-election, in preventing the transfer of policy-making power to international organizations and in increasing their organizational budgets. Political actors' prospects of re-election first and foremost depend on a good performance of the economy. A strengthening of UN human rights institutions has no impact on the German economy as Germany's assessed contributions to the UN and its additional, voluntary financial allocations to UN human rights institutions are not sufficiently large. Similarly, the strengthening of UN human rights institutions offers no opportunities for political actors to increase their organizational budget. However, political actors will oppose any substantial transfer of policy-making powers to UN human rights institutions.

The Chancellor and the *Bundestag* are the political actors involved in the foreign human rights policy network. Even though the former is highly mobilized structurally, he is situatively mobilized only if foreign human rights policy actions impact on Germany's economy, when substantial transfers of sovereignty are at stake or when intra-governmental cohesion is endangered. The *Bundestag*'s degree of structural mobilization is significant only with regard to ratification of treaties and the allocation of financial resources. The former competence plays virtually no role in the case analysed in this chapter. The latter comes into play in the context of special allocations to human rights institutions in addition to Germany's regular contribution to the UN budget. Of course, the *Bundestag* can also pass resolutions making demands on the federal government's foreign human rights policy. Many *Bundestag* members are highly situatively mobilized with regard to some issues of foreign human rights policy (Rauch 1998: 67–8). The *Länder* governments, in contrast, are generally not part of the foreign human rights policy network. They are only consulted in connection with human rights treaties whose prescriptions touch upon their competences.

Political-administrative actors are assumed primarily to be interested in retaining, or even extending, their policy-making power. They will therefore seek to retain their policy-making power vis-à-vis international organizations. Besides, they seek to fulfil their organizational purpose in order to enhance their position within the political-administrative system. In spite of having lost much of his powers in many issue areas of foreign policy (Andreae and Kaiser 1998: 31; Siwert-Probst 1998: 21), the Foreign Minister has retained the primacy over German foreign human rights policy within the UN which may thus open opportunities for him to sharpen his profile and to strengthen his position in the political-administrative system.[5] However, human rights concerns compete with other organizational purposes of the Foreign Minister's office, especially the maintenance of prosperous foreign economic relations and of good overall relations with Germany's Western partners. As a result, the Foreign Minister's situative mobilization and foreign policy preferences may vary considerably across specific issues of German foreign human rights policy. Other political-administrative actors may be part of the network in the context of some issues. The Minister of the Interior and the Minister of Justice come in where domestic politics is concerned. They will always seek to retain their competences vis-à-vis international organizations. In issues of the law of war, the Minister of Defence comes into play. He will also resist restrictions on his policy-making power. The Minister of Economics and the Minister of Finance are part of the policy network when financial allocations to the UN or domestic economic repercussions of German foreign human rights policy are at stake.

Since the founding of the FMR, consultations between the Foreign Office and human rights advocacy groups have been institutionalized (see Lottje 1998: 205–6).[6] However, no other PAS actor has entered into similarly institutionalized consultations with the FMR. The autonomy of PAS actors from the human rights advocacy groups which have joined the FMR has therefore remained high overall. In contrast, PAS actors' autonomy vis-à-vis companies and economic pressure groups is generally lower (Maier 1997). This holds especially for the Chancellor and the Minister of Economics. However, as business actors are situatively mobilized only when their prospects for economic gains are affected, they are rarely part of the foreign human rights policy network.

In sum, the German foreign human rights policy network has been marked by decentralized PAS leadership both before and after unification. The case-specific policy network structures will have to be assessed when addressing German policy towards the strengthening of UN human rights institutions more specifically.

Constructivism

The twentieth century has witnessed a 'revolutionary change concerning the place of human rights in world affairs' (Forsythe 1995b: 297). After World War II, human rights became a central element of the normative and institutional order of international society (Krasner 1999: ch. 4; Forsythe 1991). Respect for human rights is now seen as a criterion of legitimate statehood (Barkin 1998). Though specific interpretations of human rights are still challenged by reference to cultural traditions, no state today can and does abrogate the universal validity of human rights (Baehr 1994: 17, 165). Moreover, the protection of human rights domestically and internationally has become part of the identity of liberal states (Risse and Sikkink 1999: 9, 21; see also Sikkink 1993). The internationalization of human rights is not least credited to transnational advocacy coalitions which engage in human rights norm setting and compliance monitoring (see Risse and Sikkink 1999; Keck and Sikkink 1998: ch. 3). In the UN, consultative status with the Commission on Human Rights (CHR) invests these advocacy coalitions with access and legitimacy as international actors. In Germany, they serve as links between transnational and German civil society, communicating the former's expectations of appropriate behaviour to German society and German foreign policy actors.

The foundation-stone of *international human rights norms* is the UN *Charter*. Art. 1 (3) and art. 55 state that respect for human rights is a fundamental goal of the UN. Art. 56 enjoins all UN member states to cooperate for the international promotion of human rights. Though this prescription obliges states to take human rights into account in their foreign policies, it does not make specific behavioural claims. More specific expectations of appropriate behaviour may be found in legal acts issued by UN bodies. International norms pertaining to German foreign human rights policy are also contained in documents of the EU/EC. The 1973 Copenhagen Document on European Identity[7] states that the protection of human rights is a 'basic element of European identity', and thereafter human rights issues have received increasing prominence in the EC's foreign relations (Brandtner and Rosas 1998). A Declaration on Human Rights, issued by the EC Foreign Ministers at Brussels in 1986, states that '[t]he protection of human rights is the legitimate and continuous duty of the world community' (quoted in Kamminga 1992: 26). With the TEU, human rights were institutionalized as an objective of the CFSP (art. 11 para. 1 TEU). EU member states are expected to conduct their foreign policies in accordance with the CFSP (art. 11 para. 2 TEU) and, in international organizations, they shall coordinate their positions on specific issues (art. 19 para. 1 TEU). Even though the TEU does not specify substantive positions on specific issues of foreign human rights policy, EC/EU documents may have to be considered as indicators of international norms on a case-specific basis.

On the *societal level*, the commitment to the protection of human rights has become a core element of Germany's identity as a liberal state (see Kühnhardt 1994; Tomuschat 1987). The Basic Law's art. 1 states that human dignity is the central value and goal of all public policy. This general prescription also pertains to foreign policy (Rauch 1998: 66; Tomuschat 1987: 172). Further legal provisions for German foreign human rights policy do not exist. However, the domestic analogy (see chapter 5) allows for two inferences from German domestic law. First, as individual rights to liberty and integrity of the person are core rights guaranteed in Germany, their international protection will be at the centre of Germany's foreign human rights policy (see Baehr 1994: 125).[8] Second, as the independence of the judiciary, in particular of the Federal Constitutional Court, and the legal institutionalization of societal norms are central features of Germany's domestic public order (see Katzenstein 1993), Germany will generally favour judicial or quasi-judicial international human rights institutions (see Tomuschat 1991: 7, 1987: 172–4). The *programmes and platforms of German political parties* and *parliamentary debates* also reflect a broad consensus on the appropriateness of the international protection of human rights as a goal of foreign policy. The *Bundestag*'s attention to foreign human rights policy has grown markedly since the beginning of the 1980s, and the expectations of its members generally converge to a high extent (see Rauch 1998: 67–8).[9] We will thus take party programmes and platforms and parliamentary debates into account when deriving case-specific constructivist predictions.

German policy towards the strengthening of UN human rights institutions

Case description and dependent variable

For nearly half a century, the UN Centre for Human Rights (until 1982 Division of Human Rights) has been the UN Secretariat unit specializing in human rights policy matters. Besides the fulfilment of tasks assigned to it by UN organs, its mandate has included activities under its own responsibility. Thus sovereignty is delegated to it inasmuch as the Centre can act independently of UN member states. A further strengthening of this institution through the appointment of a *High Commissioner for Human Rights (HCHR)* had repeatedly been discussed at the UN since the world organization's early years (see Clark 1972). The debate was revived in the early 1990s, and an HCHR was finally appointed in February 1994 (see Kedzia and Jerbi 1998; Much 1994).

Another idea that had been considered repeatedly since the late 1940s proposed the setting up of permanent *international criminal jurisdiction over individuals responsible for the most severe types of human rights violation.* Proposals to the effect of the establishment of international criminal jurisdiction comprised the creation of an International Code of Crimes against the Peace and Security of Mankind as well as an ICC to which jurisdiction over such international crimes would be delegated (see Nanda 1998). In the 1990s, the two issues were separated, and a draft ICC statute was adopted by a diplomatic conference in Rome in 1998 (see Benedetti and Washburn 1999).[10]

Negotiations on the HCHR took place in the Third (Social and Humanitarian) Committee of the UN General Assembly (GA), in the CHR, and at the 1993 Vienna World Conference on Human Rights. The GA's Sixth (Legal) Committee and the 1998 Diplomatic Conference on an International Criminal Court in Rome dealt with international criminal jurisdiction. Thus *the behaviour of German delegations to these bodies and conferences, including statements, initiatives for, and voting on, resolutions pertaining to these issues,* is this case's dependent variable, and German policy with regard to the HCHR and ICC are the dependent variable's two indicators. At one extreme, Germany can support the establishment of an HCHR with a right of initiative to address human rights violations, and of international criminal jurisdiction, including an ICC which can try and prosecute perpetrators of gross human rights violations. At the other extreme, Germany can oppose such initiatives by voting against them, by counter-initiatives or by procedural motions with a view to delaying, or even preventing, decisions. A middle position would consist either in abstaining on initiatives or in proposing weak mandates for an HCHR and international criminal jurisdiction. Even though both institutions were only set up in the 1990s (the ICC's final establishment still awaiting the necessary number of Statute ratifications), both issues have already been subject to UN decision making prior to 1990, thus providing for comparability of (West) German foreign policy behaviour in the 1980s and 1990s.

Independent variables and predictions

Neorealism
The HCHR's mandate includes 'playing an active role in preventing the continuation of human rights violations throughout the world' (A/RES/48/141, op. para. 4f), i.e. the right to address such violations on his or her own initiative. The ICC's Prosecutor can independently commence investigations of war crimes, crimes against humanity, crimes of genocide and of aggression committed either by a citizen or on the territory of a member state of the Statute. Cases can also be brought before the Court by state members to the ICC Statute and by the UN Security Council (SC). If a case is brought by the SC, the ICC has jurisdiction over any state, not just Statute members. Both the HCHR and the ICC thus restrict Germany's autonomy. The HCHR is appointed by the UN Secretary-General with the GA's approval, and the staff of the Office of the High Commissioner for Human Rights (OHCHR) is appointed by the HCHR. The ICC's judges will be elected by the Statute's member states. Only one national of each state may be elected. Thus neither institution offers any opportunity for Germany to exert influence by securing a higher share of posts for its nationals than other states. As sovereignty is not pooled but delegated to both institutions, both *neorealism* and *modified neorealism* arrive at a conceptualization of post-unification Germany's policy towards the strengthening of UN human rights institutions as autonomy-seeking policy. Therefore, the unequivocal neorealist prediction for this case is:

> As its power position has improved, post-unification Germany will increase its opposition to the establishment of a HCHR and of international criminal jurisdiction.

Utilitarian liberalism

A strengthening of UN human rights institutions neither entails substantial costs for German society, nor affects the interests of specific core constituencies. Therefore the interest of political and political-administrative actors in re-election is not affected. However, a strengthening of UN human rights institutions may curtail the policy-making powers of both political and political-administrative actors. This applies especially to the establishment of international criminal jurisdiction. Thus, as some of the crimes listed in the Draft Code of Crimes against the Peace and Security of Mankind (e.g. the service of mercenaries) are not defined as offences by German criminal law, the Code would impose constraints on German legislation. Even though domestic criminal courts generally take precedence, the establishment of an ICC may oblige German authorities to extradite German nationals to the international court, thus contravening the proscription of such extraditions in art. 16 para. 2 of the Basic Law. An HCHR, though not empowered to make binding decisions which would impose obligations on states, may nevertheless impose constraints on German political and political-administrative actors by bringing issues of German domestic practices of rule to international attention. Thus a strengthening of UN human rights institutions affects political and political-administrative actors' basic interest in preserving their policy-making power. Accordingly, the *Bundestag*, the Chancellor and the Ministers of the Interior and of Justice are likely to oppose such an institutional strengthening in order to retain their policy-making powers. The same holds true for the Minister of Defence, who opposes the establishment of international criminal jurisdiction in order to avoid international criminal prosecution of members of the German armed forces. However, as the danger that a strengthening of UN human rights institutions will curtail the policy-making power of the aforementioned political and political-administrative actors is rather remote, the basic interest of these PAS actors in retaining their policy-making power is only indirectly affected. Their degree of situative mobilization is therefore low.

While the Foreign Minister's policy-making power is not affected in the same way, he is faced with opposition to the establishment of international criminal jurisdiction on the part of some of Germany's most important Western partners, in particular the US and France, until the final phase of the 1998 Rome Conference. As conflict with these countries would affect his interest in fulfilling his organizational purpose, the Foreign Minister will also oppose the establishment of

international criminal jurisdiction, even though the degree of his situative mobilization is also low, due to the rather small danger of such
conflicts. With regard to the establishment of an HCHR, the Foreign
Minister does not face similar problems as there was no opposition
against an HCHR on the part of any Western partner of Germany. He
will therefore have a preference in favour of an HCHR as he can claim
that the establishment of such a post would fulfil the organizational
purpose of his office. However, despite his formal primacy in the
German political-administrative system with regard to German foreign
human rights policy within the UN, the Foreign Minister's degree of
structural mobilization is generally low as he has no power to veto. The
Ministers of Justice and the Interior can also participate in decision
making, but as they do not have the power to veto either, their degree
of structural mobilization is also low. Due to the general congruity of
the preferences held by most PAS actors present in the case-specific
foreign policy network, however, the potential for intra-governmental
conflict is small. Therefore, the Chancellor will not have to make use
of his directive powers.

   As stated above, the degree of structural mobilization on the part of
human rights advocacy groups has grown in the wake of the founding
of the FMR in 1993. Human rights advocacy groups are highly mobilized
in situative terms because a strengthening of UN human rights institutions contributes to the fulfilment of their organizational purpose.
However, only the Foreign Minister's autonomy vis-à-vis human rights
advocacy groups has decreased as consultations have been institutionalized.[11] The other PAS actors present in the case-specific foreign policy
network have retained a high degree of autonomy vis-à-vis human rights
advocacy groups.

   Even if Germany strongly supported strong mandates for an HCHR
and an effective system of international criminal jurisdiction, retaliatory
economic action against Germany by other states opposing such strong
institutions would by very hypothetical, especially when Germany acts
multilaterally with a large group of states in supporting such institutions.
A strengthening of UN human rights institutions therefore affects the
basic interests of companies and economic pressure groups at best
marginally. Thus these actors are not situatively mobilized to a sufficient
degree as to be present in the case-specific foreign policy network.

   The network structure is therefore marked by a decentralized PAS
leadership both before and after unification. Due to his decreased
autonomy vis-à-vis human rights advocacy groups, the Foreign Minister

is less assertive than the other PAS actors. Accordingly, as the majority of actors present in the case-specific foreign policy network hold a low-intensity preference against a strengthening of UN human rights institutions, the utilitarian-liberal prediction for this case reads as follows:

> As there have been constant domestic interests against a strengthening of UN human rights institutions, post-unification Germany will continue to oppose the establishment of new, and the strengthening of existing, UN human rights institutions.

Constructivism

On the *international level*, no norm of sufficient specificity and commonality exists. Resolutions of UN bodies and the 1993 Vienna Declaration and Programme for action merely requested further 'consideration' of the creation of an HCHR and of international criminal jurisdiction. Transnational advocacy coalitions lobbied both for an HCHR and for international criminal jurisdiction (Benedetti and Washburn 1999; Clapham 1994) but were unable to bring about a widely shared normative consensus among UN member states. EC/EU norms on foreign human rights policy do not entail specific behavioural claims with regard to the strengthening of UN human rights institutions. A common EC/EU position on the HCHR issue was only reached in 1993, and intra-EU divisions over international criminal jurisdiction endured until the final phase of the 1998 Rome Conference (Benedetti and Washburn 1999: 31; Kaul 1997: 189). In sum, therefore, no international norm of sufficient commonality and specificity can be identified that would allow for the formulation of a constructivist prediction.

On the level of *German society*, in contrast, a widely shared expectation that Germany shall support a strengthening of UN human rights institutions has existed both before and after unification. While only some party programmes and election platforms contain general references to a strengthening of UN human rights institutions, and only few explicitly name an HCHR or international criminal jurisdiction,[12] statements in parliamentary debates that Germany shall support a strengthening of UN human rights institutions in general, and the establishment of an HCHR and international criminal jurisdiction in particular, have repeatedly been made by members of nearly all political parties. Already in 1979, *Bundestag* members from the governing coalition and opposition parties had requested that the German government press for the establishment of an HCHR and a Court for Human Rights. The HCHR should address gross human rights violations on his or her own initiative and bring them before the Court. Such statements were repeated by members of different parties in 1985 and 1986.[13] After the date of the World Conference on Human Rights had been set for 1993, demands that the German government should support the establishment of an HCHR and a human rights court were again made by both governmental and opposition parties.[14] Whereas the proposed establishment of a human rights court reflected the commitment of *Bundestag* members to judicial human rights enforcement, the first reference to international criminal jurisdiction was only made by an SPD speaker in December 1991. Requests for German support for the establishment of an ICC were then repeated by speakers from the governing coalition and opposition parties in subsequent years. Shortly before the Rome Conference, speakers from the governing coalition and the opposition parties again endorsed the ICC's establishment, insisting that it should have binding jurisdiction independent of political interference.[15]

Thus parliamentary debates indicate a continuous, widely shared commitment to the establishment of an HCHR whereas support for the establishment of international criminal jurisdiction was not expressed before the end of 1991. However, as they had long shared a commitment to the strengthening of UN human rights institutions, the parliamentary parties – the PDS being the only exception – also rallied around support for the establishment of international criminal jurisdiction once the GA had unanimously endorsed the idea in 1989. The societal norm that Germany shall support the strengthening of UN human rights institutions, including the establishment of an HCHR and of international criminal jurisdiction with strong mandates, thus possesses sufficient commonality and sufficient specificity in that it clearly rules out German opposition to a strengthening of UN human rights institutions. The *constructivist* prediction for this case can therefore be formulated as follows:

> As there has been a societal norm that Germany shall support the strengthening of UN human rights institutions, post-unification Germany will continue to support the establishment of new, and the strengthening of existing, UN human rights institutions.

German foreign policy behaviour

Establishment of an HCHR

In 1980, West Germany supported a GA resolution on the question of the establishment of an HCHR and co-sponsored a further resolution in 1981 which requested the CHR 'to consider this question with the attention it deserves' (A/RES/36/135, op. para. 1; see also UN/DOC/A/ 35/721 [1980]: para. 18; A/36/731 [1981]: para. 16). In the following years, West German delegations to the GA's Third Committee continued to endorse the creation of an HCHR in oral statements (see UN/DOC/ A/C. 3/37/SR. 40 [1982]: para. 6; A/C. 3/38/SR. 40 [1983]: para. 13; A/C. 3/39/SR. 36 [1984]: para. 19; A/C. 3/41/SR. 37 [1986]: para. 29), but no draft resolution was formally introduced by either West Germany or by other states.

In the CHR, the German delegation stated in 1980 its support for the appointment of an HCHR (UN/E/1980/13, Annexe), but no resolution was introduced. After the debate had stalled in 1981, West Germany supported a resolution in 1982 in which the CHR requested its Sub-Commission [16] to elaborate an HCHR's mandate, including a right of initiative (UN/DOC/E/1982/12: paras 397–400). In the following year, West Germany co-sponsored a resolution in which the CHR pledged itself to take a final decision on the HCHR's creation in 1984 (UN/DOC/E/1983/13: paras 201–23). At that year's session, West Germany verbally endorsed a draft resolution containing the mandate for an HCHR, including a right of initiative; yet the postponement of a decision was the CHR's final word on the issue (see UN/DOC/ E/1984/14: paras 241–74; Flood 1998: 122–3). As in the GA, West Germany refrained from launching its own initiatives in the following years.

Only in 1991 did Germany again take up the idea of establishing an HCHR; it circulated a non-paper within the EC which expressed its support for the HCHR's establishment in connection with the upcoming World Conference (Gerz 1998: 297) and continued to promote this idea in the following years. However, due to the scepticism of some EC members, Germany proposed a mandate which mainly aimed at the cooperation of the HCHR with governments (see Much 1994: 560, 562) and dropped the issue of a human rights court.[17] The outcome of intra-EC negotiations was a position paper which supported an HCHR with a right of initiative (Much 1994: 562). When the World Conference convened in Vienna,[18] the German delegation consulted informally with

HCHR supporters and opponents, as well as with NGOs (Gerz 1998: 301), but the World Conference agreed only 'at the eleventh hour' (Clapham 1994: 559) on the recommendation that the GA consider the establishment of an HCHR at its next session. When the GA convened for its forty-eighth session in the autumn of 1993, the Belgian delegation on behalf of the EU proposed a mandate for an HCHR which emphasized good services but also contained a right of initiative (UN/DOC/A/C. 3/48/SR. 41 [1993]: para. 10). As the HCHR's establishment threatened to fall victim to political blockade, the German delegation initiated an informal working group (Gerz 1998: 305) which finally reached a compromise (UN/DOC/A/C. 3/48/SR. 56 [1993]: para. 17). On 20 December 1993, the GA adopted resolution 48/141 which established the HCHR and defined the mandate, including a right of initiative, without a vote.

After the HCHR's appointment, Germany repeatedly demanded an increase in the OHCHR's budget, but concrete initiatives were not taken due to resistance from many states against changes in the allocation of UN budget resources to the UN's various activities, most notably the promotion of development (Baum 1997: 129). However, Germany has markedly increased its contributions to the Voluntary Fund for Technical Assistance in the Field of Human Rights governed by the OHCHR and has also made further donations.[19]

Establishment of international criminal jurisdiction
In 1980, West Germany supported a GA resolution which requested the UN Secretary-General to compile a report on reviving the project of an International Code of Crimes against the Peace and Security of Mankind. In the following year, West Germany supported a GA resolution which requested the UN International Law Commission (ILC)[20] to resume its work on the Draft Code. However, West Germany became sceptical about the insertion in the Draft Code of crimes such as colonialism and the service of mercenaries (see Ferencz 1981: 677) and did not show much support for the Draft Code in subsequent years (see Graefrath 1990: 76–7). When, in 1989, Trinidad and Tobago proposed an ICC for the prosecution of drug trafficking, the West German delegation to the GA's Sixth Committee insisted that jurisdiction of an ICC be restricted to war crimes and crimes against humanity. While West Germany voted against a GA resolution which requested the ILC to continue its work on the Draft Code (UN/DOC/A/44/765: para. 6), it supported a resolution requesting the

ILC to consider the establishment of an ICC, even though the resolution contained a reference to drug trafficking (UN/DOC/A/C. 6/44/SR. 28 (1989): paras 36–8). In 1990 and 1991, Germany co-sponsored GA resolutions which requested the ILC further to consider the establishment of an ICC. When, in 1992, a GA resolution requested the ILC to draft a statute, Germany endorsed the UK's co-sponsorship of that resolution on behalf of the EC. In the Sixth Committee, the German delegation spoke in favour of an ICC 'in the proper sense' but demanded that the ICC Statute should 'not be linked too closely with the Draft Code' (UN/DOC/A/C. 6/47/SR. 23 (1992): para. 23). German support for the ICC increased after it had been agreed by 1994 that the crimes falling under the ICC's jurisdiction would be defined in the Statute itself. Germany played an active role in bringing together forty-eight 'likeminded countries' which supported the ICC's creation (Kaul 1998a: 274) and cooperated closely with the NGO Coalition for an International Criminal Court (CICC) and individual NGOs, notably Human Rights Watch and Amnesty International.[21] In the Rome Conference's Preparatory Committee and at the Conference itself, Germany made proposals for an effective ICC, but also brokered compromises on delicate issues (see Benedetti and Washburn 1999: 8, 27–8).[22] In fact, 'Germany, a leading country of the Like-Minded Group (LMG), had the most extensive view of the Court's jurisdiction and powers' (Benedetti and Washburn 1999: 27–8). Germany favoured ICC jurisdiction over genocide, crimes against humanity, war crimes and aggression. At the Rome Conference, Germany supported the proposal that the ICC should deal with offences committed on the territory, by a national or against a national, of a Statute member state. In addition, the ICC should be able to start investigations against persons in the custody of a Statute member state. As this proposal did not find sufficient support, Germany played a major part in negotiating the agreement that ICC jurisdiction would pertain to crimes committed on the territory of or by a national of a Statute member state (see Kaul 1998b: 143).

Already in 1996, Germany had insisted that ICC jurisdiction over a state should be established by that state's ratification of the Statute without any further requirements (see UN/DOC/A/51/22, Suppl. 22A: 73), that no reservations by ICC Statute member states should be allowed for,[23] and that the ICC's Prosecutor should be able to start investigations on his or her own initiative (*ex officio*). A German–Argentine proposal which made the Prosecutor's investigative powers conditional upon consent by a Pre-Trial Chamber was eventually accepted (see Kaul 1998c: 128–9). Germany had proposed that the SC should be able to bring cases but not to bar proceedings but then went along with the Singaporean proposal that the SC would only be able to block further proceedings in cases with which it was itself concerned for up to twelve months.

After the Rome Conference, Germany continued to follow its policy of support for a strong ICC in the Preparatory Commission which was set up in accordance with the Final Act of the Rome Conference in order to resolve the unsettled issues of the definition of the crime of aggression, the elements of crimes, and the rules of procedure and evidence. However, even though all of these negotiations should have been concluded in June 2000, the Preparatory Commission was only able to adopt finalized texts of the elements of crimes and the rules of procedure at its fifth session on 30 June 2000 (see UN/DOC/PCNICC/2000/L. 3/Rev. 1: 2). The definition of the crime of aggression, in contrast, could not be settled due to disagreements about the role of the SC and the relation with the definition of aggression contained in GA/RES/3314 of December 1974. The US in particular used the Preparatory Commission for attempts at re-negotiating basic issues already settled in the Rome Statute regarding ICC jurisdiction. In concert with other LMG members, most notably Canada, Germany continued to support wide definitions of crimes and ICC jurisdiction against the resistance of the US and other states. With regard to aggression, however, Germany favoured a compromise granting the SC the competence to determine acts of aggression in accordance with the UN Charter. Nevertheless, even though Germany's ICC policy after the Rome Conference continued to seek compromises, it has remained dedicated to a strong and effective ICC, though focusing on rather technical issues.[24]

Germany signed the ICC Statute on 10 December 1998. However, even though the Cabinet had approved two draft laws pertaining to the incorporation of the Statute in German law and the necessary amendment of the Basic Law's art. 16 para. 2 on 1 December 1999,[25] and the *Bundestag* had held a first reading of the draft laws in which speakers of all parties urged rapid ratification in February 2000[26], technical difficulties prevented a *Bundestag* decision on ratification until both draft laws on the ICC Statute were adopted unanimously on 27 October 2000.[27]

Summary

This analysis shows that post-unification Germany supported the establishment of an HCHR and of international criminal jurisdiction with strong mandates. In the case of the HCHR, West Germany had supported the creation of the post in the 1980s but left the campaign's leadership to other countries. In contrast, during and after the 1993 Vienna World Conference, Germany was among those states most actively promoting the establishment and effective functioning of the HCHR. In the case of international criminal jurisdiction, the West German position was reserved throughout the 1980s when the Draft Code of Crimes against the Peace and Security of Mankind was at the core of UN negotiations on this issue. Only after the crimes that would fall under its jurisdiction were spelled out in the ICC's Statute itself and restricted to the most severe crimes, did Germany adopt a strongly supportive stance. Thus whereas German support for an HCHR was largely marked by continuity, Germany's policy towards the establishment of international criminal jurisdiction is marked by change.

Test of predictions

Covariance analysis

The *neorealist* prediction that post-unification Germany will increase its opposition to a strengthening of UN institutions in order to maintain its autonomy is disconfirmed by the empirical evidence. In fact, Germany intensified its support for both an HCHR and international criminal jurisdiction after unification and lobbied for strong mandates for both institutions.

Utilitarian liberalism correctly predicts Germany's opposition to the Draft Code of Crimes against the Peace and Security of Mankind. In contrast, the prediction that Germany will oppose the establishment of both an HCHR and an ICC proved incorrect. Overall, therefore, utilitarian liberalism has not been confirmed.

Constructivism rightly predicts that Germany will support an HCHR and international criminal jurisdiction. However, constructivism does not predict the defection from support for the establishment of an international court for human rights. Similarly, the fact that Germany ceased to insist on automatic jurisdiction of the ICC over all crimes and accepted an opt-out clause for war crimes is at odds with the constructivist prediction. In sum, even though constructivism has most predictive power of all the competing theories, it also has some shortcomings.

Further observable implications

Utilitarian liberalism is further disconfirmed by failing to predict correctly the preferences and the behaviour of most PAS actors. Thus the *Bundestag*'s support for international criminal jurisdiction was much stronger than predicted. Similarly, both the Foreign Minister and the Minister of Defence supported the ICC's establishment in spite of US pressure.[28] Only the Chancellor and the Minister of the Interior did not show much support for either an HCHR or international criminal jurisdiction.

An evaluation of the *constructivist* prediction's further observable implications sheds an ambiguous light on constructivism's predictive power. On the one hand, constructivism cannot explain West Germany's opposition to the Draft Code of Crimes against the Peace and Security of Mankind. On the other hand, Germany's insistence on the inclusion of aggression in the ICC's jurisdiction is best explained by domestic analogy as aggression is defined by the Basic Law (art. 26 para. 1) as a crime which must be punished.[29] In contrast to its opposition to the Draft Code of Offences against the Peace and Security of Mankind, Germany's discontinuation of its insistence of an international human rights court and of automatic ICC jurisdiction over war crimes as such do not invalidate constructivism's prediction about German foreign policy behaviour because they were the results of international interactions.[30]

In sum, even though no foreign policy theory can fully explain German foreign policy behaviour in this case, constructivism offers the most convincing explanation. German behaviour towards the strengthening of UN human rights institutions is thus best understood as *norm-consistent foreign policy*.

Continuity and change in post-unification Germany's foreign human rights policy within the UN

Summary of empirical findings

This chapter has analysed a distinct issue of German foreign human rights policy within the UN on the basis of competing theoretical predictions. Though this analysis cannot lay claim to being an all-representative study of German foreign human rights policy, it has produced some important insights into continuity and change of German foreign human rights policy since unification. Thus German policy towards the strengthening of UN human rights institutions is marked more by continuity than by change, even though change did occur when, after unification, Germany shifted its position towards international criminal jurisdiction. Overall, post-unification Germany significantly stepped up its efforts to further a strengthening of UN human rights institutions.

Evaluation of the foreign policy theories

The foreign policy theories of neorealism (including its modified variant), utilitarian liberalism and constructivism furnish competing predictions about German behaviour in this case. One theory, *constructivism*, provides a clearly superior prediction in comparison with the two others. However, in spite of its overall accuracy, constructivism cannot explain all aspects of German policy in this case, most notably its opposition to the Draft Code of Offences against the Peace and Security of Mankind. This facet of German policy was correctly predicted by *utilitarian liberalism*, whose overall predictive power, however, proved very limited. The *neorealist* prediction that post-unification Germany will oppose any further strengthening of UN human rights institutions in order to enhance its autonomy, in contrast, has been disconfirmed by the empirical evidence.

As foreign human rights policy represents a hard case for neorealism, the failure of the neorealist prediction is not at all surprising. Conversely, as the international politics of human rights is generally regarded as a strong example of the impact of social norms on international relations and foreign policy (see Risse and Sikkink 1999; Forsythe 1991), constructivism's fairly high explanatory power does not come as a surprise either. Even though utilitarian liberalism's prediction failed overall, it proved correct at least with regard to one aspect of German foreign policy behaviour, namely Germany's opposition to the Draft Code of Crimes against the Peace and Security of Mankind. In sum, however, despite the superior record of constructivism, no theory can fully explain German foreign human rights policy in the case analysed in this chapter.

Contribution to the state of the art

First and foremost, this chapter contributes to the state of the art on German foreign policy in that it provides a theory-based empirical study of one case of German foreign human rights policy within the UN. No such study has been published before. The analysis of German policy towards a strengthening of UN human rights institutions confirms previous studies of German foreign human rights policy as committed to strong and independent international human rights institutions. Furthermore, it supports both the view that the basic tenets of German foreign human rights policy, i.e. its normative foundations, have remained unchanged (Baehr 1994: 125), and the proposition that post-unification Germany has stepped up its diplomatic efforts for the international protection of human rights (Rauch 1998: 66–70). The findings of this study also confirm the view that German foreign human rights policy is influenced by societal rather than international norms (see Baehr 1994: 121; Tomuschat 1991, 1987). However, as previously stated, the analysis of German policy towards a strengthening of UN human rights institutions cannot provide a broad view of German foreign human rights policy but merely a substitute for a more broadly designed study of this issue area of German foreign policy.

Notes

1 Protocols of the interviews conducted for this case study are available from the author.
2 Most existing human rights treaties provide for member states' complaints against other member states. However, the state complaint has only been used twice under the European human rights regime and never under any other treaty-based human rights protection system.
3 The exclusion of the Council of Europe is further justified by the legal character of its human rights regime which leaves little space for manoeuvre for national foreign policies (see Moravcsik 2000; Robertson and Merrills 1994).
4 The reason that research on international relations and foreign policy has so long ignored human rights is in large part attributable to the long dominance of neorealist thinking in this field (Forsythe 1991: 173).
5 In 1993, a special human rights staff (Arbeitsstab Menschenrechte, AS-MR) was established which is mainly responsible for German human rights policy within the UN. With regard to bilateral relations, however, the AS-MR has only advisory competences.

6   Interviews at the Foreign Office, Bonn, 15 October 1998. Consultation also takes place between *Bundestag* members and the FMR (interviews with *Bundestag* members, Bonn, 14–28 October 1998, and Ludwigsburg, 5 July 1999, and with a member of the German section of Amnesty International, Bonn, 30 October 1998).

7   Quoted in Presse- und Informationsamt der Bundesregierung, Bulletin No. 165 (18 December 1973): 1651–54.

8   This priority granted to the core civil and political rights of the human individual, together with the right to national self-determination, is also reflected in the section on general principles of German foreign human rights policy of the German government's first report to the *Bundestag* on its foreign human rights policy (BT-Drs. 11/6553: 8–10).

9   This view has been confirmed by parliamentary representatives from all parties except the PDS in several interviews (Bonn, 14–28 October 1998).

10 However, the ICC will only be established after ratification of the statute by 60 states. As of 29 November 2000, 23 states had ratified it and 117 had signed it (source: http://www.igc.org/icc, December 2000). Moreover, many issues, such as the definition of the crime of aggression, the elements of crimes, and the rules of procedure and evidence, have been subject to further negotiations at the time of writing.

11 Lottje (1998: 194–5) notes that, in 1996, the FMR was at least able to enter into a dialogue with the Minister of the Interior on issues such as asylum and citizenship law. Similarly, an exchange of views took place between the FMR and the Minister of Justice with regard to the tasks of the latter's Representative for Human Rights. However, besides the ad-hoc character of these communications, which sharply distinguishes them from those that exist between the FMR and the Foreign Office, the autonomy of the Ministers of the Interior and of Justice with a view to asserting their foreign policy preferences is in no way affected.

12 General references to the strengthening of UN human rights institutions appear in: CDU 1994: 94; CSU 1993: 129; Grüne 1980a: 18; SPD 1959: 165. References to an HCHR: Bündnis 90/Grüne 1998: 2; FDP 1994: 119; FDP 1990: 21–2 References to an ICC: FDP 1997: 27; FDP 1994: 119; CDU 1994: 94; Die Grüne 1980a: 19.

13 PlPr. 8/186, 15 November 1979: 14655–707; 10/171, 7 November 1985: 12820–34; 10/192, 24 January 1986: 14476–98; 10/256, 11 December 1986: 20009–21.

14 PlPr. 12/65, 10 December 1991: 5571–98; 12/80, 21 February 1992: 11091–104; 12/128, 10 December 1992: 11091–104; 12/161, 27 May 1993: 13806–19.

15 PlPr. 12/65, 10 December 1991: 5574f.; 12/128, 10 December 1992: 11091–104; 12/161, 27 May 1993: 13806–19; 12/177, 24 September 1993: 15302–25 ; 13/240, 17 June 1998: 22127–49.

16 The Sub-Commission on Prevention of Discrimination and Protection of
    Minorities (since July 1999 the Sub-Commission for the Promotion and
    Protection of Human Rights) consists of twenty-six independent experts
    instead of governmental representatives. It will therefore not be considered
    for the present analysis of German policy.

17 Interviews at the Foreign Office, Bonn, 15 October 1998; and with a
    member of the German delegation to the Vienna Conference, Cologne, 27
    October 1998. This development in German policy is also reflected by the
    fact that, whereas Foreign Minister Genscher had proposed the creation
    of a court of human rights in his 1991 address to the GA (*Vereinte Nationen*
    5/1991: 170), such a reference was omitted in the 1992 address to the GA
    of his successor Kinkel (*Vereinte Nationen* 5/1992: 162).

18 Originally, it was planned to convene the World Conference in Berlin, but
    the German government withdrew its invitation in 1992, justifying its
    withdrawal by reference to the financial constraints imposed on it through
    unification (Gerz 1998: 298).

19 In 1988 and 1989, the German contribution amounted to US$ 24,054 and
    21,755, respectively. In 1993, it rose to US$ 71,411 and more than doubled
    in 1994 to US$ 171,454. After slight decreases in 1995 (US$ 144,927) and
    1996 (US$ 136,986), it rose again sharply in 1997 to US$ 211,132 (figures
    according to UN/DOC/E/CN. 4/1998/92, Annexe III). Thus, while German
    contributions had not exceeded DM 200,000 until 1996, they doubled in
    1997 to equal DM 400,000 (4. Bericht der Bundesregierung über ihre
    Menschenrechtspolitik in den auswärtigen Beziehungen, BT-Drs. 13/8861:
    30). In 1998 and 1999, German contributions were further raised to DM
    600,000 (5. Bericht der Bundesregierung über ihre Menschenrechtspolitik
    in den auswärtigen Beziehungen, online version, http://www. auswaertiges-
    amt.de, August 2000). Further donations comprised, among others, DM
    2 million for the Rwanda field operation and DM 1 million for the field
    operation in Bosnia (4. Bericht der Bundesregierung über ihre Menschen-
    rechtspolitik in den auswärtigen Beziehungen, BT-Drs. 13/8861: 31).

20 Because it is composed of legal experts, proceedings in the ILC are not
    considered in the analysis of German foreign policy behaviour.

21 Experts stated that the most valuable function of NGOs was that they
    ensured transparency with regard to information and warnings about
    imminent moves of delegations hostile to the ICC (interviews at the
    Foreign Office, Bonn, 29 October 1998 and 26 May 1999).

22 Thus Germany coordinated negotiations on the definition of war crimes
    and submitted a discussion paper at the end of 1997 (contained in
    UN/DOC/A/AC.149/1997/WG. 1/DP. 23 of 12 December 1997, reprinted
    in: *Humanitäres Völkerrecht* 2/1998: 90–2). Germany also circulated a pro-
    posal containing a restrictive definition of aggression (Kaul 1997: 178).

23 German position paper of May 1998, gopher://gopher.igc. apc.org/70/00/
   orgs/icc/natldocs/rome/germanposition.rm (July 1998).
24 See CICC Monitor 11(1999), http://www.igc.org/icc/html/monitor11f.
   html (August 2000).
25 FAZ, 2 December 1999.
26 See PlPr. 14/90, 24 February 2000: 8374–86.
27 See SZ, 28 October 2000: 5.
28 Shortly before the end of the Rome Conference, US Defence Secretary
   Cohen warned his German colleague Rühe that Germany's support for the
   establishment of an ICC might have repercussions for US troop deployment in Germany (FAZ, 16 July 1998; Tageszeitung, 16 July 1998).
   However, US–German tensions over the ICC were not deemed serious by
   the Foreign Office because the US administration was itself divided over
   the issue (interviews at the Foreign Office, Bonn, 26 and 28 May 1999).
29 Benedetti and Washburn (1999: 28) note that at times during the drafting
   of the ICC Statute, Germany 'seemed quite isolated on the inclusion of
   aggression'.
30 Interviews with experts revealed that the dismissal of a human rights court
   was prompted by the recognition by German foreign human rights policy
   makers that the simultaneous establishment of an HCHR and such a court
   could not be achieved, given the reservations of many states against the
   establishment of an HCHR in the first place. Similarly, automatic jurisdiction of the ICC was dropped from Germany's goals for the Rome
   Conference in order to gain wide support for the ICC Statute (interviews
   at the Foreign Office, Bonn, 15 and 29 October 1998 and 26 May 1999;
   and with a member of the German delegation to the Vienna World Conference, Cologne, 27 October 1998; see also Kaul 1998b, c).

Part IV

Comparative analysis

10

German foreign policy since unification: theories meet reality

Volker Rittberger and Wolfgang Wagner

Introduction

Notwithstanding the newest wave of analytical contributions, the bulk of the literature on post-unification Germany's foreign policy has been of a descriptive or prescriptive nature.[1] In contrast, this volume presents a theory-guided empirical analysis of post-unification Germany's foreign policy and thereby aims to contribute to both our knowledge about Germany's foreign policy behaviour *and* to the evaluation of the explanatory power of major foreign policy theories.

In the 1990s, the public debate on German foreign policy was dominated by the question of whether Germany's improved power position after unification would lead to a change in its foreign policy (see chapter 2). Therefore, we have taken neorealist foreign policy theory as our point of departure in designing our research project. In addition to 'Germany's power position', however, we have included two further independent variables, 'domestic interests' and 'social norms', in our research design. In order to test the neorealist prediction that a more powerful post-unification Germany will increase its pursuit of power politics (as well as to examine the explanatory power of 'domestic interests' and 'social norms'), we have selected eight cases from a wide range of issue areas. In this chapter we outline our criteria for case selection and give a brief overview of the sample finally chosen. We then present the findings from our research project. Following this, we give an answer to the empirical question of to what extent post-unification Germany has changed its foreign policy behaviour and to what extent it has been characterized by continuity. We then assess the explanatory power of the foreign policy theories under examination. Neorealism's explanatory record is the poorest though the modification of neorealism yields correct predictions at least in most cases of 'high politics', the home turf of neorealism. Whereas utilitarian liberalism has a mixed explanatory record, constructivism correctly predicts German behaviour in all cases, and is supported by further observable implications in many cases under consideration but, in two cases, is weakened by puzzling further observable implications. In sum, post-unification Germany's foreign policy is norm-consistent foreign policy that, at the same time, aims at enhancing its influence in the realm of high politics and seeks to achieve economic gains in the realm of foreign trade.

Research question: continuity or change in post-unification Germany's foreign policy?

Testing neorealist foreign policy theory: does an improved power position lead to increased power politics?

As outlined in chapter 2, observers agree that unification and the end of the East–West conflict opened up opportunities for Germany to step up its pursuit of power politics. Due to the largely policy-oriented character of the debate, participants were divided over the question of whether post-unification Germany's foreign policy *should* embark on such a foreign policy course. Though neorealism has hardly been mentioned explicitly in this debate, the neorealist notion that a state's foreign policy is shaped by its power position has been a major point of reference for the majority of contributors.[2] Neorealist theory therefore has taken a prominent place in the debate over post-unification Germany's foreign policy.

For a theory-led analysis of post-unification Germany's foreign policy, neorealism is therefore an obvious point of departure. The test of the neorealist prediction that, due to an improvement in Germany's power position, its foreign policy will embark on the pursuit of power politics after unification has therefore been the centrepiece of our research endeavour. Because neorealism is a theory of international politics, however, neorealist *foreign policy theory* had to be (re)constructed in the first place (chapter 3). In the neorealist view, states are rational actors that adapt their behaviour to the structural constraints of the international system. In order to safeguard their survival in an anarchic self-help system, states strive for autonomy from other actors and for influence on other actors. The more powerful a state, the more autonomy and influence it can be expected to seek. A state's power position in turn is determined by the number of great powers and the distribution of political, economic and military capabilities in the international system, i.e. its share in capabilities and the polarity of the international system. Chapter 3 examines how Germany's power position has changed from the time before unification to the time thereafter by measuring Germany's share in four key capabilities (GNP, exports, military spending and armed forces) and by discussing the impact of the transition from a bipolar to a non-bipolar international system after 1989. Though Germany's share in key capabilities has only improved modestly, its room for independent action has increased significantly. Whereas dependency on the US during the Cold War limited Germany's leverage for independent action, these constraints have lessened with the transition from a bipolar to a non-bipolar international system. Chapter 3 therefore concludes that, in sum, Germany's power position has improved moderately. *Neorealism expects Germany to step up its pursuit of power politics after unification, i.e. post-unification Germany will attempt to increase both its autonomy from, and its influence on, other actors in the international system.*

Chapter 3 takes recent debates within the neorealist school of thought into account by distinguishing two variants of neorealist foreign policy theory, i.e. neorealism and modified neorealism. Neorealism holds that states' foreign policies are based on worst-case scenarios and will thus prefer autonomy over influence when the two are at odds. Modified neorealism, in contrast, treats security pressures as an intervening variable. As a consequence, modified neorealism posits that states attribute less importance to autonomy when they are exposed to low security pressures. Thus, whenever the probability of being threatened or attacked is low, states may forgo gains in autonomy whenever substantial gains in influence can be achieved. While both variants concur in their general expectation that a more powerful post-unification Germany will intensify its pursuit of power politics, the (possible) trade-off between gains in autonomy and gains in influence has to be examined on a case-by-case basis. *Since Germany has experienced a drastic decrease of security pressures over the last decade, modified neorealism expects it to enhance its influence on others rather than its autonomy when the two are at odds.*

Evaluating the explanatory power of further independent variables:
'domestic interests' and 'social norms'

Though Germany's power position is this project's key explanatory variable, two further independent variables have been included in our research design, i.e. 'domestic interests' and 'social norms' (for an overview see table 10.1). The inclusion of these independent variables serves a double purpose. First, the impact of our key explanatory variable can better be assessed when we control for the impact of further independent variables.[3] Second, the explanatory power of domestic interests and of social norms themselves can be assessed, which may yield important findings in its own right.

Of course, in order to serve the purpose of controlling for further causal factors, further independent variables must be carefully selected. Our selection of domestic interests and of social norms reflects the state of the art in (comparative) foreign policy analysis according to which there have been two major debates. First, within the rationalist camp, the primacy of international factors (emphasized by neorealist theorizing) has been questioned by (utilitarian) liberalism, which has pointed to the importance of domestic interests as prime determinants of collective action. Second, constructivism has challenged rationalism as the dominant ontology in foreign policy analysis (underlying, among others, neorealism and utilitarian liberalism) by arguing that social action is rooted in intersubjectively shared value-based expectations of appropriate behaviour, i.e. social norms.

The claim that state behaviour is not driven by the international distribution of power but by domestic interests is long established. Going back to Kant, Hobson and Schumpeter, scholars have stressed, albeit in a critical vein, the importance of the domestic decision-making processes and the impact of influential societal groups. Starting with Allison's 'Essence of decision' (1971; Allison and Zelikow 1999), the research on bureaucratic politics has added the importance of organizational self-interest and intra-administrative decision making to this strand of foreign policy analysis. Over the course of the last two decades, liberal foreign policy analysis has increasingly been inspired by the theory development in comparative public policy analysis. Chapter 4 assembles these various research traditions into a coherent framework that allows us to derive predictions about post-unification Germany's foreign policy in all the cases examined. It distinguishes several types of actor (actors within the PAS and private actors such as companies, economic pressure groups and political advocacy groups) and attributes basic interests to them. In order to assess each actor's capacity to shape German foreign policy, its level of structural mobilization (i.e. its capacity to assert its preferences) and its level of situative mobilization (i.e. the degree to which its basic interests are affected by the matter under consideration) have to be determined. Moreover, the degree of autonomy of the most assertive actors of the PAS from the most assertive private actors must be ascertained in order to develop propositions about the domestic interests which are held to shape the foreign policy behaviour. For each step, chapter 4 carefully elaborates criteria that make possible an empirical test of utilitarian liberalism's predictions. *In general, utilitarian liberalism expects post-unification Germany to continue its pursuit of gain-seeking foreign policy in the same form and intensity as hitherto because it assumes that unification did not significantly alter Germany's constellation of domestic interests.*

More recently, rationalist theories of foreign policy (including neorealism and utilitarian liberalism) have been challenged by a growing body of constructivist research (see, among others, Hudson 1997; Goldstein and Keohane 1993). The constructivist framework assembles a heterogeneous group of scholars who have emphasized the importance of non-material factors such as 'identity', 'values', 'norms', 'culture', 'ideas', and the like. As put forward in chapter 5, social norms, i.e. intersubjectively shared, value-based expectations of appropriate behaviour, are the independent variable in a constructivist foreign policy theory. Though research on international norms, on the one hand, and on societal norms, on the other, have traditionally been separated from each other, chapter 5 integrates these two research traditions into a single coherent theory. It pays special attention to the discussion of indicators of (international and societal) norms that make the identification of shared value-based expectations of appropriate German foreign policy behaviour possible. Because the pattern of continuity and change displayed by social norms may vary across different issue areas and even across specific subjects within a single issue area, *constructivism's general prediction about German foreign policy after unification confines itself to the proposition that German foreign policy behaviour will change only if and when the norms pertaining to the issue in question have changed.*

Table 10.1 Major foreign policy theories

	Logic of action followed by actors	'Level of analysis'	Dependent variable	Independent variable
Neorealism	Logic of consequentiality	Systemic (domestic variables do not matter)	Power politics: autonomy-seeking policy, influence-seeking policy	Power position (determined by a state's share of the capabilities in, and by the polarity of, the international system)
Utilitarian liberalism	Logic of consequentiality	Subsystemic (international variables do not matter)	Gains-seeking policy (material/ immaterial gains)	Domestic interests (derived from the preferences of the domin-ant actors within a policy network)
Construct-ivism	Logic of appropriateness	Includes variables on both the systemic and the subsystemic level (both international and domestic structures matter)	Norm-consistent policy	(international and societal) norms

As for the purpose of assessing the key variable's explanatory power, further independent variables should be held constant. This is usually achieved by selecting only cases where the key explanatory variable varies while the other explanatory variables remain constant. Of course, this requires a considerable amount of information about the values of the further independent variables. With regard to 'social norms' and 'domestic interests' – the two further explanatory variables we chose to include in our design – this requirement turned out to be rather demanding. Our initial assumption borrowed from the literature on post-unification Germany, that social norms and domestic interests have, by and large, remained unchanged, was not substantiated for all cases. In fact, domestic interests and norms have changed in two cases each. In the case of Germany's net contributions to the EU budget, both social norms and domestic interests changed. Norms also changed with regard to Germany's participation in military out-of-area operations; and domestic interests changed in the case of the liberalization of agricultural trade. However, in this case norms remained the same, but the set of appropriate behavioural alternatives shifted as a consequence of the MacSharry reform, which also led constructivism to expect a foreign policy change.

As for the purpose of evaluating the explanatory power of domestic interests and of social norms, a methodological *caveat* has to be added: From a positivist point of view, a strict test of these independent variables' explanatory power is only possible if there is some variation in their values. Conversely, if both independent and dependent variables do not co-*vary* at all, no causal relationship can be established with certainty. However, if either utilitarian liberalism or constructivism correctly predicts continuity of German behaviour in a given case because of unchanged domestic interests and/or social norms, this of course serves to enhance our confidence in these theories. What is more, further observable implications may add more evidence to the presumed causal relationship between domestic interests or social norms, on the one hand, and post-unification Germany's foreign policy behaviour, on the other. Still, it is important to keep this *caveat* in mind because both domestic interests and social norms have been invariant in the majority of cases.

Research design and methodology

Three independent variables (power position, domestic interests and social norms) have been included in our research design. In order to evaluate the explanatory power of these independent variables (and the corresponding foreign policy theories), we have conducted a series of structured focused comparisons (see George 1979), each consisting of one or more observations of *post*-unification Germany's foreign policy on a certain issue and one or more observations of *pre*-unification Germany's foreign policy on the same issue. We refer to each pair or series of observations as a case.[4]

Case selection

The case selection was done in two steps. In the first step, a number of issue areas were selected, each of which has been examined in a case study. Then, in the second step, between one and three cases were singled out from the universe of cases making up each issue area.

For the first step, the selection of issue areas, three criteria were applied. Two criteria were designed to ensure a broad coverage of post-unification Germany's foreign policy behaviour. Our sample of case studies should be representative in terms of issue areas and in terms of macropolitical contexts. The third criterion was theory led: our sample should include 'hard' and 'easy' cases for neorealism as the centrepiece of our research design.

Czempiel's (1981) distinction between 'security', 'welfare' and 'system of rule' as the three broad policy areas of international politics was the first criterion that guided our selection of case studies. Following this criterion we selected case studies from each of the three policy areas. The issue area of 'security' is covered by the study of Germany's security policy within NATO (chapter 6). Germany's foreign policy in the issue area of 'welfare' is analysed by examining Germany's foreign trade policy within the EU and GATT (chapter 8). Finally, this volume includes two case studies that are concerned with German foreign policy in the issue area of 'system of rule', i.e. a case study on Germany's EU constitutional policy (chapter 7), and on Germany's human rights policy within the UN (chapter 9).

A further, though subordinate, criterion was the representativeness in terms of macropolitical contexts. By focusing on Germany's human rights policy in the UN, chapter 9 is representative of a global macropolitical context. The three other case studies are representative of different sub-contexts within the Western macropolitical context, i.e. the transatlantic context (chapter 6 and, to a lesser degree, chapter 8) and the Western European context (chapter 7 and, to a lesser degree, chapter 8).[5]

Finally, our sample of cases includes 'hard' and 'easy' cases for neorealism. This criterion reflects the widely held view that the explanatory power of any given theory (such as neorealism) varies from one issue area to another. The realm of 'high politics' is considered to be neorealism's homeground. Thus the study of Germany's security policy within NATO (chapter 6) as well as the analysis of EU constitutional policy (chapter 7) are both considered to provide 'easy' cases for neorealism. In contrast, the 'low politics' of trade and human rights are regarded as 'hard' cases for neorealism.

In a second step, for each issue area or case study, a set of cases was selected. Again, three criteria were applied to guide this process of selection. First, the issue under consideration should be politically important. Though this is certainly a rather vague criterion, it is meant to ensure that no resources are wasted for politically marginal cases. Second, the issue had to be on the political agenda both before and after unification. This criterion ensured that post-unification Germany's policy could well be compared with Germany's behaviour before unification which, in turn, is a prerequisite for deriving conclusions about continuity and change. Third, a meaningful neorealist prediction must have been possible. Though neorealism claims to cover the totality of a state's foreign policy, it does not claim to predict every single instance of state behaviour. In particular, when different behavioural options cannot be distinguished in terms of autonomy and influence, neorealism cannot predict a course of action. In sum, this volume presents eight cases listed in the table 10.2.

Table 10.2 Cases selected for studying continuity and change in German foreign policy

Issue and policy area	Case	Difficulty for neorealism
Security policy within NATO (security)	Integration of *Bundeswehr*	Easy
	Participation in military out-of-area operations	Easy
EU constitutional policy (system of rule)	Extension of QMV in the EU Council	Easy
	Strengthening of the EP's legislative powers	Easy
	Net contributions to the EU budget	Easy
Foreign trade policy within the EU and GATT (welfare)	Agricultural trade	Hard
	EC third-country provisions concerning public procurement in the telecommunications sector	Hard
Human rights policy within the UN (system of rule)	Strengthening of UN human rights institutions	Hard

Evidence and inferences

Predictions about post-unification Germany's foreign policy behaviour are derived from the three theories of foreign policy for each case. For each theory, then, the predicted value can be compared with the observed value of the dependent variable (post-unification Germany's foreign policy behaviour). According to the congruence procedure (George and McKeown 1985), the explanatory power of the theories can then be assessed by the degree of consistency between predicted and observed values of the dependent variable. Because the predictions may encompass further observable implications, additional empirical evidence will be taken into account further to enhance or diminish our confidence in the explanatory power of the theories.

Evidence based on covariance: the congruence procedure

The congruence procedure is the centre-piece of our research design. The degree of consistency between the predicted and the observed values of the dependent variable is our most important indicator of the explanatory power of our theories. If the observed value of the dependent variable turns out to be different from its value as predicted by the theory, the prediction derived from the theory in that case is falsified and the theory more generally is weakened, if not disconfirmed. In contrast, consistency between predicted and observed values of the dependent variable makes the theory survive in that test case and strengthens our confidence in its explanatory power in general.

The extent to which the explanatory power of a theory can be evaluated on the basis of co-variance also depends on the number of theories that successfully predict a given outcome. If the observed value of the dependent variable is consistent only with a single prediction, the respective theory is, *ceteris paribus*, strongly supported (e.g. constructivism in the case of Germany's policy on UN human rights institutions). In contrast, if two or more theories correctly predict a certain outcome (e.g. neorealism, utilitarian liberalism and constructivism in the case of Germany's policy on contributions to the EU budget), the congruence procedure alone cannot tell us how significant the impact of each variable is in causing that outcome.

Evidence based on further observable implications

For each of the eight cases studied, all three foreign policy theories arrive at predictions about the value of the dependent variable, i.e. about a well-defined part of post-unification Germany's foreign policy behaviour. To varying degrees, the three theories yield additional expectations about German behaviour in a certain case or about the processes leading to the predicted policy behaviour. The three foreign policy theories do not necessarily generate additional expectations about the *same* phenomena. Rather, the theories generate further expectations about different types of phenomenon (such as the policy style or the preferences of actors involved). To the extent that a theory does generate additional expectations about policy or processes, they can be treated as further observable implications which, depending on the empirical evidence, further corroborate or disconfirm the theory in question.

A prominent way of studying further observable implications is *process tracing*. Process tracing 'attempts to identify the intervening causal process – the causal chain or causal mechanism – between an independent variable (or variables) and the outcome of the dependent variable' (Bennett and George 1998: 2). It is important to note that process tracing does *not* simply take actors' definitions of the situation as primary evidence. Process tracing 'involves both an attempt to reconstruct actors' definitions of the situation and an attempt to develop a theory of action. The framework within which actors' perceptions and actions are described is given by the researcher, not by the actors themselves' (George and McKeown 1985: 35). Of course, a necessary prerequisite of process tracing is that the theory under consideration has generated predictions about causal processes, because 'then – and only then – can process tracing assess the predictions of the theory' (Bennett and George 1998: 19).

The three foreign policy theories under consideration here are suited for process tracing to varying degrees. Out of the three foreign policy theories, utilitarian liberalism offers the most elaborate theory of the composition of the policy-making network, about actor preferences and about their aggregation into policy. Thus utilitarian liberalism not only predicts a certain foreign policy behaviour but also generates predictions about who is involved in the first place, about the preferences each actor holds and about the preference(s) which finally dominate. As the case studies in this volume demonstrate, these further observable implications do serve further to corroborate or disconfirm utilitarian liberalism.

Constructivism holds that (international and societal) norms shape foreign policy behaviour because decision makers are socialized into both international society and their respective domestic society, and thereby internalize the shared expectations about appropriate behaviour dominant in these societies. This causal mechanism, however, is difficult to observe. As chapter 8 points out with respect to foreign trade policy, norms and interests may be intertwined to such an extent as to make their distinction, e.g. in expert interviews, next to impossible. However, in other cases (e.g. Germany's policy on integrating the *Bundeswehr*), interests and norms are easier to distinguish. In these cases, the way preferences are articulated and communicated and the reasons that are given to justify policies may serve to establish the influence of pertinent social norms.

Finally, neorealist foreign policy theory does not specify the processes by which structural influences on behaviour make themselves felt (Snyder 1996: 171; Risse-Kappen 1995b: 20). Instead, neorealism has black-boxed the decision-making process. Therefore, neorealism is not suited for process-tracing procedures. However, neorealist predictions may have further observable implications, too. From neorealist bargaining theory (see Krasner 1991) we may borrow the notion that a powerful state uses all means possible to compel other (less powerful) states into agreement. A state is not expected to engage in communicative action with other states but to take advantage of its power position in order to achieve its policy goals. In particular, a powerful state may exploit another state's dependence in non-related issue areas to achieve its policy goals in a given issue area. In order to do so, a powerful state may create issue linkages and may use threats and sanctions. Furthermore, whenever neorealism predicts that post-unification Germany increases its influence-seeking policy we may not only expect that policy behaviour with regard to our dependent variable (such as keeping the *Bundeswehr* integrated into NATO). We may also expect to observe related efforts of influence seeking, e.g. by laying claim to additional command posts within NATO's integrated military structure. Taken together, neorealism may be further corroborated or disconfirmed by an analysis of post-unification Germany's policy style during negotiations as well as by an examination of post-unification Germany's efforts to exploit its power position for greater influence on its partners.

The timing of a policy change may also serve as a further observable implication of importance to all foreign policy theories (see also Moravcsik 1998: 50). For example, constructivism – though correctly predicting that post-unification Germany will participate in military out-of-area operations – is weakened by the fact that pertinent societal norms evolved only *after* the policy change had already got under way.

Summary of empirical findings: continuity and change in post-unification Germany's foreign policy

Table 10.3 Continuity and change in post-unification Germany's foreign policy

Cases of foreign policy continuity	Cases of foreign policy change
Post-unification Germany continued …	Post-unification Germany …
• to have the *Bundeswehr* integrated into NATO	• began to participate in military out-of-area operations
• to support the extension of QMV in the Council of the EU	• increased its efforts to reduce its net contributions to the EU budget
• to support the strengthening of the EP's legislative powers	• no longer opposed but supported the liberalization of agricultural trade
• to oppose the EC's third-country provisions concerning public procurement in the telecommunications sector	
• to support the strengthening of UN human rights institutions	

As table 10.3 shows, post-unification Germany's foreign policy is characterized by a mixture of continuity and change, with cases of continuity in the majority. Cases of continuity can be found in all four issue areas under consideration, i.e. security policy within NATO, EU constitutional foreign policy, foreign trade policy and human rights policy. Post-unification Germany continued to support the further pooling and delegating of its sovereignty, including the integration of its military forces and the strengthening of European and global international institutions (be it the EP or the ICC). Contrary to many observers' expectations, Germany did not embark on a more unilateral foreign policy after unification.[6] Quite the opposite in fact, post-unification Germany even strengthened its multilateral ties and intensified its participation in multilateral collective action. Whereas it had opposed the liberalization of agricultural trade before unification it changed its policy in the early 1990s and agreed to new GATT provisions, including agricultural trade. Moreover, Germany began to participate in multilateral military out-of-area operations after unification. The remaining case in which post-unification Germany changed its foreign policy also took place within the framework of multilateral institutions. Here, post-unification Germany's increased efforts to achieve a reduction in its net contributions to the EU budget marks a gradual intensification of pre-unification Germany's policy.

Evaluation of theories

This section discusses the explanatory power of neorealism (in both of its variants), utilitarian liberalism and constructivism. All three foreign policy theories arrive at predictions for each of the eight cases examined (in four cases, there are two competing neorealist predictions). Moreover, additional evidence further to corroborate or disconfirm the theories has been gathered by observing further implications of a theory's prediction.

Neorealism and modified neorealism

Neorealism

Table 10.4 Neorealism's explanatory record

Neorealism correctly predicts that post-unification Germany ...	Neorealism wrongly predicts that post-unification Germany ...
• will increase its efforts to achieve a reduction of its net contributions to the EU budget	• will reduce the integration of the *Bundeswehr* into NATO
	• will participate in military out-of-area operations in ad-hoc coalitions while keeping its armed forces under national command
	• will increase its opposition against the extension of QMV in the Council of the EU
	• will increase its opposition to the strengthening of the EP's legislative powers
	• will increase its opposition to the liberalization of agricultural trade
	• will increase its support for the EC's third-country provisions concerning public procurement in the telecommunications sector
	• will increase its opposition to the strengthening of UN human rights institutions

As table 10.4 shows, neorealism's explanatory record for post-unification Germany's foreign policy is extremely one sided. It wrongly predicts German behaviour in all cases but one. Contrary to neorealist expectations, post-unification Germany did not strive to enhance its autonomy by opposing the further pooling and delegation of sovereignty. Given the general neorealist expectation that post-unification Germany will change the course of its foreign policy, neorealism's weak explanatory record hardly comes as a surprise since five out of eight cases are characterized by continuity. It should be noted, however, that neorealism cannot explain even two of those cases in which German behaviour indeed changed (participation in military out-of-area operations and support for the liberalization of agricultural trade). Moreover, it is important to note that neorealism fails to explain post-unification Germany's foreign policy even in a number of 'easy' cases such as 'military integration into NATO', 'participation in military out-of-area operations', 'extension of QMV in the EU Council' and 'strengthening of the EP's legislative powers'.

Neorealism correctly predicts only that post-unification Germany will increase its efforts to achieve a reduction of its (net) contributions to the EU budget. However, this policy behaviour is predicted by all three foreign policy theories. In this case, neorealism is further supported by additional observations (notably Germany's preparedness to use threats and to violate European norms in order to achieve its policy goals). However, the available evidence only disconfirms constructivism but does not allow discrimination between Germany's improved power position, on the one hand, and intensified domestic interests in reduced EU contributions, on the other, as likely causes of Germany's policy change in this case.

In sum, post-unification German foreign policy behaviour does not seem to be driven by an (increased) quest for autonomy. In the neorealist variant of the concept, post-unification Germany's foreign policy cannot be explained as power politics.

Modified neorealism

In order to account for recent debates within neorealism, we have distinguished two variants of neorealist foreign policy theory, i.e. neorealism and modified neorealism (see chapter 3). In contrast to neorealism, modified neorealism holds that a state's foreign policy is not only shaped by its power position but also by its exposure to varying security pressures. As a consequence of Germany's decreased exposure

Table 10.5 Modified neorealism's explanatory record

Modified neorealism correctly predicts that post-unification Germany ...	Modified neorealism wrongly predicts that post-unification Germany ...
• will continue to have the *Bundeswehr* integrated into NATO (though low-key approach towards claiming command posts remains puzzling)	• will increase its opposition to strengthening of the EP's legislative powers*
	• will increase its opposition to the liberalization of agricultural trade*
• will participate in military out-of-area operations (though time lag remains puzzling)	• will increase its opposition to the EC's third-country provisions for public procurement in the telecommunications sector*
• will continue to support the extension of QMV in the Council (though issue area-specific preferences disconfirm the theory)	
	• will increase its opposition to the strengthening of UN human rights institutions*
• will increase its efforts to achieve a reduction of its net contributions to the EU budget*	

* Modified neorealism arrives at the same prediction as neorealism.

to security pressures after the end of the Cold War, modified neorealism expects post-unification Germany to forgo gains in autonomy whenever substantial gains in influence can thereby be achieved.

Post-unification Germany faced trade-offs between gains in autonomy and gains in influence in three cases (integration of the *Bundeswehr*, out-of-area operations, and extension of QMV). Here, modified neorealism arrives at predictions different from neorealism. In most cases, however, there have been no trade-offs between gains in autonomy and gains in influence, and both variants of neorealism generate the same prediction.

As table 10.5 demonstrates, modified neorealism's explanatory record is much better than the neorealist one. Modified neorealism correctly predicts post-unification Germany's foreign policy behaviour in half of the cases examined: in addition to the one case in which the modified neorealist prediction concurs with the correct neorealist prediction (Germany's net contributions to the EU budget), modified neorealism also correctly predicts the three cases in which a trade-off between autonomy and influence can be observed. With the exception of Germany's policy on strengthening the EP's legislative powers, modified neorealism correctly predicts post-unification German foreign policy in all 'easy' cases for neorealism (including all cases of security policy). At the same time, among the 'hard' cases (i.e. in the issue areas of foreign trade and human rights), modified neorealism fails to predict German behaviour correctly in all but a single case. Though modified neorealism, in general, expected an increase in German power politics after unification (i.e. change), the theory accounts not only for two cases of change (net contributions to the EU budget and military out-of-area operations) but also for two cases of continuity (QMV and integration of the *Bundeswehr* into NATO).

If further observable implications are taken into account, modified neorealism's record becomes less impressive. In one case (military out-of-area operations), Germany's behaviour is best explained by modified neorealism, even though Germany's reluctance to participate in those operations up to IFOR remains puzzling (see chapter 6). In another case (net contributions to the EU budget), no other theory offers a better explanation though the available evidence does not allow discrimination between modified neorealism and utilitarian liberalism. In the two remaining cases (integration of the *Bundeswehr* and extension of QMV in the EU Council), modified neorealism correctly predicts Germany's behaviour but is disconfirmed by further observable implications (i.e. Germany's reluctance to lay claim to command posts in NATO and its issue-specific preferences on QMV and unanimity).

As the explanatory record demonstrates, the modification of neorealism has improved neorealism's explanatory power. The inclusion of 'security pressures' as an intervening variable, as well as the ensuing stronger emphasis on influence-seeking rather than autonomy-seeking behaviour, has enabled modified neorealism better to capture Germany's power politics *within* international institutions. However, post-unification Germany's willingness to *delegate* sovereignty, e.g. to the EP or an ICC, remains puzzling for modified neorealism. What is more, modified neorealism cannot account for post-unification Germany's preparedness to agree to liberalization in areas where no relative economic gains vis-à-vis the United States could be achieved, i.e. in agricultural trade in the EC public procurement in the telecommunications sector.

Taken together, modified neorealism fails to account for Germany's foreign policy behaviour in areas of 'low politics' in which relative economic gains and the delegation of sovereignty have been at stake. Conversely, modified neorealism has a strong record in explaining post-unification Germany's foreign policy in areas of 'high politics' in which sovereignty is pooled and substantial influence gains within international institutions can be achieved.

Utilitarian liberalism

Table 10.6 Utilitarian liberalism's explanatory record

Utilitarian liberalism correctly predicts that post-unification Germany ...	Utilitarian liberalism wrongly predicts that post-unification Germany ...
• will continue to have the *Bundeswehr* integrated into NATO (though the creation of capacities for planning, command and control remains puzzling)	• will continue to refrain from participating in military out-of-area operations
• will no longer oppose but will support the liberalization of agricultural trade	• will continue to oppose the extension of QMV in the Council
• will continue to oppose the EC's third-country provisions concerning public procurement in the telecommunications sector	• will continue to oppose the strengthening of the EP's legislative powers
• will increase its efforts to achieve a reduction of its net contributions to the EU budget	• will continue to oppose the strengthening of UN human rights institutions

As table 10.6 shows, Utilitarian liberalism's overall explanatory record is modest. It correctly predicts post-unification Germany's foreign policy in half of the cases examined. Utilitarian liberalism can explain both cases of post-unification German foreign trade policy as well as one case of security policy (military integration of the *Bundeswehr*) and one case of EU constitutional foreign policy (net contributions). As this record demonstrates, utilitarian liberalism is well suited to explain both continuity and change in post-unification German foreign policy. However, in all of these cases, at least one other theory is equally successful in correctly predicting Germany's foreign policy behaviour. Thus there is not a single case in which domestic interests have undoubtedly caused Germany's foreign policy behaviour.

Utilitarian liberalism performs especially well in the issue area of foreign trade. This corresponds to two features that characterize this issue area in particular. First, the issue area of foreign trade policy is marked by a particularly high level of private actors' influence on policy. In both cases, we encounter 'corporatist policy networks' in which the actors of the PAS were dependent on powerful economic pressure groups that were highly mobilized since their basic interest in improving members' opportunities for increasing their income was directly affected.

Second, material gains are comparatively easy to calculate in foreign trade policy. Though the actors involved in foreign trade policy may not be able to estimate the exact gains or losses resulting from trade agreements, they are certainly able to anticipate whether (and to what extent) an agreement benefits them or their competitors. The other two cases in which utilitarian liberalism correctly predicts Germany's foreign policy behaviour also share this feature: in both cases (military integration of the *Bundeswehr* and net contributions to the EU budget), the actors involved in policy making can easily anticipate whether or not they will have to contribute additional financial resources. However, material losses turned out to be of no explanatory power in the case of post-unification Germany's participation in military out-of-area operations. Here, utilitarian liberalism wrongly predicts that Germany will not participate in out-of-area operations with combat troops because of the high costs of such operations. Utilitarian liberal predictions *always* proved mistaken whenever *only* PAS actors' interests in retaining their decision-making power was affected. Thus it seems to be a necessary, though not a sufficient condition, for utilitarian-liberal predictions to prove correct that calculable material gains are at stake. At the same time, the two cases of foreign trade policy indicate that a high level of private actors' influence on policy making may even be a sufficient condition for utilitarian-liberal predictions to prove correct.

In sum, utilitarian liberalism's explanatory power turned out to be modest. However, utilitarian liberalism's explanatory record shows interesting patterns which certainly deserve further attention. Further research is needed to examine the robustness of our finding that utilitarian liberalism's explanatory power strongly depends on the nature of the policy network as well as on the nature of the gains and losses to be expected.

Constructivism
As shown in table 10.7, Constructivism clearly has the best record in explaining post-unification Germany's foreign policy behaviour. As far as co-variation is concerned, constructivism always predicts post-unification Germany's policy correctly. The constructivist record is all the more impressive since it comprises not only four 'easy' but also three 'hard' cases for constructivism.[7] Moreover, constructivism explains cases of both continuity and change. As pointed out in chapter 5, constructivism claims high predictive power when there are convergent expectations of appropriate behaviour of a sufficient degree of com-

Table 10.7 Constructivism's explanatory record

Constructivism correctly predicts that post-unification Germany ...

- will continue to have the *Bundeswehr* integrated into NATO
- will participate in military out-of-area operations (though the sequence between the policy change and the evolution of societal norms, as well as Germany's participation in the air strikes against the FRY, disconfirm the constructivist account)
- will continue to support the extension of QMV in the EU Council
- will continue to support the strengthening of the EP's legislative powers
- will increase its efforts to achieve a reduction of its net contributions to the EU budget (though specific policy proposals and the negotiation style disconfirm constructivism)
- will no longer oppose but will support the liberalization of agricultural trade
- will continue to oppose the EC's third-country provisions concerning public procurement in the telecommunications sector
- will continue to support the strengthening of UN human rights institutions

monality and specificity on both the international and the societal level of analysis. The integration of the *Bundeswehr* into NATO, the participation in military out-of-area operations and the extension of both QMV and the EP's legislative powers are such 'easy' cases in which the international community of states and domestic society hold the same, convergent, expectations of appropriate German foreign policy behaviour. In contrast, with regard to the strengthening of UN human rights institutions, to the EC's third-country provisions concerning public procurement and to the net contributions to the EU budget there are no pertinent international but only societal norms. These cases are considered 'hard' cases because the constructivist prediction rests on social norms on only one level of analysis.

In three out of eight cases, constructivist foreign policy theory is the *only* theory whose predictions are fully corroborated by the observable behaviour. Only constructivism explains post-unification Germany's continued support for an extension of QMV in the EU Council, for a strengthening of the EP's legislative powers and for a strengthening of UN human rights institutions. What is more, in the case of the integration of the *Bundeswehr* in NATO, the three competing theories converge in their predictions but only constructivism is not disconfirmed by further observable implications. Thus constructivism provides the best explanation for half of the cases under examination, including one 'hard' case (UN human rights institutions).

Altogether, constructivism correctly predicts the entire range of post-unification Germany's foreign policy studied and provides the best explanation for half of the cases under examination. Thus post-unification Germany's foreign policy can best be characterized as norm-consistent foreign policy.

At the same time, however, there is one case in which the constructivist prediction is only partly correct: constructivism predicts that post-unification Germany will participate in military out-of-area operations *if* the operation has a firm international legal basis and a strong peace keeping character. This prediction is entirely correct with regard to half of the out-of-area operations under consideration. As regards German participation in SFOR and KFOR, however, Germany's contribution of combat troops does not fully correspond to the constructivist condition that a strong peace keeping character is to be expected. Finally, Germany's participation in the air strikes of 1999 against the former republic of Yugoslavia is not in line with the constructivist prediction either since a firm international legal basis did not exist. Taken together, constructivism correctly predicts the *pattern* of post-unification German foreign policy behaviour in that case but misses several specific instances of Germany's security policy behaviour.

In another case, constructivism correctly predicts post-unification Germany's foreign policy behaviour but is disconfirmed by further observable implications. Constructivist foreign policy theory correctly predicts that Germany will increase its efforts to reduce its net contribution to the EU budget, but it is disconfirmed by the German government's deliberate violation of EU norms in doing so, namely its demand for a rebate.

Finally, pertinent norms and domestic interests are almost indistinguishably linked in two cases, i.e. post-unification Germany's support for the liberalization of agricultural trade and its opposition to the EC's third-country provisions concerning public procurement in the telecommunications sector. Thus in the issue area of foreign trade, the societal norm to support free trade and the domestic interest in open markets coincide. In both cases, it has proved next to impossible to distinguish between the influence of societal norms and domestic interests. Therefore, it remains unclear in these cases whether post-unification Germany's foreign policy is best characterized as norm-consistent or as gain-seeking foreign policy.

Two further *caveats* must be added. First, if we accept that constructivism's explanatory power will be particularly strong in a highly

institutionalized environment, our sample of cases may be criticized for
having a selection bias because it comprises only cases of German foreign
policy within or towards international institutions.[8] As a matter of fact,
however, Germany has been embedded in an especially dense network
of international institutions. Thus, even if we accept that our sample
of cases does favour constructivism, this is due to Germany as our
object of inquiry rather than to a selection bias. Of course, the *caveat*
builds on the notion that a highly institutionalized environment is likely
to encompass widely shared expectations about appropriate (German)
behaviour.[9] However, as the occasionally low levels of specificity and
commonality of member states' expectations in our sample of cases
demonstrate, this notion does not necessarily prove correct. In fact, our
sample includes four cases in which there are no sufficiently specific
and widely shared norms on the international level (net contributions
to the EU budget, agricultural trade, EC third-country provisions, and
UN human rights institutions). Predictions have therefore been
generated on the basis of societal norms only, which, from a constructivist point of view, constitutes a 'hard' case (see chapter 4). In one of
these four 'hard' cases (the strengthening of UN human rights institutions), constructivism is the *only* theory offering a correct prediction.
In two other 'hard' cases (agricultural trade and EC third-country
provisions concerning public procurement in the telecommunications
sector), constructivism is not disconfirmed by further observable implications though utilitarian liberalism offers an equally plausible
explanation. Only in the last 'hard' case (Germany's net contributions
to the EU budget) is constructivism disconfirmed by further observable
implications.

The second *caveat* addresses our selection of indicators for the
identification of social norms. We are aware that party programmes
and election platforms, in particular, may not only identify social norms
but interests as well.[10] By linking the identification of a norm to a certain
level of commonality (e.g. a consensus among the major political parties)
we did try to avoid mixing up societal norms and domestic interests to
the best possible extent. However, domestic interests may simply acquire
a high level of acceptance in domestic society and may become part of
a society's political culture. Then, our indicators cannot, of course, or
only with great difficulty, discriminate between societal norms and
domestic interests. It is important to note, however, that our indicators
do not mistake domestic interests for societal norms but may simply
be unable to distinguish between the two because the two may indeed

be indistinguishably intertwined (the case study on foreign trade policy is a case in point). After all, adherents of constructivism do not argue that norms *replace* interests as a causal variable. Constructivism even concedes that norms may originate from interests in the first place. What distinguishes constructivism from rationalist approaches, however, is the former's claim that norms, once established, do have an impact in their own right. In order to evaluate the respective explanatory power of (societal) norms, as opposed to domestic interests, we would have to select cases in which (societal) norms change whereas domestic interests remain constant. That is to say, we would have to design a new research project which has constructivist (instead of neorealist) foreign policy theory as its centrepiece.

Summary

The evaluation of the foreign policy theories has yielded a number of remarkable results (table 10.8 gives an overview of our findings). First, the eight cases examined strongly disconfirm neorealism. The modification of neorealism clearly improves its explanatory record. However, modified neorealism's explanatory power remains limited to, but does not include all, cases of 'high politics'. Second, social norms turned out to yield the best explanation of post-unification Germany's foreign policy behaviour, capturing both cases of continuity and change as well as 'hard' and 'easy' cases for the theory. Finally, utilitarian liberalism's explanatory power seems to depend on the policy network structure dominating in the issue under consideration. Though its overall explanatory power may be modest, it can be regarded as a useful theory which is suited for the explanation of those cases of foreign policy in which PAS actors do not dominate the policy network (sufficient condition) and costs and benefits are material and calculable (necessary condition).

Table 10.8 Overview of foreign policy theories' explanatory records

Case	Neorealism	Modified neorealism	Utilitarian liberalism	Constructivism
Integration of the Bundeswehr in NATO	Disconfirmed	Correct prediction but puzzling further observables	Correct prediction but puzzling further observables	Confirmed
Participation in military out-of-area operations	Disconfirmed	Correct prediction but puzzling further observables	Disconfirmed	Correct prediction but puzzling further observables
Extension of QMV in the EU Council	Disconfirmed	Correct prediction but puzzling further observables	Disconfirmed	Confirmed
Strengthening of the EP's legislative powers	Disconfirmed		Disconfirmed	Confirmed
Net contributions to the EU budget	Confirmed		Confirmed	Correct prediction but puzzling further observables
Liberalization of agricultural trade	Disconfirmed		Confirmed	Confirmed
EC third-country provisions concerning public procurement	Disconfirmed		Confirmed	Confirmed
Strengthening of UN human rights institutions	Disconfirmed		Disconfirmed	Confirmed

Conclusion

Contrary to the expectation that post-unification Germany was about to step up the pursuit of power politics (see chapter 2), post-unification Germany's foreign policy was marked by a mixture of continuity and change, with cases of continuity in the majority. Notwithstanding an increased preparedness to participate in multilateral military out-of-area operations and a more assertive policy on financial burden sharing within the EU, post-unification Germany continued to support the establishment of new international institutions (e.g. the ICC), the strengthening of existing international institutions (e.g. the EP) and the pooling of sovereignty (e.g. by keeping the *Bundeswehr* integrated in NATO and by supporting the extension of QMV in the EU Council). In the area of agricultural trade, post-unification Germany turned to a more cooperative policy.

Neorealism's record in explaining post-unification Germany's foreign policy, even in its modified variant, turned out to be comparatively weak. Of course, adherents of neorealism may point to a time lag between a change in a state's power position and a change in its foreign policy behaviour. They may also point to the fact that the two most obvious cases of apparent power politics (post-unification Germany's policy on military out-of-area operations and on net contributions to the EU budget) have taken place in the second half of the 1990s. However, critics of neorealism may well regard the neorealist reference to time lags as yet another attempt to escape empirical falsification.[11]

This volume conveys three major findings. Post-unification Germany's foreign policy can first and foremost be characterized as norm-consistent foreign policy. As predicted by constructivism, post-unification Germany's foreign policy has almost always adhered to the value-based expectations of appropriate behaviour shared within the international and domestic society. At the same time, however, post-unification Germany has intensified its influence-seeking policy. Particularly in the 'high politics' issue areas, it has stepped up its efforts to increase its influence on collective decision making and collective action. Finally, and in line with its tradition as an institutionally integrated trading state, post-unification Germany has pursued a gain-seeking policy, in the making of which demands of assertive private actors have played a prominent role.[12]

Notes

1   For recent theory-led research see, among others, Banchoff 1999a, b; Berger 1998; Duffield 1999, 1998; Katzenstein 1997a; and Kirste 1998. For the debate geared towards analysis of and for policy, see chapter 2 and Hellmann 1996.

2 As chapter 2 shows, only a minority of observers have referred to that notion affirmatively. The majority of commentators have done so rather disapprovingly.

3 It should be noted, however, that a longitudinal analysis of a single country poses less severe problems of control than the analysis of different countries in different time periods. This is because a broad range of country-specific variables is held constant automatically (Lijphart 1975: 159).

4 The term 'case' has been used in a variety of ways (see Ragin and Becker 1992). Following Lijphart's definition of a case as 'an entity on which only one basic observation is made and in which the independent and dependent variables do not change during the period of observation' (1975: 160), one could argue that each observation of Germany's foreign policy on a certain issue at a specific point in time constitutes a case of its own. However, our research question does not refer to instances of German foreign policy but to instances of German foreign policy continuity or change. A single case in the sense in which Lijphart uses the term cannot give an answer to our central research questions. Only a pair or series of observations can provide an answer to these questions. It is thus appropriate to refer to each pair or series of observations as a case.

5 We have to acknowledge that our original goal of including a maximum of macropolitical contexts has not been achieved. For instance, cases concerned with Eastern Europe (e.g. German policy on the issue of enlargement of NATO and the EU) had to be omitted from our sample of cases because post-unification Germany's policy can hardly be compared with its policy before unification because these enlargement issues were not then on the political agenda.

6 The (in)famous case of the diplomatic recognition of Yugoslav successor states in the early 1990s cannot be dealt with here because it defies the research design of a comparison between pre- and post-unification Germany.

7 The liberalization of agricultural trade is difficult to assess in these terms because international ('protect agricultural market!') and societal ('support trade liberalization!') norms may be compatible (though not convergent) (as in the 1990s) as well as contradictory (as in the late 1980s).

8 We owe this point to Bernhard Zangl.

9 Of course, Germany has also been influential in shaping international institutions in the first place. Thus if we use international norms as independent variables to predict German behaviour, we seem to run the risk of circular reasoning. However, this danger is all the smaller the longer the time period between norm creation and its expected impact on German behaviour.

10 We owe this point to Markus Jachtenfuchs in particular.

11 For a discussion on neorealism as a degenerative research programme, see Vasquez 1997 and Legro and Moravcsik 1999 and the ensuing debates in the *American Political Science Review* and *International Security*.

12 These results basically confirm earlier findings (Rittberger 1999). However, in the light of the more differentiated results of this volume, two modifications seem in order. First, although continuity prevails in post-unification Germany's foreign policy, it is now clear that, nonetheless, there appear to be some systematic changes which may indeed be attributable to Germany's improved power position in the international system and which can be explained by modified neorealism. Second, it can now be stated with more confidence that, in general, German foreign policy is decisively shaped by social norms.

References

Party programmes and election platforms

CDU/CSU

CSU (1976), Grundsatzprogramm der Christlich Sozialen Union.

CDU (1978), Grundsatzprogramm der CDU.

CDU/CSU (1980), Für Frieden und Freiheit. Das Wahlprogramm der CDU/CSU.

CDU/CSU (1983), Arbeit, Frieden, Zukunft. Miteinander schaffen wir's. Das Wahlprogramm der CDU/CSU.

CDU/CSU (1987), Weiter so, Deutschland. Für eine gute Zukunft. Das Wahlprogramm von CDU und CSU für die Bundestagswahl 1987.

CDU (1988), Unsere Verantwortung in der Welt. Christlich-demokratische Perspektiven zur Deutschland-, Außen-, Sicherheits-, Europa- und Entwicklungspolitik.

CDU (1990), Ja zu Deutschland – Ja zur Zukunft. Wahlprogramm der Christlich Demokratischen Union Deutschlands zur gesamtdeutschen Bundestagswahl am 2. Dezember 1990.

CSU (1990), Heimat Bayern. Zukunft Deutschland. Mit uns. CSU. Programm der Christlich-Sozialen Union zur Bundestagswahl am 2. Dezember 1990.

CSU (1992), Die Welt im Umbruch: Frieden in Freiheit sichern. Europa gestalten. Deutsche Interessen vertreten.

CSU (1993), In Freiheit dem Gemeinwohl verpflichtet. Grundsatzprogramm der Christlich-Sozialen Union in Bayern.

CDU (1994), Freiheit in Verantwortung. Grundsatzprogramm der Christlich Demokratischen Union Deutschlands.

CDU/CSU (1994), Wir sichern Deutschlands Zukunft. Regierungsprogramm von CDU und CSU.

CDU (1998), Das 21. Jahrhundert menschlich gestalten. Zukunftsprogramm der CDU.

CDU/CSU (1998), Wahlplattform der CDU und CSU 1998–2002.

Bündnis 90/Die Grünen and Die Grünen

Die Grünen (1980a), Bundesprogramm.

Die Grünen (1980b), Wahlplattform zur Bundestagswahl 1980.

Die Grünen (1983), Diesmal die GRÜNEN – warum? Ein Aufruf zur Bundestagswahl 1983.

Die Grünen (1987), Programm Bundestagswahl 1987. Farbe bekennen. DIE GRÜNEN.

Die Grünen (1990), DIE GRÜNEN: Das Programm zur 1. gesamtdeutschen Wahl 1990.

Die Grünen/Bündnis 90 (1990), DIE GRÜNEN/Bündnis 90. Wahlplattform.

Bündnis 90/Die Grünen (1994a), Bündnis 90/DIE GRÜNEN. Politische Grundsätze.

Bündnis 90/Die Grünen (1994b), Nur mit uns. Wahlprogramm zur Bundestagswahl 1994.

Bündnis 90/Die Grünen (1998), Grün ist der Wechsel (Magdeburger Programm).

FDP

FDP (1980), Unser Land soll auch morgen liberal sein. Wahlprogramm der Freien Demokratischen Partei für die Bundestagswahlen am 5. Oktober 1980.

FDP (1983), Freiheit braucht Mut. Wahlaussage '83 der Freien Demokratischen Partei für die Bundestagswahlen am 6. März 1983.

FDP (1985), Zukunftschance Freiheit. Liberales Manifest für eine Gesellschaft im Umbruch.

FDP (1987), Zukunft durch Leistung. Wahlplattform der F.D.P. zur Bundestagwahl 1987.

FDP (1990), Das liberale Deutschland. Programm der F.D.P. zu den Bundestagswahlen am 2. Dezember 1990.

FDP (1994), Liberal denken. Leistung wählen. Das Programm der F.D.P. zur Bundestagswahl 1994.

FDP (1997), Wiesbadener Grundsätze. Für die liberale Bürgergesellschaft.

FDP (1998), Es ist Ihre Wahl. Das Wahlprogramm der Liberalen zur Bundestagswahl 1998.

PDS

PDS (1990), Programm.

PDS (1993), Programm der Partei des Demokratischen Sozialismus.

PDS (1994), Opposition gegen Sozialabbau und Rechtsruck. Wahlprogramm der PDS 1994.

PDS (1996), Sicherheit und Abrüstung. Vorschläge und Forderungen der PDS-

Gruppe des Deutschen Bundestages. Eine Dokumentation, PDS Pressedienst Nr. 31/96 und Nr. 32/96.
PDS (1998), PDS-Wahlprogramm 1998.

SPD

SPD (1959), Grundsatzprogramm der Sozialdemokratischen Partei Deutschlands (Godesberger Programm).
SPD (1980), Sicherheit für Deutschland. Wahlprogramm 1980.
SPD (1983), SPD-Wahlprogramm 1983.
SPD (1987), Zukunft für alle – arbeiten für soziale Gerechtigkeit und Frieden. Regierungsprogramm 1987–1990 der Sozialdemokratischen Partei Deutschlands.
SPD (1989), Grundsatzprogramm Sozialdemokratische Partei Deutschlands, reprinted in: Programme der deutschen Sozialdemokratie, Bonn, Dietz, 169–243.
SPD (1990), Der neue Weg: ökologisch, sozial, wirtschaftlich stark. Regierungsprogramm 1990–1994.
SPD (1994), Reformen für Deutschland. Das Regierungsprogramm der SPD.
SPD (1998), Arbeit, Innovation und Gerechtigkeit. SPD-Programm für die Bundestagswahl 1998.

Books and articles

Ahner, Dirk (1996), 'Gemeinsame Agrarpolitik – Herzstück und Sorgenkind', in Moritz Röttinger and Claudia Weyringer (eds), Handbuch der europäischen Integration. Strategie-Struktur-Politik der Europäischen Union, Vienna, Manzsche Verlags- und Universitätsbuchhandlung, 846–70.
Akehurst, Michael (1987), A Modern Introduction to International Law, 6th edn, London, Routledge.
Albrecht, Ulrich (1993), 'Konfliktfelder in einer neuen Weltordnung', in Hans-Peter Hubert and Bundesarbeitsgemeinschaft Frieden und Internationalismus der Grünen (eds), Grüne Außenpolitik – Aspekte einer Debatte, Göttingen, Die Werkstatt, 63–8.
Allison, Graham T. (1971), Essence of Decision. Explaining the Cuban Missile Crisis, Boston, Little, Brown.
Allison, Graham T. and Zelikow, Philip (1999), Essence of Decision. Explaining the Cuban Missile Crisis, 2nd edn, New York, Longman.
Alten, Jürgen von (1994), Die ganz normale Anarchie. Jetzt erst beginnt die Nachkriegszeit, Berlin, Siedler.
Anderson, Jeffrey J. (1997), 'Hard Interests, Soft Power, and Germany's Changing

Role in Europe', in Peter Katzenstein (ed.), *Tamed Power. Germany in Europe*, Ithaca, NY, Cornell University Press, 80–107.

Anderson, Jeffrey J. (1999), *German Unification and the Union of Europe. The Domestic Politics of Integration Policy*, Cambridge, Cambridge University Press.

Anderson, Jeffrey J. and Goodman, John B. (1993), 'Mars or Minerva? A United Germany in a Post-Cold War Europe', in Robert O. Keohane, Joseph S. Nye and Stanley Hoffmann (eds), *After the Cold War. International Institutions and State Strategies in Europe, 1989–1991*, Cambridge, MA, Harvard University Press, 23–62.

Andreae, Lisette and Kaiser, Karl (1998), 'Die "Außenpolitik" der Fachministerien', in Wolf-Dieter Eberwein and Karl Kaiser (eds), *Deutschlands neue Außenpolitik, Vol. 4: Institutionen und Ressourcen*, Munich, Oldenbourg, 29–46.

Arend, Anthony Clark (1996), 'Toward an Understanding of International Legal Rules', in Robert J. Beck, Anthony Clark Arend and Robert D. Vander Lugt (eds), *International Rules. Approaches from International Law and International Relations*, Oxford, Oxford University Press, 289–310.

Armstrong, David (1993), *Revolution and World Order. The Revolutionary State in International Society*, Oxford, Clarendon Press.

Armstrong, David (1994), 'The Socialization of States', paper presented at the ISA Annual International Convention, 28 March – 1 April 1994, Washington, DC.

Arnim, Joachim von (1995), 'Was ist des Deutschen Außenpolitik?', in Jörg Calließ and Bernhard Moltmann (eds), *Die Zukunft der Außenpolitik: Deutsche Interessen in den internationalen Beziehungen*, Loccumer Protokolle, 67/94, Rehburg-Loccum, Evangelische Akademie Loccum, 470–5.

Art, Robert (1996), 'American Foreign Policy and the Fungibility of Force', *Security Studies*, 5: 4, 7–42.

Atkinson, Michael M. and Coleman, William D. (1989), 'Strong States and Weak States: Sectoral Policy Networks in Advanced Capitalist Economies', *British Journal of Political Science*, 19: 1, 47–67.

Auswärtiges Amt (ed.) (1995), *Außenpolitik der Bundesrepublik Deutschland. Dokumente von 1949 bis 1994*, Bonn, Auswärtiges Amt.

Axelrod, Robert and Keohane, Robert O. (1985), 'Achieving Cooperation under Anarchy: Strategies and Institutions', *World Politics*, 38: 1, 226–54.

Bach, Jonathan P. G. (1999), *Between Sovereignty and Integration. German Foreign Policy and National Identity after 1989*, Münster, Lit.

Baehr, Peter R. (1994), *The Role of Human Rights in Foreign Policy*, Basingstoke, Macmillan.

Bahr, Egon and Mutz, Reinhard (1998), 'Deutsche Interessen und die Sicherheit Europas: Zur militärischen Verengung eines politischen Begriffs', in Reinhard Mutz, Bruno Schoch and Friedhelm Solms (eds), *Friedensgutachten 1998*, Münster, Lit, 236–49.

Banchoff, Thomas (1997), 'German Policy Toward the European Union: The Effect of Historical Memory', *German Politics*, 6: 1, 60–76.

Banchoff, Thomas (1999a), *The German Problem Transformed. Institutions, Politics, and Foreign Policy, 1945–1995*, Ann Arbor, MI, University of Michigan Press.

Banchoff, Thomas (1999b), 'German Identity and European Integration', *European Journal of International Relations*, 5: 3, 259–89.

Baring, Arnulf (1994), '"Germany, What Now?"', in Arnulf Baring (ed.), *Germany's New Position in Europe*, Oxford, Berg, 1–20.

Barkin, J. Samuel (1998), 'The Evolution of the Constitution of Sovereignty and the Emergence of Human Rights Norms', *Millennium: Journal of International Studies*, 27: 2, 229–52.

Bartl, Peter (1997), 'Kosovo – historische Ursachen eines aktuellen Konflikts', *Die Friedenswarte*, 72: 4, 351–60.

Baum, Gerhart R. (1997), 'Menschenrechte in den Vereinten Nationen – ein aktueller Lagebericht', *Vereinte Nationen*, 45: 4, 126–30.

Bauman, Rainer and Kerski, Basil (1994), 'Deutschlandpolitisches Faustpfand oder bloße Verhandlungsmasse? Sowjetische Truppenpräsenz und die Neugestaltung des sicherheitspolitischen Status Deutschlands, in Gunther Hellman (ed.), *Alliierte Präsenz und deutsche Einheit. Die politischen Folgen militärischer Macht*, Baden-Baden, Nomos, 195–227.

Baumann, Rainer, Rittberger, Volker and Wagner, Wolfgang (1999), 'Macht und Machtpolitik. Neorealistische Außenpolitiktheorie und Prognosen über die deutsche Außenpolitik nach der Vereinigung', *Zeitschrift für Internationale Beziehungen*, 6: 2, 245–86.

Bellers, Jürgen (1990), *Außenwirtschaftspolitik der Bundesrepublik Deutschland 1949–1989*, Münster, Lit.

Benedetti, Fanny and Washburn, John L. (1999), 'Drafting the International Criminal Court Treaty: Two Years to Rome and an Afterword on the Rome Diplomatic Conference', *Global Governance*, 5: 1, 1–37.

Bennett, Andrew and George, Alexander (1998), 'Process Tracing with Notes on Causal Mechanisms and Historical Explanation', paper presented at the Diplomatic History and International Relations Theory Conference, Arizona State University, January 1998.

Bentinck, Marc (1986), *NATO's Out-of-Area Problem*, Adelphi Papers, 211, London, The International Institute for Strategic Studies.

Benz, Arthur (1993), 'Commentary on O'Toole and Scharpf: The Network Concept as a Theoretical Approach', in Fritz W. Scharpf (ed.), *Games in Hierarchies and Networks. Analytical and Empirical Approaches to the Study of Governance Institutions*, Frankfurt a.M., Campus, 167–76.

Bergem, Wolfgang (1993), *Tradition und Transformation: eine vergleichende Untersuchung zur politischen Kultur in Deutschland*, Opladen, Westdeutscher Verlag.

Berger, Thomas U. (1996), 'Norms, Identity, and National Security in Germany and Japan', in Peter J. Katzenstein (ed.), *The Culture of National Security. Norms and Identity in World Politics*, New York, Columbia University Press, 317–56.

Berger, Thomas U. (1998), *Cultures of Antimilitarism: National Security in Germany and Japan*, Baltimore, Johns Hopkins University Press.

Bergner, Jeffrey T. (1991), *The New Superpowers: Germany, Japan, the U.S.A. and the New World Order*, New York, St. Martin's Press.

Berndt, Michael (1997), *Deutsche Militärpolitik in der 'neuen Weltunordnung'. Zwischen nationalen Interessen und globalen Entwicklungen*, Münster, Agenda.

Bertram, Christoph (1997), 'Determinanten deutscher Außenpolitik', in Jörg Calließ and Christoph Hüttig (eds), *Deutsche Interessen in den internationalen Beziehungen*, Loccumer Protokolle, 62/95, Loccum, Evangelische Akademie Loccum, 13–24.

Beyme, Klaus von (1989), 'Gesellschaftliche Interessen und gesellschaftliche Organisationen in der Bundesrepublik Deutschland', in Werner Weidenfeld and Hartmut Zimmermann (eds), *Deutschland-Handbuch. Eine doppelte Bilanz 1949–1989*, Bonn, Bundeszentrale für politische Bildung, 141–55.

Bieber, Roland (1991), 'Verfassungsentwicklung und Verfassungsgebung in der Europäischen Gemeinschaft', in Rudolf Wildenmann (ed.), *Staatswerdung Europas?*, Baden-Baden, Nomos, 393–414.

Billing, Peter, Kittel, Gabriele, Rittberger, Volker and Schimmelfennig, Frank (1993), 'State Characteristics and Foreign Policy. Industrialized Countries and the UNESCO Crisis', *Cooperation and Conflict*, 28: 2, 143–80.

Black, David R. (1999), ' "No Cricket": The Effects and Effectiveness of the Sport Boycott', in Neta C. Crawford and Audie Klotz (eds), *How Sanctions Work. Lessons from South Africa*, New York, St. Martin's Press, 213–31.

Blair, John P. and Maser, Steven M. (1978), 'A Reassessment of Axiomatic Models in Policy Studies', in Gordon Tullock and Richard E. Wagner (eds), *Policy Analysis and Deductive Reasoning*, Lexington, MA, Lexington Books, 3–16.

Blume, Gerd and Rex, Alexander Graf von (1998), 'Weiterentwicklung der inhaltlichen und personellen Mitwirkung der Länder in Angelegenheiten der EU nach Maastricht', in Franz H. U. Borkenhagen (ed.), *Europapolitik der deutschen Länder*, Opladen, Leske+Budrich, 29–49.

Bogdandy, Armin von (1991), 'Europäische und nationale Steuerung des Außenhandels', in Heinrich Siedentopf (ed.), *Europäische Integration und nationalstaatliche Verwaltung: Deutsche Vereinigung und institutionelle Weiterentwicklung der Gemeinschaft*, Stuttgart, Franz Steiner Verlag, 135–54.

Bogdandy, Armin von and Wernicke, Stephan (1993), 'Transatlantischer Streit um das öffentliche Auftragswesen', *EuZW*, 4: 7, 216–21.

Boli, John and Thomas, George M. (eds) (1999), *Constructing World Culture. International Nongovernmental Organizations Since 1875*, Stanford, CA, Stanford University Press.

Borchmann, Michael (1994), 'Die Aktivitäten der deutschen Länder: Das Beispiel

Hessen', in Franz H. U. Borkenhagen *et al.* (eds), *Die deutschen Länder in Europa. Politische Union und Wirtschafts- und Währungsunion*, Baden Baden, Nomos, 110–19.

Bourgeois, Jacques (1995), 'The EC in the WTO and Advisory Opinion 1/94', *Common Market Law Review*, 32: 3, 763–87.

Boutros-Ghali, Boutros (1995), *An Agenda for Peace*, 2nd edn with supplement and related UN documents, New York, United Nations (DPI/1623/PKO, E.95.0.15).

Brandtner, Barbara and Rosas, Allan (1998), 'Human Rights and the External Relations of the European Community: An Analysis of Doctrine and Practice', *European Journal of International Law*, 9: 3, 468–90.

Breuning, Marijke (1995), 'Words and Deeds: Foreign Assistance Rhetoric and Policy Behaviour in the Netherlands, Belgium, and the United Kingdom', *International Studies Quarterly*, 39: 2, 235–54.

Breuning, Marijke (1997), 'Culture, History, Role: Belgian and Dutch Axioms and Foreign Assistance Policy', in Valerie Hudson (ed.), *Culture and Foreign Policy*, Boulder, CO, Lynne Rienner, 99–123.

Brooks, Stephen G. (1997), 'Dueling Realisms', *International Organization*, 51: 3, 445–77.

Brösse, Ulrich (1999), *Industriepolitik*, 2nd rev. edn, Munich, Oldenbourg.

Brunner, Manfred (1996), 'Europa und Nation: Über die Notwendigkeit der Souveränität', in Heimo Schwilk and Ulrich Schacht (eds), *Die selbstbewußte Nation: 'Anschwellender Bocksgesang' und weitere Beiträge zu einer deutschen Debatte*, 3rd edn, Berlin, Ullstein, 381–9.

Buchanan, James M. (1989), 'Rational Choice Models in the Social Sciences', in James M. Buchanan and Robert D. Tollison (eds), *Explorations into Constitutional Economics*, Houston, Texas A & M University Press, 37–50.

Buchanan, James M. and Tullock, Gordon (1962), *The Calculus of Consent. Logical Foundations of Constitutional Democracy*, Ann Arbor, MI, University of Michigan Press.

Bühl, Walter (1994), 'Gesellschaftliche Grundlagen der deutschen Außenpolitik', in Karl Kaiser and Hanns Maull (eds), *Deutschlands neue Außenpolitik, Vol. 1: Grundlagen*, Munich, Oldenburg, 175–202.

Bull, Hedley (1977), *The Anarchical Society. A Study of Order in World Politics*, Basingstoke, Macmillan.

Bulmer, Simon (1991), 'Analysing EPC: The Case for Two-Tier-Analysis', in Martin Holland (ed.), *The Future of European Political Cooperation. Essays on Theory and Practice*, Basingstoke, Macmillan, 70–94.

Bulmer, Simon (1997), 'Shaping the Rules? The Constitutive Politics of the European Union and German Power', in Peter Katzenstein (ed.), *Tamed Power. Germany in Europe*, Ithaca, NY, Cornell University Press, 49–79.

Bulmer, Simon and Paterson, William (1987), *The Federal Republic of Germany and the European Community*, Boston, Allen & Unwin.

Bulmer, Simon, Jeffery, Charlie and Paterson, William (1998), 'Deutschlands europäische Diplomatie: Die Entwicklung des regionalen Milieus', in Werner Weidenfeld (ed.), *Deutsche Europapolitik: Optionen wirksamer Interessenvertretung*, Bonn, Europa Union Verlag, 11–102.

Bundesminister der Verteidigung (1985), *Weißbuch. Zur Lage und Entwicklung der Bundeswehr*, Bonn, Bundesministerium der Verteidigung.

Bundesminister der Verteidigung (1992), *Verteidigungspolitische Richtlinien*, Bonn, Bundesministerium der Verteidigung.

Bundesminister der Verteidigung (1994), *Weißbuch zur Sicherheit der Bundesrepublik Deutschland und zur Lage und Zukunft der Bundeswehr*, Bonn, Bundesministerium der Verteidigung.

Bundesminister der Verteidigung (1995), *Die konzeptionelle Leitlinie zur Weiterentwicklung der Bundeswehr* (reprinted by: Presse- und Informationsamt der Bundesregierung, Referat Außen- und Sicherheitspolitik, Bonn).

Bundesminister der Verteidigung (1999), *Bestandsaufnahme. Die Bundeswehr an der Schwelle zum 21. Jahrhundert*, Bonn, Bundesministerium der Verteidigung.

Bundesministerium der Finanzen (1997), *Finanzbericht 1997*, Bonn, Bundesanzeiger.

Bundespresseamt (1995), *Alliierte Truppen und multinationale Streitkräftestrukturen in Deutschland*, Bonn, Presse- und Informationsamt der Bundesregierung, Referat Außen- und Sicherheitspolitik.

Burley, Anne-Marie (1993a), 'Regulating the World: Multilateralism, International Law, and the Protection of the New Deal Regulatory State', in John Gerard Ruggie (ed.), *Multilateralism Matters. The Theory and Praxis of an Institutional Form*, New York, Columbia University Press, 125–56.

Burley, Anne-Marie (1993b), 'International Law and International Relations Theory: A Dual Agenda', *American Journal of International Law*, 87: 2, 205–39.

Buzan, Barry (1991), *People, States and Fear. An Agenda for International Security Studies in the Post-Cold War Era*, 2nd edn, New York, Harvester Wheatsheaf.

Buzan, Barry (1993a), 'Rethinking System and Structure', in Barry Buzan, Charles Jones and Richard Little (eds), *Logic of Anarchy. Neorealism to Structural Realism*, New York, Columbia University Press, 19–80.

Buzan, Barry (1993b), 'From International System to International Society. Structural Realism and Regime Theory Meet the English School', *International Organization*, 47: 3, 327–52.

Byers, Michael (1999), *Custom, Power and the Power of Rules. International Relations and Customary International Law*, Cambridge, Cambridge University Press.

Calic, Marie-Janine (1996), *Krieg und Frieden in Bosnien-Herzegovina*, 2nd edn, Frankfurt a.M., Suhrkamp.

Carleton, David and Stohl, Michael (1985), 'The Foreign Policy of Human Rights: Rhetoric and Reality from Jimmy Carter to Ronald Reagan: A Critique and Reappraisal', *Human Rights Quarterly*, 7: 2, 205–29.

Carlsnaes, Walter (1992), 'The Agency-Structure Problem in Foreign Policy Analysis', *International Studies Quarterly*, 36: 3, 245–70.

Carr, Edward H. (1939), *The Twenty Years' Crisis 1919–1939: An Introduction to the Study of International Relations*, London, Macmillan.

Carrubba, Clifford F. (1997), 'Net Financial Transfers in the European Union. Who Gets What and Why?', *Journal of Politics*, 59: 2, 469–96.

Cassese, Antonio (1999), 'Ex iniuria ius orientur: Are We Moving Towards International Legitimation of Forcible Humanitarian Countermeasures in the World Community?', *European Journal of International Law*, 10: 1, 23–30.

Cawson, Alan (1985), 'Introduction. Varieties of Corporatism: The Importance of the Meso-Level of Interest Intermediation', in Alan Cawson (ed.), *Organized Interests and the State: Studies in Meso-Corporatism*, London, Sage, 1–21.

Chan, Steve (1997), 'In Search of Democratic Peace: Problems and Promise', *Mershon International Studies Review*, 41: 1, 59–91.

Chayes, Abram and Chayes, Antonia Handler (1993), 'On Compliance', *International Organization*, 47: 2, 175–205.

Checkel, Jeffrey T. (1997), 'International Norms and Domestic Politics: Bridging the Rationalist–Constructivist Divide', *European Journal of International Relations*, 3: 4, 473–95.

Checkel, Jeffrey T. (1998), 'The Constructivist Turn in International Relations Theory', *World Politics*, 50: 2, 324–48.

Christe, Hans-Joachim (1995), *Die USA und der EG-Binnenmarkt. Die amerikanische Außenwirtschaftspolitik gegenüber der EG 1985–1992. Strukturen, Entwicklungen, Entscheidungsprozesse*, Baden-Baden, Nomos.

Christensen, Thomas J. and Snyder, Jack (1997), 'Progressive Research on Degenerate Alliances', *American Political Science Review*, 91: 4, 919–22.

Clapham, Andrew (1994), 'Creating the High Commissioner for Human Rights: The Outside Story', *European Journal of International Law*, 5: 4, 556–68.

Clark, Roger Stenson (1972), *A United Nations High Commissioner for Human Rights*, The Hague, Martinus Nijhoff.

Clostermeyer, Claus-Peter (1992), 'Die Mitwirkung der Länder in EG-Angelegenheiten', in Franz H. U. Borkenhagen *et al.* (eds), *Die deutschen Länder in Europa. Politische Union und Wirtschafts- und Währungsunion*, Baden-Baden, Nomos, 171–82.

Clostermeyer, Claus-Peter (1997), 'Deutschland – "Zahlmeister" Europas?', in Rolf Caesar (ed.), *Zur Reform der Finanzverfassung und Strukturpolitik der EU*, Baden-Baden, Nomos, 141–52.

Cooper, Alice H. (1997), 'When Just Causes Conflict with Accepted Means: The German Peace Movement and Military Intervention in Bosnia', *German Politics and Society*, 15: 3, 99–118.

Coplin, William (1969), 'International Law and Assumptions about the State System', in James Rosenau (ed.), *International Politics and Foreign Policy*, rev. edn, New York, Free Press, 142–52.

Corbett, Richard (1987), 'The 1985 Intergovernmental Conference', in Roy Pryce (ed.), *The Dynamics of European Union*, London, Croom Helm, 238–72.

Corbett, Richard (1993), *The Treaty of Maastricht: From Conception to Ratification*, Harlow, Longman.

Corbett, Richard, Jacobs, Francis and Shackleton, Michael (1995), *The European Parliament*, 3rd edn, London, Catermill.

Cortell, Andrew and Davis, James (1996), 'How Do International Institutions Matter? The Domestic Impact of International Rules and Norms', *International Studies Quarterly*, 40: 4, 451–78.

Crozier, Michel and Friedberg, Erhard (1979), *Macht und Organisation. Die Zwänge kollektiven Handelns*, Königstein, Athenaeum Verlag.

Czada, Roland M. (1991), 'Interest Groups, Self-Interest, and the Institutionalization of Political Action', in Roland M. Czada and Adrienne Windhoff-Héritier (eds), *Political Choice. Institutions, Rules, and the Limits of Rationality*, Boulder, CO, Westview, 257–99.

Czada, Roland (1994), 'Konjunkturen des Korporatismus: Zur Geschichte eines Paradigmenwechsels in der Verbändeforschung', in Wolfgang Streeck (ed.), *Staat und Verbände*, PVS-Sonderheft 25, Opladen, Westdeutscher Verlag, 37–64.

Czada, Roland (1996), 'Interessenvermittlung und Anpassungslernen in der Vereinigungspolitik', in Andreas Eisen and Hellmut Wollmann (eds), *Institutionenbildung in Ostdeutschland. Zwischen externer Steuerung und Eigendynamik*, Opladen, Leske+Budrich, 337–58.

Czempiel, Ernst-Otto (1981), *Internationale Politik. Ein Konfliktmodell*, Paderborn, Schöningh.

Czempiel, Ernst-Otto (1993), 'Die neue Souveränität – ein Anachronismus? Regieren zwischen nationaler Souveränität, europäischer Integration und weltweiten Verflechtungen', in Hans-Hermann Hartwich and Göttrik Wewer (eds), *Regieren in der Bundesrepublik V. Souveränität, Integration, Interdependenz – Staatliches Handeln in der Außen- und Europapolitik*, Opladen, Leske + Budrich, 145–58.

Czempiel, Ernst-Otto (1999), *Kluge Macht. Außenpolitik für das 21. Jahrhundert*, Munich, Beck.

Czempiel, Ernst-Otto (2000), 'Determinanten zukünftiger deutscher Außenpolitik', *Aus Politik und Zeitgeschichte*, B24/2000, 13–21.

Dalvi, Sameera (1998), 'The Post-Cold War Role of the Bundeswehr: A Product of Normative Influences', *European Security*, 7: 1, 97–116.

Daugbjerg, Carsten and Marsh, David (1998), 'Explaining Policy Outcomes: Integrating the Policy Network Approach With Macro-level and Micro-level Analysis', in David Marsh (ed.), *Comparing Policy Networks*, Buckingham, Open University Press, 52–71.

Deile, Volkmar (1998), 'Können Nichtregierungsorganisationen einen Beitrag zum Menschenrechtsschutz leisten?', in Gerhart Baum, Eibe Riedel and

Michael Schaefer (eds), *Menschenrechtsschutz in der Praxis der Vereinten Nationen*, Baden-Baden, Nomos, 101–18.

Deile, Volkmar (1999), 'Gibt es eine glaubwürdige deutsche Menschenrechtspolitik?', in Franz-Josef Hutter and Carsten Tessmer (eds), *Menschenrechte und Bürgergesellschaft in Deutschland*, Opladen, Leske + Budrich, 201–18.

Deiseroth, Dieter (1985), 'Die Bundesrepublik – Transit-Stelle für US-Militäreinsätze außerhalb des NATO-Gebiets? Anmerkungen zum "Wartime-Host-Nation-Support-Abkommen" zwischen den USA und der Bundesrepublik Deutschland vom 15. April 1982', *Kritische Justiz*, 18, 412–34.

Dessler, David (1989), 'What's at Stake in the Agent-Structure Debate?', *International Organization*, 43: 3, 441–73.

Deubner, Christian (1995), *Deutsche Europapolitik. Von Maastricht nach Kerneuropa*, Baden-Baden, Nomos.

Devuyst, Youri (1995), 'The European Community and the Conclusion of the Uruguay Round', in Carolyn Rhodes and Sonia Mazey (eds), *The State of the European Union, Vol. 3: Building a European Polity?*, Boulder, CO, Lynne Rienner, 449–67.

Dinan, Desmond (1994), *Ever Closer Union? An Introduction to the European Community*, Basingstoke, Macmillan.

Dinan, Desmond (1998), *Encyclopedia of the European Union*, Basingstoke, Macmillan.

Dobler, Wolfgang (1989), *Außenpolitik und öffentliche Meinung*, Frankfurt a.M., Haag + Herchen.

Donges, Juergen B. (1995), *Deutschland in der Weltwirtschaft. Dynamik sichern, Herausforderungen bewältigen*, Mannheim, BI-Taschenbuchverlag.

Donnelly, Jack (1989), *Universal Human Rights in Theory and Practice*, Ithaca, NY, Cornell University Press.

Dowding, Keith (1995), 'Model or Metaphor? A Critical Review of the Policy Network Approach', *Political Studies*, 43: 1, 136–58.

Dowding, Keith and King, Desmond (1995), 'Introduction', in Keith Dowding and Desmond King (eds), *Preferences, Institutions, and Rational Choice*, Oxford, Clarendon Press, 1–19.

Downs, Anthony (1967), *Inside Bureaucracy*, Boston, MA, Little, Brown.

Duffield, John S. (1994), 'German Security Policy after Unification: Sources of Continuity and Restraint', *Contemporary Security Policy*, 15: 3, 170–98.

Duffield, John S. (1998), *World Power Forsaken: Political Culture, International Institutions, and German Security Policy After Unification*, Stanford, CA, Stanford University Press.

Duffield, John S. (1999), 'Political Culture and State Behavior: Why Germany Confounds Neorealism', *International Organization*, 53: 4, 765–803.

Duijm, Bernhard and Winter, Helen (1992), 'Für eine neue Dimension der Handelspolitik', *Wirtschaftsdienst*, 72: 7, 374–9.

Edinger, Lewis J. (1993), 'Pressure Group Politics in West Germany', in Jeremy J. Richardson (ed.), *Pressure Groups*, Oxford, Oxford University Press, 175–90.

Egeland, Jan (1988), *Impotent Superpower – Potent Small State: Potentials and Limitations of Human Rights Objectives in the Foreign Policies of the United States and Norway*, Oslo, Norwegian University Press.

Elgie, Robert (1995), *Germany. Dispersed Leadership*, Basingstoke, Macmillan.

Elias, Norbert (1969), *Über den Prozeß der Zivilisation. Soziogenetische und psychogenetische Untersuchungen*, Bern, Francke.

Elias, Norbert (1985), *Humana conditio. Beobachtungen zur Entwicklung der Menschheit am 40. Jahrestag eines Kriegsendes (8. Mai 1985)*, Frankfurt a.M., Suhrkamp.

Ellger, Reinhard (1992), 'Deutsches und internationales Wirtschaftsrecht der grenzüberschreitenden Telekommunikation', in Reinhard Ellger and Thomas-Sönke Kluth (eds), *Das Wirtschaftsrecht der Internationalen Telekommunikation in der Bundesrepublik Deutschland*, Baden-Baden, Nomos, 171–215.

Elman, Colin (1996a), 'Horses for Courses. Why Not Neo-realist Theories of Foreign Policy?', *Security Studies*, 6: 1, 7–53.

Elman, Colin (1996b), 'Cause, Effect, and Consistency: A Response to Kenneth Waltz', *Security Studies*, 6: 1, 58–61.

Elman, Colin and Elman, Miriam Fendius (1997), 'Lakatos and Neorealism: A Reply to Vasquez', *American Political Science Review*, 91: 4, 923–6.

Erdmann-Keefer, Vera (1991), *Agrarhandelskonflikte EG-USA. Analyse eines Dauerproblems*, Kehl, N. P. Engel Verlag.

European Commission (1998), *Financing the EU. Commission Report on the Operation of the Own Resources System*, Brussels, KOM (1998) 560.

European Parliament (1997), 'Resolution of 4 December 1997 on Agenda 2000: 2000–2006 Financial Framework for the Union and the Future Financing System (Rapporteur: Colom i Naval)', A4–0331/97.

Feldmeyer, Karl (1993), 'Die NATO und Deutschland nach dem Ende des Ost-West-Gegensatzes', in Rainer Zitelmann, Karlheiz Weißmann and Michael Großheim (eds), *Westbindung: Chancen und Risiken für Deutschland*, Frankfurt a.M., Propyläen, 459–76.

Ferencz, Benjamin B. (1981), 'The Draft Code of Offences Against the Peace and Security of Mankind', *American Journal of International Law*, 75: 4, 674–9.

Fichter, Michael and Reister, Hugo (1996), 'Die Gewerkschaften', in Oskar Niedermayer (ed.), *Intermediäre Strukturen in Ostdeutschland*, Opladen, Leske+Budrich, 309–33.

Finlayson, Jock A. and Zacher, Mark W. (1981), 'The GATT and the Regulation of Trade Barriers: Regime Dynamics and Functions', *International Organization*, 35: 4, 561–602.

Finnemore, Martha (1993), 'International Organizations as Teachers of Norms: The United Nations Educational, Scientific, and Cultural Organization and Science Policy', *International Organization*, 47: 4, 565–97.

Finnemore, Martha (1996a), *National Interests in International Society*, Ithaca, NY, Cornell University Press.

Finnemore, Martha (1996b), 'Norms, Culture, and World Politics: Insights from Sociology's Institutionalism', *International Organization*, 50: 2, 325–47.

Finnemore, Martha and Sikkink, Kathryn (1998), 'International Norm Dynamics and Political Change', *International Organization*, 52: 4, 887–917.

Fischer, Thomas (1999), 'Die Außenpolitik der deutschen Länder. Transföderale Beziehungen zwischen Kooperation und Konkurrenz', *Der Bürger im Staat*, 49: 1/2, 133–9.

Flood, Patrick James (1998), *The Effectiveness of UN Human Rights Institutions*, New York, Praeger.

Florini, Ann (1996), 'The Evolution of International Norms', *International Studies Quarterly*, 40: 3, 363–90.

Forsythe, David P. (1990), 'The United States, the United Nations, and Human Rights', in Margaret P. Karns and A. Karen Mingst (eds), *The United States and Multilateral Institutions. Patterns of Changing Instrumentality and Influence*, Boston, Unwin Hyman, 261–88.

Forsythe, David P. (1991), *The Internationalization of Human Rights*, Lexington, MA, Lexington Books.

Forsythe, David P. (1995a), 'Human Rights and US Foreign Policy: Two Levels, Two Worlds', in David Beetham (ed.), *Politics and Human Rights*, Political Studies, Special Issue, 43, Oxford, Blackwell, 111–30.

Forsythe, David P. (1995b), 'The UN and Human Rights at Fifty: An Incremental but Incomplete Revolution', *Global Governance*, 1: 3, 297–318.

Forsythe, David P. (2000), *Human Rights and Comparative Foreign Policy*, Tokyo, United Nations University Press.

Franck, Thomas M. (1990), *The Power of Legitimacy among Nations*, New York, Oxford University Press.

Frank, Kirsten Michaela (2000), *Die Koordinierung der Vergabe öffentlicher Aufträge in der Europäischen Union*, Berlin, Duncker & Humblot.

Frenkler, Ulf (1998), 'Die Maastricht-Politik der Bundesrepublik Deutschland: Machtpolitik oder Zivilmacht', paper presented at the workshop 'Zivilmacht Bundesrepublik – erste Befunde der empirischen Forschung' at the University of Trier, 11–12 December 1998.

Freytag, Andreas (1995), *Die strategische Handels- und Industriepolitik der EG – eine politökonomische Analyse*, Untersuchungen zur Wirtschaftspolitik, 99, Cologne: Institute for Economic Policy, University of Cologne.

Friedman, Gil and Starr, Harvey (1997), *Agency, Structure, and International Politics: From Ontology to Empirical Enquiry*, New York, Routledge.

Gabler Wirtschaftslexikon (1998), 14th edn, Wiesbaden, Gabler.

Gabriel, Jens-Peter (1993), *Grundstrukturen agrarpolitischer Willensbildungsprozesse in der Bundesrepublik Deutschland (1949–1989). Zur politischen Konsens- und Konfliktregelung*, Opladen, Leske + Budrich.

Gaddum, Eckart (1994), *Die deutsche Europapolitik in den 80er Jahren: Interessen, Konflikte und Entscheidungen der Regierung Kohl*, Studien zur Politik, 22, Paderborn, Schöningh.

Gamble, Andrew (1995), 'The New Political Economy', *Political Studies*, 43: 3, 516–30.

Garrett, Geoffrey and Lange, Peter (1996), 'Internationalization, Institutions, and Political Change', in Robert O. Keohane and Helen V. Milner (eds), *Internationalization and Domestic Politics*, Cambridge, Cambridge University Press, 48–75.

Gehring, Thomas (1997), 'Die Europäische Union: Legitimationsstrukturen eines Regimes mit föderativen Bestandteilen', in Klaus-Dieter Wolf (ed.), *Projekt Europa im Übergang? Probleme, Modelle und Strategien des Regierens in der Europäischen Union*, Baden-Baden, Nomos, 125–54.

George, Alexander L. (1979), 'Case Studies and Theory Development: The Method of Structured, Focused Comparison', in Paul Gordon Lauren (ed.), *Diplomacy: New Approaches in History, Theory and Policy*, New York, Free Press, 43–68.

George, Alexander L. and McKeown, Timothy J. (1985), 'Case Studies and Theories of Organizational Decision Making', in L. S. Sproull and P. D. Larkey (eds), *Advances in Information Processing in Organizations*, Greenwich, CT, JAI Press, 21–58.

George, Stephen (1998), *An Awkward Partner. Britain in the European Community*, 3rd edn, Oxford, Oxford University Press.

Gerke, Kinka (1994), *Vom GATT zur Welthandelsorganisation*, HSFK Report, 5/1994, Frankfurt a.M., Hessische Stiftung Friedens- und Konfliktforschung.

Gerz, Wolfgang (1998), 'Die Menschenrechtsweltkonferenz fünf Jahre nach Wien – Erfolg oder Flop?', in Gerhart Baum, Eibe Riedel and Michael Schaefer (eds), *Menschenrechtsschutz in der Praxis der Vereinten Nationen*, Baden-Baden, Nomos, 295–309.

Gibowski, Wolfgang G. (1991), 'Wie wirkt sich die wirtschaftliche Lage auf das Wahlverhalten aus? Forschungsstand und eigene Untersuchung', in Hans-Georg Wehling (ed.), *Wahlverhalten*, Stuttgart, Kohlhammer, 122–38.

Giessmann, Hans J. (1999), *The 'Cocooned Giant': Germany and European Security*, Hamburger Beiträge zur Friedens- und Sicherheitspolitik, 116, Hamburg, Institut für Friedensforschung und Sicherheitspolitik.

Gillessen, Günther (1994), 'Germany's New Position in the Centre of Europe: The Significance of Germany's Position and Misunderstandings about German Interests', in Arnulf Baring (ed.), *Germany's New Position in Europe*, Oxford, Berg, 21–33.

Gillies, David (1996), *Between Principle and Practice. Human Rights in North-South Relations*, Montreal, McGill-Queen's University Press.

Gilpin, Robert (1981), *War and Change in World Politics*, Cambridge, Cambridge University Press.

Gilpin, Robert (1986), 'The Richness of the Tradition of Political Realism', in Robert O. Keohane (ed.), *Neorealism and Its Critics*, New York, Columbia University Press, 301–22.

Glaser, Charles (1995), 'Realists as Optimists. Cooperation as Self-Help', *International Security*, 19: 3, 50–90.

Gluchowski, Peter and Wilamowitz-Moellendorff, Ulrich von (1997), 'Sozialstrukturelle Grundlagen des Parteienwettbewerbs in der Bundesrepublik Deutschland', in Oscar W. Gabriel, Oskar Niedermayer and Richard Stöss (eds), *Parteiendemokratie in Deutschland*, Bonn, Bundeszentrale für politische Bildung, 179–208.

Goertz, Gary and Diehl, Paul F. (1992), 'Toward a Theory of International Norms. Some Conceptual and Measurement Issues', *Journal of Conflict Resolution*, 36: 4, 634–64.

Goetz, Klaus H. (1996), 'Integration Policy in a Europeanized State: Germany and the Intergovernmental Conference', *Journal of European Public Policy*, 3: 1, 23–44.

Goldmann, Kjell (1988), *Change and Stability in Foreign Policy: The Problems and Possibilities of Detente*, Princeton, NJ, Princeton University Press.

Goldstein, Judith and Keohane, Robert O. (1993), 'Ideas and Foreign Policy. An Analytical Framework', in Judith Goldstein and Robert O. Keohane (eds), *Ideas and Foreign Policy. Beliefs, Institutions, and Political Change*, Ithaca, NY, Cornell University Press, 3–30.

Gordon, Philip H. (1996), *NATO's Transformation. The Changing Shape of the Atlantic Alliance*, Lanham, MD, Rowman & Littlefield.

Gose, Stefan (1997), 'Rüstungsbeschaffung: Parlamentarische Kontrolle unmöglich', *Antimilitarismus Information*, 27: 3, 22–7.

Gow, James (1997), *Triumph of the Lack of Will. International Diplomacy and the Yugoslav War*, London, Hurst.

Gowa, Joanne (1994), *Allies, Adversaries, and International Trade*, Princeton, NJ, Princeton University Press.

Graefrath, Bernhard (1990), 'Universal Criminal Jurisdiction and an International Criminal Court', *European Journal of International Law*, 1: 1/2, 67–88.

Graf Vitzthum, Wolfgang (1997), 'Begriff, Geschichte und Quellen des Völkerrechts', in Wolfgang Graf Vitzthum (ed.), *Völkerrecht*, Berlin, de Gruyter, 1–100.

Grande, Edgar (1989), *Vom Monopol zum Wettbewerb? Die neokonservative Reform der Telekommunikation in Großbritannien und der Bundesrepublik Deutschland*, Wiesbaden, Deutscher Universitäts-Verlag.

Grieco, Joseph M. (1988a), 'Anarchy and the Limits of Cooperation. A Realist Critique of the Newest Liberal Institutionalism', *International Organization*, 42: 3, 485–507.

Grieco, Joseph M. (1988b), 'Realist Theory and the Problem of International Cooperation. Analysis with an Amended Prisoner's Dilemma', *Journal of Politics*, 50: 3, 600–24.

Grieco, Joseph M. (1990), *Cooperation among Nations. Europe, America, and Non-Tariff Barriers to Trade*, Ithaca, NY, Cornell University Press.

Grieco, Joseph M. (1995), 'The Maastricht Treaty, Economic and Monetary Union and the Neo-Realist Research Programme', *Review of International Studies*, 21: 1, 21–40.

Grimm, Dieter (1993), 'Der Staat in der kontinentaleuropäischen Tradition', in Rüdiger Voigt (ed.), *Abschied des Staates – Rückkehr des Staates?*, Baden-Baden, Nomos, 27–50.

Groß, Jürgen (1995), *Die eingebildete Ohnmacht. Internationale Staatengemeinschaft und lokale Kriege*, Hamburger Beiträge zur Friedensforschung und Sicherheitspolitk, 95, Hamburg, Institut für Friedensforschung und Sicherheitspolitik.

Großheim, Michael, Weißmann, Karlheinz and Zitelmann, Rainer (1993), 'Einleitung: Wir Deutschen und der Westen', in Rainer Zitelmann, Karlheinz Weißmann and Michael Großheim (eds), *Westbindung: Chancen und Risiken für Deutschland*, Frankfurt a.M., Propyläen, 9–17.

Großmann, Harald (1993), 'Kommt es zum Handelskrieg?', *Wirtschaftsdienst*, 73: 4, 166–7.

Gross Stein, Janice (1988/89), 'The Wrong Strategy in the Right Place. The US and the Gulf', *International Security*, 13: 3, 142–67.

Grosser, Dieter (1985), 'Das Verhältnis von Staat und Wirtschaft in der Bundesrepublik Deutschland, in Dieter Grosser (ed.), *Der Staat in der Wirtschaft der Bundesrepublik Deutschland*, Opladen, Leske + Budrich, 13–60.

Gwartney, James D. and Wagner, Richard E. (1988), 'Public Choice and the Conduct of Representative Government', in James D. Gwartney and Richard E. Wagner (eds), *Public Choice and Constitutional Economics*, Greenwich, CT, JAI Press, 3–28.

Haas, Peter M. (1992), 'Introduction. Epistemic Communities and International Policy Coordination', *International Organization*, 46: 1, 1–35.

Hacke, Christian (1988), *Weltmacht wider Willen. Die Außenpolitik der Bundesrepublik Deutschland*, Stuttgart, Klett-Cotta.

Hacke, Christian (1994), 'Die neue Bundesrepublik in den internationalen Beziehungen', in Hartmut Jäckel (ed.), *Die neue Bundesrepublik*, Baden-Baden, Nomos, 57–96.

Hacke, Christian (1997), *Die Außenpolitik der Bundesrepublik Deutschland. Weltmacht wider Willen?*, rev. edn, Frankfurt a.M., Ullstein.

Hacke, Christian (1998), 'Die nationalen Interessen der Bundesrepublik Deutschland an der Schwelle zum 21. Jahrhundert', *Aussenpolitik*, 49: 2, 5–26.

Hacke, Christian (1999), 'Hans-Peter Schwarz, die deutsche Frage und die Außenpolitik der Bundesrepublik Deutschland', in Peter R. Weilemann, Hanns Jürgen Küsters and Günter Buchstab (eds), *Macht und Zeitkritik: Festschrift für Hans-Peter Schwarz zum 65. Geburtstag*, Paderborn, Schöningh, 189–208.

Haftendorn, Helga (1986), *Sicherheit und Entspannung. Zur Außenpolitik der Bundesrepublik Deutschland 1955–1982*, 2nd edn, Baden-Baden, Nomos.

Haftendorn, Helga (1993), 'Führungsmacht Deutschland? Ein Rückblick auf die Rolle der Deutschen in Europa', in Werner Weidenfeld (ed.), *Was ändert die Einheit? Deutschlands Standort in Europa*, Gütersloh, Bertelsmann Stiftung, 31–43.

Haftendorn, Helga (1994), 'Gulliver in der Mitte Europas. Internationale Verflechtung und nationale Handlungsmöglichkeiten', in Karl Kaiser and Hanns W. Maull (eds), *Deutschlands neue Außenpolitik, Vol. 1: Grundlagen*, Munich, Oldenbourg, 129–52.

Haftendorn, Helga (1999a), 'German Foreign Policy in a Strategic Triangle: Bonn–Paris–Washington', *German Politics and Society*, 17: 1, 1–31.

Haftendorn, Helga (1999b), 'Der gütige Hegemon und die unsichere Mittelmacht: Deutsch–amerikanische Beziehungen im Wandel', *Aus Politik und Zeitgeschichte*, B29–30/99, 3–11.

Haftendorn, Helga and Riecke, Henning (1996), '… *die volle Macht eines souveränen Staates …'. Die Alliierten Vorbehaltsrechte als Rahmenbedingungen westdeutscher Außenpolitik 1949–1990*, Baden-Baden, Nomos.

Hahn, Karl-Eckhard (1996), 'Westbindung und Interessenlage: Über die Renaissance der Geopolitik', in Heimo Schwilk and Ulrich Schacht (eds), *Die selbstbewußte Nation: "Anschwellender Bocksgesang" und weitere Beiträge zu einer deutschen Debatte*, 3rd edn, Berlin, Ullstein, 327–44.

Hall, Peter A. (1997), 'The Role of Interests, Institutions, and Ideas in the Comparative Political Economy of the Industrialized Nations', in Mark Irving Lichbach and Alan S. Zuckerman (eds), *Comparative Politics. Rationality, Culture, and Structure*, Cambridge, Cambridge University Press, 174–207.

Hall, Peter A. and Taylor, Rosemary C. R. (1996), 'Political Science and the Three New Institutionalisms', *Political Studies*, 44: 4, 936–57.

Hallerbach, Rolf (1991), 'Zauberformel der Zukunft: Multinationale NATO-Truppen', *Europäische Sicherheit*, 40: 1, 21–3.

Hamann, Rudolf, Matthies, Volker and Vogt, Wolfgang R. (1995), 'Deutsche Soldaten in alle Welt? Zur Problematik einer militärischen Instrumentalisierung der deutschen Außenpolitik', in Jörg Calließ and Bernhard Moltmann (eds), *Die Zukunft der Außenpolitik. Deutsche Interessen in den internationalen Beziehungen*, Loccumer Protokolle, 67/94, Rehburg-Loccum, Evangelische Akademie Loccum, 355–66.

Hanf, Kenneth (1978), 'Introduction', in Kenneth Hanf and Fritz W. Scharpf (eds), *Interorganizational Policy Making. Limits to Coordination and Central Control*, London, Sage, 1–15.

Hanf, Kenneth and O'Toole, Laurence J. Jr (1992), 'Revisiting Old Friends. Networks, Implementation Structures and the Management of Interorganizational Relations', *European Journal of Political Research*, 21: 1–2, 163–80.

Harnisch, Sebastian (1996), *Europa und Amerika: Die US–amerikanische Haltung zur westeuropäischen Integration 1987–1994*, Sinzheim, Pro Universitate Verlag.

Hart, Herbert L. (1961), *The Concept of Law*, Oxford, Clarendon Press.

Hart, Jeffrey (1976), 'Three Approaches to the Measurement of Power in International Relations', *International Organization*, 30: 2, 289–305.

Hasenclever, Andreas, Mayer, Peter and Rittberger, Volker (1997), *Theories of International Regimes*, Cambridge, Cambridge University Press.

Haungs, Peter (1992), 'Die CDU: Prototyp einer Volkspartei', in Alf Mintzel and Heinrich Oberreuter (eds), *Parteien in der Bundesrepublik Deutschland*, Opladen, Leske + Budrich, 158–98.

Hauser, Heinz and Schanz, Kai-Uwe (1995), *Das neue GATT. Die Welthandelsordnung nach Abschluß der Uruguay-Runde*, Munich, Oldenbourg.

Hayes, J. P. (1993), *Making Trade Policy in the European Community*, New York, St. Martin's Press.

Hayes-Renshaw, Fiona and Wallace, Helen (1997), *The Council of Ministers*, Basingstoke, Macmillan.

Hellmann, Gunther (1996), 'Goodbye Bismarck? The Foreign Policy of Contemporary Germany', *Mershon International Studies Review*, 40: 1, 1–39.

Hellmann, Gunther (1997), 'The Sirens of Power and German Foreign Policy: Who Is Listening?', *German Politics*, 6: 2, 29–57.

Hellmann, Gunther (1998), 'Die prekäre Macht: Deutschland an der Schwelle zum 21. Jahrhundert', in Wolf-Dieter Eberwein and Karl Kaiser (eds), *Deutschlands neue Außenpolitik, Vol. 4: Institutionen und Ressourcen*, Munich, Oldenbourg, 265–82.

Hellmann, Gunther (1999), 'Machtbalance und Vormachtdenken sind überholt: Zum außenpolitischen Diskurs im vereinigten Deutschland', in Monika Medick-Krakau (ed.), *Außenpolitischer Wandel in theoretischer und vergleichender Perspektive. Die USA und die Bundesrepublik Deutschland*, Baden-Baden, Nomos, 97–126.

Hellmann, Gunther and Wolf, Reinhard (1993), 'Neorealism, Neoliberal Institutionalism, and the Future of NATO', *Security Studies*, 3: 1, 3–43.

Helms, Ludger (1996), 'Das Amt des deutschen Bundeskanzlers in historisch und international vergleichender Perspektive', *Zeitschrift für Parlamentsfragen*, 27: 4, 697–711.

Henkin, Louis (1968), *How Nations Behave. Law and Foreign Policy*, New York, Praeger.

Henkin, Louis (1995), *International Law: Politics and Values*, Dordrecht, Martinus Nijhoff.

Henneberger, Fred (1996), 'Die Unternehmerverbände', in Oskar Niedermayer (ed.), *Intermediäre Strukturen in Ostdeutschland*, Opladen, Leske + Budrich, 335–55.

Henson, Penny and Malhan, Nisha (1995), 'Endeavours to Export a Migration

Crisis: Policy Making and Europeanisation in the German Migration Dilemma', *German Politics*, 4: 3, 128–44.

Héritier, Adrienne (1993a), 'Policy-Analyse. Elemente der Kritik und Perspektiven der Neuorientierung', in Adrienne Héritier (ed.), *Policy-Analyse. Kritik und Neuorientierung*, PVS-Sonderheft 24, Opladen, Westdeutscher Verlag, 9–36.

Héritier, Adrienne (1993b), 'Policy-Netzwerkanalyse als Untersuchungsinstrument im europäischen Kontext: Folgerungen aus einer empirischen Studie regulativer Politik', in Adrienne Héritier (ed.), *Policy-Analyse. Kritik und Neuorientierung*, PVS-Sonderheft, 24, Opladen, Westdeutscher Verlag, 432–47.

Hilf, Meinhard (1986), 'Die Anwendung des GATT im deutschen Recht', in Meinhard Hilf and Ernst-Ulrich Petersmann (eds), *GATT und die europäische Gemeinschaft*, Baden-Baden, Nomos, 11–62.

Hilf, Meinhard and Pache, Eckhard (1995a), 'Artikel C EUV', in Eberhard Grabitz (ed.), *Kommentar zur Europäischen Union*, Munich, Beck.

Hilf, Meinhard and Pache, Eckhard (1995b), 'Präambel zum EUV', in Eberhard Grabitz (ed.), *Kommentar zur Europäischen Union*, Munich, Beck.

Hofer, Ralf (1993), 'Einige Aspekte zum Thema "Rüstungsexporte in der Bundesrepublik Deutschland"', in Hans-Peter Hubert and Bundesarbeitsgemeinschaft Frieden und Internationalismus der Grünen (eds), *Grüne Außenpolitik – Aspekte einer Debatte*, Göttingen, Die Werkstatt, 69–74.

Hofferbert, Richard I. and Klingemann, Hans-Dieter (1990), 'The Policy Impact of Party Programmes and Government Declarations in the Federal Republic of Germany', *European Journal of Political Research*, 18: 3, 277–304.

Holsti, Ole R. (1992), 'Public Opinion and Foreign Policy: Challenges to the Almond–Lippmann Consensus', *International Studies Quarterly*, 36: 4, 439–66.

Holsti, Ole R. (1996), *Public Opinion and American Foreign Policy*, Ann Arbor, MI, University of Michigan Press.

Hopf, Ted (1998), 'The Promise of Constructivism in International Relations Theory', *International Security*, 23: 1, 171–200.

Hort, Peter (1997), 'Die deutsche Europa-Politik wird "britischer"', *Frankfurter Allgemeine Zeitung*, 30 October.

Howell, Thomas R. and Hume, Gregory I. (1992), 'Germany', in Thomas R. Howell (ed.), *Conflict among Nations. Trade Policies in the 1990s*, Boulder, CO, Westview Press, 145–203.

Hrbek, Rudolf (1997), 'Die Auswirkungen der EU-Integration auf den Föderalismus in Deutschland', *Aus Politik und Zeitgeschichte*, B24/1997, 12–21.

Huber, Peter M. (1992), 'Die Rolle des Demokratieprinzips im Europäischen Integrationsprozeß', *Staatswissenschaften und Staatspraxis*, 3: 3, 349–78.

Hudson, Valerie M. (ed.) (1997), *Culture and Foreign Policy*, Boulder, CO, Lynne Rienner.

Hurrell, Andrew (1993), 'International Society and the Study of Regimes: A Reflective Approach', in Volker Rittberger (ed.), *Regime Theory and International Relations*, Oxford, Clarendon Press, 49–72.

Hurrell, Andrew (1995), 'Regionalism in Theoretical Perspective', in Louise Fawcett and Andrew Hurrell (eds), *Regionalism in World Politics*, Oxford, Oxford University Press, 37–73.

Ikenberry, John, Lake, David and Mastanduno, Michael (1988), 'Introduction: Approaches to Explaining American Foreign Economic Policy', in John Ikenberry, David Lake and Michael Mastanduno (eds), *The State and American Foreign Economic Policy*, Ithaca, NY, Cornell University Press, 1–14.

Inacker, Michael J. (1996), 'Macht und Moralität: Über eine neue deutsche Sicherheitspolitik', in Heimo Schwilk and Ulrich Schacht (eds), *Die selbstbewußte Nation: "Anschwellender Bocksgesang" und weitere Beiträge zu einer deutschen Debatte*, 3rd edn, Frankfurt a.M., Ullstein, 364–80.

Ipsen, Knut (1999), 'Der Kosovo-Einsatz – Illegal? Entschuldbar? Gerechtfertigt?', *Die Friedens-Warte*, 74: 1–2, 19–23.

Ipsen, Knut and Haltern, Ulrich R. (1991), *Reform des Welthandelssystems? Perspektiven zum GATT und zur Uruguay-Runde*, Frankfurt a.M., Peter Lang.

Jachtenfuchs, Markus (1999), *Ideen und Integration. Verfassungsideen in Deutschland, Frankreich und Großbritannien und die Entwicklung der EU*, Habilitationsschrift, Fakultät für Sozialwissenschaften, Universität Mannheim.

Jachtenfuchs, Markus, Diez, Thomas and Jung, Sabine (1997), 'Ideas and Integration. Conflicting Models of a Legitimate European Political Order', paper for presentation at the Fifth Biannual ECSA Conference, Seattle, 29 May 1997.

Jackson, Peter McLeod (1983), *The Political Economy of Bureaucracy*, Totowa, NJ, Barnes & Noble.

Janning, Josef (1996a), 'A German Europe – a European Germany? On the Debate over Germany's Foreign Policy', *International Affairs*, 72: 1, 33–41.

Janning, Josef (1996b), 'Deutschland und die Europäische Union: Integration und Erweiterung', in Karl Kaiser and Joachim Krause (eds), *Deutschlands neue Außenpolitik, Vol. 3: Interessen und Strategien*, Munich, Oldenbourg, 31–54.

Jansen, Bernhard (1996), 'Die EG und die WTO (GATT)', in Moritz Röttinger and Claudia Weyringer (eds), *Handbuch der europäischen Integration. Strategie-Struktur-Politik der Europäischen Union*, Vienna, Manzsche Verlagsund Universitätsbuchhandlung, 514–35.

Jervis, Robert (1978), 'Cooperation under the Security Dilemma', *World Politics*, 30: 2, 167–214.

Jessen, Christoph (1999), 'Agenda 2000: Das Reformpaket von Berlin, ein Erfolg für Gesamteuropa', *Integration*, 22: 3, 167–75.

Jestaedt, Thomas, Kemper, Klaus, Marx, Fridhelm and Prieß, Hans-Joachim (1999), *Das Recht der Auftragsvergabe. Auftraggeber, ausschreibungspflichtige Aufträge, Vergabeverfahren, Sektoren, Rechtsschutz*, Neuwied, Luchterhand.

Johnson, Nevil (1978), 'Law as the Articulation of the State in Western Germany: A German Tradition Seen from a British Perspective', *West European Politics*, 1: 2, 177–92.

Johnston, Alastair Iain (1996), 'Cultural Realism and Strategy in Maoist China', in Peter J. Katzenstein (ed.), *The Culture of National Security. Norms and Identity in World Politics*, New York, Columbia University Press, 216–68.

Johnstone, Ian (1994), *Aftermath of the Gulf War: An Assessment of UN Action*, Boulder, CO, Lynne Rienner.

Jordan, Grant and Schubert, Klaus (1992), 'A Preliminary Ordering of Policy Network Labels', *European Journal of Political Research*, 21: 1–2, 7–27.

Joyner, Christopher C. (1997), 'Conclusion: The United Nations as International Law-Giver', in Christopher C. Joyner (ed.), *The United Nations and International Law*, Cambridge, Cambridge University Press, 432–57.

Kaarbo, Juliet (1996), 'Power and Influence in Foreign Policy Decision Making: The Role of Junior Coalition Partners in German and Israeli Foreign Policy', *International Studies Quarterly*, 40: 4, 501–30.

Kaiser, Karl (1991), *Deutschlands Vereinigung: Die internationalen Aspekte*, Bergisch Gladbach, Lübbe.

Kaiser, Karl (1993), 'Die ständige Mitgliedschaft im Sicherheitsrat. Ein berechtigtes Ziel der neuen deutschen Außenpolitik', *Europa Archiv*, 48: 19, 541–52.

Kaiser, Karl (1995), 'Deutsche Außenpolitik in der Ära des Globalismus', *Internationale Politik*, 50: 1, 27–36.

Kaiser, Karl and Becher, Klaus (1992), *Deutschland und der Irak-Konflikt: Internationale Sicherheitsverantwortung Deutschlands und Europas nach der deutschen Vereinigung*, Arbeitspapiere zur Internationalen Politik, 68, Bonn, Europa Union Verlag.

Kamminga, M. T. (1992), *Inter-State Accountability for Violations of Human Rights*, Philadelphia, PA, University of Pennsylvania Press.

Kappelhoff, Peter (1995), 'Macht in Politiknetzwerken – Modellvergleich und Entwurf eines allgemeinen Entscheidungsmodells', in Dorothea Jansen and Klaus Schubert (eds), *Netzwerke und Politikproduktion: Konzepte, Methoden, Perspektiven*, Marburg, Schüren, 24–51.

Karunaratne, Neil Dias (1993), 'The Reality and the Rhetoric of Free Trade in Services. The Case of Telecommunications', *Intereconomics*, 28: 2, 95–102.

Katzenstein, Peter J. (ed.) (1978), *Between Power and Plenty. Foreign Economic Policies of Advanced Industrial States*, Madison, WI, University of Wisconsin Press.

Katzenstein, Peter J. (1987), *Policy and Politics in West Germany: The Growth of a Semisovereign State*, Philadelphia, PA, Temple University Press.

Katzenstein, Peter J. (1993), 'Coping with Terrorism: Norms and Internal Security in Germany and Japan', in Judith Goldstein and Robert Keohane (eds), *Ideas and Foreign Policy: Beliefs, Institutions and Political Change*, Ithaca, NY, Cornell University Press, 265–96.

Katzenstein, Peter J. (ed.) (1997a), *Tamed Power: Germany in Europe*, Ithaca, NY, Cornell University Press.

Katzenstein, Peter J. (1997b), 'United Germany in an Integrating Europe', in Peter J. Katzenstein (ed.), *Tamed Power. Germany in Europe*, Ithaca, NY, Cornell University Press, 1–48.

Kaul, Hans-Peter (1997), 'Auf dem Weg zum Weltstrafgerichtshof: Verhandlungsstand und Perspektiven', *Vereinte Nationen*, 45: 5, 177–81.

Kaul, Hans-Peter (1998a), 'Internationaler Strafgerichtshof – ein bedeutender Anfang in Rom', in Gerhart Baum, Eibe Riedel and Michael Schaefer (eds), *Menschenrechtsschutz in der Praxis der Vereinten Nationen*, Baden-Baden, Nomos, 273–8.

Kaul, Hans-Peter (1998b), 'Der Internationale Strafgerichtshof: Das Ringen um seine Zuständigkeit und Reichweite', *Humanitäres Völkerrecht*, 11: 3, 138–44.

Kaul, Hans-Peter (1998c), 'Durchbruch in Rom: Der Vertrag über den Internationalen Strafgerichtshof', *Vereinte Nationen*, 46: 4, 125–30.

Keck, Margaret E. and Sikkink, Kathryn (1998), *Activists Beyond Borders: Advocacy Networks in International Politics*, Ithaca, NY, Cornell University Press.

Kedzia, Zdislaw and Jerbi, Scott (1998), 'The United Nations High Commissioner for Human Rights', in Gerhart Baum, Eibe Riedel and Michael Schaefer (eds), *Menschenrechtsschutz in der Praxis der Vereinten Nationen*, Baden-Baden, Nomos, 85–99.

Kenis, Patrick and Schneider, Volker (1991), 'Policy Networks and Policy Analysis. Scrutinizing a New Analytical Toolbox', in Bernd Marin and Renate Mayntz (eds), *Policy Networks. Empirical Evidence and Theoretical Considerations*, Frankfurt a.M., Campus, 25–59.

Keohane, Robert O. (1983), 'The Demand for International Regimes', in Stephen D. Krasner (ed.), *International Regimes*, Ithaca, NY, Cornell University Press, 141–71.

Keohane, Robert O. (1986), 'Theory of World Politics: Structural Realism and Beyond', in Robert O. Keohane (ed.), *Neorealism and Its Critics*, New York, Columbia University Press, 158–203.

Keohane, Robert O. (1989a), 'International Institutions. Two Approaches', in Robert O. Keohane, *International Institutions and State Power. Essays in International Relations Theory*, Boulder, CO, Westview Press, 158–79.

Keohane, Robert O. (1989b), 'Neoliberal Institutionalism. A Perspective on World Politics', in Robert O. Keohane, *International Institutions and State Power. Essays in International Relations Theory*, Boulder, CO, Westview Press, 1–20.

Keohane, Robert O. (1989c), *International Institutions and State Power. Essays in International Relations Theory*, Boulder, CO, Westview Press.

Keohane, Robert O. and Hoffmann, Stanley (1991), 'Institutional Change in Europe in the 1980s', in Robert O. Keohane and Stanley Hoffmann (eds), *The New European Community. Decisionmaking and Institutional Change*, Boulder, CO, Westview Press, 1–40.

Keohane, Robert O. and Nye, Joseph S. (eds) (1972), *Transnational Relations and World Politics*, Cambridge, MA, Harvard University Press.

Keohane, Robert O. and Nye, Joseph S., Jr (1977), *Power and Interdependence. World Politics in Transition*, Boston, MA, Little, Brown.

Keohane, Robert O. and Nye, Joseph S. (1993), 'Introduction: The End of the Cold War in Europe', in Robert O. Keohane, Joseph S. Nye and Stanley Hoffmann (eds), *After the Cold War. International Institutions and State Strategies in Europe, 1989–1991*, Cambridge, MA, Harvard University Press, 1–19.

King, Anthony (1994), '"Chief Executives" in Western Europe', in Ian Budge and David McKay (eds), *Developing Democracy. Comparative Research in Honour of J. F. P. Blondel*, London, Sage Publications, 150–64.

Kirchgässner, Gebhard (1991), *Homo Oeconomicus. Das ökonomische Modell individuellen Verhaltens und seine Anwendung in den Wirtschafts- und Sozialwissenschaften*, Tübingen, Mohr.

Kirchner, Emil (1992), 'The European Community: Seeds of Ambivalence', in Gordon Smith, William Paterson, Peter Merkl and Stephen Padgett (eds), *Developments in German Politics*, London, Macmillan, 172–84.

Kirste, Knut (1998), *Rollentheorie und Außenpolitikanalyse: Die USA und Deutschland als Zivilmächte*, Frankfurt a.M., Lang.

Kirste, Knut and Maull, Hanns W. (1996), 'Zivilmacht und Rollentheorie', *Zeitschrift für Internationale Beziehungen*, 3: 2, 283–312.

Klein, Eckart (1997), 'Die Internationalen und Supranationalen Organisationen als Völkerrechtssubjekte', in Wolfgang Graf Vitzthum (ed.), *Völkerrecht*, Berlin, de Gruyter, 267–391.

Klein, Paul (1990), *Deutsch-französische Verteidigungskooperation – Das Beispiel der deutsch-französischen Brigade*, Baden-Baden, Nomos.

Kleinfeld, Ralf (1999), 'Verbände', in Werner Weidenfeld and Karl-Rudolf Korte (eds), *Handbuch zur deutschen Einheit. 1949–1989–1999*, Frankfurt a.M., Campus, 765–80.

Klingemann, Hans-Dieter and Volkens, Andrea (1997), 'Struktur und Entwicklung von Wahlprogrammen in der Bundesrepublik Deutschland 1949–1994', in Oscar W. Gabriel, Oskar Niedermayer and R. Stöss (eds), *Parteiendemokratie in Deutschland*, Opladen, Westdeutscher Verlag, 517–36.

Klingemann, Hans-Dieter, Hofferbert, Richard I. and Budge, Ian (1994), *Parties, Policies, and Democracy*, Boulder, CO, Westview Press.

Klotz, Audie (1995), *Norms in International Relations: The Struggle Against Apartheid*, Ithaca, NY, Cornell University Press.

Klotz, Audie (1999), 'Diplomatic Isolation', in Neta C. Crawford and Audie Klotz (eds), *How Sanctions Work. Lessons from South Africa*, New York, St. Martin's Press, 195–212.

Knoke, David, Pappi, Franz Urban, Broadbent, Jeffrey and Tsujinaka, Yutaka

(1996), *Comparing Policy Networks. Labor Politics in the US, Germany, and Japan*, Cambridge, Cambridge University Press.

Knyphausen-Aufseß, Dodo zu (1997), 'Auf dem Weg zu einem ressourcenorientierten Paradigma? Resource-Dependence-Theorie der Organisation und Resource-based View des Strategischen Managments im Vergleich', in Günther Ortmann, Jörg Sydow and Klaus Türk (eds), *Theorien der Organisation. Die Rückkehr der Gesellschaft*, Opladen, Westdeutscher Verlag, 452–80.

Koch, Eckart (1992), *Internationale Wirtschaftsbeziehungen. Eine praxisorientierte Einführung*, Munich, Vahlen.

Koester, Ulrich (1996), 'Gemeinsame Agrarmarktordnungen der EU', in Renate Ohr (ed.), *Europäische Integration*, Stuttgart, Kohlhammer, 141–72.

Kohler-Koch, Beate (1998), 'Bundeskanzler Kohl – Baumeister Europas. Randbemerkungen zu einem zentralen Thema', in Göttrik Wewer (ed.), *Bilanz der Ära Kohl*, Opladen, Leske + Budrich, 283–311.

Koopmann, Georg, Kreienbaum, Christoph and Borrmann, Christine (1997), *Industrial and Trade Policy in Germany*, Baden-Baden, Nomos.

Korte, Karl-Rudolf (1998), 'Unbefangen und gelassen: Über die außenpolitische Normalität der Berliner Republik', *Internationale Politik*, 53: 12, 3–12.

Krasner, Stephen D. (1978), *Defending the National Interest: Raw Materials Investments and US Foreign Policy*, Princeton, NJ, Princeton University Press.

Krasner, Stephen D. (1983a), 'Regimes and the Limits of Realism. Regimes as Autonomous Variables', in Stephen D. Krasner (ed.), *International Regimes*, Ithaca, NY, Cornell University Press, 355–68.

Krasner, Stephen D. (1983b), 'Structural Causes and Regime Consequences: Regimes as Intervening Variables', in Stephen D. Krasner (ed.), *International Regimes*, Ithaca, NY, Cornell University Press, 1–21.

Krasner, Stephen D. (1984), 'Approaches to the State. Alternative Conceptions and Historical Dynamics', *Comparative Politics*, 16: 2, 223–46.

Krasner, Stephen D. (1991), 'Global Communications and National Power: Life on the Pareto Frontier', *World Politics*, 43: 3, 336–66.

Krasner, Stephen D. (1993a), 'Power, Polarity, and the Challenge of Disintegration', in Helga Haftendorn and Christian Tuschoff (eds), *America and Europe in an Era of Change*, Boulder, CO, Westview Press, 21–42.

Krasner, Stephen D. (1993b), 'Sovereignty, Regimes, and Human Rights', in Volker Rittberger (ed.), *Regime Theory and International Relations*, Oxford, Clarendon Press, 139–67.

Krasner, Stephen D. (1995), 'Sovereignty and Intervention', in Gene M. Lyons and Michael Mastanduno (eds), *Beyond Westphalia? State Sovereignty and International Intervention*, Baltimore, Johns Hopkins University Press, 228–49.

Krasner, Stephen D. (1999), *Sovereignty: Organized Hypocrisy*, Princeton, NJ, Princeton University Press.

Kratochwil, Friedrich V. and Ruggie, John Gerard (1986), 'International Organization. A State of the Art on an Art of the State', *International Organization*, 40: 4, 753–75.

Kreile, Michael (1993), 'Übernimmt Deutschland eine Führungsrolle in der Europäischen Gemeinschaft?', in Werner Weidenfeld (ed.), *Was ändert die Einheit? Deutschlands Standort in Europa*, Gütersloh, Bertelsmann Stiftung, 44–62.

Kretzschmar, Gotthard (1996), 'Die Agrarverbände', in Oskar Niedermayer (ed.), *Intermediäre Strukturen in Ostdeutschland*, Opladen, Leske + Budrich, 379–99.

Kuebart, Jörg (1991), 'Perspektiven und Parameter der Luftwaffenstruktur. Umbau nicht zum Nulltarif', *Europäische Sicherheit*, 40: 9, 504–6.

Kühnhardt, Ludger (1991), *Die Universalität der Menschenrechte*, Schriftenreihe der Bundeszentrale für politische Bildung, 256, 2nd edn, Bonn, Bundeszentrale für politische Bildung.

Kühnhardt, Ludger (1994), 'Wertgrundlagen der deutschen Außenpolitik', in Karl Kaiser and Hanns Maull (eds), *Deutschlands neue Außenpolitik, Vol. 1: Grundlagen*, Munich, Oldenburg, 99–128.

Kuper, Ernst (1999), 'Zwischen Unterordnung und Vorherrschaft: Deutschland im künftigen Europa', in Peter R. Weilemann, Hanns Jürgen Küsters and Günter Buchstab (eds), *Macht und Zeitkritik: Festschrift für Hans-Peter Schwarz zum 65. Geburtstag*, Paderborn, Schöningh, 407–19.

Laffan, Brigid (1997), *The Finances of the European Union*, London, Macmillan.

Laffan, Brigid and Shackleton, Michael (1996), 'The Budget', in Helen Wallace and William Wallace (eds), *Policy-Making in the European Union*, 3rd edn, Oxford, Oxford University Press, 71–96.

Lang, Ruth (1997), *Die Mitwirkungsrechte des Bundesrates und des Bundestages in Angelegenheiten der Europäischen Union gemäß Artikel 23 Abs. 2 bis 7 GG*, Berlin, Duncker & Humblot.

Lange, Peter (1992), 'The Politics of the Social Dimension', in Alberta M. Sbragia (ed.), *Euro-Politics. Institutions and Policymaking in the 'New' European Community*, Washington, DC, Brookings Institution, 225–56.

Langen, Klaus-Peter (1992), 'Multinationale Marineverbände. Der deutsche Beitrag', *Europäische Sicherheit*, 41: 12, 667–9.

Langguth, Gerd (1993), 'Die EG nach dem Ost–West-Konflikt – deutsche Positionen und Interessen in Europa', in Werner Weidenfeld (ed.), *Was ändert die Einheit? Deutschlands Standort in Europa*, Gütersloh, Bertelsmann Stiftung, 17–27.

Langhammer, Rolf J. (1993), *Die Handelspolitik der EG nach 1992. Die 'Integrationsdividende' in Gefahr*, Kieler Diskussionsbeiträge, 214, Kiel, Institut für Weltwirtschaft.

Laufer, Heinz and Münch, Ursula (1997), *Das föderative System der Bundesrepublik Deutschland*, Bonn, Bundeszentrale für politische Bildung.

Laursen, Finn and Vanhoonacker, Sophie (1992), *The Intergovernmental Conference on Political Union: Institutional Reform, New Policies, and International Identity of the European Community*, Dordrecht, Martinus Nijhoff.

Layne, Christopher (1993), 'The Unipolar Illusion: Why New Great Powers Will Rise', *International Security*, 17: 4, 5–51.

Lebow, Richard (1994), 'The Long Peace, the End of the Cold War, and the Failure of Realism', *International Organization*, 48: 2, 249–77.

Legro, Jeffrey (1997), 'Which Norms Matter? Revisiting the "Failure" of Internationalism', *International Organization*, 51: 1, 31–64.

Legro, Jeffrey W. and Moravcsik, Andrew (1999), 'Is Anybody still a Realist?', *International Security*, 24: 2, 5–55.

Lehmbruch, Gerhard (1984), 'Concertation and the Structure of Corporatist Networks', in John Goldthorpe (ed.), *Order and Conflict in Contemporary Capitalism*, Oxford, Oxford University Press, 60–80.

Lehmbruch, Gerhard (1987), 'Administrative Interessensvermittlung', in Adrienne Windhoff-Héritier (ed.), *Verwaltung und ihre Umwelt*, Opladen, Westdeutscher Verlag, 11–43.

Lehmbruch, Gerhard (1991), 'The Organization of Society, Administrative Strategies, and Policy Networks. Elements of a Developmental Theory of Interest Systems', in Roland M. Czada and Adrienne Windhoff-Héritier (eds), *Political Choice. Institutions, Rules, and the Limits of Rationality*, Frankfurt a.M., Campus, 121–58.

Lehmbruch, Gerhard (1994), 'Dilemmata verbandlicher Einflußlogik im Prozeß der deutschen Vereinigung', in Wolfgang Streeck (ed.), *Staat und Verbände*, PVS-Sonderheft 24, Opladen, Westdeutscher Verlag, 370–92.

Lehmbruch, Gerhard (1996), 'Die ostdeutsche Transformation als Strategie des Institutionentransfers: Überprüfung und Antikritik', in Andreas Eisen and Hellmut Wollmann (eds), *Institutionenbildung in Ostdeutschland. Zwischen externer Steuerung und Eigendynamik*, Opladen, Leske + Budrich, 63–78.

Lewis-Beck, Michael (1988), *Economics and Elections: The Major Western Democracies*, Ann Arbor, MI, University of Michigan Press.

Lijphart, Arend (1975), 'The Comparable-Cases Strategy in Comparative Research', *Comparative Political Studies*, 8: 2, 158–77.

Lijphart, Arend (1980), 'The Structure of Inference', in Gabriel Almond and Sidney Verba (eds), *The Civic Culture Revisited*, Boston, MA, Little, Brown, 37–56.

Link, Werner (1992), 'Kooperative Machtbalance und europäische Föderation als außenpolitische Orientierung', in Wolfgang Heydrich *et al.* (eds), *Sicherheitspolitik Deutschlands: Neue Konstellationen, Risiken, Instrumente*, Baden-Baden, Nomos, 601–11.

Link, Werner (1993), 'Perspektiven der europäischen Integration', in Karl Kaiser and Hanns W. Maull (eds), *Die Zukunft der europäischen Integration: Folgerungen für die deutsche Politik*, Arbeitspapiere zur Internationalen Politik, 78, Bonn, Europa Union Verlag, 7–26.

Link, Werner (1998), *Die Neuordnung der Weltpolitik: Grundprobleme globaler Politik an der Schwelle zum 21. Jahrhundert*, Munich, Beck.

Link, Werner (1999), 'Alternativen deutscher Außenpolitik', *Zeitschrift für Politik*, 46: 2, 125–43.

Link, Werner (2000), 'Deutschland im multipolaren Gleichgewicht der großen Mächte und Regionen', *Aus Politik und Zeitgeschichte*, B24/2000, 22–30.

Little, Richard and Smith, Steve (1988), *Belief Systems and International Relations*, Oxford, Blackwell.

Lottje, Werner (1998), 'Das "Forum Menschenrechte". Chancen und Grenzen der Kooperation nichtstaatlicher Menschenrechtsorganisationen in Deutschland', in Anmesty International (ed.), *Menschenrechte im Umbruch. 50 Jahre Allgemeine Erklärung der Menschenrechte*, Neuwied, Luchterhand, 189–206.

Lowi, Theodore (1972), 'Four Systems of Policy, Politics and Choice', *Public Administration Review*, 33: 4, 298–310.

Lübkemeier, Eckhard (1998), *Interdependenz und Konfliktmanagement: Deutsche Außenpolitik am Beginn des 21. Jahrhunderts*, Studie zur Außenpolitik, 74, Bonn, Friedrich-Ebert-Stiftung.

Luhmann, Niklas (1981), *Politische Theorie im Wohlfahrtsstaat*, Munich, Olzog.

Lumsdaine, David Halloran (1993), *Moral Vision in International Politics. The Foreign Aid Regime, 1949–1989*, Princeton, NJ, Princeton University Press.

Lutz, Dieter S. (1999), 'Dem Frieden dienen! Zur deutschen Sicherheitspolitik nach dem Krieg', in Bruno Schoch, Ulrich Ratsch and Reinhard Mutz (eds), *Friedengutachten 1999*, Münster, Lit, 48–59.

Maier, Jürgen (1997), 'Dominanz von Wirtschaftsinteressen? Die Rolle der Menschenrechte in der deutschen Außenpolitik', in Stiftung Entwicklung und Frieden (ed.), *UN-williges Deutschland. Der WEED-Report zur deutschen UNO-Politik*, Bonn, Dietz, 168–200.

Malcolm, Noel (1998), *Kosovo. A Short History*, London, Macmillan.

Mancini, Frederico (1991), 'The Making of a Constitution for Europe', in Robert O. Keohane and Stanley Hoffmann (eds), *The New European Community. Decisionmaking and Institutional Change*, Boulder, CO, Westview, 177–94.

Mangaliso, Nomazengele A. (1999), 'Cultural Boycotts and Political Change', in Neta C. Crawford and Audie Klotz (eds), *How Sanctions Work. Lessons from South Africa*, New York, St. Martin's Press, 232–43.

Maoz, Zeev and Russett, Bruce M. (1993), 'Normative and Structural Causes of Democratic Peace, 1946–1986', *American Political Science Review*, 87: 3, 624–38.

March, James G. and Olsen, Johan P. (1989), *Rediscovering Institutions. The Organizational Basis of Politics*, New York, Free Press.

March, James G. and Olsen, Johan P. (1998), 'The Institutional Dynamics of International Political Orders', *International Organization*, 52: 4, 943–69.

Marin, Bernd and Mayntz, Renate (1991), 'Introduction. Studying Policy Networks', in Bernd Marin and Renate Mayntz (eds), *Policy Networks. Empirical Evidence and Theoretical Considerations*, Frankfurt a.M., Campus, 11–23.

Markovits, Andrei S. and Reich, Simon (1997), *The German Predicament. Memory and Power in the New Europe*, Ithaca, NY, Cornell University Press.

Marsh, David (1998), 'The Utility and Future of Policy Network Analysis', in David Marsh (ed.), *Comparing Policy Networks*, Buckingham, Open University Press, 185–97.

Marsh, David and Rhodes, R.A.W. (1992), 'Policy Communities and Issue Networks. Beyond Typology', in David Marsh and R.A.W. Rhodes (eds), *Policy Networks in British Government*, Oxford, Clarendon Press, 249–68.

Maull, Hanns W. (1990), 'Germany and Japan: The New Civilian Powers', *Foreign Affairs*, 69: 5, 91–106.

Maull, Hanns W. (1992), 'Zivilmacht Bundesrepublik Deutschland – Vierzehn Thesen für eine neue deutsche Außenpolitik', *Europa Archiv*, 43: 10, 269–78.

Maull, Hanns W. (1997), 'Quo vadis, Germania? Außenpolitik in einer Welt des Wandels', *Blätter für Deutsche und Internationale Politik*, 42: 10, 1245–56.

Maull, Hanns W. (1999), 'Rot-grüne Außenpolitik – von den Höhen guter Absichten in die Niederungen globalisierter Politik', in Hanns W. Maull, Christoph Neßhöver and Bernhard Stahl (eds), *Lehrgeld: Vier Monate rot-grüne Außenpolitik*, Trierer Arbeitspapiere zur Internationalen Politik, 1, Trier, Lehrstuhl für Außenpolitik und Internationale Beziehungen, 1–11.

Maurer, Andreas and Grunert, Thomas (1998), 'Der Wandel in der Europapolitik der Mitgliedstaaten', in Mathias Jopp, Andreas Maurer and Heinrich Schneider (eds), *Europapolitische Grundverständnisse im Wandel. Analysen und Konsequenzen für die politische Bildung*, Bonn, Europa Union Verlag, 213–300.

May, Bernhard (1984), 'Der deutsche Beitrag zum Gemeinschaftshaushalt – die "Nettozahler"-Diskussion', in Rudolf Hrbek and Wolfgang Wessels (eds), *EG-Mitgliedschaft: ein vitales Interesse der Bundesrepublik Deutschland?*, Bonn, Europa Union Verlag, 357–87.

Mayer, Peter (1999), 'War der Krieg der NATO Gegen Jugoslawien Moralisch Gerechtfertigt? Die Operation "Allied Force" im Lichte der Lehre vom Gerechten Krieg', *Zeitschrift für Internationale Beziehungen*, 6:2, 287–321.

Mayer, Peter, Rittberger, Volker and Zürn, Michael (1993), 'Regime Theory. State of the Art and Perspectives', in Volker Rittberger (ed.), *Regime Theory and International Relations*, Oxford, Clarendon Press, 391–430.

Mayntz, Renate (1992), 'Modernisierung und die Logik von interorganisatorischen Netzwerken', *Journal für Sozialforschung*, 32: 1, 19–32.

Mayntz, Renate (1993), 'Policy-Netzwerke und die Logik von Verhandlungssystemen', in Adrienne Héritier (ed.), *Policy-Analyse. Kritik und Neuorientierung*, PVS-Sonderheft 24, Opladen, Westdeutscher Verlag, 39–56.

McElroy, Robert W. (1992), *Morality and American Foreign Policy. The Role of Ethics in International Affairs*, Princeton, NJ, Princeton University Press.

McNeely, Connie L. (1995), *Constructing the Nation-State. International Organization and Prescriptive Action*, Westport, CT, Greenwood Press.

Mearsheimer, John J. (1990), 'Back to the Future. Instability in Europe After the Cold War', *International Security*, 15: 1, 5–56.

Mearsheimer, John J. (1995), 'The False Promise of International Institutions', *International Security*, 19: 3, 5–49.

Mercer, Jonathan (1996), *Reputation and International Politics*, Ithaca, NY, Cornell University Press.

Messner, Dirk (1995), *Die Netzwerkgesellschaft. Wirtschaftliche Entwicklung und internationale Wettbewerbsfähigkeit als Probleme gesellschaftlicher Steuerung*, Schriftenreihe des Deutschen Instituts für Entwicklungspolitik, 108, Cologne, Weltforum Verlag.

Messner, Dirk and Nuscheler, Franz (1996a), *Global Governance: Challenges to German Politics on the Threshold of the Twenty-First Century*, Policy Paper, 2, Bonn, Stiftung Entwicklung und Frieden.

Messner, Dirk and Nuscheler, Franz (1996b), *Weltkonferenzen und Weltberichte: Ein Wegweiser durch die internationale Diskussion*, Bonn, Dietz.

Meyer, John W. (1987), 'The World Polity and the Authority of the Nation-State', in George M. Thomas *et al.* (eds), *Institutional Structure. Constituting State, Society, and the Individual*, Beverly Hills, CA, Sage, 41–70.

Meyer, John W. , Ramirez, Francisco O., Robinson, Richard and Boli-Bennett, John (1979), 'The World Educational Revolution, 1950–1970', in John W. Meyer and Michael T. Hannan (eds), *National Development and the World System. Educational, Economic and Political Change, 1950–1970*, Chicago, IL, University of Chicago Press, 37–55.

Millotat, Christian E. O. (1996), 'NATO and Germany. A Renaissance in Strategy', *Parameters: Journal of the US Army War College*, 26: 1, 51–61.

Milner, Helen (1992), 'International Theories of Cooperation. Strengths and Weaknesses', *World Politics*, 44: 3, 466–96.

Milner, Helen V. (1997), 'Industries, Governments, and Regional Trade Blocs', in Edward D. Mansfield and Helen V. Milner (eds), *The Political Economy of Regionalism*, New York, Columbia University Press, 77–106.

Mitchell, Timothy (1991), 'The Limits of the State: Beyond Statist Approaches and Their Critics', *American Political Science Review*, 85: 1, 77–96.

Molsberger, Josef and Duijm, Bernhard (1997), 'Deutsche Wirtschaftsordnung und internationales Handelssystem', *ORDO. Jahrbuch für die Ordnung von Wirtschaft und Gesellschaft*, 48, 549–72.

Moravcsik, Andrew (1991), 'Negotiating the Single European Act', in Robert O. Keohane and Stanley Hoffmann (eds), *The New European Community. Decision-Making and Institutional Change*, Boulder, CO, Westview, 41–84.

Moravcsik, Andrew (1997a), 'Taking Preferences Seriously: A Liberal Theory of International Politics', *International Organization*, 51: 4, 513–53.

Moravcsik, Andrew (1997b), 'Warum die Europäische Union die Exekutive stärkt: Innenpolitik und internationale Kooperation', in Klaus Dieter Wolf (ed.), *Projekt Europa im Übergang? Probleme, Modelle und Strategien des Regierens in der Europäischen Union*, Baden-Baden, Nomos, 211–69.

Moravcsik, Andrew (1998), *The Choice for Europe: Social Purpose and State Power from Messina to Maastricht*, Ithaca, NY, Cornell University Press.

Moravcsik, Andrew (2000), 'The Origin of Human Rights Regimes: Democratic Delegation in Postwar Europe', *International Organization*, 54: 2, 217–52.

Moravcsik, Andrew and Nicolaïdis, Calypso (1999), 'Explaining the Treaty of Amsterdam: Interests, Influence, Institutions', *Journal of Common Market Studies*, 37: 1, 59–85.

Morgenthau, Hans (1948), *Politics Among Nations. The Struggle for Power and Peace*, New York, Knopf.

Morgenthau, Hans J. (1973), *Politics among Nations: The Struggle for Power and Peace*, 5th edn, New York, Knopf.

Mower, A. Glenn, Jr (1987), *Human Rights and American Foreign Policy: The Carter and Reagan Experiences*, New York, Greenwood Press.

Much, Christian (1994), 'Der begrenzte Handlungsspielraum des UN-Hochkommissars für Menschenrechte', *Europa Archiv*, 49: 19, 560–6.

Mueller, Dennis C. (1989), *Public Choice II. A Revised Edition of Public Choice*, Cambridge, Cambridge University Press.

Müller, Harald (1993a), 'The Internalization of Principles, Norms, and Rules by Governments. The Case of Security Regimes', in Volker Rittberger (ed.), *Regime Theory and International Relations*, Oxford, Clarendon Press, 361–88.

Müller, Harald (1993b), *Die Chance der Kooperation. Regime in den internationalen Beziehungen*, Darmstadt, Wissenschaftliche Buchgesellschaft.

Müller, Harald and Schoch, Bruno (1999), 'Der Spagat wird schwieriger: Die deutsche Politik vor neuen Herausforderungen', in Bruno Schoch, Ulrich Ratsch and Reinhard Mutz (eds), *Friedensgutachten 1999*, Münster, Lit, 37–47.

Müller-Rommel, Ferdinand (1988a), 'Federal Republic of Germany', in Jean Blondel and Ferdinand Müller-Rommel (eds), *Cabinets in Western Europe*, Basingstoke, Macmillan, 151–66.

Müller-Rommel, Ferdinand (1988b), 'Interessengruppenvertretung im Deutschen Bundestag', in Uwe Thaysen (ed.), *US-Kongreß und Deutscher Bundestag*, Opladen, Westdeutscher Verlag, 300–22.

Nanda, Ved P. (1998), 'The Establishment of a Permanent International Criminal Court: Challenges Ahead', *Human Rights Quarterly*, 20: 3, 413–28.

Nassauer, Otfried (1993), 'Das Militär im wiedervereinigten Deutschland', in Hans-Peter Hubert and Bundesarbeitsgemeinschaft Frieden und Internationalismus der Grünen (eds), *Grüne Außenpolitik – Aspekte einer Debatte*, Göttingen, Die Werkstatt, 75–83.

Nentwich, Michael and Falkner, Gerda (1997), *The Treaty of Amsterdam: Towards a New Institutional Balance*, IEF Working Papers, 28, Wien, Forschungsinstitut für Europafragen der Wirtschaftsuniversität Wien.

Nerlich, Uwe (1991), 'Deutsche Sicherheitspolitik und Konflikte außerhalb des NATO-Gebiets', *Europa Archiv*, 46: 10, 303–10.

Neumann, Hans Adolf and Welge, Gerhard-Hannes (1996), 'Die Gemeinsame

Handelspolitik und ihre Instrumente', in Moritz Röttinger and Claudia Weyringer (eds), *Handbuch der europäischen Integration. Strategie-Struktur-Politik
der Europäischen Union*, Vienna, Manzsche Verlags- und Universitätsbuchhandlung, 624–69.

Nicolaysen, Gert (1996), *Europarecht II. Das Wirtschaftsrecht im Binnenmarkt*,
Baden-Baden, Nomos.

Nicoll, William and Salmon, Trevor C. (1994), *Understanding the New European
Community*, New York, Harvester Wheatsheaf.

Niskanen, William A. Jr (1971), *Bureaucracy and Representative Government*,
Chicago, IL, Aldine.

Noël, Alain and Thérien, Jean-Philippe (1995), 'From Domestic to International
Justice: The Welfare State and Foreign Aid', *International Organization*, 49:
3, 523–53.

Nye, Joseph S. (1990), *Bound to Lead. The Changing Nature of American Power*,
New York, Basic Books.

Offe, Claus (1987), 'Die Staatstheorie auf der Suche nach ihrem Gegenstand.
Beobachtungen zur aktuellen Diskussion', *Jahrbuch zur Staats- und Verwal-
tungswissenschaft 1987*, 309–20.

Olson, Mancur (1971), *The Logic of Collective Action. Public Goods and the Theory
of Groups*, Cambridge, MA, Harvard University Press.

Olson, Mancur (1982), *The Rise and Decline of Nations*, New Haven, RI, Yale
University Press.

Onuf, Nicholas Greenwood (1989), *World of Our Making. Rules and Rule in
Social Theory and International Relations*, Columbia, SC, University of South
Carolina Press.

Oppermann, Thomas and Beise, Marc (1993), 'GATT-Welthandelsrunde und
kein Ende? Die Gemeinsame EG-Handelspolitik auf dem Prüfstand', *Europa
Archiv*, 48: 1, 1–11.

Oppermann, Thomas and Classen, Claus Dieter (1993), 'Europäische Union:
Erfüllung des Grundgesetzes', *Aus Politik und Zeitgeschichte*, B28/1993, 11–20.

Orden, Geoffrey van (1991), 'The Bundeswehr in Transition', *Survival*, 33: 4,
352–70.

Ortmann, Günther, Sydow, Jörg and Windeler, Arnold (1997), 'Organisationen
als reflexive Strukturen', in Günther Ortmann, Jörg Sydow and Klaus Türk
(eds), *Theorien der Organisation. Die Rückkehr der Gesellschaft*, Opladen,
Westdeutscher Verlag, 315–54.

Oschatz, Georg-Berndt and Risse, Horst (1995), 'Die Bundesregierung an der
Kette der Länder? Zur europapolitischen Mitwirkung des Bundesrates', *Die
Öffentliche Verwaltung*, 48:11, 437–52.

Pappi, Franz Urban (1993), 'Policy-Netze. Erscheinungsformen moderner Poli-
tiksteuerung oder methodischer Ansatz?', in Adrienne Héritier (ed.), *Policy-
Analyse. Kritik und Neuorientierung*, PVS-Sonderheft 24, Opladen,
Westdeutscher Verlag, 84–94.

Parsons, Talcott (1951), *The Social System*, London, Routledge & Kegan Paul.

Parsons, Talcott (1961), 'Order and Community in the International System', in James N. Rosenau (ed.), *International Politics and Foreign Policy. A Reader in Research and Theory*, New York, Free Press, 120–9.

Paterson, William E. (1996), 'Beyond Semi-Sovereignty: The New Germany in the New Europe', *German Politics*, 5: 2, 167–84.

Patterson, Lee Ann (1997), 'Agricultural Policy Reform in the European Community: A Three-Level Game Analysis', *International Organization*, 51: 1, 135–65.

Peters, Guy (1998), 'Policy Networks: Myth, Metaphor and Reality', in David Marsh (ed.), *Comparing Policy Networks*, Buckingham/Philadelphia, PA, Open University Press, 21–32.

Petersmann, Ernst-Ulrich (1989), 'Wie kann Handelspolitik konstitutionalisiert werden? Verfassungsrechtliche Bindungen der Außenhandelspolitik', *Europa Archiv*, 45: 2, 55–64.

Pfeffer, Jeffrey and Salancik, Gerald R. (1978), *The External Control of Organizations. A Resource Dependence Perspective*, New York, Harper Row.

Philippi, Nina (1997), *Bundeswehreinsätze als außen- und sicherheitspolitisches Problem des geeinten Deutschland*, Fankfurt a.M., Lang.

Pollack, Mark (1997), 'Delegation, Agency, and Agenda Setting in the European Community', *International Organization*, 51: 1, 99–134.

Powell, G. Bingham Jr and Whitten, Guy D. (1993), 'A Cross-National Analysis of Economic Voting. Taking Account of Political Context', *American Journal of Political Science*, 37: 2, 391–414.

Preuss, Ulrich K. (1995), 'Chancen und Grenzen einer Verfassungsgebung für Europa', in Michael Zürn and Ulrich Preuss (eds), *Probleme einer Verfassung für Europa*, ZERP Diskussionspapier, 3/95, Bremen, Zentrum für Europäische Rechtspolitik, 41–76.

Projektgruppe UNO von WEED (1995), '10 Punkte für eine neue deutsche UNO-Politik', in Jörg Calließ and Bernhard Moltmann (eds), *Die Zukunft der Außenpolitik. Deutsche Interessen in den internationalen Beziehungen*, Loccumer Protokolle, 67/94, Rehburg-Loccum, Evangelische Akademie Loccum, 457–68.

Ragin, Charles S. and Becker, Howard S. (1992), *What is a Case? Exploring the Foundations of Social Inquiry*, Cambridge, Cambridge University Press.

Ragnitz, Joachim (1996), 'Deutschland und die Gestaltung der Weltwirtschaft', in Karl Kaiser and Joachim Krause (eds), *Deutschlands neue Außenpolitik, Vol. 3: Interessen und Strategien*, Munich, Oldenbourg, 63–76.

Ramirez, Francisco O. and Weiss, Jane (1979), 'The Political Incorporation of Women', in John W. Meyer and Michael T. Hannan (eds), *National Development and the World System. Educational, Economic and Political Change*, Chicago, IL, University of Chicago Press, 238–49.

Randelzhofer, Albrecht (1994), 'Art. 24, Abs. 2', in Theodor Maunz and Günter Dürig (eds), *Grundgesetz Kommentar*, Munich, Beck.

Rauch, Andreas M. (1998), 'Die auswärtige Menschenrechtspolitik des wiedervereinigten Deutschland', *Aussenpolitik*, 49: 1, 64–73.

Rawls, John (1955), 'Two Concepts of Rules', *Philosophical Review*, 64: 1, 3–32.

Raymond, Gregory A. (1997), 'Problems and Prospects in the Study of International Norms', *Mershon International Studies Review*, 41: 2, 205–45.

Reblin, Jörg (1993), *Das GATT und der Weltagrarhandel*, Hamburg, Kovac.

Rehbinder, Manfred (1993), *Rechtssoziologie*, 3rd edn, Berlin, de Gruyter.

Reister, Erwin (1975), *Haushalt und Finanzen der Europäischen Gemeinschaften*,
Baden-Baden, Nomos.

Reus-Smit, Christian (1997), 'The Constitutional Structure of International Society and the Nature of Fundamental Institutions', *International Organization*,
51: 4, 555–89.

Reuter, Alexander (1995), *Außenwirtschafts- und Exportkontrollrecht Deutsch-
land/ Europäische Union. Systematische Darstellung mit Praxisschwerpunkten*,
Munich, Beck.

Rhodes, R.A.W. and Marsh, David (1992), 'New Directions in the Study of
Policy Networks', *European Journal of Political Research*, 21: 1–2, 181–205.

Rieger, Elmar (1996), 'The Common Agricultural Policy: External and Internal
Dimensions', in Helen Wallace and William Wallace (eds), *Policy-Making in
the European Union*, 3rd edn, Oxford, Oxford University Press, 97–123.

Risse, Thomas (2000), 'Communicative Action in World Politics', *International
Organization*, 54: 1, 1–40.

Risse, Thomas and Sikkink, Kathryn (1999), 'The Socialization of International
Human Rights Norms into Domestic Practices: Introduction', in Thomas
Risse, Stephen C. Ropp and Kathryn Sikkink (eds), *The Power of Human
Rights. International Norms and Domestic Political Change*, Cambridge, Cam-
bridge University Press, 1–38.

Risse, Thomas, Engelmann, Daniela, Knopf, Hans-Joachim and Roscher, Klaus
(1999), 'To Euro or Not to Euro? The EMU and Identity Politics in the
European Union', *European Journal of International Relations*, 5: 2, 147–87.

Risse-Kappen, Thomas (1991), 'Public Opinion, Domestic Structure, and
Foreign Policy in Liberal Democracies', *World Politics*, 43: 4, 479–512.

Risse-Kappen, Thomas (1994), 'Ideas Do Not Float Freely. Transnational Coalitions, Domestic Structures, and the End of the Cold War', *International
Organization*, 48: 2, 185–214.

Risse-Kappen, Thomas (1995a), 'Bringing Transnational Relations Back In: In-
troduction', in Thomas Risse-Kappen (ed.), *Bringing Transnational Relations
Back In. Non-State Actors, Domestic Structures, and International Institutions*,
Cambridge, Cambridge University Press, 3–33.

Risse-Kappen, Thomas (1995b), *Cooperation Among Democracies. The European
Influence on US Foreign Policy*, Princeton, NJ, Princeton University Press.

Risse-Kappen, Thomas (1996), 'Collective Identity in a Democratic Community:
The Case of NATO', in Peter J. Katzenstein (ed.), *The Culture of National*

Security. Norms and Identity in World Politics, New York, Columbia University Press, 357–99.

Rittberger, Volker (1992), 'Nach der Vereinigung – Deutschlands Stellung in der Welt', Leviathan, 20: 2, 207–29.

Rittberger, Volker (1995), 'Conferences', in Rüdiger Wolfrum (ed.), United Nations: Law, Policies and Practice, Munich, Beck, 160–7.

Rittberger, Volker (1999), 'Deutschlands Außenpolitik nach der Vereinigung. Zur Anwendbarkeit theoretischer Modelle der Außenpolitik: Machtstaat, Handelsstaat oder Zivilstaat?', in Wolfgang Bergem, Volker Ronge and Georg Weißeno (eds), Friedenspolitik in und für Europa. Festschrift für Gerda Zellentin zum 65. Geburtstag, Opladen, Leske + Budrich, 83–108.

Rittberger, Volker and Mogler, Martin (1997), 'Reform des Sicherheitsrats der Vereinten Nationen und ständige Mitgliedschaft Deutschlands', in Deutsche Gesellschaft für die Vereinten Nationen (ed.), Die Reform des UN-Sicherheitsrats: Ein ständiger Sitz für Deutschland?, Blaue Reihe, 70, Bonn, DGVN, 18–40.

Rittberger, Volker and Zangl, Bernhard (1995), Internationale Organisationen. Politik und Geschichte, 2nd edn, Opladen, Leske + Budrich.

Rittberger, Volker, Mogler, Martin and Zangl, Bernhard (1997), Vereinte Nationen und Weltordnung: Zivilisierung der internationalen Politik?, Opladen, Leske + Budrich.

Rittberger, Volker, Schrade, Christina and Schwarzer, Daniela (1999), 'Introduction: Transnational Civil Society and the Quest for Security', in Muthiah Alagappa and Takashi Inoguchi (eds), International Security Management and the United Nations, Tokyo, United Nations University Press, 109–38.

Robertson, A. H. and Merrills, J. G. (1994), Human Rights in Europe. A Study of the European Convention on Human Rights, 3rd edn, Manchester, Manchester University Press.

Rode, Reinhard (1996), Deutsche Außenpolitik, Amsterdam, G+B Verlag Fakultas.

Rohe, Karl (1994), 'Politische Kultur. Zum Verständnis eines theoretischen Konzepts', in Oskar Niedermayer and Klaus von Beyme (eds), Politische Kultur in Ost- und Westdeutschland, Berlin, Akademie Verlag, 1–21.

Röhl, Klaus (1987), Rechtssoziologie, Cologne, Carl Heymanns Verlag.

Röhl, Klaus Rainer (1996), 'Morgenthau und Antifa: Über den Selbsthaß der Deutschen', in Heimo Schwilk and Ulrich Schacht (eds), Die selbstbewußte Nation: 'Anschwellender Bocksgesang' und weitere Beiträge zu einer deutschen Debatte, 3rd edn, Frankfurt a.M., Ullstein, 85–100.

Rosenau, James N. (1966), 'Pre-theories and Theories of Foreign Policy', in Barry R. Farrell (ed.), Approaches to Comparative and International Politics, Evanston, Northwestern University Press, 27–92.

Rosenau, James N. (1990), Turbulence in World Politics, Princeton, NJ, Princeton University Press.

Rosenbauer, Claus (1997), 'Das Führungszentrum der Bundeswehr', Europäische Sicherheit, 46: 2, 16–18.

Roth, Claudia (1993), 'Der Pazifismus und Kampf gegen Rassismus und Völkermord (1)', in Hans-Peter Hubert and Bundesarbeitsgemeinschaft Frieden und Internationalismus der Grünen (eds), *Grüne Außenpolitik – Aspekte einer Debatte*, Göttingen, Die Werkstatt, 212–28.

Rudzio, Wolfgang (1996), *Das politische System in der Bundesrepublik Deutschland*, 4th edn, Opladen, Leske + Budrich.

Ruggie, John Gerard (1983), 'International Regimes, Transactions, and Change: Embedded Liberalism in the Postwar Economic Order', in Stephen D. Krasner (ed.), *International Regimes*, Ithaca, NY, Cornell University Press, 195–231.

Ruggie, John Gerard (1993), 'Territoriality and Beyond: Problematizing Modernity in International Relations', *International Organization*, 47: 1, 139–74.

Ruggie, John Gerard (1994), 'Trade, Protectionism and the Future of Welfare Capitalism', *Journal of International Affairs*, 48: 1, 1–12.

Ruggie, John Gerard (1998), 'Introduction: What Makes the World Hang Together? Neo-Utilitarianism and the Social Constructivist Challenge', in John Gerard Ruggie (ed.), *Constructing the World Polity. Essays on International Relations*, London, Routledge, 1–44.

Russett, Bruce (1990), *Controlling the Sword: The Democratic Governance of National Security*, Cambridge, MA, Harvard University Press.

Russett, Bruce (1993), *Grasping the Democratic Peace. Principles for a Post-Cold War World*, Princeton, NJ, Princeton University Press.

Sabatier, Paul (1993), 'Advocacy-Koalitionen, Policy-Wandel und Policy-Lernen: Eine Alternative zur Phasenheuristik', in Adrienne Héritier (ed.), *Policy-Analyse. Kritik und Neuorientierung*, PVS-Sonderheft 24, Opladen, Westdeutscher Verlag, 116–48.

Sauder, Axel (1995), *Souveränität und Integration. Deutsche und französische Konzeptionen europäischer Sicherheit nach dem Ende des Kalten Krieges*, Baden-Baden, Nomos.

Schaber, Thomas and Ulbert, Cornelia (1994), 'Reflexivität in den Internationalen Beziehungen. Literaturbericht zum Beitrag kognitiver, reflexiver und interpretativer Ansätze zur dritten Theoriedebatte', *Zeitschrift für Internationale Beziehungen*, 1: 1, 139–69.

Scharpf, Fritz (1997), *Games Real Actors Play. Actor-Centered Institutionalism in Policy Research*, Boulder, CO, Westview Press.

Scherpenberg, Jens van (1992), *Ordnungspolitik im EG-Binnenmarkt: Auftrag für die Politische Union*, Baden-Baden, Nomos.

Schiller, Theo (1997), 'Parteien und Interessenverbände', in Oscar W. Gabriel, Oskar Niedermayer and Richard Stöss (eds), *Parteiendemokratie in Deutschland*, Bonn, Bundeszentrale für politische Bildung, 459–77.

Schimmelfennig, Frank (1994), 'Internationale Sozialisation neuer Staaten. Heuristische Überlegungen zu einem Forschungsdesiderat', *Zeitschrift für Internationale Beziehungen*, 1: 2, 335–55.

Schimmelfennig, Frank (1998), 'Liberal Norms and the Eastern Enlargement of the European Union: A Case for Sociological Institutionalism', *Österreichische Zeitschrift für Politikwissenschaft*, 27: 4, 459–72.

Schlör, Wolfgang F. (1993), *German Security Policy. An Examination of the Trends in German Security Policy in a European and Global Context*, Adelphi Papers, 277, London: The International Institute for Strategic Studies.

Schmid, Josef and Voelzkow, Helmut (1996), 'Funktionsprobleme des westdeutschen Korporatismus in Ostdeutschland', in Oskar Niedermayer (ed.), *Intermediäre Strukturen in Ostdeutschland*, Opladen, Leske + Budrich, 421–40.

Schmidt, Max (1995), 'Elemente eines Konzepts ziviler deutscher Außenpolitik', in Jörg Calließ and Bernhard Moltmann (eds), *Die Zukunft der Außenpolitik. Deutsche Interessen in den internationalen Beziehungen*, Loccumer Protokolle, 67/94, Rehburg-Loccum, Evangelische Akademie Loccum, 314–29.

Schmillen, Achim (1993), 'Außenpolitische Konfliktlösung zwischen Gewaltfreiheit und militärischen Einsätzen', in Hans-Peter Hubert and Bundesarbeitsgemeinschaft Frieden und Internationalismus der Grünen (eds), *Grüne Außenpolitik – Aspekte einer Debatte*, Göttingen, Die Werkstatt, 84–8.

Schmillen, Achim (1995), 'Stolpern in das 21. Jahrhundert. Thesen zur bündnisgrünen Außen- und Friedenspolitik vor der Jahrtausendwende', in Jörg Calließ and Bernhard Moltmann (eds), *Die Zukunft der Außenpolitik. Deutsche Interessen in den internationalen Beziehungen*, Loccumer Protokolle, 67/94, Rehburg-Loccum, Evangelische Akademie Loccum, 511–31.

Schmuck, Otto (1993), 'Der Gipfel von Edinburgh: Erleichterung nach einem europapolitisch schwierigen Jahr', *Integration*, 16: 1, 33–6.

Schöllgen, Gregor (1993), *Angst vor der Macht. Die Deutschen und ihre Außenpolitik*, Berlin, Ullstein.

Schöllgen, Gregor (1994), 'National Interest and International Responsibility: Germany's Role in World Affairs', in Arnulf Baring (ed.), *Germany's New Position in Europe*, Oxford, Berg, 35–49.

Schöllgen, Gregor (1998), 'Die Berliner Republik als internationaler Akteur: Gibt es noch eine deutsche Interessenpolitik?', *Aussenpolitik*, 49: 2, 27–37.

Schöllgen, Gregor (2000), 'Zehn Jahre als europäische Großmacht: Eine Bilanz deutscher Außenpolitik seit der Vereinigung', *Aus Politik und Zeitgeschichte*, B24/2000, 6–12.

Scholz, Rupert (1996), 'Artikel 23', in Theodor Maunz and Günther Dürig (eds), *Kommentar zum Grundgesetz*, Munich, C. H. Beck.

Schomaker, Astrid and Detken, Dirk (1996), 'Die EU und die USA', in Moritz Röttinger and Claudia Weyringer (eds), *Handbuch der Europäischen Integration: Strategie, Struktur, Politik der Europäischen Union*, Vienna, Manz, 536–53.

Schönweiß, Reinhard (1984), *Die Agrarpolitik der Bundesrepublik Deutschland. Ziele, Maßnahmen und Kritik staatlicher Interventionen auf dem Agrarsektor unter besonderer Berücksichtigung der struktur- und markt-/preispolitischen Beschlüsse*, Munich, tuduv.

Schreyögg, Georg (1997), 'Kommentar: Theorien organisatorischer Ressourcen', in Günther Ortmann, Jörg Sydow and Klaus Türk (eds), *Theorien der Organisation. Die Rückkehr der Gesellschaft*, Opladen, Westdeutscher Verlag, 481–6.

Schubert, Klaus (1995), 'Struktur-, Akteur- und Innovationslogik. Netzwerkkonzeptionen und die Analyse von Politikfeldern', in Dorothea Jansen and Klaus Schubert (eds), *Netzwerke und Politikproduktion. Konzepte, Methoden, Perspektiven*, Marburg, Schüren, 222–40.

Schubert, Klaus von, Bahr, Egon and Krell, Gert (eds) (1988), *Friedensgutachten 1988*, Heidelberg, FEST.

Schwarz, Hans-Peter (1985), *Die gezähmten Deutschen. Von der Machtbesessenheit zur Machtvergessenheit*, Stuttgart, DVA.

Schwarz, Hans-Peter (1994a), *Die Zentralmacht Europas. Deutschlands Rückkehr auf die Weltbühne*, Berlin, Siedler.

Schwarz, Hans-Peter (1994b), 'Das deutsche Dilemma', in Karl Kaiser and Hanns W. Maull (eds), *Deutschlands neue Außenpolitik, Vol. 1: Grundlagen*, Munich, Oldenbourg, 81–97.

Schwarz, Hans-Peter (1999), 'Die Zentralmacht Europas auf Kontinuitätskurs. Deutschland stabilisiert den Kontinent', *Internationale Politik*, 54: 11, 1–10.

Schweller, Randall L. (1994), 'Bandwagoning for Profit. Bringing the Revisionist State Back In', *International Security*, 19: 1, 72–107.

Schweller, Randall L. (1996), 'Neorealism's Status-Quo Bias: What Security Dilemma?', in Benjamin Frankel (ed.), *Realism: Restatements and Renewal*, London, Frank Cass, 90–121.

Schweller, Randall L. (1997), 'New Realist Research on Alliances: Refining not Refuting Waltz's Balancing Proposition', *American Political Science Review*, 91: 4, 927–30.

Schweller, Randall (1998), *Deadly Imbalances. Tripolarity and Hitler's Strategy of World Conquest*, New York, Columbia University Press.

Schweller, Randall L. and Priess, David (1997), 'A Tale of Two Realisms: Expanding the Institutions Debate', *Mershon International Studies Review*, 41: 1, 1–32.

Schwilk, Heimo and Schacht, Ulrich (1996), 'Einleitung', in Heimo Schwilk and Ulrich Schacht (eds), *Die selbstbewußte Nation: 'Anschwellender Bocksgesang' und weitere Beiträge zu einer deutschen Debatte*, 3rd edn, Frankfurt a.M., Ullstein, 11–17.

Schwok, René (1991), *US-EC Relations in the Post-Cold War Era. Conflict or Partnership?*, Boulder, CO, Westview Press.

Scott, W. Richard (1986), *Grundlagen der Organisationstheorie*, Frankfurt a.M., Campus.

Sebaldt, Martin (1997), *Organisierter Pluralismus. Kräftefeld, Selbstverständnis und politische Arbeit deutscher Interessengruppen*, Opladen, Westdeutscher Verlag.

Seebacher-Brandt, Brigitte (1996), 'Norm und Normalität: Über die Liebe zum eigenen Land', in Heimo Schwilk and Ulrich Schacht (eds), *Die selbstbewußte Nation: 'Anschwellender Bocksgesang' und weitere Beiträge zu einer deutschen Debatte*, 3rd edn, Frankfurt a.M., Ullstein, 43–56.

Seidl-Hohenveldern, Ignaz (1997), *Völkerrecht*, 9th edn, Cologne, Carl Heymanns.

Seidl-Hohenveldern, Ignaz and Loibl, Gerhard (1996), *Das Recht der Internationalen Organisationen einschließlich der Supranationalen Gemeinschaften*, 6th edn, Cologne, Carl Heymanns.

Seitz, Klaus and Windfuhr, Michael (1989), *Landwirtschaft und Welthandelsordnung: Handbuch zu den Agrarverhandlungen der Uruguay-Runde im GATT*, Texte, 45, Hamburg, Verlag Dienste in Übersee.

Senghaas, Dieter (1993), 'Was sind der Deutschen Interessen?', *Blätter für Deutsche und Internationale Politik*, 38: 6, 673–87.

Senghaas, Dieter (1994), *Wohin driftet die Welt? Über die Zukunft friedlicher Koexistenz*, Frankfurt a.M., Suhrkamp.

Shackleton, Michael (1990), *Financing the European Community*, London, Pinter.

Shackleton, Michael (1993), 'Keynote Article: The Delors II Budget Package', *Journal of Common Market Studies*, 31 (Annual Review of Activities), 11–25.

Siebert, Christian and Svindland, Eirik (1992), *Nationalstaat und Interdependenz – kooperative Interaktionsmuster in der EG-Handelspolitik*, DIW Sonderheft, Berlin, Duncker & Humblot.

Siedschlag, Alexander (1995), *Die aktive Beteiligung Deutschlands an militärischen Aktionen zur Verwirklichung kollektiver Sicherheit*, Frankfurt a.M., Lang.

Sikkink, Kathryn (1993), 'The Power of Principled Ideas: Human Rights Policies in the United States and Western Europe', in Judith Goldstein and Robert O. Keohane (eds), *Ideas and Foreign Policy. Beliefs, Institutions, and Political Change*, Ithaca, NY, Cornell University Press, 139–70.

Simma, Bruno (1999), 'NATO, the UN, and the Use of Force: Legal Aspects', *European Journal of International Law*, 10: 1, 1–22.

Simon, Herbert A. (1985), 'Human Nature in Politics. The Dialogue of Psychology with Political Science', *American Political Science Review*, 79: 2, 293–304.

SIPRI (1991), *SIPRI Yearbook 1991. World Armaments and Disarmament*, Oxford, Oxford University Press.

Siwert-Probst, Judith (1998), 'Die klassischen außenpolitischen Institutionen', in Wolf-Dieter Eberwein and Karl Kaiser (eds), *Deutschlands neue Außenpolitik, Vol. 4: Institutionen und Ressourcen*, Munich, Oldenbourg, 13–28.

Skocpol, Theda (1985), 'Bringing the State Back In: Strategies of Analysis in Current Research', in Peter B. Evans, Dietrich Rueschemeyer and Theda Skocpol (eds), *Bringing the State Back In*, Cambridge, Cambridge University Press, 3–27.

Smith, Gordon (1991), 'The Resources of a German Chancellor', *West European Politics*, 14: 2, 48–61.

Smith, Jackie, Chatfield, Charles and Pagnucco, Ron (1997), *Transnational Social*

Movements and Global Politics: Solidarity Beyond the State, Syracuse, NY, Syracuse University Press.

Smith, Martin J. (1993), *Pressure, Power and Policy. State Autonomy and Policy Networks in Britain and the United States*, New York, Harvester Wheatsheaf.

Snidal, Duncan (1985a), 'The Limits of Hegemonic Stability Theory', *International Organization*, 39: 4, 579–614.

Snidal, Duncan (1985b), 'The Game Theory of International Politics', *World Politics*, 38: 1, 25–57.

Snidal, Duncan (1991), 'International Cooperation Among Relative Gains Maximizers', *International Studies Quarterly*, 35: 4, 387–402.

Snyder, Glenn H. (1996), 'Process Variables in Neorealist Theory', *Security Studies*, 5: 3, 167–92.

Snyder, Jack (1991), *Myths of Empire: Domestic Politics and International Ambition*, Ithaca, NY, Cornell University Press.

Spirtas, Michael (1996), 'A House Divided. Tragedy and Evil in Realist Theory', *Security Studies*, 5: 3, 385–423.

Spruyt, Hendrik (1994), *The Sovereign State and Its Competitors: An Analysis of Systems Change*, Princeton, NJ, Princeton University Press.

Staack, Michael (2000), *Handelsstaat Deutschland: Deutsche Außenpolitik in einem neuen internationalen System*, Paderborn, Schöningh.

Staeck, Nicola (1997), *Politikprozesse in der Europäischen Union. Eine Policy-Netzwerkanalyse der europäischen Strukturfondspolitik*, Baden-Baden, Nomos.

Stark, Jürgen (1997), 'Finanzierung der Europäischen Union: Rückblick, Zwischenbilanz und Ausblick', in Elmar Brok et al. (eds), *Das Finanzsystem der EU: Neue Ansätze und Perspektiven*, Interne Studien der Konrad Adenauer Stiftung, 142/97, Sankt Augustin, Konrad Adenauer Stiftung, 23–34.

Statz, Albert (1993a), 'Nationale Selbstbeschränkung – internationale Einbindung – transnationale Verflechtung: Thesen zur grün-alternativen Außenpolitik', in Hans-Peter Hubert and Bundesarbeitsgemeinschaft Frieden und Internationalismus der Grünen (eds), *Grüne Außenpolitik – Aspekte einer Debatte*, Göttingen, Die Werkstatt, 93–112.

Statz, Albert (1993b), 'Migranten als Brücke. Migrationsverträglicher Umbau unserer Gesellschaften und gemeinsame Entwicklung in Europa', in Caroline Thomas and Klaus-Peter Weiner (eds), *Auf dem Weg zur Hegemonialmacht? Die deutsche Außenpolitik nach der Vereinigung*, Cologne, PapyRossa, 130–48.

Stein, E. Eric (1981), 'Lawyers, Judges, and the Making of a Transnational Constitution', *American Journal of International Law*, 75: 1, 1–27.

Stigler, George J. (1975), 'The Theory of Economic Regulation', in George J. Stigler (ed.), *The Citizen and the State. Essays on Regulation*, Chicago, IL, University of Chicago Press, 114–41.

Stokman, Frans N. (1995), 'Entscheidungsansätze in politischen Netzwerken', in Dorothea Jansen and Klaus Schubert (eds), *Netzwerke und Politikproduktion: Konzepte, Methoden, Perspektiven*, Marburg, Schüren, 160–84.

Streeck, Wolfgang (1994), 'Einleitung des Herausgebers. Staat und Verbände: Neue Fragen. Neue Antworten', in Wolfgang Streeck (ed.), *Staat und Verbände*, PVS-Sonderheft 25, Opladen, Westdeutscher Verlag, 7–34.

Stuart, D. and Tow, W. (1990), *The Limits of Alliance. NATO Out-of-Area Problems since 1949*, Baltimore, MD, Johns Hopkins University Press.

Stürmer, Michael (1994), 'Deutsche Interessen', in Karl Kaiser and Hanns W. Maull (eds), *Deutschlands neue Außenpolitik, Vol. 1: Grundlagen*, Munich, Oldenbourg, 39–61.

Szasz, Paul C. (1997), 'General Law-Making Process', in Christopher C. Joyner (ed.), *The United Nations and International Law*, Cambridge, Cambridge University Press, 27–64.

Taylor, Paul (1983), *The Limits of European Integration*, London, Croom Helm.

Teasdale, Anthony (1996), 'The Politics of Majority Voting in Europe', *Political Quarterly*, 67: 2, 101–15.

Theiler, Olaf (1997), 'Der Wandel der NATO nach dem Ende des Ost–West-Konflikts', in Helga Haftendorn and Otto Keck (eds), *Kooperation jenseits von Hegemonie und Bedrohung. Sicherheitsinstitutionen in den internationalen Beziehungen*, Baden-Baden, Nomos, 101–36.

Thies, Jochen (1993), 'Perspektiven deutscher Außenpolitik', in Rainer Zitelmann, Karlheinz Weißmann and Michael Grossheim (eds), *Westbindung: Chancen und Risiken für Deutschland*, Frankfurt, Propyläen, 523–36.

Thies, Jochen (1994), 'Germany and Eastern Europe between Past and Future', in Arnulf Baring (ed.), *Germany's New Position in Europe*, Oxford, Berg, 65–78.

Thun, Konstantin (1993), 'Menschenrechtsdefizite in der deutschen Außenpolitik', in Heiner Bielefeldt, Volkmar Deile and Bernd Thomsen (eds), *Menschenrechte vor der Jahrtausendwende*, Frankfurt, Fischer, 143–51.

Tomuschat, Christian (1987), 'Die Herrschaft des Rechts. Deutsche Außenpolitik im Dienste der Menschenrechte und des Völkerrechts', in H. -D. Genscher (ed.), *Nach vorn gedacht … Perspektiven deutscher Außenpolitik*, Stuttgart, Verlag Bonn Aktuell, 169–76.

Tomuschat, Christian (1991), 'Bewährung, Stärkung, Ausgestaltung. Zur künftigen Menschenrechtspolitik Deustchlands in der Weltorganisation', *Vereinte Nationen*, 39: 1, 6–10.

Tuschhoff, Christian (1994), 'Machtverschiebungen und künftige Bruchstellen im Bündnis. Die politischen Folgen der Truppenpräsenz nach den NATO-Reformen', in Gunther Hellmann (ed.), *Alliierte Präsenz und deutsche Einheit. Die politischen Folgen militärischer Macht*, Baden-Baden, Nomos, 365–401.

Tuschoff, Christian (1999), 'Alliance Cohesion and Peaceful Change in NATO', in Helga Haftendorn, Robert O. Keohane and Celeste A. Wallander (eds), *Imperfect Unions. Security Institutons Over Time and Space*, Oxford, Oxford University Press, 140–61.

Ulbert, Cornelia (1997), 'Ideen, Institutionen und Kultur. Die Konstruktion (inter-)nationaler Klimapolitik in der BRD und in den USA', *Zeitschrift für Internationale Beziehungen*, 4: 1, 9–40.

Vad, Erich and Meyers, Manfred (1996), 'Multinationalität der Streitkräfte. Instrument deutscher Sicherheitspolitik', *Europäische Sicherheit*, 45: 9, 33–8.

Vahl, Remco (1997), *Leadership in Disguise. The Role of the European Commission in EC Decision-Making on Agriculture in the Uruguay Round*, Aldershot, Ashgate.

Varwick, Johannes and Woyke, Wichard (1999), *NATO 2000. Transatlantische Sicherheit am Ausgang des Jahrhunderts*, Opladen, Leske + Budrich.

Vasquez, John A. (1997), 'The Realist Paradigm and Degenerative versus Progressive Research Programs: An Appraisal of Neotraditional Research on Waltz's Balancing Proposition', *American Political Science Review*, 91: 4, 899–912.

Vincent, R. J. (1986), *Human Rights and International Relations*, Cambridge, Cambridge University Press.

Voeth, Markus (1996), *Entmonopolisierung von Märkten – Das Beispiel Telekommunikation*, Baden-Baden, Nomos.

Voigt, Rüdiger (1993), 'Abschied vom Staat – Rückkehr zum Staat?', in Rüdiger Voigt (ed.), *Abschied vom Staat – Rückkehr zum Staat?*, Baden-Baden, Nomos, 9–24.

Voigt, Rüdiger (1995), 'Der kooperative Staat: Auf der Suche nach einem neuen Steuerungsmodus', in Rüdiger Voigt (ed.), *Der kooperative Staat. Krisenbewältigung durch Verhandlung?*, Baden-Baden, Nomos, 33–92.

Waarden, Frans van (1992a), 'Dimensions and Types of Policy Networks', *European Journal of Political Research*, 21: 1–2:, 29–52.

Waarden, Frans van (1992b), 'The Historical Institutionalization of Typical National Patterns in Policy Networks between State and Industry. A Comparison of the USA and Netherlands', *European Journal of Political Research*, 21: 1–2, 131–62.

Waarden, Frans van (1993), 'Über die Beständigkeit nationaler Politikstile und Politiknetzwerke. Eine Studie über die Genese ihrer institutionellen Verankerung', in Roland Czada and Manfred G. Schmidt (eds), *Verhandlungsdemokratie, Interessenvermittlung, Regierbarkeit. Festschrift für Gerhard Lehmbruch*, Opladen, Westdeutscher Verlag, 191–212.

Wachtler, Günther (1983), *Militär, Krieg, Gesellschaft: Texte zur Militärsoziologie*, Frankfurt a.M., Campus.

Wagner, Wolfgang (1999), 'Interessen und Ideen in der europäischen Verfassungspolitik. Rationalistische und konstruktivistische Erklärungen mitgliedstaatlicher Präferenzen', *Politische Vierteljahresschrift*, 40: 3, 415–41.

Wallace, Helen (1999), 'Piecing the Integration Jigsaw Together', *Journal of European Public Policy*, 6: 1, 155–9.

Walt, Stephen M. (1987), *The Origins of Alliances*, Ithaca, NY, Cornell University Press.

Walt, Stephen M. (1997), 'The Progressive Power of Realism', *American Political Science Review*, 91: 4, 931–5.

Waltz, Kenneth N. (1979), *Theory of International Politics*, New York, McGraw-Hill.

Waltz, Kenneth N. (1986), 'Reflections on Theory of International Politics. A Response to My Critics', in Robert O. Keohane (ed.), *Neorealism and Its Critics*, New York, Columbia University Press, 322–45.

Waltz, Kenneth N. (1993), 'The Emerging Structure of International Politics', *International Security*, 18: 2, 44–79.

Waltz, Kenneth N. (1996), 'International Politics is not Foreign Policy', *Security Studies*, 6: 1, 52–5.

Waltz, Kenneth N. (1997), 'Evaluating Theories', *American Political Science Review*, 91: 4, 913–17.

Wapner, Paul (1996), *Environmental Activism and World Civic Politics*, Albany, NY, State University of New York Press.

Watzal, Ludwig (1993), 'Der Irrweg von Maastricht', in Rainer Zitelmann, Karlheinz Weißmann and Michael Großheim (eds), *Westbindung: Chancen und Risiken für Deutschland*, Frankfurt a.M., Propyläen, 477–500.

Weart, Spencer (1994), 'Peace among Democratic and Oligarchic Republics', *Journal of Peace Research*, 31: 3, 299–316.

Weede, Erich (1996), *Economic Development, Social Order, and World Politics. With Special Emphasis on War, Freedom, the Rise and Decline of the West, and the Future of East Asia*, Boulder, CO, Lynne Rienner.

Weidemaier, Jürgen (1995), 'Das Führungszentrum der Bundeswehr', *Europäische Sicherheit*, 44: 10, 41–2.

Weidenfeld, Werner (1996), *Kulturbruch mit Amerika. Das Ende transatlantischer Selbstverständlichkeit*, Gütersloh, Bertelsmann.

Weidenfeld, Werner (1998), *Außenpolitik für die deutsche Einheit*, Geschichte der deutschen Einheit, 4, Stuttgart, DVA.

Weiler, Joseph (1999), *The Constitution of Europe*, Cambridge, Cambridge University Press.

Weiss, Frank D. (1989), 'Die außenwirtschaftlichen Beziehungen der Bundesrepublik Deutschland', in Werner Weidenfeld and Hartmut Zimmermann (eds), *Deutschland-Handbuch. Eine doppelte Bilanz. 1949–1989*, Bonn, Bundeszentrale für politische Bildung, 621–38.

Weiß, Wolfgang W. (1986), 'Sozialisation', in Bernhard Schäfers (ed.), *Grundbegriffe der Soziologie*, 2nd edn, Opladen, Leske + Budrich, 269–71.

Weißhuhn, Reinhard (1993), 'Menschenrechte in der Außenpolitik', in Hans-Peter Hubert and Bundesarbeitsgemeinschaft Frieden und Internationalismus der Grünen (eds), *Grüne Außenpolitik – Aspekte einer Debatte*, Göttingen, Die Werkstatt, 191–6.

Weißmann, Karlheinz (1996), 'Herausforderung und Entscheidung: Über einen politischen Verismus für Deutschland', in Heimo Schwilk and Ulrich Schacht (eds), *Die selbstbewußte Nation: 'Anschwellender Bocksgesang' und weitere Beiträge zu einer deutschen Debatte*, 3rd edn, Berlin, Ullstein, 309–26.

Welck, Georg von (1991), *Die Bundesländer und die einheitliche europäische Akte*, Europarecht – Völkerrecht. Studien und Materialien, 36, Munich, VVF.

Weller, Marc (1999), 'The Rambouillet Conference on Kosovo', *International Affairs*, 75: 2, 211–52.

Wendt, Alexander E. (1987), 'The Agent-Structure Problem in International Relations Theory', *International Organization*, 41: 3, 335–70.

Wendt, Alexander (1991), 'Bridging the Theory/Meta-theory Gap in International Relations', *Review of International Studies*, 17: 4, 383–92.

Wendt, Alexander (1992), 'Anarchy is What States Make of It. The Social Construction of Power Politics', *International Organization*, 46: 2, 391–425.

Wendt, Alexander (1994), 'Collective Identity Formation and the International State', *American Political Science Review*, 88: 2, 384–96.

Wendt, Alexander (1999), *Social Theory of International Politics*, Cambridge, Cambridge University Press.

Wendt, Alexander and Duvall, Raymond (1989), 'Institutions and International Order', in Ernst-Otto Czempiel and James N. Rosenau (eds), *Global Changes and Theoretical Challenges. Approaches to the World Politics for the 1990s*, Lexington, MA, Lexington Books, 51–73.

Wernicke, Christian (1998), 'Bonn bremst', *Die Zeit*, 28 March, 3.

Wessels, Wolfgang (1991), 'The EC Council: The Community's Decisionmaking Center', in Robert O. Keohane and Stanley Hoffmann (eds), *The New European Community. Decisionmaking and Institutional Change*, Boulder, CO, Westview Press, 133–54.

Wessels, Wolfgang (1999), 'Zentralmacht, Zivilmacht oder Ohnmacht? Zur deutschen Außen- und Europapolitik nach 1989', in Peter R. Weilemann, Hanns Jürgen Küsters and Günter Buchstab (eds), *Macht und Zeitkritik. Festschrift für Hans-Peter Schwarz zum 65. Geburtstag*, Paderborn, Schöningh, 389–406.

Westerhoff, Horst-Dieter (1998), 'Die Gestaltung der Wirtschaftspolitik bei wachsender internationaler Verflechtung', in Wolf-Dieter Eberwein and Karl Kaiser (eds), *Deutschlands neue Außenpolitik, Vol. 4: Institutionen und Ressourcen*, Munich, Oldenbourg, 100–20.

Wette, Wolfram (1994), 'Rückkehr zur 'Normalität' und Weltmachtdenken. Die Renaissance des Militärischen im neuen Deutschland', *Blätter für Deutsche und Internationale Politik*, 39: 8, 981–90.

Wette, Wolfram (1996), 'Sonderweg oder Normalität? Zur Diskussion um die internationale Position der Bundesrepublik', *Blätter für Deutsche und Internationale Politik*, 41:1, 61–70.

Weyel, Volker (1997), 'Deutsche Menschenrechtspolitik – Aufgabe nicht nur nach außen, sondern auch nach innen', in Stiftung Entwicklung und Frieden (ed.), *UN-williges Deutschland: Der WEED-Report zur deutschen UNO-Politik*, Bonn, Dietz, 148–67.

Whitford, Jon and Young, Thomas-Durell (1997), 'Multinational Command Authorities: The Need for Change in NATO', *Defense Analysis*, 13: 1, 35–57.

Wielgohs, Jan and Wiesenthal, Helmut (1995), 'Konkurrenz–Ignoranz–Kooperation: Interaktionsmuster west- und ostdeutscher Akteure beim Aufbau von Interessenverbänden', in Helmut Wiesenthal (ed.), *Einheit als Interessenpolitik. Studien zur sektoralen Transformation Ostdeutschlands*, Frankfurt a.M., Campus Verlag, 298–333.

Wildenmann, Rudolf (1992), Wahlforschung, Mannheim, B. I. Taschenbuchverlag.

Wilkinson, David (1999), 'Unipolarity without Hegemony', *International Studies Review*, 1:1, 141–72.

Willke, Helmut (1992), *Ironie des Staates. Grundlinien einer Staatstheorie polyzentrischer Herrschaft*, Frankfurt a.M., Suhrkamp.

Winkelmann, Ingo (ed.) (1994), *Das Maastricht-Urteil des Bundesverfassungsgerichts vom 12. Oktober 1993. Dokumentation des Verfahrens mit Einführung*, Berlin, Duncker und Humblot.

Winkler, Rainer (1995), 'Deutschlands geopolitische Lage im sich wandelnden Europa', *WeltTrends* 3:6, 98–111.

Winter, Helen (1994), *Interdependenzen zwischen Industrie- und Handelspolitik der Europäischen Gemeinschaft*, Baden-Baden, Nomos.

Wolf, Anita (1992), 'Bundesrepublik Deutschland', in Werner Weidenfeld and Wolfgang Wessels (eds), *Jahrbuch Europäische Integration 1991/92*, Bonn, Europa Union Verlag, 310–20.

Wolf, Frieder Otto (1993), 'Außenpolitik und Menschenrechte: Thesen für eine Untersuchung', in Hans-Peter Hubert and Bundesarbeitsgemeinschaft Frieden und Internationalismus der Grünen (eds), *Grüne Außenpolitik – Aspekte einer Debatte*, Göttingen, Die Werkstatt, 197–211.

Wolf, Klaus (1998), 'Von offenen, verdeckten und vergessenen Interessen: Deutschlands Außenpolitik und der Globalismus', *Zeitschrift für Politik*, 45: 4, 367–83.

Wolf, Klaus-Dieter (1995), 'Eine neue Rolle Deutschlands?', in Hans-Georg Wehling (ed.), *Sicherheitspolitik unter geänderten weltpolitischen Rahmenbedingungen*, Stuttgart, Kohlhammer, 173–86.

Wolf, Reinhard (1996), 'Renationalisation of Western Defence and Security Policies: A German View on a Hesitant Spectre', in Snezana Trifunovska (ed.), *The Transatlantic Alliance on the Eve of the New Millennium*, The Hague, Kluwer Law International, 129–41.

Woolcock, Stephen (1992), *Trading Partners or Trading Blows? Market Access in EC–US Relations*, New York, Council on Foreign Relations Press.

Woolcock, Stephen and Hodges, Michael (1996), 'EU Policy in the Uruguay Round', in Helen Wallace and William Wallace (eds), *Policy-Making in the European Union*, 3rd edn, Oxford, Oxford University Press, 301–24.

Woolcock, Stephen, Hodges, Michael and Schreiber, Kirstin (1991), *Britain, Germany and 1992. The Limits of Deregulation*, London, Pinter.

Yost, David S. (1998), *NATO Transformed*, Washington, DC, United States Institute of Peace Press.

Young, Oran R. (1989), *International Cooperation. Building Regimes for Natural Resources and the Environment*, Ithaca, NY, Cornell University Press.

Young, Thomas-Durell (1992a), *The 'Normalization' of the Federal Republic of Germany's Defense Structures*, Carlisle, PA, Strategic Studies Institute, US Army War College.

Young, Thomas-Durell (1992b), 'Bundeswehr Plans for a National Command and Control Structure', *Defense Analysis*, 8: 3, 315–18.

Young, Thomas-Durrell (1995), 'Nationalization or Intergration? The Future Direction of German Defense Policy', *Defense Analysis*, 11: 2, 109–20.

Young, Thomas-Durell (1996), 'German National Command Structures after Unification: A New German General Staff?', *Armed Forces & Society*, 22: 3, 379–417.

Zakaria, Fareed (1992), 'Realism and Domestic Politics: A Review Essay', *International Security*, 17: 1, 177–98.

Zangl, Bernhard (1999), *Interessen auf zwei Ebenen. Internationale Regime in der Agrarhandels-, Währungs- und Walfangpolitik*, Baden-Baden, Nomos.

Zitelmann, Rainer (1996), 'Position und Begriff: Über eine neue demokratische Rechte', in Heimo Schwilk and Ulrich Schacht (eds), *Die selbstbewußte Nation: 'Anschwellender Bocksgesang' und weitere Beiträge zu einer deutschen Debatte*, 3rd edn, Frankfurt a.M., Ullstein, 163–81.

Zuleeg, Manfred (1982), 'Demokratie und Wirtschaftsverfassung', *Europarecht*, 17: 1, 21–9.

Zuleeg, Manfred (1993), 'Demokratie in der Europäischen Gemeinschaft', *Juristen Zeitung*, 48: 22, 1069–74.

Zürn, Michael (1992), *Interessen und Institutionen in der internationalen Politik. Grundlegung und Anwendung des situationsstrukturellen Ansatzes*, Opladen, Leske + Budrich.

Zürn, Michael (1993), 'Bringing the Second Image (Back) in. About the Domestic Sources of Regime Formation', in Volker Rittberger (ed.), *Regime Theory and International Relations*, Oxford, Clarendon Press, 282–311.

Zürn, Michael (1997), 'Assessing State Preferences and Explaining Institutional Choice. The Case of Intra-German Trade', *International Studies Quarterly*, 41: 2:, 295–320.

Index

Note: 'n' after a page reference indicates a note on that page; page numbers given in *italic* refer to information contained in tables.

1

Introduction

Volker Rittberger

When in 1989/90 the East–West conflict ended and the division of Germany into two states was overcome through unification, many observers expected these changes to entail significant consequences not only for Germany's internal affairs, but also for its foreign policy. As it was perceived, unification had profoundly altered Germany's position in Europe in many respects. First of all, the 'new' Germany was bigger: its territory, population and, in absolute terms at least, its economy were obviously larger than those of either German state during the Cold War. Moreover, Germany had regained full sovereignty as a result of the Two-plus-Four Treaty. Finally, after the end of the East–West conflict, Germany was no longer precariously located at the front line of a global conflict, but lay right in the heart of Europe. While the division of Germany after World War II had been deliberately designed to limit German power, which had been big enough to destabilize Europe twice, leading to two world wars, unification now undid this division and thus also removed the limitations to German power. There were fears in Europe that this gain in power would prompt Germany to change its foreign policy and to become a destabilizing factor in Europe again. Politically, therefore, unification met initially with some resistance.

The expectation that a more powerful Germany would turn away from its multilateral, low-profile approach to foreign policy was found not only with some European politicians but was expressed also in the academic discourse. In particular, authors whose writings were informed by the realist and neorealist schools of thought about international relations voiced the expectation that Germany's post-unification foreign policy behaviour would become less cooperative and that Germany might even strive for hegemony in Europe. The neorealist view, however, was challenged by authors who held that a fundamental change in German foreign policy was not to be expected. They pointed, for instance, to post-unification Germany's continued embeddedness in a multitude of international institutions or to its continuing trade dependence, and argued that such factors would make for continuity in Germany's foreign policy behaviour.

Meanwhile, more than ten years have passed since unification and it seems worthwhile to examine how German foreign policy has actually developed since then. Such an endeavour would seem rewarding in two respects. First of all, it would allow us to evaluate the competing expectations just outlined about Germany turning away from, or maintaining, its cooperative approach to foreign policy and thus to establish whether *empirically* continuity prevailed in German foreign policy or whether a profound change induced by Germany's gain in power occurred. Yet secondly, an analysis of Germany's post-unification foreign policy behaviour would also have *theoretical* merit. For Germany's post-unification foreign policy appears to be an almost ideal test case for neorealism. The basic causal claim of neorealist foreign policy theory is that a state's power position in the international system determines its foreign policy behaviour. In the case of Germany, the value of neorealism's basic causal variable – Germany's power position – has changed as a result of unification, whereas many of those variables which are regarded as determinants of foreign policy by other theories, e.g. international and domestic institutions, can be assumed to have remained fairly constant over the course of unification. Thus, by comparing Germany's foreign policy before and after unification, the impact of Germany's improved power position on its foreign policy behaviour can be singled out and hence neorealism's basic theoretical claim can be evaluated.

To use Germany's foreign policy after unification as a test case for neorealism was the basic idea behind a research project which was launched in 1997 at the Centre for International Relations/Peace and Conflict Studies of the University of Tübingen and whose results are presented in this volume. The main objective of this research project was to establish, across a wide range of issue areas, whether continuity or change prevailed in Germany's post-unification foreign policy and, when changes could be detected, to determine whether they were attributable to Germany's improved power position. In order to rule out the possibility that other explanatory factors for possible changes in German foreign policy behaviour were overlooked, our goal was not to focus solely on the impact of Germany's power position but also to control for the influence both of domestic interests and of international and societal norms on German foreign policy.

To achieve these goals, we had to formulate three theories of foreign policy which could be submitted to an empirical test. The theories had to spell out how the proposed independent variables – Germany's power position, domestic interests, and international and societal norms – shape Germany's foreign policy behaviour. Moreover, the theories had to be applicable across different issue areas and had to specify how the value of the respective independent variables was to be determined in empirical research. It soon turned out that foreign policy theories meeting these requirements were not readily available in the literature. Instead, we had to (re)construct such theories, which could be submitted to hypothesis testing, and we did so building on the state of the art in the most influential schools of thought in international relations theory and foreign policy analysis.

This (re)construction resulted in the formulation of three foreign policy theories. *Neorealism*, our first theory, explains a state's foreign policy behaviour by reference to its power position. To do justice to recent developments in the neorealist literature, however, we distinguish two variants of neorealist foreign policy theory. Both variants rely on the same basic causal variable, i.e. a state's power position, and characterize a state's foreign policy behaviour as power politics. Both variants hold that states in their foreign policies above all seek to gain autonomy from, and influence on, their international environment. Yet they disagree about how states weigh up the goals of autonomy and influence when the two are in conflict. Neorealism, on the one hand, assumes that states are subject to invariably high security pressures. It therefore holds that states will always prefer autonomy over influence, if the two are at odds. States, for instance, will not be willing to participate in international institutions which constrain their autonomy, even if they can achieve substantial influence on other states through the institution, and the more powerful states are, the more reluctant they will be to give up autonomy in such circumstances. Therefore, from a neorealist perspective, a state such as Germany, whose power position has improved, will tend to sever its ties to international institutions and seek to enhance its autonomy.

Modified neorealism, on the other hand, posits that the security pressures to which states are exposed are variable. If a state is exposed to low security pressures, it may be willing to give up part of its autonomy when it can gain substantial influence in return. From a modified neorealist perspective, therefore, a state gaining power will not necessarily try to disengage from international institutions restricting its autonomy, but will instead seek more influence and attempt to use the institutions as a means to influence other states.

While both variants of neorealist foreign policy theory focus on the impact that a state's power position in the international system has on its foreign policy, *utilitarian liberalism*, our second theory, focuses on subsystemic determinants of foreign policy behaviour. Its basic causal claim is that the interests of domestic actors decisively shape a state's foreign policy. Hence this theory must provide an answer to two questions: Who are the actors whose interests will shape a state's foreign policy behaviour with regard to a given issue? And, which course of action is preferred by these actors, i.e. in which concrete foreign policy behaviour will the dominant domestic actors' interests translate? The theory answers the first of these two questions by means of a policy network analysis. This tool allows predictions about which domestic actors will be able to assert their preferences in a given situation. The second question, aiming at the substance of the dominant domestic actors' preferences, is answered by deriving concrete policy preferences from theoretically assumed basic interests of the respective actors. Different kinds of actor are assumed to hold different basic interests. Political actors, for instance, are primarily interested in protecting their incumbency, e.g. by securing their re-election, administrative actors chiefly want to preserve their competences, companies aim at increasing their income, etc. From these basic interests, preferences about foreign policy in a given situation can be derived. Together with the policy network analysis, they allow us to make predictions about German foreign policy behaviour in a given situation. Thus the theory is able to generate hypotheses about the influence of domestic interests on foreign policy across issue areas which can be submitted to an empirical test.

Both neorealism and utilitarian liberalism are rooted in the assumption that actors – states in the former, individuals in the latter – are rational utility maximizers with given interests. More recently, an important strand of international relations theory and foreign policy analysis has developed that rejects this notion of rational utility-maximizing actors. Instead, *constructivism* holds that actors follow a logic of appropriateness and that their behaviour is shaped by social norms, i.e. by value-based shared expectations about appropriate behaviour. Hence constructivist foreign policy theory has international and societal norms